ETHNIC ORIGINS

ETHNIC ORIGINS
THE ADAPTATION OF CAMBODIAN AND HMONG REFUGEES IN FOUR AMERICAN CITIES

JEREMY HEIN

A Volume in the American Sociological Association's
Rose Series in Sociology

Russell Sage Foundation • New York

Library of Congress Cataloging-in-Publication Data

Hein, Jeremy.
  Ethnic origins : the adaptation of Cambodian and Hmong
  refugees in four American cities / Jeremy Hein.
     p. cm.
  Includes bibliographical references and index.
  ISBN 0-87154-336-2
     1. Cambodian Americans—Social conditions—Case studies. 2. Cambodian
  Americans—Cultural assimilation—Case studies. 3. Cambodian Americans—Ethnic
  identity—Case studies. 4. Hmong Americans—Social conditions—Case studies.
  5. Hmong Americans—Cultural assimilation—Case studies. 6. Hmong Americans—
  Ethnic identity—Case studies. 7. Refugees—United States—Social conditions—
  Case studies. 8. Assimilation (Sociology)—Case studies. 9. Sociology, Urban—
  United States—Case studies. 10. United States—Ethnic relations—Case studies. I. Title.

  E184.K45H45 2006
  305.895′93073—dc22

                                                                    2005044937

The paper used in this publication meets the minimum requirements of American
National Standard for Information Sciences—Permanence of Paper for Printed Library
Materials.   ANSI Z39.48-1992.

Text design by Suzanne Nichols.

RUSSELL SAGE FOUNDATION
112 East 64th Street, New York, New York 10021
10 9 8 7 6 5 4 3 2 1

Previous Volumes in the Series

Beyond College For All: Career Paths for the Forgotten Half
James E. Rosenbaum

Making Hate a Crime: From Social Movement to Law Enforcement
Valerie Jenness and Ryken Grattet

Trust in Schools: A Core Resource for Improvement
Anthony S. Bryk and Barbara Schneider

America's Newcomers and the Dynamics of Diversity
Frank D. Bean and Gillian Stevens

Egalitarian Capitalism: Jobs, Incomes, and Growth in Affluent Countries
Lane Kenworthy

Forthcoming Titles

Changing Rhythms of the American Family
Suzanne M. Bianchi, John Robinson, and Melissa Milkie

Citizens, Markets, and Transnational Labor Activism
Gay Seidman

Good Jobs, Bad Jobs, No Jobs: Changing Work and Workers in America
Arne L. Kalleberg

Morality by Choice: Politics, Personal Choice, and the Case of Covenant Marriage
Scott Feld and Katherine Rosier

Passing the Torch: Does Higher Education for the Disadvantaged Pay Off Across the Generations
Paul Attewell and David Lavin

Pension Puzzles: Questions of Principle and Principal
Melissa Hardy and Lawrence Hazelrigg

*The Production of Demographic Knowledge: States, Societies, and Census
Taking in Comparative and Historical Perspective*
Rebecca Emigh, Dylan Riley, and Patricia Ahmed

Race, Place, and Crime: Structural Inequality, Criminal Inequality
Ruth D. Peterson and Lauren J. Krivo

*Repressive Injustice: Political and Social Processes in the Massive
Incarceration of African Americans*
Pamela E. Oliver and James E. Yocum

*Retrenching Welfare, Entrenching Inequality: Gender, Race, and Old Age in
the United States*
Madonna Harrington Meyer and Pamela Herd

*Re-Working Silicon Valley: Politics, Power and the Informational
Labor Process*
Seán Ó Riain and Chris Benner

Who Counts as Kin: How Americans Define the Family
Brian Powell, Lala Carr Steelman, Catherine Bolzendahl,
Danielle Fettes, and Claudi Giest

The Rose Series in Sociology

The American Sociological Association's Rose Series in Sociology publishes books that integrate knowledge and address controversies from a sociological perspective. Books in the Rose Series are at the forefront of sociological knowledge. They are lively and often involve timely and fundamental issues on significant social concerns. The series is intended for broad dissemination throughout sociology, across social science and other professional communities, and to policy audiences. The series was established in 1967 by a bequest to ASA from Arnold and Caroline Rose to support innovations in scholarly publishing.

DOUGLAS L. ANDERTON
DAN CLAWSON
NAOMI GERSTEL
JOYA MISRA
RANDALL G. STOKES
ROBERT ZUSSMAN

EDITORS

To my students in Sociology 312,
"Race and Ethnic Relations in the United States."

We all move, one after the other, along the same roads mapped out for us by our origins and our hopes.

—W. G. Sebald, *The Rings of Saturn*

Contents

About the Author

Jeremy Hein is professor of sociology at the University of Wisconsin—Eau Claire.

═ Preface ═

In 1997 President Clinton announced his intention to create a national dialogue about race. No American president had ever voluntarily confronted this social problem. Clinton unveiled his ambitious Initiative on Race in a commencement address at the University of California—San Diego. He proclaimed (Clinton 1997):

> A half century from now when your own grandchildren are in college there will be no majority race in America. Now, we know what we will look like, but what will we be like? Can we be one America, respecting, even celebrating, our differences, but embracing even more what we have in common? Can we define what it means to be an American, not just in terms of the hype in showing our ethnic origins, but in terms of our primary allegiance to the values America stands for and values we really live by? Our hearts long to answer yes, but our history reminds us that it will be hard. To be sure, there is old, unfinished business between black and white Americans, but the classic American dilemma has now become many dilemmas of race and ethnicity. That is why I have come here today to ask the American people to join me in a great national effort, to perfect the promise of America for this new time as we seek to build our more perfect union.

The day before giving this speech Clinton issued executive order 13050, creating the President's Advisory Board on Race. Included in its goals were "promote a constructive national dialogue to confront and work through challenging issues that surround race" and "bridge racial divides by encouraging leaders in communities throughout the Nation to develop and implement innovative approaches to calming racial tensions" (President's Advisory Board on Race 1998, A-1).

To achieve these goals the advisory board held forums for dozens of religious and corporate leaders, supported a nationwide "Campus Week of Dialogue," and organized hundreds of town hall–style meetings around the country. President Clinton attended three of these meetings, including one that was broadcast on national television. The Initiative on Race also obtained funding from fifteen federal departments and agencies for "an historic gathering of the nation's leading scholars on racial and ethnic relations," which resulted in a two-volume anthology more than a thousand pages long (Smelser, Wilson, and Mitchell 2001, 1). One year into the initiative, CNN reported a poll that found that 48 percent of the American public believed the initiative would improve race relations.[1]

President Clinton's goals are still shared by many people in the United States, yet few of us now remember his Initiative on Race. Its moment in the public spotlight passed quickly, leaving in its wake no new program or policy nor even an enduring image of reconciliation. One reason for the initiative's shortcomings was the very problem President Clinton identified when announcing it: "The classic American dilemma has now become many dilemmas of race and ethnicity."

Since the 1940s social scientists have used the phrase "the American dilemma" as shorthand for the seemingly irreconcilable conflict between blacks and whites over the questions of why racial inequality exists and what should be done about it. Sustained international migration since the 1970s means that many other groups are now encountering these issues. As a result, one branch of the social science literature on immigrants examines the repercussions of demographic changes as whites of European ancestry become a smaller proportion of American society. Another branch focuses on immigrants' economic adaptation, looking for signs of upward mobility. With mid-twentieth-century African American history in mind, many scholars ponder "the potential for deep social conflict resulting from the immigrant quest for progress and the obstacles that such a search entails" (Waldinger 2001b, 329). Social conflict, however, involves symbols and not just material conditions such as population and poverty. Thus another aspect of the new American dilemmas concerns racial and ethnic adaptation: how immigrants interpret and respond to new identities and inequalities that result from perceived physical and cultural differences.

I examine racial and ethnic adaptation among immigrants (of which refugees are a subgroup) with the help of some inconspicuous people living in some obscure places. Most U.S. residents have never met Hmong (pronounced "mung") and Khmer (commonly called Cambodian) refugees and have never heard of Eau Claire, Wisconsin, and Rochester, Minnesota.[2] These groups and places appear marginal to the "real diversity" typically studied in international cities such as Los Angeles, Miami, and New York. Yet policy makers, journalists, and social scientists can learn much about American society's new racial and ethnic dilemmas by looking at diversity in less-well-known places. According to the sociologist Howard Becker (1998), we should more often study "cases that don't fit" in order to counterbalance the tendency of scientific inquiry to focus on a narrow range of topics dictated by conventional wisdom.

I compare Cambodian and Hmong refugees because these two groups are commonly subsumed within aggregates such as Southeast Asian, Asian American, and even the residual category "other Asian." In addition to belonging to the same race (according to the American system of classification), both groups have a low socioeconomic status and a common migration history rooted in failed U.S. foreign policy. Despite these similarities, the Hmong in Laos and the Khmer in Cambodia belong to very different ethnic groups. By beginning my analysis with this distinction in ethnic origins I am able to analyze how the histories, politics, and cultures that Cambodian and Hmong refugees bring with them shape their adaptation to American race and ethnic relations.

The Hmong in Eau Claire and the Cambodians in Rochester would in any case be worthy of investigation if only to learn about immigrants in small cities, since most research is conducted in large urban areas. But the previously insular midwestern cities that now have significant Asian (and Hispanic) populations are much more than interesting "deviant cases"—sociologists' term for situations whose atypical qualities reveal exceptions to accepted generalizations. Carefully choosing cases using precise theoretical and methodological criteria creates a powerful comparative research design on human behavior in social groups. My analysis therefore compares the Hmong in Eau Claire with those in Milwaukee, Wisconsin, and Cambodians in Rochester with those in Chicago, Illinois (see figure P.1).

In this comparative context minor groups and out-of-the-way places suddenly become very important because they raise fascinating theoretical questions. Perhaps Cambodians and the Hmong have similar forms of racial and ethnic adaptation regardless of where they reside because they are Asians with low or moderate incomes in an affluent and predominantly white society. Conversely, living in a large or small American city may determine the refugees' adjustment to new social identities and inequalities. Another theoretical possibility is that being Hmong or Khmer shapes responses to contested identities and inequalities no matter what social environment the refugees live in. Finally, the interaction between the refugees' ethnicity and the urban social structure could produce a hybridity of patterns in their racial and ethnic adaptation.

In fact, all of these outcomes are evident among Cambodians and the Hmong in the Midwest because racial and ethnic adaptation is a multidimensional process. The refugees are adjusting to different types of social

Figure P.1   The Upper Midwest of the United States

Source: Graphics Division, Learning and Technology Services, University of Wisconsin–Eau Claire.

identities, such as "Asian American" and "American citizen," and varied forms of inequality, such as stereotypes and institutional discrimination.

Yet despite this complexity a central pattern is evident: the refugees' ethnic origins are the primary influence on their racial and ethnic adaptation. Cambodians in Rochester have views of American diversity that are more like those of their compatriots in Chicago than they are like the views of the Hmong in Eau Claire. Similarly, the Hmong in Milwaukee have views about race, ethnicity, and inequality in the United States that are much closer to those of the Hmong in Eau Claire than to those of Cambodians in Chicago. This finding supports the transnational perspective on migration and its premise that explanations of immigrant adaptation must include circumstances in their homeland. It also suggests the need to revise prevailing theories that are based on examinations of assimilation, ethnic competition, and modes of incorporation, which focus almost exclusively on events in the host society.

To demonstrate the importance of ethnic origins for immigrants' adaptation, I start with two chapters on concepts and theories from two related yet distinct fields of research: immigration and race and ethnic relations. Chapter 1 makes the case that despite an incremental increase in research on immigrants' homelands, prevailing theories about immigrant adaptation minimize or ignore cultural variations among immigrants. Chapter 2 presents the concept of ethnic origins and explains how cultures, as well as homeland histories and politics, establish ethnic boundaries and ethnic identities that influence how immigrants respond to new boundaries and identities in the host society. It also discusses the research design I developed to test the ethnic- origins hypothesis on two ethnic groups in four cities.

The next two chapters focus on Southeast Asia and establish that Cambodians and the Hmong have distinctive ethnic origins. Chapter 3 examines the historical, political, religious, and kinship components of Khmer ethnic origins in Cambodia, and chapter 4 examines the same factors for the Hmong in Laos (for readers who wish to proceed to the book's core chapters, this information is summarized in table 2.4, "Components and Qualities of Khmer and Hmong Ethnic Origins"). Two subsequent chapters on places describe the midwestern urban environments in which the refugees resettled from the mid 1970s through the 1980s. Chapter 5 presents the experience of small-town hospitality and hate as the refugees became the first nonwhite populations to live in Eau Claire and Rochester. Chapter 6 presents the refugees' encounter with ethnic succession in the urban pecking order as they established enclaves in distressed neighborhoods in Chicago and Milwaukee.

Chapters 7 through 12 compare the refugees' racial and ethnic adaptation in large and small cities. In most chapters I first use survey data to reveal the main similarities and differences by ethnicity and urban locale. I present some of these quantitative data as descriptive statistics, such as percentages and means, but I also employ OLS (ordinary least squares) regression analysis to pinpoint particularly interesting findings. Rather than expect the statistics to prove the significance of ethnic origins, I use the quantitative data to establish the general contours of the empirical terrain. I then turn to qualitative data to explore the salient features in more detail (see appendix A for an overview of my methodologies and appendix B for a detailed discussion).

My comparative analysis of the refugees' responses to the urban pecking order and small-town hospitality and hate begins with the meanings they attach to two prominent social identities: that of Asian American and of American citizen. Chapter 7 shows that ethnic origins profoundly shape the degree to which Cambodians and the Hmong develop a sense of pan-Asian ethnicity at the micro-level. Chapter 8 determines if these refugees feel they become "Americans" when they become citizens. Few of them do, largely because racial polarization undermines national unity in the United States. Instead, urban locale and ethnic origins influence what becoming an "American citizen" means to them.

Four subsequent chapters compare the refugees' perceptions of and reactions to racial and ethnic inequality. Chapter 9 evaluates what Cambodians and the Hmong like most about the United States and whether racism is among the things they most dislike. Urban locale explains their dislikes, whereas homeland social structure (not ethnic origins) explains why the two groups differ in their assessment of the positive aspects of American society.

When Cambodians and the Hmong think about the United States as a whole they tend to emphasize the positive attributes of American society and downplay racism. Their views are quite different when they discuss specific forms of inequality. Chapter 10 examines Cambodians' and the Hmong's sensitivity to three common stereotypes about them: eating dogs, lacking a work ethic, and not belonging in the United States because they are foreign-born. Chapter 11 analyzes their perceptions of institutional discrimination in the workplace, housing market, and criminal justice system. Ethnic origins strongly influence the refugees' perceptions of prejudice and discrimination, but ethnicity also interacts with urban locale to shape their views.

Severe prejudice and discrimination against a people distinguished by race or ethnicity transform them into a minority group. Chapter 12 explores Cambodians' and the Hmong's communal reactions to inequality. In 1996 the U.S. Congress significantly restricted immigrants' access to federal social welfare programs by making U.S. citizenship an eligibility requirement. Cambodians and the Hmong have suffered from the law in similar ways, but they have reached different conclusions about its ramifications and what to do about it. Discussion among peers reveal that ethnic origins influence how groups mobilize and plan collective action to achieve equality. Ethnic origins thus help us understand why there are now "many dilemmas of race and ethnicity" in the United States and how they differ from those in the past.

Acknowledgments

R esearching two ethnic groups in four cities using four different methodologies often felt like climbing Mount Everest without an oxygen supply or a map. Reaching the summit was only possible because I had the assistance of a support team.

The venture would never have begun in 1996 without a grant from the American Sociological Association's Fund for the Advancement of the Discipline. Once the study was under way, additional material support came from the Office of University Research at the University of Wisconsin–Eau Claire, the Southeast Asian Studies Center at the University of Wisconsin–Madison, and the National Science Foundation (grant no. SBR-9801152). I am very grateful for this funding, but even more for the encouragement it gave me to pursue a daunting research project when my primary professional responsibilities are teaching in an undergraduate sociology department.

Funding, however generous, only established the base camps for my ascent. Negotiating passage to the summit required local guides. For that I thank Pang Cher Vue and Ron Buzard, who helped me put together an extraordinary team of Cambodian and Hmong research assistants: Pheap Chhorm, Samantha Keo, Chava Lee, Mayhoua L. Moua, Reth Oum, Ponnareay Peng, Mai Vang, See J. Vang, Ge Xiong, and Touly Xiong. They took time from their jobs, family commitments, and volunteer work in the ethnic community to help me on what at the time seemed like an almost impossible task. Their efforts and insights are the only reason I was able to gather survey data, contact informants to interview, organize peer-group conversations, and have reliable interpreters and translators.

Although I traveled light I had help with the heavy lifting. Mindy Meyer, Chris Moore, Shoua Thao, and Nou Yang—all sociology majors at the University of Wisconsin–Eau Claire—coded and entered data and transcribed and translated tape recordings. Goodson Vue, a sociology major at the University of Wisconsin–White Water, also has my gratitude for helping me retrieve data from a rare CD-ROM of *Milwaukee Journal Sentinel* articles. Nahal Toosi, a reporter at the *Milwaukee Journal Sentinel,* provided me with copies of articles from the paper's archives, which are not open to the public.

For their comments on drafts of this book I thank my colleagues Daniel Strouthes, Melissa Bonstead-Bruns, Katherine Rhoades, and Steve Baumgardner. Two former students, Chris Moore and Hwa-Ji Shin, provided me with valuable comments and have since launched their own careers in sociology. I also obtained helpful feedback when I first presented the manuscript's thesis in April 1998 at the Asian American Studies Symposium at the University of Wisconsin–Madison. I owe a special thanks to Elliot Barkan, Erik Davis, and Mark Pfeifer for sharing with me their extensive expertise on immigrants, Cambodians, and the Hmong, respectively. I benefited enormously from comments by Sucheng Chan, the author of three exquisite books on the Hmong and Cambodians (Chan 1994, 2003, 2004), which are landmarks in the field of Asian American studies.

Locating the summit was only made possible by cogent advice from the editors of the American Sociological Association's Rose Series: Douglas Anderton, Dan Clawson, Naomi Gerstel, Joya Misra, Randall Stokes, and principal editor Robert Zussman. Our meeting on March 5th, 2004, at the University of Massachusetts–Amherst will always remain one of my most treasured intellectual experiences. I want to particularly acknowledge Bob Zussman's extraordinary editorial talent and his willingness to read my manuscript three times as it evolved. His wisdom helped me to make the correct choices at several forks in the road and enabled me to jettison paraphernalia that I needed during early stages of writing this book but that hindered my final ascent.

Once at the summit I suffered from altitude sickness and had trouble discerning the topography below. I am indebted to the veteran mountaineers Nazli Kibria and Min Zhou for their assistance at this last stage. These two external reviewers provided insightful criticism that immeasurably helped me refine my thinking about how ethnic origins influence immigrants' racial and ethnic adaptation.

= Part I =

Ideas

═ Chapter 1 ═

Immigrants and Culture

The colonization by France of Vietnam, Laos, and Cambodia in the mid-nineteenth century initiated the historical forces that would bring Southeast Asian refugees to the United States in the late twentieth century. During the intervening years the Russian Revolution in 1917 and the Chinese Revolution in 1949 augmented national liberation movements in French Indochina. American military intervention to oppose the spread of Communism began as the colonies gained independence in 1953 and 1954. The United States directly entered combat in 1965 and withdrew its troops in 1973, although fighting between pro-American and Communist troops continued for another two years (Chan 1994, 2003).

When the governments in South Vietnam, Laos, and Cambodia finally collapsed in April and May of 1975, all of the soldiers, politicians, and civilians who had backed the United States suddenly became targets for revenge by the new Communist governments (Hein 1995; Robinson 1998). These brutal regimes then began persecuting many people who had no connection to the previous regimes. By the early 1990s more than 2 million refugees had fled Vietnam, Laos, and Cambodia. For each one who reached the comparative safety of refugee camps in Thailand or another adjacent country, one died during the escape or at the hands of compatriots before flight was even possible.

Some of these refugees eventually returned to their homelands, but most did not. More than 1.5 million of them entered a global resettlement system with such disparate destinations as France, Canada, Australia, Sweden, Japan, and China, but it was the United States that admitted the largest number of Southeast Asian refugees, more than 1 million (Hein 1993). They now live in all fifty states. Within this flow of people, one resettlement current brought Hmong refugees from Laos and Khmer refugees from Cambodia to small and large cities in the Midwest.

Heng was among these refugees. Born in Cambodia, he lived for ten years in a Thai refugee camp with his family and arrived in Chicago at the age of fourteen. He graduated from high school, then enrolled at an adjacent state university but dropped out his first year because he lacked

3

adequate English proficiency to do the course work. Now twenty-four years old, Heng is taking English and math classes at a community college while working at a Burger King. He aspires to be a teacher.

As we sat in an office at the Cambodian Association of Illinois in Chicago's Uptown, I asked Heng to elaborate on an incident he had described when completing a survey about six months earlier.

Heng: The first day in high school I still wore the clothes I had brought from Thailand. My shoes were Thai shoes and they looked strange. In Thailand nobody laughed at me. Here some black students laughed at me. It was insulting, I had low self-esteem. Their shoes were expensive Nikes.

Author: You also said [on the survey] that some black students beat you up. Did you tell anyone about it?

Heng: No. I was walking in a group with four other students. It was not a bad beating. They just hit us like this [makes shoving motion with hands]. I just walked away. I thought "If I fight back it will happen again next time. I will hit them and they will hit me." To be a loser is sometimes better than to be a winner.

Author [in an incredulous tone]: To be a loser is sometimes better than to be a winner?

Heng: That's a Cambodian expression.[1] We believe in Buddhism. We defend but we never are offensive. I think that other people have their problems too.

Author: Have other Cambodians ever told you about their experiences with prejudice?

Heng: Everybody has heard about prejudice. It's a normal thing. Like eating rice, wearing the same clothes. We get used to it. Sometimes I feel angry but I think that I shouldn't. Maybe they [people who show prejudice] have problems so that's why they say things like that. It's really hard in this society. It's easy to get into conflicts. I go to church. They [church members] teach me to think first, to forgive. It's hard to forgive.

Author: What type of church is it?

Heng: A Korean church.

One need not be a specialist on Southeast Asia to recognize the salient themes in this passage. Heng cites Buddhist values to explain his response to prejudice. He also invokes the Buddhist concept of karma when he notes that hitting back would produce more hitting in the future. Yet despite Heng's adherence to the traditional religion of Cambodia, he sees no contradiction in attending a church and blending the Buddhist value of compassion with the Christian value of forgiveness.

Mee, a twenty-two-year-old Hmong woman in Eau Claire, Wisconsin, also considers it self-evident that homeland values and norms influence how newcomers respond to American diversity and adversity. Born in Laos, she arrived in the United States at the age of five and is now a secondary education major at the local university. At the Hmong Mutual Assistance Association we talked about race and ethnic relations in the United States, including how Hmong parents and children communicate with each other. As Mee explained to me:

> In Hmong culture it's more common to walk up to a Hmong person and start talking to them just like you were friends. You see them as close to you. The Hmong are close knit, a clan people. Like my parents. They told me because I am a Vang, that I can always treat any other Vang like my brother.[2] But if I want to date a white person, no. If I ask my parents if I can bring a Caucasian guy over to the house they will say no.
>
> It's the same if the person is African American. They will say no and not explain. If I say I want to marry a Hmong, they will say "Maybe, it depends on the family." It makes you think, "Okay, maybe I shouldn't try to get to know another people because I can't bring them to my house."

What seems so obvious to Heng and Mee is actually at odds with current social science theories about immigrants. There is mounting evidence that immigrants' histories, politics, and cultures shape their adaptation to American race and ethnic relations.[3] Yet these insights have not changed assimilation, ethnic competition, and modes of incorporation theories, the prevailing explanations for immigrant adaptation. For example, it is now widely recognized that immigrants bring with them ideas about race. Hispanic immigrants from the Caribbean conceptualize race as a continuum rather than the black-white dichotomy common in American society (Landale and Oropesa 2002). Those who do not define themselves as white or black have a distinctive pattern of residential settlement (Denton and Massey 1989). Similarly, the identity "la raza" has a political meaning for Chicanos but an international one for Mexican immigrants (Hurtado, Gurin, and Peng 1994). Only among the former is the "la raza" identity correlated with support for bilingual education and a preference for Spanish-language media.

Religion is also acknowledged to be a highly durable feature of immigrants' homeland experiences. Iranian immigrants who were religious minorities in Iran are more likely to resist assimilation in the United States than those from the majority group (Bozorgmehr 1997). Immigrants from

their homeland's majority ethnic group also have greater difficulty building religious solidarity than those from homeland minority groups, since
the latter arrive with a heightened sense of ethnic identity (Ebaugh and
Chafetz 2000). These and other studies reveal that immigrants' experiences with race and ethnicity prior to migration influence their adaptation to race and ethnic relations after migration.

The sociologist Mary Waters's (1999, 6) pathbreaking study of West
Indians in New York City makes this point more clearly than any previous research: "Black immigrants from the Caribbean come to the
United States with a particular identity/culture/worldview that reflects
their unique history and experiences." She demonstrates how attitudes
developed in their homelands shape a number of adaptation outcomes
in the United States, including views of race relations and social mobility. Yet Waters does not conceptualize Caribbean immigrants' homeland experiences in a way that can be applied to other immigrant groups.
Her main purpose in reviewing Caribbean history is to demonstrate that
it has produced "the quintessential postmodern peoples" who operate
with "situational, multilayered, and socially constructed identities" (329).
Nor does Waters use her evidence of homeland effects to develop an
alternative explanation to theories based on assimilation, ethnic competition, and modes of incorporation. In fact, she repudiates a new theoretical approach—the transnational perspective—by stating, "I think the
notion of a transnational identity or a transnational cultural space is quite
exaggerated" (92).

Homeland effects have not resulted in revisions to existing theories
about immigrant adaptation because doing so requires emphasizing
cultural variation among immigrants. Two developments created this
theoretical dilemma. First, the War on Poverty during the 1960s and
especially the neoconservative policy paradigm of the 1980s made cultural explanations for racial and ethnic inequality a social-science taboo.
Second, the postmodernist reinterpretation of culture during the 1980s
and 1990s banished one of its essential meanings that is particularly
appropriate for immigrants: values and norms internalized through
socialization. These two developments have profound theoretical consequences. With culture deemed a neoconservative ploy or an ephemeral
construction, theories about immigrants continue to avoid analyzing
culture and other aspects of immigrants' pre-migration experiences.
Even the rise of the transnational perspective on migration, which
emphasizes conditions in immigrants' homelands, has not changed the
host-society focus in theories of assimilation, ethnic competition, and
modes of incorporation.

In this book I use the observations of Heng, Mee, and many other
Cambodian and Hmong refugees to develop and test what I term the

ethnic-origins hypothesis. Ethnic origins comprise aspects of culture such as religious values and kinship norms, as well as patterns of nation-state formation and political cleavage. Owing to global diversity in history, politics, and culture, each group of emigrants takes with it a unique worldview of what it means to be a member of society. These home-grown conceptions of societal membership influence how immigrants interpret and respond to new identities and inequalities in a host society. The concept of ethnic origins helps us appreciate that immigrants add more than demographic breadth to diversity in the United States. Immigrants also change the meaning of diversity because they have distinctive ethnic origins. Yet the proposition that values and norms from immigrants' homelands influence their new lives in the United States immediately raises a heated controversy that has raged since the 1960s.

From the Culture of Poverty to the Ethnic Myth

Sociology is acknowledged to have taken a "cultural turn" as a discipline during the 1970s and 1980s (Bonnell and Hunt 1999), largely owing to developments in anthropology (Sewell 1999a). But the fields of immigration and race and ethnicity did not follow suit, for political reasons. The first roadblock was put in place during the 1960s, when the concept of culture became stigmatized as a result of its misuse. The anthropologist Oscar Lewis (1959, 1965) developed a culture-of-poverty theory to explain how dysfunctional behaviors among Mexicans and Puerto Ricans passed from one generation to the next and trapped them in a cycle of poverty. According to Lewis (1965, xlv): "By the time slum children are age six or seven they have usually absorbed the basic values and attitudes of their subculture and are not psychologically geared to take full advantage of changing conditions or increased opportunities which may occur in their lifetime."

Although now considered pejorative, the culture of poverty theory was initially considered a progressive view of social problems. Many liberals used it to explain why poor people could not help themselves advance economically. Michael Harrington (1962/1986), a leader of the New Left, strongly endorsed the theory in his classic work *The Other America*: "Poverty in the United States is a culture, an institution, a way of life" (17). By arguing that poor people were trapped, Harrington and others established the moral rationale for government antipoverty programs.

Daniel Patrick Moynihan, then a political scientist at the U.S. Department of Labor, considered himself among these advocates for the poor. He applied the culture-of-poverty theory to African Americans in a study, *The Negro Family*, published in 1965, hoping it would make "the case for national action" (Moynihan 1967, 93). Subsequently dubbed the Moynihan Report, it attributed poverty among blacks to a dysfunctional family structure that had originated during slavery and was character-ized by illegitimate births, single mothers, and a form of matriarchy that undermined fathers and husbands. Moynihan (1967, 76) concluded, "At the center of the tangle of pathology is the weakness of the family struc-ture." A storm of criticism erupted when President Lyndon Johnson reit-erated this point in a speech at Howard University, a historically black college (Rainwater 1967). By the late 1960s the culture-of-poverty theory stood as a testament to all that can go wrong when the social sciences use values and norms to explain patterns of race and ethnic relations.

Paradoxically, during the mid-1960s, cultural explanations were just beginning to gain credence in American immigration historiography. At the time there was not much need for the concept of culture as it per-tained to contemporary immigrants. In 1960 the foreign-born made up only 6 percent of the U.S. population and went down to 5 percent in 1970, the lowest point during the twentieth century. American society was overwhelmingly white (88 percent) in 1960, and blacks accounted for 92 percent of the minority population (Kent et al. 2001; Richie 2000), proportions that were largely unchanged ten years later.

Rudolph Vecoli (1964) was one of the first historians to critique ear-lier work that portrayed European immigrants as uprooted peasants who left Old World traditions behind and rapidly Americanized. He argued that "the historian of immigration must study the distinctive cultural character of each ethnic group and the manner in which this influenced its adjustments" (Vecoli 1964, 417). Stephan Thernstrom (1964/1975) shared Vecoli's perspective and examined the worldviews of Irish immigrants and its impact on their social mobility. Thernstrom found that they did not progress as rapidly as American mythology claimed, and he advanced a cultural argument to explain this outcome: "The land hunger and the religious devotion of the working class Catholic led him to seek property at the cost of education and the forms of social mobility which required education" (177).

Although there is a degree of class bias in Thernstrom's thesis, the importance of immigrants' pre-migration values and norms became widely accepted among historians following the publication of Herbert Gutman's (1973) highly influential article "Work, Culture, and Society in Industrializing America." He examined nineteenth-century immigrants' "premodern culture" to explain how "habits and values" shaped their responses to factory work, again to discredit myths about the rapidity of Americanization among European immigrants. Gutman (1976, xxi) then bolstered the concept of cultural continuity by systematically refuting the pejorative portrayal of the black family in the Moynihan Report, noting that "it is through families that historically derived beliefs usually pass from generation to generation." After studying African American folklore, the historian Lawrence Levine (1977, 5) reached a similar conclusion concerning culture's durability. He demonstrated "that with Africans, as with European and Asian immigrants, aspects of the traditional cultures and worldview they came with may have continued to exist not as mere vestiges but as dynamic, living, creative parts of group life in the United States."

Cultural explanations in the fields of immigration and race and ethnicity came under intense criticism from the mid-1970s to the mid-1980s. The historians Alan Dawley (1976), David Montgomery (1979), Oliver Zunz (1982), and John Bodnar (1985), and the sociologists Stanley Lieberson (1980) and especially Stephen Steinberg (1981/1989), provided two widely accepted alternative explanations for patterns of adaptation: class and racism. Class arguments focused on the skills that immigrants brought with them and the inequalities created by capitalism. Arguments based on racism focused on the structure of opportunity in American society and how a color hierarchy facilitated advancement for some groups and blocked it for others. Proponents of these explanations either dismissed cultural differences as irrelevant or, when they acknowledged them at all, considered them less important than racial subordination and class stratification. Steinberg (1981/1989, xiv) provides the definitive synopsis of this perspective in his iconic book *The Ethnic Myth*:

> The reification of ethnic values has made a mystique of ethnicity, creating the illusion that there is something ineffable about ethnic phenomena that does not lend itself to rational explanation. This is especially the case when ethnic groups are assumed to be endowed with a given set of cultural values, and no attempt is made to understand these values in terms of their material sources.

American society was already much more culturally diverse by the time class and race theories supplanted those based on culture. By 1980 the proportion of immigrants in the U.S. population had risen to 7 percent. Whites had fallen to 80 percent of the population. The increasing numbers of Hispanic and Asian immigrants reduced blacks to 57 percent of the minority population (Kent et al. 2001; Richie 2000). In 1985 *Time* magazine dedicated an entire issue to immigrants, proclaiming that "they are rapidly and permanently changing the face of America. They are altering the nation's racial makeup, its cities, its tastes, its entire perception of itself and its way of life" (*Time,* July 8, 1985, 1).

This new diversity during the 1980s should have been enough to bring culture back in to social-science theories of immigrant adaptation. But politics once again intervened as the neoconversative lexicon gained a monopoly on the terms "values" and "culture" during President Ronald Reagan's two administrations. Reagan's policies revived notions of culture in ways that intensified suspicions among most social scientists. His scholarly supporters, such as the historian Charles Murray (1984, 220), dismissed policies like public assistance as "social engineering" that were doomed to fail because they merely "encourage dysfunctional values and behaviors." According to Murray (1984, 220) cultural explanations had found a sponsor in the White House: "It is now intellectually respectable, as until recently it was not, to argue that welfare children should be indoctrinated with middle-class values."

As a result of this new political rhetoric, social-science theories about immigrants, race, and ethnicity came to be judged by whether they supported the neoconservative policy paradigm. Some did so explicitly, such as the economist Thomas Sowell's (1981, 296) *Ethnic America,* which sought to shift explanations for inequality away from "racist teachers and biased tests." Instead he argued that values and norms explain variation in socioeconomic achievement among racial and ethnic groups in the United States.

Other scholars advanced more complex reinterpretations of inequality but still sounded like Reagan's neoconservative coterie. The sociologist William Julius Wilson (1987) attempted to call attention to the consequences of concentrated poverty among urban blacks. In doing so he reinvented the culture-of-poverty thesis by attributing poverty among blacks to a "tangle of pathology" (a phrase taken from the Moynihan Report), including "black crime, teenage pregnancy, female-headed families, and welfare dependency" (21).

Cultural arguments about race and socioeconomic status became even more discredited from the late 1960s to the 1980s as the media propagated the view that Asian Americans are a "model minority." *U.S. News and World Report* claimed that "few groups are as determined to get ahead as those whose roots are in the Pacific and Far East" (McBee 1984, 41). This assertion implies the invidious question: Which groups lack such determination? The answer, apparently, is groups with a cultural deficiency. The *Wall Street Journal* argued that Southeast Asian refugees adapted quickly because of "values that spell success: work, school, thrift, family."[4] Similarly, a *New York Times Magazine* article explained that "Asian-Americans thrive by transplanting old values" (Oxnam 1986, 70). Not to be outdone, *Fortune* magazine called Asians "America's super minority" and asserted that they "have wasted no time laying claim to the American dream. They are smarter and better educated and make more money than everyone else" (Ramirez 1986, 148).

The politicization of the model-minority myth further stigmatized concepts such as values for social scientists in the fields of immigration and race and ethnicity. During the 1992 presidential campaign the Republican vice-presidential candidate, Dan Quayle, announced the formation of the group "Asian Americans for Bush-Quayle." He claimed that "the Bush administration shares so many values with the Asian-American community, including an emphasis on entrepreneurship, close-knit families, crime prevention, hard work, and education" (quoted in Hoang 1992, 17). To this day culture is often used as a test for divining the conservative or liberal sympathies of social scientists who study immigrants, race, and ethnicity. As Waters (1999, 334) notes in self-defense: "In arguing that there are cultural expectations about race that explain some of the dynamics of West Indian success in the service economy, I am not in agreement with the classical 'cultural' explanations for West Indian success." Thus, despite some efforts to balance cultural and structural analysis of immigrant economic adaptation (van Niekerk 2004; Perlmann 1988; Vermeulen and Perlmann 2000), invoking culture in the field of race and ethnic relations is not for those with thin skin. According to Steinberg (2000, 61): "The pairing of 'culture' with 'socioeconomic position' is a red flag signaling a discourse that is fraught with problems and anything but politically innocent."

From Values and Norms to Ethnic Options

Culture has traditionally been defined as values and norms internalized through a socialization process (Griswold 2004). Values refer to ideals that people hope they and others will live up to, whereas norms refer to rules regarding conduct. It is now recognized that culture is less programmed than once thought and that individuals have considerable agency in how they enact values and norms (Swidler 1986). Nonetheless, ideals and conduct are heavily influenced by the place where people experience the early stages of the life course and the significant others who shape this process. For example, a majority of middle and high school students in central Mexico want to work in the United States someday because "international migration is cultural in the sense that the aspiration to migrate is transmitted across generations" (Kandel and Massey 2002, 981).

Where culture can be conceptualized as a way of life defined by values and norms, ethnicity refers to the cultural markers that distinguish group boundaries and sustain a sense of membership and identity (Barth 1969a). During the 1980s, social scientists moved away from thinking of ethnic identity as rooted in "primordial bonds," as Clifford Geertz (1963) had argued to explain why newly independent states in Asia and Africa often failed to embrace modernity. Instead, social scientists increasingly viewed ethnicity as an emergent identity shaped by structural factors such as work and housing patterns (Yancey, Erickson, and Juliani 1976) and resource competition (Hannan 1979; Nagel and Olzak 1982).

This pragmatic conception of ethnicity seemed particularly persuasive in contrast to more "essentialist" notions of cultural identity rooted in a suspect sociobiology. The political scientist Harold Isaacs (1975, 27) felt that "tribal solidarity" is "lodged in the old limbic system of the brain rather than in the neocortex." Similarly, the sociologist Pierre L. van den Berghe (1981, 8) argued that ethnicity stemmed from kinship ties based on a "genetically selected propensity for nepotism." Henceforth any suggestion that ethnicity had deep cultural roots now carried the stigma of biological determinism.

The growing consensus that ethnic identity is emergent rather than primordial gained credence from the postmodernist paradigm that swept through the social sciences during the 1980s and 1990s. Postmodernism rejects notions of objectivity and fixed meanings. Its proponents argue that "culture is only a play of images without reference to some underlying reality" (Griswold 2004, 48) and therefore a person's or group's "identity is multiple, problematic, fluid, self-reflexive, 'plural,' and 'decentered' " (Lamont 2000, 244). In the area of race and ethnic relations this postmodernist view became known as the social-constructionist perspective, according to which "the origin, content, and form of ethnicity reflect the creative choices of individuals and groups as they define themselves and others in ethnic ways" (Nagel 1994, 152). Following Ann Swidler's (1986) metaphor of culture as a tool kit, Joane Nagel (1994) suggested that "ethnic culture" could be conceived of as a shopping cart.

The experiences of European Americans best typify this voluntaristic conception of ethnicity. Herbert Gans (1979) called identities such as Irish American "symbolic ethnicity" because they lacked a material basis in neighborhoods and work places. Waters's (1990) brilliant book on Irish, Italian, and other European Americans epitomized this view in the title *Ethnic Options: Choosing Identities in America*. Waters carefully noted that the race and generational status of European Americans distinguished them from other groups in the United States. Nevertheless, her study quickly became the archetype for the social-constructionist perspective of ethnicity in general. Thus, according to Nagel (1994, 162, emphasis in original):

> It is important that we discard the notion that culture is simply an historical legacy; culture is *not* a shopping cart that comes to us already loaded with a set of historical cultural goods. Rather we construct culture by picking and choosing items from the shelves of the past and present.

By the time, around 1990, that ethnicity came to be seen as a form of consumerism, immigrants had risen to 8 percent of the U.S. population on their way to more than 10 percent by 2000 (del Pinal and Singer 1997; Kent et al. 2001; Lee 1998; Richie 2000). Other momentous changes had also occurred. By 1990 non-Hispanic whites had fallen to 76 percent of the population and for the first time in postcolonial American history blacks constituted less than half of the minority population (48 percent). In the previous two decades the Hispanic population had increased by 133 percent and by 2000 it outnumbered the African American population. In addition to the historic flow from Cuba and Mexico, Hispanic immigrants now came from new source countries including the Dominican Republic, El Salvador, and Colombia. The Asian American population had increased even more rapidly, by 353 percent from 1970 to 1990. Immigrants from India, Korea, China, and the Philippines augmented their historic presence, and entirely new populations also arrived from places such as Vietnam, Laos, and Cambodia. Asian Americans became so diverse that the largest ethnic group (Chinese) only constituted 24 percent of their population (by contrast, Mexicans account for 59 percent of Hispanic Americans). Even the black population diversified through the arrival of immigrants from Jamaica, Haiti, Guyana, Nigeria, and Ethiopia.

American society is now more culturally diverse than at any other point in its history (Reimers 2005). Yet the postmodernist perspective has so eviscerated the concepts of culture and ethnicity that they can hardly do justice to this new pluralism. Ignoring cultural variation among immigrants undermines the public credibility of the social sciences. It also incapacitates theoretical development. In the next section, I briefly review theories based on assimilation, ethnic competition, and modes of incorporation, as well as the transnational perspective. I show how each one makes a significant contribution to understanding immigrants' adaptation to new patterns of race and ethnic relations. I also demonstrate that they largely neglect cultural variation among immigrants and thus the importance of immigrants' ethnic origins.

Assimilation

The distinctive histories, politics, and cultures among immigrants did not interest the first sociologists who studied them. Robert Park (1950; 1914/1967) and others tended to treat European immigrants as an undifferentiated mass of premodern peasants. In their view international migration disrupted traditional communal ties and caused social disorganization among immigrants, such as familial conflict and alcoholism. Assimilation—replacing one's original culture with the culture of a dominant group—would solve these problems by eventually merging the newcomers with the native population. This depiction of a linear and inevitable assimilation into American society eventually became the conventional view of immigrants among sociologists (Warner and Srole 1945) and historians (Handlin 1951/1973).

Although difficult to appreciate now, in the early 1900s the assimilation model represented an optimistic view of immigrants. It arose during the Progressive Era, when urban reformers, journalists, and scholars sought to expose and ameliorate social problems (Zaretsky 1996). Park and other sociologists vigorously disputed the views of contemporary nativists who attributed crime, vice, and poverty among eastern and southern European immigrants to racial and cultural inferiority. According to the nativists of the 1920s, these newest immigrants lacked the capacities of earlier arrivals from northern and western Europe and thus threatened the integrity of American society (Higham 1974). Since many native elites used immigrants' culture against them, it is not surprising that assimilation theory focuses on immigrants' future in the host society rather than their lives in their past and homelands.

Despite its progressive intellectual origins, the assimilation model became unpopular among social scientists for almost two decades. The civil rights and ethnic pride movements of the 1960s and 1970s appeared to contradict its premise that racial and cultural differences would increasingly wane. Yet reform of U.S. immigration policy in the midst of these political and social developments set the stage for the reemergence of the assimilation model. The numbers of immigrants from Asia, Latin America, and the Caribbean increased dramatically in the decades following passage of new immigration laws in 1965.

Since then, social scientists have increasingly returned to the assimilation model to explain the reduction of differences between immigrants and natives over time, particularly in fertility rates, familial roles, intermarriage, and segregation. Douglas Massey (1981) reviewed the immigrant literature from 1965 to 1980 and concluded that most Asian and Hispanic immigrants "appear to be well-launched on the path to assimilation with the core of American life" (77–78). Richard Alba and Victor Nee (2003, 270) surveyed the research on immigrants during the 1980s and early 1990s and reached the same assessment: "Assimilation remains a pattern of major import for immigrant groups entering the United States." Assimilation theory even gained a renewed credence among historians, who are well known for parsing nuances and avoiding grand generalizations. According to Elliott Barkan (1995, 46), a president of the Immigration and Ethnic History Society, "Multitudes of individuals of many ethnic ancestries have assimilated into the broader general society—and indeed into the expanded Anglo-American core group." This renewed interest in the assimilation model, however, did not change the fact that it analytically deemphasizes cultural variation among immigrants at the time of arrival.

A partial breakthrough in acknowledging the diversity among immigrants came from recognition that immigrant groups exhibit different types of assimilation patterns. Termed segmented assimilation (Portes and Rumbaut 2001; Portes and Zhou 1993; Zhou 1997), the theory suggests that the outcomes of immigrant adaptation are contingent on several factors, including government policy, prejudice, and the size and class composition of the ethnic community. For example, West Indian youth in some New York City neighborhoods assimilate the adversarial subculture of their inner-city peers, thus alienating parents and other adults in the ethnic community and losing crucially needed social capital (Waters 1999). Conversely, many Vietnamese American children in New Orleans have a high level of scholastic achievement because they maintain a strong attachment to the ethnic traditions of their parents and community (Zhou and Bankston 1998).

Segmented assimilation theory does not, however, analyze cultural variation among immigrants at the time of arrival. Instead, it examines a conglomeration of social and structural factors subsumed under the rubric of nationality, such as "legal Mexicans," "Cuban refugees, 1960–80" and "Haitian boat people, 1979–83" (Portes and Zhou 1993, 84). Thus even this revised assimilation model retains a resemblance to the original theory developed by Park. Its explanation focuses on conditions in the host society and minimizes the importance of culture and other aspects of immigrants' ethnic origins.

Ethnic Competition

A number of studies in the 1940s and 1950s began questioning the validity of the assimilation model (see Kazal 1995 for a historiography of this literature). Nathan Glazer and Daniel Patrick Moynihan (1963) launched the most decisive challenge in their classic book *Beyond the Melting Pot.* They argued that ethnicity still mattered to the Irish, Italians, and other ethnic groups in New York City because it helped organize their participation in unions, elections, and other political activities. Reducing their thesis to a slogan, Glazer and Moynihan concluded that "the ethnic groups in New York are also *interest groups*" (17, emphasis in original).

From this perspective, ethnicity is not a liability that prevents assimilation but a highly functional adaptation because groups with greater solidarity are better able to achieve collective goals. In refuting assimilation theory, however, *Beyond the Melting Pot* shifted attention away from cultural issues entirely and gave priority to materialistic outcomes.

Glazer and Moynihan's (1963) insight that ethnicity can be a resource, and that its importance is heightened by intergroup conflict, is now known as ethnic-competition theory. Assimilation theory posits that segregation and isolation perpetuate attachment to ethnic identities, whereas proximity and interaction reduces them. Ethnic-competition theory reverses this argument: increased contact among previously separated groups actually intensifies ethnic differences (Hannan 1979; Nagel and Olzak 1982; Olzak 1992). Interaction that entails competition for resources increases in-group solidarity even more. Based on a social-ecology model, the theory points to trends in urbanization, immigration, and labor markets to explain the shifting salience of ethnicity. Competition theory's essential insight into ethnic identity is that "ethnic group boundaries coincide with niche boundaries" (Hannan 1979, 260).

Research on Hispanic Americans supports the claims of ethnic-competition theory (Itzigsohn, Giorguli, and Vazquez 2005; Ono 2002; Portes 1984; Portes and Bach 1985; Portes and McLeod 1996; Sizemore and Milner 2004). In general, those who are the most integrated into the society and have achieved the most economic success report the strongest perceptions of discrimination against their group (but compare Aguirre, Saenz, and Hwang 1989; Floyd and Gramman 1995; Kleugel and Bobo 2001). A similar relationship between higher socioeconomic status and increased awareness of inequality has also been documented for Asian Americans (Bell, Harrison, and McLaughlin 1997; Hein 1994; Kleugel and Bobo 2001; Roberts 1988; Zhou 2001). Research on African Americans' perceptions of inequality finds the same pattern: blacks with higher-status occupations and more education report the most discrimination against blacks (Adams and Dressler 1988; Bobo and Hutchings 1996; Moghaddam et al. 1995; Sigelman and Welch 1992). Jennifer Hochschild (1995, 73) concludes from four decades of survey data that "well-off African Americans see more racial discrimination than do poor blacks, see less decline in discrimination, expect less improvement in the future, and claim to have experienced more in their own lives."

Ethnic-competition theory clearly poses a challenge to assimilation theory. There is substantial empirical support for its position that awareness of social inequality is greatest among those members of racial and ethnic groups who would appear to be the most assimilated. The more groups interact, the more the importance of group differences is perpetuated and even heightened, especially when they contend for scarce resources. Yet ethnic-competition theory examines immigrants entirely from the perspective of the host society and assumes that their homeland histories, politics, and cultures do not influence the forms or outcomes of conflict with natives.

Modes of Incorporation

A second challenge to assimilation theory began after some sociologists (Glazer 1971), historians (Handlin 1962), and political commentators (Kristol 1966) applied the theory to the migration of African Americans from the rural South to northern cities during the 1950s and 1960s. They asserted that these newcomers would experience an adaptation process similar to that of European immigrants during the early twentieth century. The sociologist Robert Blauner challenged this prediction.

In a widely cited journal article (1969) and subsequently a book (1972), Blauner argued that the form of a group's entry into American society—its mode of incorporation—has profound long-run consequences for its position in the society. Groups that enter a new society through voluntary incorporation, such as European Americans, temporarily become immigrant minorities. They wait their turn in a queuing process and eventually gain freedom to change areas of settlement, political influence, control over cultural change, and access to all sectors of the economy. Conversely, groups that experience coercive incorporation through conquest, such as African Americans, Native Americans, and Chicanos, become permanent colonized minorities. Involuntary incorporation excludes them from the queuing process in which newer groups gradual move up the societal rungs. Instead, colonized minorities experience economic exploitation, geographic marginalization, forced assimilation, and social control by the political system. Because of these differences, Blauner predicted that blacks migrating to northern cities would not replicate the adaptation of European immigrants and he has obviously been proved correct. Yet in debunking assimilation theory Blauner suggested that all voluntary immigrants have the same pattern of adaptation and thus that their cultural variation is irrelevant.

Despite its origins in a unique period of American race relations, the theory of immigrant and colonized minorities remains central to social-science understanding of racial and ethnic inequality (Omi and Winant 1994; Pedraza 1994; Portes and Bach 1985). Because of its intuitively obvious distinction between voluntary and involuntary modes of incorporation, Blauner's theory is included in anthologies (Takaki 1994) and textbooks (Aguirre and Turner 1998; Marger 1997; McLemore 1998). According to one popular textbook (Healy 1997, 68–69): "Blauner's typology has proven to be an extremely useful conceptual tool for the analysis of U.S. dominant-minority relations and it is used extensively in this text. In fact, when we conduct case studies of minority groups starting in chapter 5, we cover the groups in approximate order from those created by colonization to those created by immigration." This approach is not merely simplistic history for undergraduates. John Higham (1982, 1452), one of the most eminent authorities on ethnicity and immigration, notes that "historians, while comparing the advancement of certain white ethnic groups, have generally been unwilling to compare the various races because the circumstances of their incorporation into American society were so different."

One of the most enduring applications of the modes-of-incorporation theory concerns the educational disadvantage of African American students compared to their immigrant peers, such as Asian Americans. Following Blauner, the anthropologist John Ogbu (1978) explains variation in academic achievement by distinguishing between immigrant and caste minorities. Because of their different "initial terms of incorporation," Ogbu argues (1991a; 1991b, 8; Fordam and Ogbu 1986) that caste minorities develop oppositional identities and cultures which define mainstream institutions (such as schools) as sources of group oppression. In contrast, immigrant minorities consider mainstream institutions as sources of opportunity because they emphasize individual success and acceptance by a dominant group.

The merits of Ogbu's theory have been questioned (Ainsworth-Darnell and Downey 1998), but research on the Hmong supports his argument. In both St. Paul (McNall, Dunnigan, and Mortimer 1994) and Madison, Wisconsin (Lee 2001), Hmong students exhibit high educational aspirations and achievement compared to native students. Similarly, Waters (1999) relies on Ogbu's theory to explain why West Indian blacks, who migrate from a former slave society, are often more successful in the United States than African Americans. According to Waters: "The movement to the United States seems to provide the immigrants with a 'foreign' status, which makes their reactions to discrimination and prejudice more likely to resemble those of other voluntary immigrants in the United States, than to resemble those of black Americans" (144).

Bimodal theories like that of Blauner and Ogbu have limitations: they cannot explain variation among immigrants, since by definition they all share the same voluntary mode of incorporation. Alejandro Portes and Ruben Rumbaut (2001) ingeniously resolve this problem with a multi-factor mode of incorporation theory applied to immigrant youths. They attribute level of educational achievement to several variables in the context of reception, including government policy toward different types of immigrants and the degree of societal prejudice they face. These and other factors shape the extent to which immigrant parents and students actualize "the values and resources that they themselves have brought" (276). This view casts a glance back at the homeland but ultimately rests on the belief in a universal "immigrant achievement drive" that is channeled by conditions in the host society (281). In the end, all variants of the mode-of-incorporation theory assume that the cultures in immigrants' homelands are a constant rather than a variable.

Transnationalism

The emergence of a transnational perspective on migration during the 1980s and 1990s should have revived the concept of culture in theories about immigrant adaptation, particularly since the primary credit for this new perspective goes to three anthropologists: Linda Basch, Nina Glick Schiller, and Christina Szanton Blanc (1994; Glick Schiller, Basch, and Blanc-Szanton 1992, 1995). Although they had intellectual predecessors (Georges 1990; Sutton 1987), Basch, Glick Schiller, and Szanton Blanc (1994, 7) provided the first comprehensive conceptualization of transnationalism, defining it as "the processes by which immigrants forge and sustain multi-stranded social relations that link together their societies of origin and settlement. We call these processes transnationalism to emphasize that many immigrants today build social fields that cross geographic, cultural, and political borders."

Transnationalism was a fact well before it had a name. Chicano studies had long emphasized the need to examine both sides of national borders (Barrera 1979). But the increased flow of legal and illegal immigrants from Mexico during the 1980s gave the issue great relevance for U.S. public policy. The sociologist Douglas Massey and a team of Mexican anthropologists (Massey et al. 1987) addressed this issue in a novel way by collecting data in both western Mexico and California. Their pathbreaking book *Return to Aztlan* revealed how the social networks linking Mexican cities with daughter communities in the United States created a cumulative process of circular migration rather than a definitive emigration. On the basis of these findings Massey and colleagues (1987) accurately predicted that U.S. immigration policy could never end illegal immigration because it was a self-sustaining social process that transcended political borders. This was a stunning finding during the 1980s, given public hysteria about illegal immigration and subsequent passage of the Immigration Reform and Control Act of 1986, which only diminished the flow for a few years.

Caribbean immigration provided an even earlier impetus for a transnational perspective. The social links between Puerto Rico and New York City were well known to social scientists during the 1960s.

Glazer and Moynihan (1963, 99–100) described New York Puerto Ricans as an "island centered community," noting that "many would be hard put to say whether they belonged to the city or the island." Indeed, if not for his ill-fated culture of poverty theory, Oscar Lewis (1965) might be remembered as a pioneer of transnationalism, since he studied kinship networks in San Juan and New York City. The "bidirectional" quality of Caribbean migration continued to be emphasized during the 1970s (Sutton and Makiesky 1975). The big empirical breakthrough, however, came from research undertaken by the sociologist Sherri Grasmuck and the anthropologist Patricia Pessar (1991) in the Dominican Republic and New York City. In *Between Two Islands* they established the importance of social networks in organizing household, extended family, and communal migration in both directions. Absent the concept of transnationalism, Grasmuck and Pessar (1991, 199) situated their findings within world-systems theory, a neo-Marxist perspective developed in the 1960s and early 1970s which argues that "international migration follows the political and economic organization of an expanding global market" (Massey et al. 1998, 41).

With world-systems theory as an intellectual stepping stone, the transnational perspective offered by Basch, Glick Schiller, and Szanton Blanc (1994) quickly captured the interest of many scholars studying immigrants. It seemed self-evident that international migration was just one of several trends requiring a global view of issues once thought of as primarily or exclusively centered in the nation-state (Bauböck 1994; Sassen 1991; Soysal 1994). Events during the 1980s and 1990s provided abundant evidence that globalization was eroding national boundaries: larger multinational corporations, more international trade and human rights accords, rising dual citizenship, increasingly globalized forms of consumerism and entertainment, and especially the invention of the Internet. Taken together these developments suggested that the view of immigrants as belonging to only one nation-state—the homeland or the host society—had become an anachronism. Some researchers even proposed the concept of a transnational diaspora in which social networks, the media, and geographic mobility link immigrants from the same ethnic group in multiple host societies (Clifford 1994; Lie 1995).

By the early twenty-first century, journal articles examining immigrants or migration from a transnational perspective were appearing virtually every month, with 431 citations listed in the database Sociological Abstracts for 2000 to 2005. The growth of this research front was in part the result of increasing debate over the validity of the transnational perspective. Was it really a new development among immigrants? Did it apply only to those with homelands adjacent to the host society? Would transnationalism quickly fade among second and later generations? (See Foner [2000] and Levitt, DeWind, and Vertovec [2003] for reviews of these arguments and Portes [2003] for a judicious verdict.)

Such debates will not be settled quickly, but one outcome is clear: the rise of the transnational perspective did not bring culture back in to theories about immigrants' adaptation. This surprising and unfortunate development is another legacy of postmodernism. In the opening chapter of their monumental book *Nations Unbound*, Basch, Glick Schiller, and Szanton Blanc note (1994, 10) how "post-modern ethnographies are arguing for a world of multiple paths," and they defensively state that "by even proposing the term 'analytical framework' we run the risk of being dismissed as being in the sway of 19th century Western positivism." Under this lurking postmodernist threat, they timidly define culture as "all human practice, understood to include both thought and action" and then make almost no analytical use of it in the remainder of the book (12).

This missed opportunity notwithstanding, the explosion of interest in transnationalism has created the ideal intellectual environment in which to reintroduce values, norms, and culture to the conceptual lexicon of research on immigrants. From the start, research on transnationalism examined global cultural diffusion, such as how the Western consumerism and more egalitarian gender roles among immigrants impacted those who never left (Georges 1990; Grasmuck and Pessar 1991). Based on these findings and her own research on Dominicans in Boston and on the island, the sociologist Peggy Levitt (2001, 60) concludes that immigrants' cultural adaptation in the host society leads to "social remittances" when "they communicate the values and norms they have observed to those at home." Only a small step is now required to acknowledge that the values and norms that immigrants bring with them shape their adaptation as well. Indeed, these venerable concepts are vital to fully achieving one goal of the transnational perspective: understanding how "the manner in which immigrants . . . articulate their sense of estrangement from the United States is shaped by their own national constructions about race and nationality formed in their home countries" (Basch, Glick Schiller, and Szanton Blanc 1994, 234).

Conclusion

There is universal agreement that the United States is experiencing unprecedented demographic change as a result of international migration from Latin America, Asia, Africa, and the Caribbean (Reimers 2005). Each year about 800,000 immigrants become legal residents of the United States. These new members of American society include approximately 50,000 immigrants picked annually by lottery through a "diversity program" under legislation passed by Congress "to introduce more variety into the stream of immigrants to the United States" (Martin and Midgley 2003, 7). President Clinton's Advisory Board on Race appreciated these dramatic developments: "We are becoming a new society, based on a fresh mixture of immigrants, racial groups, religions, and cultures" (President's Advisory Board on Race 1998, 54). The director of the U.S. Census, Kenneth Prewitt, gives an even bolder assessment: "The twenty-first century will be the century in which we redefine ourselves as the first country in world history which is literally made up of every part of the world."[5] Yet despite the obvious need for the concept culture in research on immigrants, two developments in the fields of immigration and race and ethnic relations during the 1960s, 1970s, and 1980s placed it off limits.

The first development was theoretical. Many social scientists now view ethnicity as an epiphenomenon lacking deep cultural roots. For postmodernists, ethnicity is a symbolic identity based on individual choice, not socialization. For neo-Marxists in the tradition of Steinberg's (1981/1989) *The Ethnic Myth*, ethnicity reflects underlying resource competition and other features of class. Both views resist efforts to link ethnicity with values and norms internalized through socialization, one widely accepted definition of culture (Griswold 2004).

The second development was political. Many social scientists impulsively reject any conceptualization of racial and ethnic inequality that even hints at the influence of values and norms. In their view an approach to social problems that includes culture is de facto endorsement of the neoconservative policy paradigm that dismisses the influence of race, class, gender, and other forms of domination.

To appreciate these paradigmatic changes in the study of race, ethnicity, and immigration, consider the reception of the sociologist Ewa Morawska's (1985) book on east-central European immigrants in Johnstown, Pennsylvania, between 1890 and 1940. Among its many topics, *For Bread with Butter* examined how "peasant cultural values," including work ethic, fatalism, and attitudes toward formal education, influenced the immigrants' adaptation to an urban industrial society (23). Reviews in leading journals justly praised the book as "required reading" (Alexander 1988, 144), "theoretically sophisticated" (Bensman 1988, 173), "state-of-the-art" (Light 1988, 455), and "definitive" (Prpic 1987, 761). Yet a comparable study of contemporary immigrants from agricultural societies risks accusations of racism and reification.

These political and postmodernist pitfalls in the fields of immigration and race and ethnicity constrain theoretical explanations of immigrant adaptation. They create disincentives to analyze immigrants' homelands, since that is the site of distinctive values and norms. Thus, theories based on assimilation, ethnic competition, and modes of incorporation are the same in one important respect, despite considerable differences in their conceptual premises and historical origins: they ignore cultural variation among immigrants. Even the transnational perspective of immigrant adaptation does not emphasize how immigrants' values and norms shape their adaptation. Reclaiming culture as a vital concept for the analysis of immigrant adaptation is therefore the first step in recognizing the significance of their ethnic origins.

Immigrants' ethnic origins comprise history and politics but also cultural values and norms internalized through socialization. This definition of culture is admittedly one of the simplest. It combines the anthropologist Clifford Geertz's idea of culture as a system of symbols with an older notion of culture as learned behavior (Sewell 1999b). There are, however, several advantages in using this definition in research on immigrants.

First, conceptualizing culture as value, norms, and socialization fits well with the way immigrants talk about their experiences. For example, in this chapter's opening vignettes Heng states that "we believe in Buddhism," while Mee notes that "Hmong culture" makes them "a clan people." Taking people at their word risks merely endorsing folk theories, a disparaging term that social scientists use to mean commonsense, but inaccurate, explanations for complex social problems. But a much more serious error occurs when social scientists deny people the right to speak for themselves. In fact, scholars who study immigrants usually respect them as informants and rely on them to help us understand a social world with which we often have little or no personal experience.

Second, the simplicity of values, norms, and socialization means that the concepts can be operationalized in empirical research. Obtaining information from individuals through surveys and semistructured personal interviews are the main methodologies used to study immigrants. It is thus essential to easily move from concepts to data collection. More complex definitions of culture are needed when social scientists analyze agency and ideology in phenomena such as social movements, scientific paradigms, and movies. Yet the vast majority of research on immigrants aspires to achieve something much more basic: understanding groups by examining the characteristics of individuals.

Third, one of the central concerns in immigration research is the adaptation process, or how individuals as members of households, networks, and communities meet their needs in a new social environment. Adaptation is a form of resocialization. Many of the central debates in the field concern whether resocialization is positive or negative for immigrants (for example, does Americanization improve or hinder school achievement) and to what degree it is ever fully completed (for example, how rapidly do immigrants adopt American gender roles). Interest in these processes indicate the necessity of including learned behavior in the definition of culture.

Finally, culture as a concept is largely absent from theories of immigrant adaptation based on assimilation, ethnic competition, and modes of incorporation and appears only in a diluted form in the transnational perspective, where race, nationality, and politics are paramount. Proponents of these explanations have little incentive to include culture, given the political and postmodernist critiques of the past forty years. It therefore seems reasonable to start with a simple definition of culture before theories of immigrant adaptation move on to more complex definitions.

═ Chapter 2 ═

Ethnic Origins

The sociologists Michael Omi and Howard Winant's (1994, 60) influential theory of racial formation is based on the idea that "everybody learns some combination, some version of the rules of racial classification." This socialization occurs very differently for natives and immigrants, however. Members of a native minority, such as African Americans, develop a racial identity and an awareness of racial inequality from an early age through parental and peer socialization (Demo and Hughes 1990; Jackson et al. 1991). Conversely, immigrants undergo a process of resocialization as they encounter new racial and ethnic identities and inequalities in the United States.

Racial and ethnic resocialization is just one of numerous adjustments required when immigrants reside in a new social environment. Well-known forms of adaptation include economic (Bailey and Waldinger 1991), familial (Kibria 1993), and gender (Hondagneu-Sotelo 1994), as well as less-studied forms such as religious (Warner 1998), legal (Hein and Beger 2001), and medical adaptation (Menjívar 2002). I use the term "racial and ethnic adaptation" to describe immigrants' adjustment to the attitudinal, behavioral, and institutional system of race and ethnicity in a host society.

All forms of immigrant adaptation involve an interaction between immigrants' conditioning in their homeland and conditions in the host society. In the case of racial and ethnic adaptation, the relevant features of the host society are identities and inequalities based on perceived physical appearance and culture. Until immigrants are fully assimilated (if that ever happens), they rely heavily on their homeland histories, politics, and cultures to interpret and respond to American diversity. Cambodian and Hmong refugees exemplify this process because they had little or no prior knowledge of American race and ethnic relations before they arrived. As a result, their ethnic origins have an enormous influence on how they feel about identities such as Asian American, how they perceive inequalities such as racism, and how they react to political injustice.

Learning About American Diversity

Globalization has become such a buzzword that it is easy to assume that everybody has a world map in their head. Such was not the case for Cambodian refugees arriving in the United States. Villagers near Cambodia's capital in about 1960 had only the barest understanding of the features of the globe (Ebihara 1968, 577): "The world beyond Cambodia's borders is largely terra incognita. The country's immediate neighbors, Thailand, Laos, and Vietnam, are the only nations whose exact locations are known and whose names are recognized in some meaningful fashion. . . . The rest of the world floats in a nebulous haze somewhere 'out there.' "

Hmong villagers were traditionally even more isolated because they lived in mountainous areas at elevations of 3,000 to 5,000 feet without any forms of modern communication. The small size of villages and transportation problems compounded this isolation even more, according to Yang Dao (Yang 1975/1993, 17): "Hmong villages contain an average of 10 or 20 houses. Those having more than 50 houses are a rarity. Villages are often several hours', sometimes even several days', walk apart. . . . During the rainy season, when vegetation is profuse and the forests are crawling with leeches, villagers do as little traveling as possible."

As a result of such insularity, almost all of the 179 Cambodians and Hmong I surveyed in Eau Claire, Rochester, Chicago, and Milwaukee (using procedures described in appendices A and B) report knowing little or nothing about blacks, American Indians, Hispanics, and other Asians in the United States (see table 2.1).

Only a few respondents had learned about American racial and ethnic minorities through education in their homeland. Suom had fifteen years of schooling in Cambodia (making him one of my most educated respondents) and had been a teacher before the Khmer Rouge revolution. During a follow-up interview I asked Suom what American meant to Cambodians prior to arrival in the United States and he responded:

> They just mean white. Over there, if you say black they think you mean African. They don't believe blacks live in America. They're surprised. When African Americans go to Cambodia they believe they're from Africa, not America. I read and heard that it's mixed over here. Before, during the slave time, they buy people from Africa, that's part of the mix here. Some Cambodians never read about that and now they are surprised that it's not only white people here. They're surprised to see mostly blacks in sports on TV. They say they cannot be American. They don't believe it. But if they went to school in Cambodia then they understand.

About 10 percent of respondents had learned about American minority groups in schools in a refugee camp. Nonetheless, these

Table 2.1   Refugees' Sources of Information About American Diversity by Size of Current U.S. City (Percentages; Multiple Answers Accepted)

	Big City	Small City
Pre-arrival		
Homeland school	5	3
Refugee camp school	15	8
Post-arrival		
School	80	69*
Media	81	68*
Whites	54	18***
Minorities	66	23***
Own group	63	40**

Source: Author's compilation.
Note: N = 82 in big cities, 97 in small cities.
*p < .10; **p < .01; ***p < .001

schools sometimes failed to provide an accurate picture of race and ethnicity in the United States. Heng reported during a follow-up interview that actually interacting with African Americans was far different from the abstract knowledge he had received in a refugee camp school in Thailand:

> I was surprised the first time I saw black people. They were standing in front of my building the first morning after I arrived. Maybe I didn't notice them at the airport because I was so sleepy. When I saw them I thought, "They look strange." [He quickly interjects.] Not discrimination. I just never saw people like that. Then I knew there were different kinds of people in the U.S. They spoke fast, like "whitwhitwhitwhit" [he makes a whistling sound]. In Thailand I studied about America, about slavery, I knew there were blacks and whites in the U.S. But . . . [pauses then laughs] I never knew what a black person looked like.

As Suom and Heng suggest, Cambodian and Hmong refugees arrive with very little knowledge about the range of racial and ethnic groups in the United States. The diversity they encounter can therefore be quite surprising to them. For example, on the survey Rebecca stated that she had not learned about American society in a homeland nor refugee camp school. During a follow-up interview, she described being startled by the extent of American diversity:

> When I first came to the United States and I saw black people, people with a different color, it was so amazing. I had never seen other groups before.

Living in Cambodia I didn't know there was another world because Cambodia's not so modern. It was like "Wow!" Like amazing. I never thought about different people. It was weird to see people with other height, other color, not Cambodian like myself. Not prejudice, but seeing differences just as unique. It was only five, ten years after, then I went to school and other students called me names. That's when I started thinking about prejudice.

Rebecca's final comments are particularly intriguing because they indicate the considerable resocialization that occurs as Southeast Asian refugees learn about American race and ethnic relations. Like Suom and Heng, Rebecca explains that she did not realize how many "different people" live in the United States. Yet she also notes that she did not anticipate experiencing prejudice, either. In fact, some refugees are initially unable to even determine when natives are expressing prejudice because they cannot understand English nor even interpret nonverbal communication. During an oral history interview (D.C. Everest Area Schools 2000, 35) in Wausau, Wisconsin, a Hmong man was asked, "Did you and your family experience any discrimination upon your arrival?" Shu Blong Her responded:

When I came to America, for myself, I didn't have the concept of discrimination or prejudice. We didn't have that terminology. And so whatever people did to us, whether it was bad or good, we couldn't tell anyway, because we couldn't speak English. And the gestures with their hands and the facial gestures, whether it was negative or positive, I couldn't identify them. But afterwards, I began to learn the English language, I noticed that some of those languages are not quite positive. I began to learn the terminology of people hating other people, especially of a different race.

Although newly arrived refugees often lack any comprehension of American diversity, they gradually piece together a portrait from a variety of groups and institutions where they live. Schools and the media are their primary sources of information, especially for younger refugees. In big but not in small cities, the refugees are likely to talk about American diversity with whites, racial and ethnic minorities, and members of their own ethnic group.

Cambodians and the Hmong draw upon a wide range of sources to learn about the United States but their knowledge is often incomplete (see table 2.2). Slightly less than one-half of the 179 refugees surveyed (49 percent) correctly answer four basic questions about racial and ethnic groups in the United States. About one in ten do not answer any of the questions correctly (9 percent) or have only one correct answer (another 10 percent).

This variation in knowledge of American diversity is mostly determined by age and education. Older respondents know much less than

Table 2.2   Refugees' Factual Knowledge About American Diversity (Percentage Answering Correctly)

"What is the name of the group whose ancestors were slaves in the United States?"	80
"What language do people from Mexico speak?"	72
"What is the name of the group whose ancestors were the first people to live in what is now the United States?"	70
"Where did the ancestors of most white people in the United States come from?"	65
All four answers correct	49

Source: Author's compilation.
Note: N = 179

younger ones and more years of U.S. education substantially increase knowledge. Yet years of U.S. residence is only moderately correlated with the number of correct answers (r = .165; p < .05) and there is no meaningful difference between respondents living in small or big cities. Immigrants add to the country's demographic diversity upon arrival, yet their understanding of this diversity often involves a lengthy process of resocialization.

Demonstrating that Cambodian and Hmong refugees are learning about American diversity raises the question of what worldview guides them during the process of racial and ethnic adaptation. I posit that ethnic origins serve this function. Homeland history, politics, and culture create specific types of ethnic boundaries which in turn shape how immigrants respond to new identities and inequalities following migration.

Ethnic Boundaries

The theory of symbolic interaction in sociology (Fine 1993) and intergroup behavior in psychology (Brewer and Brown 1998) explain how an individual's sense of self results from interaction with other people and produces a relational identity based on social categorization. These theoretical insights are often applied to ethnic groups via the anthropologist Fredrik Barth's (1969a) concept of an ethnic boundary. Barth explained how membership in an ethnic group (or in-group) is determined by comparison and often interaction with other groups (or out-groups). Each ethnic group develops "criteria for membership" and thus a distinct identity through a boundary-maintenance process that defines what makes the in-group different from out-groups (Barth 1969a, 38). Research in the field of social psychology supports this premise, particularly the findings on group schemas and in-group favoritism (see Fiske 1998 and Howard 2000 for a review of this literature).

Barth's (1969a) seminal essay is frequently cited in the social-constructionist literature on immigrants and ethnicity. Yet his own analysis of the Pathan in Pakistan repudiates the prevailing conceptualization of ethnicity that ignores how socialization creates durable values and norms. He noted that Pathan ethnicity is based on a "universal" acceptance of patrilineal descent, that "a Pathan must be an orthodox Moslem," and that the Pashto language is "a necessary and diacritical feature" of their identity (1969b, 119). In addition, Barth identified "core Pathan values" related to male sexuality, dominance, and patriarchy (123). He deemed these attributes "the essential characteristics of Pathans which, if changed, would change their ethnic categorization vis-à-vis one or several contrasting groups" (132).

Barth's compelling insight, therefore, is not that ethnicity results from an individual's choices but that "ethnic identities function as categories of inclusion/exclusion" between different groups (1969b, 132). All ethnic groups have a boundary, but these boundaries vary in the extent to which they include and exclude. Like a Venn diagram depicting the intersection of circles, an ethnic identity can overlap with those of other groups to varying degrees or be totally distinct.

The ethnic boundary of the Old Order Amish provides an excellent example of in-group and out-group polarization. This type of boundary creates a powerful sense of ethnic-group membership for the Amish through contrast with a negative reference group (Kraybill and Bowman 2001). Conversely, the ethnic boundary of Irish Americans involves subtle shadings of difference between in- and out-groups and greater flexibility on the criteria for group membership (Waters 1990) than that of the Amish. This discretionary approach to ethnic identity explains why the proportion of the American population claiming some Irish ancestry actually exceeds what is demographically possible on the basis of immigration and natural increase (Hout and Goldstein 1994). Ethnic boundaries thus range from hermetic to porous. Some have a "gate-keeping function protecting ethnically generated resources" while others have a "bridging function encouraging intergroup association" (Sanders 2002, 348; see Cornell 1996 for a more elaborate typology of ethnic boundaries).

I posit that when immigrants arrive in a host society their homeland ethnic boundaries filter new experiences and shape their responses to them. My approach to ethnic boundaries thus fits within the social-constructionist perspective of race and ethnicity. The ethnic-origins hypothesis emphasizes how interactions at one point in time (in immigrants' homelands) shape interactions later on (in the host society). Most applications of the social-constructionist perspective, on the other hand, examine only a single place and time and therefore find less continuity and more discretionary behavior. Conversely, the concept of ethnic origins emphasizes the durability of history, politics, and culture while still recognizing that ethnicity is not primordial.

Ethnic Origins: History, Politics, and Culture

Social scientists are justifiably suspicious of a cultural explanation because it can be an intellectual Trojan horse. Proponents of cultural arguments sometimes start with values and norms but then surreptitiously expand the conceptual meaning of these concepts. For example, Thomas Sowell (1996, 49) compares six immigrant diasporas in order to determine "the role of culture in the economic and social fates of peoples." He begins with a nuanced discussion of homeland geography, chain migration, and other factors. Three hundred pages later, however, "cultural capital" is used indiscriminately to explain everything from "intellect, sex, and art" (379) to "modern medical science" (382) and "life-style differences" (383). Cultural arguments self-destruct when they lack analytical precision.

Rather than elide the cultural and noncultural, the ethnic-origins hypothesis delineates four aspects of immigrants' homeland experiences that influence their racial and ethnic adaptation. Two are cultural: ideals concerning spiritual goals (religious values) and guidelines for determining ancestry (kinship norms). A third is historical: the forming of national borders around diverse peoples (nation-state formation). The fourth is political: conflict over the exercise of power (political cleavage). Each one of these components of immigrants' ethnic origins contributes to a particular conception of societal membership and what it means to belong to a people (see table 2.3).

A second reason that social scientists are justifiably suspicious of cultural arguments is that they often advance a simplistic, monocausal explanation. For example, one study of the high GPAs among Vietnamese and Lao children concludes, "We have accounted for the achievements of the refugees by emphasizing cultural values and the family setting in which these values are transmitted" (Caplan, Whitmore, and Choy 1989, 127). This statement is problematic because it analyzes culture in isolation from historical and structural factors in the homeland and the host society. Conversely, James Loewen's (1971/1988) study of economic success among Chinese Americans in Mississippi provides one of the earliest

Table 2.3   Culture, History, and Politics in the Formation of Ethnic Origins[a]

	Characteristics of Ethnic Origins
Culture	
Religious values	Degree of individualism and collectivism in spiritual aspirations
Kinship norms	Ratio of choice and constraint in social-network membership
Nation-state formation	Level of subordination, equality, and dominance in national institutions
Political cleavage	Salience of intra- and inter-ethnic conflict over power

Source: Author's compilation.
[a]Ethnic origins include components that I do not examine in this book, such as region and urban or rural residence, or hold constant, such as race and class. I subsume migration history and transnational ties within the component nation-state formation, although they could be analyzed separately.

examples of analysis that combines cultural and noncultural factors rather than prioritizing one over the other.

To avoid the common inadequacies of cultural arguments, I conceptualize Cambodian (or more accurately Khmer) and Hmong ethnic origins as a holistic combination of historical, political, and cultural components rather than individual causal variables (see Ragin 1987 for a detailed discussion of this distinction between case and variable analysis). Consequently, I do not specify the magnitude of the difference between Cambodian and Hmong ethnic origins, only that they represent fundamentally different types or sociological cases (see Becker 1992 and Ragin 1992 for a definition of what is a case). Cambodian ethnic origins are characterized by a porous ethnic boundary and a liminal ethnic identity. Hmong ethnic origins are characterized by a hermetic ethnic boundary and a polarized ethnic identity (see table 2.4, which summarizes the material presented in chapters 3 and 4).

A case-based analysis of culture has two analytical advantages over variable-based analysis. First, it does not prioritize or rank the four components of Cambodian and Hmong ethnic origins. Their influences are synthetic rather than additive. For example, in the case of the Hmong it would be futile to argue that being military allies of the U.S. CIA during the 1960s and then being abandoned at the war's end in 1975 is more influential for their ethnic origins than the diaspora from China circa 1800. Such an argument would fall into the historical fallacy of claiming that recent events are more powerful than those in the distant past. The

Table 2.4   Components and Qualities of Khmer and Hmong Ethnic Origins

	Khmer	Hmong
Components		
Religious values	Theravada Buddhism Merit and personal karma	Animism Ancestor worship
Kinship norms	Bilateral Discretionary ancestry	Patrilineal Clan and lineage
Nation-state formation	Hybrid culture with nation-state Dominant group	Diaspora without nation-state Minority group
Political cleavage (1960s to 1970s)	Intra-ethnic Limited intervention by U.S.	Inter-ethnic Extensive intervention by U.S.
Qualities	Porous boundary, liminal identity	Hermetic boundary, polarized identity

Source: Author's compilation.

converse is equally erroneous: that events occurring over a longer period of time (the diaspora) have a greater impact than those of shorter duration (the failed military alliance with the United States).

Similarly, when one is analyzing the ethnic origins of Cambodians it would be impossible to argue that their view of social relations derives mostly from Khmer Rouge atrocities or mostly from the value of merit shaping a person's karma. Any attempt to pursue this line of reasoning would quickly result in absurd counterfactual arguments. One would face the impossibility of guessing what the worldview of modern Cambodians would be like if the Khmer Rouge revolution had not occurred or if Theravada Buddhism did not have a notion of ethically influenced rebirth. Instead of pitting one variable against another in a fight for explanatory supremacy, the concept of ethnic origins respects the organic integrity of history, politics, and culture.

A second advantage of case analysis is that it avoids presenting culture as primordial. Ethnic origins are dynamic, not perpetual, because they result from the interaction of cultural and noncultural factors. Among immigrants, values and norms emerge from the group's adaptation to historical and structural conditions both prior to and after migration. A primordial approach to culture would argue that values and norms are invariant. Events in Cambodia easily disprove this argument, since the horrors of the Khmer Rouge revolution occurred in a society of devout Buddhists (for an explanation for this anomaly see Hinton 2005).

Hypothesis and Research Design

The ethnic-origins hypothesis states that immigrant groups with distinct ethnic origins will have different forms of racial and ethnic adaptation, even when these groups are similar in physical appearance, mode of incorporation, and socioeconomic status. More specifically, a group's ethnic origins will influence four dimensions of racial and ethnic adaptation (see table 2.5).

One set of outcomes concerns identities. Those based on affiliation require immigrants to consider how membership in their own ethnic group implicitly or explicitly connects them to other ethnic groups. Pan-ethnicity, or subsuming a specific identity such as Hmong or Cambodian within a broader one such as Asian American, is a good example of an affiliation-based identity. Other affiliation-based identities for immigrants include broad categories based on race (for example, "people of color"), religion ("Buddhist" and "Muslim"), and region ("Caribbean"). Conversely, an identity based on affinity requires immigrants to consider adding a new identity in response to changes in other identities. U.S. citizen is a good example of an affinity-based identity, since it is a way for immigrants to claim rights and membership in American society. Other affinity-based identities for immigrants in the United States include those based on neighborhood and city.

Where racial and ethnic identities involve a social-psychological evaluation of the meanings of group membership, racial and ethnic inequalities concern stigmatizing hierarchies, such as group stereotypes, and unfair outcomes, such as mistreatment by employers. Since immigrants experience a process of resocialization, it is necessary to examine how they

Table 2.5   Dimensions of Racial and Ethnic Adaptation

Identities		Inequalities	
Affiliation	Affinity	Perceiving	Reacting
Pan-ethnicity	U.S. citizen	Societal racism	Mobilization
		Group stereotypes	Collective action
		Institutional	
		discrimination	

Source: Author's compilation.

become aware of inequality in the host society. They may not have known about it prior to migration, and if they did, they may have learned considerably more after arrival. Thus it is important to analyze immigrants' perceptions of inequality, since the objective facts of inequality (such as immigrants' median income) cannot be used to infer immigrants' knowledge of these facts.

Immigrants' perceptions of racism, stereotypes, and discrimination are significant, but they only reveal the individual component of their adaptation to racial and ethnic inequality. Evaluating the communal component requires analysis of immigrants' reactions to inequality. Reactions can be as mundane as telling other members of the ethnic community about a discriminatory experience or go so far as participation in a social movement to redress an injustice. Immigrants' racial and ethnic adaptation may therefore include meeting with co-ethnics to discuss the need for social change (mobilization) and then challenging a dominant group (collective action).

The ethnic-origins hypothesis has some metatheoretical similarities with the theory of segmented assimilation (Portes and Rumbaut 2001; Portes and Zhou 1993). Unlike classical assimilation theory, both posit that there are multiple outcomes in immigrants' adaptation rather than a single, inevitable result for all immigrants. According to the ethnic-origins hypothesis, immigrant groups will evince stronger or weaker pan-ethnic identities, heightened or diminished perceptions of inequality, and more or less mobilization and collective action. Similarly, the ethnic-origins hypothesis and segmented-assimilation theory point to differences among immigrant groups at the time of arrival to explain variation in adaptation outcomes. Finally, both approaches presume that characteristics upon arrival do not unilaterally determine adaptation outcomes but instead interact with the social environment in which immigrants settle.

The ethnic-origins hypothesis differs from the theory of segmented assimilation in that it begins with conditions in immigrants' homelands, thus incorporating the fundamental insight of the transnational perspective. The hypothesis posits that immigrants use memory and imagination to continuously tap into the histories, politics, and cultures of their homelands—an orientation termed "bifocality" (Vertovec 2004)—even when they do not engage in literal forms of transnationalism (Espiritu 2003). Conversely, the first chronological variable in segmented-assimilation theory is host-government reception policy toward legal immigrants, illegal immigrants, and refugees (Portes and Rumbaut 2001; Portes and Zhou 1993). The ethnic-origins hypothesis commences with homeland history, politics, and culture. Of course, many studies of immigrants include information on their history in order to appraise their human and social capital (Portes and Bach 1985), social networks (Kyle 2000; Massey et al. 1987), and communal bonds (Menjívar 2000). Rather than studying homeland conditions to understand characteristics of individuals, networks, or even communities, the ethnic-origins hypothesis examines something much broader: how notions of peoplehood that were developed in the homeland shape adaptation outcomes after migration.

This focus on homeland histories, politics, and cultures enables the concept of ethnic origins to make more nuanced distinctions among immigrants than is possible with the variables in segmented-assimilation theory. For example, Alejandro Portes and Min Zhou (1993, 84) cite Cambodian and Hmong refugees as examples of the same mode of incorporation: receptive government policy because they received resettlement assistance, prejudiced societal response because they are Asian, and weak co-ethnic community because on arrival they were few in number and "composed primarily of manual workers." All true. Yet the Hmong and Cambodians have very different experiences with nation-state formation and political cleavage in their homelands, as well as different religions and kinship structures. Thus, the ethnic- origins hypothesis predicts that they will exhibit different patterns of racial and ethnic adaptation despite having the same mode of incorporation.

Testing the ethnic origins-hypothesis requires a complex comparative research design. First, two immigrant groups with significantly different ethnic origins must be selected. Second, other factors well known to influence immigrant adaptation must be evaluated. It is self-evident that Cambodian and Hmong refugees belong to the same race, according to the American system of classification (Asian) and come from adjacent agricultural societies in Southeast Asia (Cambodia and Laos). In addition to race and region of origin, social scientists typically evaluate four other factors when analyzing immigrants' adaptation: migration motive, host-state response to the immigrants, class background, and region and city of settlement in the host society. Cambodian and Hmong refugees meet these comparative criteria because they differ in their ethnic origins but are very similar or even identical in other relevant respects.

Migration Motive and the Host State

Two of the most fundamental variables in international migration are exit conditions from the homeland and the response of the host state to the immigrants' arrival (Portes and Rumbaut 1990). In these respects Cambodian and Hmong refugees occupy the same point on the spectrum of international migration to the United States.

Both groups fled to refugee camps in Thailand because of persecution by Communist regimes that took power in 1975 following the collapse of anti-Communist U.S. foreign policy in the region (Chan 1994, 2004). U.S. immigration officials interviewed the refugees in the Thai camps, designated them political migrants because they fit U.S. foreign policy objectives in the region, and began admitting them in large numbers during the late 1970s and early 1980s (Hein 1995). Both groups participated in the federal refugee resettlement program, which provided funds to states and nonprofit organizations to promote the refugees' adaptation (Hein 1993). Thus Cambodian and Hmong refugees experienced identical treatment by the U.S. state. Their encounter with immigration policy is quite distinct from that of illegal immigrants who arrive to work or gain political asylum and of legal immigrants who arrive through family sponsors or because they have professional skills.

Class Background and Socioeconomic Status

Class background is often considered the single most important factor shaping immigrants' adaptation, particularly among contemporary immigrants to the United States who exhibit a bimodal pattern (Portes and Rumbaut 1990). Many immigrants arrive with levels of human capital above that of natives. Often they use these job skills and educational credentials to obtain professional employment or operate their own businesses. Many other immigrants, however, arrive with little human capital. They face very bleak economic prospects in a services and information economy that demands ever higher levels of education and technical skills.

Most Cambodians and Hmong refugees fall within the lower-human-capital segment of contemporary immigrants (Chan 1994, 2004). They came from rural areas and small towns in Cambodia and Laos with limited opportunities for education. About one-third of Cambodians, and the majority of the Hmong, arrived in the United States illiterate in their native language. Men and women tended to be farmers, particularly the Hmong, and often supplemented their income by selling produce in open-air markets. About one-quarter of Cambodian men, and two-thirds of Hmong men, were soldiers before arriving in the United States, a legacy of the wars in Southeast Asia which further limited their education and deprived them of transferable job skills.

Cambodians and the Hmong therefore assumed the lowest position in the American class hierarchy when they began arriving during the mid- and late 1970s (Hein 1995). The 1990 U.S. Census provides a picture of conditions among the refugees during the initial phase of their adaptation, since 84 percent of foreign-born Cambodians and 61 percent of foreign-born Hmong entered the United States between 1975 and 1989 (Reeves and Bennett 2004). It found that the majority of Cambodian and Hmong adults had an eighth-grade education or less compared to 10 percent for the U.S. population as a whole. About one-third of Cambodians and the Hmong worked as operators and laborers, the lowest occupational category (only 15 percent of all U.S. workers had this type of employment). As a result, median household income was extremely low. Compared to an income of $30,000 for the average family in the United States, the median was $14,300 for the Hmong and $18,800 for Cambodians (the latter tended to have more workers per family, thus generating more income). About 40 percent of Cambodian families met the official criteria for poverty, but only 10 percent of all U.S. families did not have sufficient income to meet their basic material needs. The poverty rate was above 60 percent for Hmong families, in part due to a greater number of children (six on average) compared to Cambodians (typically four). Thus both groups faced enormous economic disadvantage as they began their adaptation to American society.

Cambodians and the Hmong made significant economic progress during the 1990s, particularly by entering the labor force and ending public assistance (Southeast Asian Resource Action Center 2004). Nonetheless, by 2000 both Cambodians and the Hmong remained more disadvantaged than African Americans, Native Americans, and Hispanic Americans as measured by college completion, poverty, and per capita income. For example, 29 percent of Cambodians and 38 percent of the Hmong meet the federal government's definition of being in poverty, compared to only 12 percent of the total U.S. population (Reeves and Bennett 2004). It would take generations, not decades, for Cambodians and the Hmong to overcome the enormous hardships created by migration from agricultural societies ravaged by war to an urban, postindustrial society where 52 percent of the population had at least some college education.

Host-Society Region and City

Immigrants' adaptation is greatly influenced by the region and city in which they live (Waldinger 2001b). To exclude the influence of region I analyze Cambodians and the Hmong in a region of the upper Midwest comprising southern Minnesota, Wisconsin, and northern Illinois. Although the plurality of both the Hmong and Cambodians live in California (about 35 percent and 40 percent, respectively, in 2000), there are significant populations in other parts of the country. Minnesota and Wisconsin have the second and third largest Hmong populations in the United States (about 25 percent and 20 percent, respectively). Few

Cambodians reside in Wisconsin and they are more dispersed than the Hmong, with only one state other than California having more than one-tenth of the population (Massachusetts, with 11 percent). Minnesota has the sixth largest population of Cambodians (3 percent of their national population) and Illinois has the eleventh largest (2 percent).

In addition to holding region constant I also control for urban locale. I examine the adaptation of Cambodians and the Hmong in small cities that were almost entirely white prior to their arrival and in large cities with racial and ethnic diversity. St. Paul has both Hmong and Cambodian populations and I considered it as the large-city research site. According to the 2000 U.S. Census, more than 25,000 Hmong reside there (making them the largest Asian group in the city) but only about 1,000 Cambodians. This immense demographic disparity invalidates a comparison of the groups' racial and ethnic adaptation.

Instead of St. Paul, I compare Cambodians in Chicago with the Hmong in Milwaukee, two cities less than one hundred miles apart on the western shore of Lake Michigan. In Milwaukee the Hmong population grew over time, from community estimates of 3,250 in 1990 to 15,000 in 2000 (Lo 2001), although the 2000 U.S. Census only enumerated about 8,000 Hmong in Milwaukee. In Chicago the Cambodian population remained stable during the 1990s. Community estimates suggest that the population numbered 5,000 in both 1989 (North and Sok 1989) and 2000 (Cambodian Association of Illinois 2000). Despite this demographic difference, in both cities the Hmong and Cambodians are small ethnic groups engulfed by much larger populations of native minorities and other immigrants.

I compare the refugees' adaptation in these large cities to that of Cambodians in Rochester, Minnesota, and the Hmong in Eau Claire, Wisconsin. Only about 90 miles separate these two towns. I chose to study the Hmong in Eau Claire because of my prior research on this community, although there are Hmong communities in several other small Wisconsin cities. Rochester is the only choice for a Cambodian community in a small upper midwestern city. When I started my research in the mid 1990s local sources informed me that approximately 1,400 Cambodians resided in Rochester and 2,000 Hmong resided in Eau Claire. At the time Rochester was comparable to Eau Claire in population size (70,000 and 57,000, respectively) and in the proportion of residents that were white when the refugees arrived (98 percent and 99 percent, respectively, in 1980). Rochester is better known than Eau Claire because of the internationally recognized Mayo Clinic. Yet Eau Claire has a comparable economic base through the presence of a university, a community college, and two large hospitals.

Although a strong case can be made for the comparability of my research sites, I endorse the view that race and ethnic relations in the

United States are localized and that no two cities are identical. Nonetheless, on the spectrum of urban areas in the United States, Eau Claire and Rochester cluster together as do Chicago and Milwaukee. International migration has brought to these adjacent midwestern cities refugees who differ significantly in their ethnic origins but are quite similar in physical appearance, region of origin, migration motive, and class background. The host-state response is also similar. The result is a natural experiment in how the adaptation process is shaped by the places in which immigrants settle and the historically, politically, and culturally embedded understandings of societal membership they bring to these places.

To demonstrate how ethnic origins shape immigrant adaptation in small and large cities I conducted a sequentially designed ethnosurvey (Massey 1987; Massey and Zenteno 2000) from 1996 to 1999. I first examined archival sources to determine how Cambodian and Hmong refugees arrived in each research site and the patterns of race and ethnic relations that unfolded with their settlement. I then used a standardized survey to obtain identical statistics on the refugees in each place. After the survey I conducted semistructured follow-up interviews with some survey respondents to obtain qualitative data. Finally, I organized peer-group conversations in each city with new participants in order to have multilevel qualitative data. The characteristics of these samples are provided in appendix A and a detailed description of how I implemented each methodology is available in appendix B.

Conclusion

The ethnic-origins hypothesis posits that when immigrants arrive in a host society they begin a process of racial and ethnic adaptation. During this resocialization immigrants must cope with new identities and inequalities that are based on perceived physical and cultural differences. To interpret host-society patterns of diversity, immigrants draw upon preexisting conceptualizations of social relations and peoplehood, which I term immigrants' ethnic origins. Some immigrants think of ethnic boundaries as porous and fluid and for them ethnic identities are liminal. Others assume that ethnic boundaries are hermetic and rigid; they think of ethnic identities as polarized.

Multiple experiences in immigrants' homelands shape how they situate ethnic boundaries and evaluate ethnic identities. Historical developments determine whether or not they have a nation-state and how minority and dominant groups lay claims to national institutions. Political cleavages divide people into competing groups in ways that reinforce or alter racial and ethnic boundaries. Religious values and kinship norms create assumptions about discretion and collective commitments to spiritual aspirations and social networks. Once immigrants arrive in a host society these preexisting boundaries and identities influence how they adapt to new ones.

The ethnic-origins hypothesis identifies four dimensions of racial and ethnic adaptation. Two adjustment issues concern identities based on affiliation (for example, Asian American) and identities based on affinity (for example, U.S. citizen). Two others concern perceptions of inequalities (for example, group stereotypes) and reactions to inequalities (for example, readiness to participate in a social movement). The ethnic-origins hypothesis predicts that a group with ethnic origins like those of the Hmong (hermetic boundary and polarized identity) will have a looser affiliation with Asian pan-ethnicity and a weaker affinity for U.S. citizenship than a group with ethnic origins like those of Cambodians (porous boundaries and liminal identities). Similarly, the hypothesis predicts that awareness of inequality, such as the prevalence of institutional discrimination, will be greater for a group like the Hmong than for a group like Cambodians. Finally, the hypothesis predicts that a group with ethnic origins similar to the Hmong's will display a higher propensity to mobilize and engage in collective action to combat inequality than a group with ethnic origins like those of Cambodians. These are plausible hypotheses given the histories, politics, and cultures of the Khmer in Cambodia and the Hmong in Laos.

= Part II =

Peoples

= Chapter 3 =

Khmer

Cambodian refugees come from a "hybrid culture" (Chandler 1996, 80) and thus arrive in the United States thinking that ethnic boundaries are porous and that ethnic identities are liminal. A well-known origin story symbolizes their worldview. It concerns an Indian prince named Kambu, who travels to Southeast Asia and marries a dragon-princess (Osborne 2000). The region at this time is covered by ocean and the father-in-law dragon drinks enough water to leave dry land for the couple to live on. This new country is named Kambuja, after the prince, from which the name Cambodia is derived. Milton Osborne (1988, 22) interprets this origin story as a statement about the value of inter-ethnic contact: "It is not surprising that the Cambodian national birth legend, to take only one example, sees the legendary marriage of a Brahman with a local princess as the beginning of Cambodia's rise to greatness that culminated in the Angkorian period." In fact, several historically significant Cambodian kings married princesses from neighboring countries, including one king who subsequently converted to Islam (Chandler 1996; Higham 2001). This theme of bridging and blending cultures reoccurs in multiple ways throughout Cambodian history.

A Hybrid Nation-State

Khmer-speaking Theravada Buddhists constituted about 85 to 90 percent of Cambodia's population prior to 1975 (Steinberg 1959). Ethnic Chinese, Vietnamese, and Cham (Muslims) accounted for about 13 percent of the population, with mountain-dwelling ethnic groups constituting the remainder. Although lacking racial and ethnic diversity as measured by American indicators of pluralism, the central theme in Khmer history is cultural fusion.

Some of the most significant features of the Khmer nation-state came from India (Coe 2003; Coedès 1968). Indian merchants began arriving by ship circa A.D. 100, part of a larger flow of trade from the Middle East and China to Southeast Asia. The annual east to west shift in the monsoon winds made the region a natural terminus for commerce, as did the

45

resources in its tropical jungles. From Funan in the southern part of present-day Vietnam, Indian civilization spread through cultural osmosis rather than conquest. It made a lasting impact on the Khmer (Chandler 1996, 12), one that transcended the period of kings and feudal states:

> In the nineteenth century, for example, Cambodian peasants still wore recognizably Indian costumes, and in many ways they behaved more like Indians than they did like their closest neighbors, the Vietnamese. Cambodians eat with spoons and fingers [not chopsticks], for example, and carried goods on their heads; they wore turbans rather than straw hats and skirts rather than trousers. Musical instruments, jewelry, and manuscripts were also Indian in style.

In addition to material imports from India, Cambodian civilization incorporated Hinduism and Buddhism (Coe 2003; Coedès 1968). As in other parts of Southeast Asia, Cambodian rulers encouraged this cultural transfer because the new ideologies transformed them from an aristocracy into deified mediators with divine powers (Kulke 1984). India's more bureaucratically advanced political system provided Southeast Asian kings with a means of better administering their states. Hinduism also promoted caste distinctions and respect for title and authority. Brahmanist values are reflected in Cambodians' hierarchical status distinctions and deference for rank such as teacher, monk, and government official (Steinberg 1959). Buddhism provided an elaborate cultural legitimation for this hierarchy, since it stressed nonviolence and acceptance of the existing social order (Houtart 1977). To encourage their subjects' adherence to Buddhism, kings became the benefactors of the sangha—celibate monks who devoted their lives to Buddhist practice—by granting monasteries land and donating food.

Cambodian kings promoted the adoption of a Hindu and Buddhist social order for political reasons, but economy and geography grounded this process of cultural amalgamation (Coedès 1968). The cycle of monsoon rice agriculture exists in southern India and Cambodia. These conditions provided a common material foundation in both regions even prior to contact. Rather than Indian influence being imposed on Cambodia, numerous features of Cambodian society facilitated the incorporation and modification of a new culture.

The arrival of Indian civilization initiated cultural hybridization in Cambodia, and the process continued as a result of demography (Higham 2001). Land was more plentiful than people, and scarcity of people meant scarcity of labor. As a result, slavery was central to the Indianized economy and social order that preceded the great Khmer kingdom of Angkor as well as during Angkor itself (circa 800–1431).

Many slaves were captives in wars of expansion in the east and west, but others came from local mountain-dwelling groups. Thus, cultural hybridization had a geopolitical rationale based on rulers' desire to increase the population.

Cambodia's location on a plain between Thailand and Vietnam also meant an inevitable flow of external influences that made isolation impossible and cultural accommodation a necessity (see figure 3.1). David

Figure 3.1   Southeast Asia

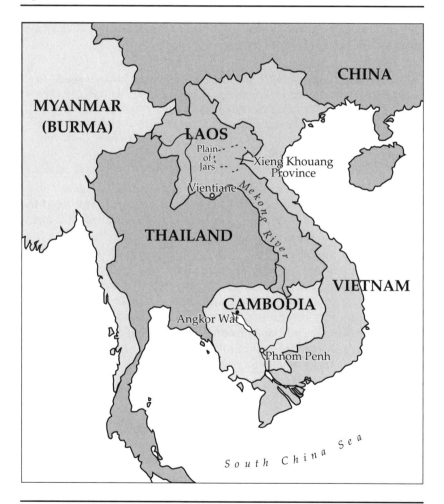

Source: Graphics Division, Learning and Technology Services, University of Wisconsin–Eau Claire.

Chandler (1996, 4) describes Cambodia's position between a Buddhist cultural zone to the west and a Sinicized one to the east as "a cultural fault line." Rather than seeking to socially impose what geography had denied them, premodern Khmer states accepted a fluid ethnic boundary. According to Osborne (1988, 40–41), "If the pyramid is a useful symbol to depict the disposition of power in Vietnam, a series of concentric circles might be taken to represent the nature of power in the Buddhist kingdoms. . . . The Buddhist rulers of mainland Southeast Asia, again in contrast to Vietnam, accepted that [borders] were uncertain and porous." This more amorphous and less hierarchical social order among the Khmer had profound effects for their conception of ethnicity. It meant that we-they dichotomies never prevailed in their worldview of other ethnic groups. As Coedès (1968, 24) notes:

> The social structure of India, dominated by the caste system, seems to have undergone profound modification upon contact with native societies. The genealogies of ancient Cambodia often present a curious mixture of Sanskrit and Khmer names, a fact that prompted Auguste Barth to say that the Brahmans of Cambodia "do not appear to have been very scrupulous about racial purity."

Cultural hybridization accelerated when Cambodia's western neighbor invaded in 1431 (Higham 2001). That year, Thailand conquered the Angkor kingdom and captured Angkor Wat, the monumental stone temples built during the twelfth century, which remain the largest religious structure in the world. After the fifteenth-century invasion Thailand supplanted India as a source of cultural and especially religious influence on the Khmer. Of particular importance was the transition from the more hierarchical and elite Hinduism to Theravada Buddhism, with its emphasis on lay participation and accommodation of local animism. The fall of Angkor also shifted the country's political center to the present-day capital of Phnom Penh on the banks of the Mekong River. This navigable river route further opened Cambodia to influences from abroad.

The next phase of amalgamation in Cambodia's history occurred in the early 1600s and involved its more populous neighbor to the east (Chandler 1996). Vietnam had a long history of expansion from the densely settled north to the sparsely populated south. The Khmer had historically inhabited large portions of the Mekong Delta. Vietnam's conquest of this Khmer region in what became southern Vietnam disrupted trade between Phnom Penh and Saigon (now called Ho Chi Minh City). It also cut off the Khmer population in the area from the rest of the country, to this day called Khmer Krom, or low Cambodians.

These "Cambodian Vietnamese" added to the Khmer melting pot when they emigrated to Cambodia during French colonization to meet labor demands caused by increasing rice exports. The proximity of Thailand and Vietnam continued to mean frequent invasion for Cambodia, particularly from the mid-1700s to the mid-1800s.

Thus, from Indianization onward, historical developments in Cambodia moved in the same direction: the formation of an ethnic boundary characterized by cultural hybridization rather than promoting in-group solidarity through exclusion of outsiders. As a result of this trend, Khmer ethnic origins are described by different observers of Cambodia in remarkably similar ways. David Steinberg (1959, 37) succinctly states: "The modern Khmer are the end-product of countless centuries of intricate cultural and racial blending." According to Michael Coe (2003, 59), "An amalgam of the native and the foreign has characterized Khmer civilization for the past two millennia." Chandler (1996, 80) enumerates the ingredients:

> The mixture contained elements of Hinduized kingship, traceable to Angkor, and Theravada monarchic accessibility, traceable to the Mon kingdom of Davaravati, perhaps, which had practiced Theravada Buddhism for almost a thousand years, as well as remnants of paternalistic, village-oriented leadership traceable to the ethnic forerunners of the Thai, tribal peoples from the mountains of southern China.

As these quotations suggest, the main features of Khmer ethnic origins are porous borders and mutable identities. This cultural syncretism, set in motion by events over a thousand years ago, remains an enduring element in the worldview of contemporary Cambodians. In 2005 several Cambodian dancers in St. Paul joined others from India, Sri Lanka, and Indonesia to perform the Ramayana. The director of the performance, Rita Mustaphi, describes the foundations of this "pan-Asian collaboration" by noting that "the sea route that connected Southern and Eastern Asia allowed for strong Indian influences in dance, drama and music on many Asian cultures. For many the Ramayana is the most popular story for dance and drama and has a central role even today" (Mustaphi 2005). Called Ramakerti in Cambodia, this classical Indian tale about adversity and morality became a fixture of Khmer poetry and theater as artistic adaptation transformed it into an expression of Buddhist values (Pou 1992).

Buddhist Values

Cambodians in the United States are noted for their strong adherence to their homeland religion (Chan 2004; Hopkins 1996; Mortland 1996;

Smith-Hefner 1999). Among Cambodians in Long Beach, California, the largest Khmer community in the United States, 80 percent or more identify themselves as Buddhists (Chan 2003). When asked their religion, 79 percent of respondents in my sample of ninety-nine Cambodians in Rochester and Chicago reported being Buddhist and another 8 percent chose Buddhism and Christianity.

Animism, however, predated Buddhism's arrival in Cambodia from India circa A.D. 100. It would have been totally inconsistent with Cambodians' penchant for cultural hybridization to reject this older belief in spirits of the material and nonmaterial world. In typical Khmer fashion they produced a spiritual amalgam. According to Ang Chouléan (1988, 36), "Since the time of ancient Cambodia the main enduring characteristic in the elaboration of Khmer religious thought was the search for harmony between the local animistic foundation and Indian philosophical-spiritual contributions." Fortune-telling, exorcising spirits, and using incantations to cure illness have all been woven into the Buddhist practices of Cambodians and are often performed by Buddhist monks themselves (Ebihara 1968; Men 2002; Smith-Hefner 1994). Thus, in modern Cambodia, "Buddhism exists side-by-side with, and to some extent intermingles with, pre-Buddhist animism and Brahman practices" (Headley 1990, 120).

The principles of Buddhism itself greatly facilitated this process of religious fusion and as a theology "lends itself to syncretism" (Rutledge 1986, 147). Four beliefs are central to Buddhism: humans suffer; suffering is caused by the impossibility of permanently gratifying human desires; reducing desire reduces suffering; ethical conduct can replace the illusive quest for gratification (Nhat Hanh 1998). Living these precepts requires close attention to personal behavior in order to adhere to meritorious ethical standards known as the eightfold path.

One of the most important social implications of Buddhism is that individuals are responsible for their own suffering and its remediation. This assessment logically follows from the belief that suffering results from one's own attitudes and behavior, not those of other people. Personal reactions that avoid compounding suffering are more important to Buddhists than avoiding suffering itself, which is deemed futile. This individualistic view of society is particularly pronounced in the Theravada Buddhist tradition practiced in Cambodia. Conversely, the Mahayana Buddhist tradition in Vietnam and Tibet has a more social perspective that focuses on generating compassion for the suffering of others.

Earning merit through ethical conduct, and thus positive personal karma, is a core belief in Buddhism. This value further fosters individualism, since each "Buddhist is his own authority and must learn Truth for himself through study, self-discipline, and right practice" (Rutledge 1986, 149). "Do good get good, do bad get bad" is a common Khmer Buddhist saying. Nancy Smith-Hefner (1999, 35) elaborates on this worldview:

> Many Khmer invoke the concept of karma to make sense of social inequalities. The wealthy and powerful are said to be those who accumulated significant merit in their previous lives. Those who are poor or in difficult circumstances explain their condition by referring to putative misdeeds in a prior existence. Karma, however, is not absolute. . . . Most important, the individual is always free to choose whether to engage in meritorious or demeritorious acts, thereby directing his or her future in a negative or positive way.

Buddhism's profound influence on Khmer culture eventually became significant for U.S. foreign policy during the Vietnam War. When the U.S. Department of the Army (1970, 248) assessed the military potential of the Khmer it concluded (apparently with regret) that they lacked a warrior spirit: "The Khmer are a gentle, patient people who seek harmonious social relationships through mutually self-imposed submission. . . . Very flexible in social situations, they are also highly tolerant of variations in human behavior as long as basic precepts of politeness are not violated."

Loose Kinship Norms

Kinship norms structure an ethnic group internally and thus create a template for understanding the significance of membership in social networks. By the standards of several cultures in Asia, Khmer kinship practices are loose and give much discretion to the individual. Based on fieldwork in a Khmer village during the late 1950s and early 1960s, May Ebihara (1968, 157) concluded: "There are no rigidly defined, obligatory rules of behavior toward kinsmen. . . . An individual has considerable freedom to act as he pleases toward kinsmen, and the quality of his interaction with particular relatives depends in large part upon personal inclination."

The less structured character of Khmer kinship has much in common with practices among the Lao and Thai, but is quite distinct from the pattern found among the Chinese, Vietnamese, and the Hmong. Steinberg (1959, 77–78) summarizes these differences:

> In contrast to the Vietnamese and Chinese, Cambodians do not attach special importance to tracing descendants through the male line. The Cambodian kinship system is bilateral—relations among kin members,

marriage ties, inheritance patterns are all regulated without maternal or paternal bias. . . . While formal respect is paid to both paternal and maternal ancestors at weddings and funerals, ancestor worship is not a major family function as in China.

Smith-Hefner (1999, 12–13) offers a similar cross-cultural comparison. She goes further than simple categorization by suggesting how kinship structures a group's worldview:

Unlike the Chinese or Vietnamese, Khmer lack any kind of unilineal descent group. Instead, as in many other Southeast Asian (and, for that matter, Western European) cultures, family structure is loosely neolocal, cognatic ("bilateral"), and focused on the nuclear family. By many accounts, too, Khmer are more individualistic than collective when compared to some of their neighbors, especially those influenced by Chinese tradition. Behavior among kin is less rigidly prescribed and more dependent on individual likes and dislikes.

Conversely, ancestral lineage is of paramount importance to the Hmong, since they belong to clans. Members of the same clan, such as Vang or Xiong, are considered descendants of a single male ancestor described in folklore on Hmong origins. Clans, therefore, must practice exogamy in order not to violate the incest taboo. Among the Khmer, on the other hand, choice of marriage partner is guided by parents' wishes but not kinship norms on exogamy or endogamy (Hopkins 1996; Smith-Hefner 1999). In fact, during much of Khmer history bilateral norms combined with polygyny problematized political succession rights, and "the potential for factionalism and dissension was ever present" when it was time to replace a king (Higham 2001, 11).

What would most startle the Hmong about Khmer kinship is their attitude toward family names. Cambodians did not use surnames until required to do so by a colonial decree in 1910 (Steinberg 1959). Even after this administrative stipulation, Cambodian parents commonly used either the mother's or father's personal name as a child's surname, clearly an indication that preserving an ancestral lineage was not of great interest to them. The haphazard use of surnames among Cambodians was still prevalent in the 1970s and 1980s, much to the consternation of U.S. immigration officials creating documents for Cambodian families bound for the United States. The relative importance of ancestry for Cambodians should not be misconstrued. They are concerned with the reincarnation of their ancestors and believe in ancestral ghosts (Ebihara 1968). Yet they do not practice the type of ancestor worship that is common to ethnic groups influenced by Confucianism, such as the Vietnamese (Hickey 1964).

The more egocentric approach to kinship among Cambodians is further evidenced by the prevalence of fictive kinship. Cambodians often create kin relations through the use of terms like "cousin" or "aunt" and "uncle" to refer to significant people in their social network to whom they are not related by blood or marriage (Ebihara 1968; Hein 1995). Fictive kinship also occurs among the Hmong but is more structured. Rather than being egocentric, fictive kinship for the Hmong is determined for individuals by their clan. Other clan members are considered relatives and can be called by kin names such as cousin, aunt, or "brother."

The relaxed approach to kinship among Cambodians minimizes the importance of groups and maximizes personal choice, since individuals are free to create kin-like relations rather than being obliged to accept preexisting ones, such as clan membership. Ebihara (1968, 171) concludes that "among the Khmer the 'personal kindred' is not a very tangible phenomenon: it is not clearly bounded; it has no formal organization; it does not crystallize as a group except in periodic 'assemblages ad hoc' of only part of its total possible membership." It is no surprise, therefore, that groups have only episodic importance for Cambodians rather than being a constant reference point. Combined with a hybrid culture, this discretionary approach to membership in social networks has manifested in one unfortunate feature of the refugees' adaptation in the United States: Cambodian youth gangs. Sody Lay (2004, 226) notes that they are "accepting of ethnic and racial diversity within their ranks, and youth may often become a part of the gang the same way a new person is introduced to a circle of friends."

Intra-Ethnic Political Conflict and the Khmer Rouge

French colonization of Cambodia from 1863 to 1953 offered an opportunity for Cambodians to develop an oppositional identity. They could have produced a strident independence movement, such as occurred in neighboring Vietnam. Instead, according to Chandler (1996, 13), "Cambodian nationalism, unlike its Vietnamese counterpart, has not generally pictured itself as the product of struggle against foreign invaders."

Cambodians did not come to think of the French as an oppositional out-group because they were political realists. Khmer kings faced a perennial need for protection from Thai and Vietnamese incursions. In the 1590s, for example, the king of Cambodia sought support from the Portuguese colony in Malacca "to prop up his regime against the ever-present threat of invasion from the ruler of Siam" (Osborne 2000, 47). Cambodia's acquiescence to French colonization in the 1860s stemmed in part from its hope that protectorate status would prevent partial or even complete encroachment by Thailand and Vietnam. In fact, Thailand ruled large portions of western Cambodia from 1794 until the French colonial government forced it out in 1906. During World War II, Thailand again occupied the western region of Cambodia. When independence initiatives began in Cambodia after the war, nationalists worried that French departure would once more leave them vulnerable to Thai intrusions (Chandler 1996).

Not only did French colonization secure Cambodia's borders but it revitalized Khmer cultural identity. Angkor Wat had lain in forgotten jungle-covered ruins for hundreds of years until it was rediscovered by Henri Mouhot in 1860 (Osborne 2000). When Thailand relinquished control of the area in 1906 the French colonial administration began serious restoration and archaeological investigation of the site. French scholars spent the next five decades analyzing the wall sculptures and statues, thus contributing to a Khmer national heritage. Largely because of the work of a colonial power, the Angkor Wat "monuments are a source of pride and provide a strong sense of ethnic identity to Khmer refugees" (Welaratna 1993, 13). It appears on the country's flag and is the centerpiece of the country's flourishing tourism industry. Far from experiencing colonization as a cultural challenge, Cambodia was "mummified by ninety years of a French colonial protectorate, which preserved, even enhanced the country's traditional monarchy and social structure" (Kiernan 1996, 4–5).

The comparatively limited impact of France on its Cambodian colony resulted in limited mobilization against colonization (Chandler 1996). Anti-French activities occurred from 1885 to 1886 and a French official was assassinated in 1925. By contrast, Communist-led peasant revolts in Vietnam posed a significant challenge to France and resulted in atrocious repression. Colonial troops and the French Foreign Legion killed more than 10,000 Vietnamese peasants in 1931 alone (Paige 1975). Such atrocities never occurred during Cambodia's colonial history, and the country's "first modern political demonstration" against the French was in 1942 (Kiernan 1996, 12). Thus, the development of a nationalist independence movement in Cambodia was late, weak, and less violent than what occurred in Vietnam (Osborne 1988).

Variation in the development of a Western educated middle class is one reason for the different forms of nationalism in Cambodia and Vietnam. This elite group spearheaded many anticolonial struggles in Africa and Asia but developed slowly in Cambodia (Kiernan 2004). Khmer-language newspapers and literature did not appear until the 1920s and 1930s (Young 1976). High schools and colleges established by the French, the most advanced educational institutions in the country, emerged at about the same time. When the Cambodian middle class did become politically active it took a decidedly materialistic approach to national identity. The nationalists were more concerned with resources and status than with cultural issues. They felt deprived by the French colonial administration's recruitment of Vietnamese for civil service jobs in Cambodia and the administration's policy of allowing the Chinese to monopolize commerce. To this day in Cambodia the paramount conflicts are between Cambodians and other Asians—with the Vietnamese over power; with the Chinese over class—and there is virtually no resentment at the cultural legacy of French colonization.

With the assistance of the Vietnamese Communist party, a militant and armed independence movement did eventually develop in Cambodia in 1945 (Kiernan 2004). But Cambodian independence in 1953 was largely a side effect of the intense anticolonial struggle in Vietnam, which culminated in the French military defeat at the battle of Dien Bien Phu in 1954. The lack of a decisive revolt against French colonialism in Cambodia foreclosed the first modern opportunity for political conflict among Cambodians to generate a polarized ethnic boundary.

A second political conflict began in the late 1960s during the Vietnam War (Kiernan 2004). Cambodia was drawn into the war in Vietnam as the North Vietnamese Army and the Communist Viet Cong in South Vietnam established base camps and supply routes along the Vietnam-Cambodia border. The U.S. military believed these activities constituted a serious threat, although subsequent investigation proved they were of only minor strategic importance (Karnow 1983). For thirteen months in 1969 and 1970, President Nixon ordered U.S. air and ground forces to secretly attack the Communist bases and supply routes in Cambodia without congressional approval (Shawcross 1977).

Prince Norodom Sihanouk had ruled Cambodia since independence from France and he kept the country neutral during most of the Vietnam War. In 1970, however, General Lon Nol took power in a coup supported by the U.S. military, which wanted a pro-American government in Phnom Penh (Kiernan 2004; Shawcross 1977). U.S. bombings in Cambodia dramatically escalated during the early 1970s as the Cambodian Communist guerrillas known as the Khmer Rouge expanded their own military activity with the support of China and North Vietnam. The U.S. military subjected approximately one-third of Cambodia to almost unrestricted and indiscriminate bombing. One off-course B-52 bomber killed 125 civilians and wounded more than 250 others in a government-held town. Catastrophes with lower casualties were common. As a result, American military intervention in Cambodia during the early 1970s actually increased popular support for the Khmer Rouge by enabling them to blame the United States for killing civilians (Kiernan

1996). While bombings did not halt the advance of the Khmer Rouge, they did displace tens of thousands of Cambodian civilians, who fled their homes for the safety of the capital and a few other large cities.

Some Cambodians are aware of the United States' complicity in the political and military conflict in their homeland. In an oral history (Tenhula 1991, 46), one refugee recalls: "I remember those not-so-secret bombings that destroyed my country. Really, none of that was secret. I went to bed and I felt my bed make motions because of the bombs. My bed shook! We heard about the bombings on the radio and in the coffeehouse. It was all that we talked about."

The U.S. bombings in Cambodia during the 1970s also came up spontaneously in several of my follow-up interviews with Cambodians. Buon was a teenager at this time and knew about U.S. military intervention in Cambodia from firsthand experience: "When I grew up during the war, people said, 'American bad.' They put bombs in Cambodia, in my province." Sombat also raised the topic during his interview, although he was only one year old in 1973 (the last year of the U.S. bombings). His knowledge of and concern about the U.S. bombings are significant because it indicates the transmission of this history to new generations. We were talking about American nativism, and after explaining his feelings toward this prejudice he concluded: "I have the right to be here. The [U.S.] government damaged my country. One bomb did so much damage it takes thirty years to build back. The bombs killed morality, self-esteem. The whole thing killed the country. Someday I want to use my skills and go back to Cambodia, to rebuild."

Although some Cambodians, like Buon and Sombat, are aware that the United States contributed to the destabilization of their homeland, far more important in their minds are the atrocities perpetrated by the Khmer Rouge. Following the collapse of the pro-American Lon Nol government in 1975, the victorious Khmer Rouge, led by Pol Pot, embarked on a revolution to level Cambodian society in order to rebuild it according to their vision of Socialism (Jackson 1989; Kiernan 1996). They followed principles derived from Mao Zedong, the leader of the Chinese Revolution and the chairman of the Chinese Communist party from 1949 to 1976. The Khmer Rouge started their revolution by moving urban populations into rural areas. Most Cambodians had been farmers before 1975. Now all were required to work the land with little food and they received severe punishment for disobedience.

But the Khmer Rouge revolution aimed to reshape an entire culture, not merely the country's economy (Becker 1986; Ponchaud 1989; Chan 2003, 2004). The possession of literacy, professional skills, and symbols of modernity as trivial as eyeglasses became grounds for execution. The Khmer Rouge also dismantled Buddhist temples, profaned statues of the Buddha, and disrobed monks. They indoctrinated youths to switch their loyalty from parents and relatives to the new political regime. Conditions worsened steadily until December 1978, when Vietnam invaded Cambodia. More an effort to gain control over its neighbor than an act of humanitarianism, Vietnamese troops defeated the Khmer Rouge in early 1979 and remained in the country until 1989. From a population of 7 million, at least 1.7 million died of starvation, disease, and execution during the four years of the Khmer Rouge regime.

The Khmer Rouge revolution was so traumatic that it created a historical chasm difficult or impossible for many Cambodians to bridge. During an oral history interview, one refugee cites this void in response to a question about her experiences before she came to the United States: "Please understand that your life as a Cambodian is divided into two periods: life before and life after Pol Pot. Most of us try to forget the first period" (Tenhula 1991, 151). Similarly, an elderly refugee yearns for his homeland but also feels it does not exist: "I want to be able to go to the pagoda and to walk in my gardens. This will not be possible ever again. . . . I would like to be able to return to Cambodia someday, but I know that would not be possible. I think that the Khmer Rouge destroyed it completely" (115). Thus, unlike the Hmong who became refugees due to persecution by the Communist Lao for their direct support of the U.S. military, Cambodians were persecuted by members of their own ethnic group. As a result, Cambodians rarely attribute their collective trauma to the actions of the U.S. state, despite its massive bombing of Cambodia in the early 1970s. In fact, unexploded ordnance still litters the country. In September 2003, four children and a young adult were killed by a thirty-year-old U.S. bomb which they found and attempted to dismantle to sell as scrap metal.[1] Nonetheless, Cambodians blame their tragedy on other Cambodians and often refer to the Khmer Rouge era as the time when "Khmer killed Khmer."

The Khmer Rouge revolution not only made co-ethnics the source of Cambodians' contemporary suffering, it also negatively impacted their sense of national identity. A hypernationalist movement, the Khmer Rouge hunted for traitors who often were identified as such on the basis of Chinese or Vietnamese ancestry (Kiernan 1996). Many Cambodians cannot fathom how Cambodians could kill each other, only to be "saved" by Vietnamese invaders. One refugee in San Francisco concludes, "Since we had Communism, I don't want to be Cambodian. Why should I want to be like those people, those crazy people who killed my husband, my sister, their own flesh and blood?" (Welaratna 1993, 217–18). In Chicago, the organizer of a program for Cambodian youth found the same problem: "One of the worst things Cambodia has been through is the Khmer Rouge regime, and you see a lot of bad visuals, bad feelings from this. Most kids say they don't want to be Cambodians because there are so many bad things happening" (Chan 2003, 143). Nationalism and, by extension, ethnic identity became tainted for Cambodian refugees; meanwhile, in Cambodia itself there is evidence of a resurgent Khmer nationalism against more powerful neighbors, such as the anti-Thai riots in January 2003.

A large portion of the American public first became aware of the Khmer Rouge atrocities with the release in 1984 of *The Killing Fields*, a movie about a Cambodian photojournalist's experiences during the regime. The film's significance, however, went beyond informing Americans about the aftermath of the war in Southeast Asia. Many Cambodians in the United States came to use the film as a synopsis of their own experiences. During my interview with Ruon I asked her what she tells Americans about Cambodia and she responded: "I used to say that it was like Hawaii, with coconut and banana trees. That we look like Thai. Now when Americans ask me about Cambodia, I say, 'Did you see *The Killing Fields*? That's the country I'm from. That's what it was like before.' " Margaret, too, mentioned that the film is a reference point for defining her identity. Here's how she describes what she tells Americans about Cambodia: "I say, 'Do you know Vietnam and Thailand?' People know those countries, and then I tell them they are Cambodia's neighbors. I also tell them about *The Killing Fields*. Some know and some don't know. I tell them I'm a part of that story."

Following the success of the film, Haing Ngor, the Cambodian refugee who played the lead role, became a spokesperson for Cambodians in the United States. In 1989, Chinese gang members in Los Angeles killed him during a street robbery. But two years before his death Ngor published one of the first autobiographical accounts of life under the Khmer Rouge regime. In his book, Ngor (1987, 1) articulates the revolutionary rupture that marks all Cambodian refugees in the United States and provides a final insight into their ethnic origins:

> I have been many things in life. A trader walking barefoot on paths through the jungle. A medical doctor, driving to his clinic in a shiny Mercedes. In the past few years to the surprise of many people, and above all myself, I have been a Hollywood actor. But nothing has shaped my life as much as surviving the Pol Pot Regime. I am a survivor of the Cambodian holocaust. That's who I am.

Conclusion

It is a truism that countries around the world differ in their histories, politics, and cultures. When immigrants leave their homelands, these ethnic origins continue to shape their definitions of societal membership and the meanings they attach to group boundaries. For refugees from Cambodia, a history of cultural amalgamation is one of the central components of their ethnic origins. Trade and religious diffusion from India heavily influenced Cambodia's development as a nation-state, as did managing uncertain borders with other kingdoms in Southeast Asia. These events created a hybrid culture and an amorphous conception of ethnicity.

Theravada Buddhism is another component of ethnicity among the Khmer. It has a highly accommodative view of social differences and does not polarize insiders and outsiders. As a theology Buddhism emphasizes individual ethical conduct to earn merit toward positive reincarnation; individuals are not judged by their conformity to canonical standards.

Khmer kinship norms further contribute to a porous ethnic boundary. Unlike the pattern in China and Vietnam, the Khmer do not emphasize ancestral lineage. Similarly, Khmer kinship neither values endogamy nor discourages exogamy. Instead, kinship norms among the Khmer are comparatively unstructured, since descent, if it matters at all, is traced through both the father's and the mother's bloodlines, and fictive kin may be as important as blood kin. This balancing of individualism with kin commitments promotes a discretionary view of membership in groups and social networks.

Intra-ethnic violence prior to arrival in the United States is a final component of Khmer ethnic origins. The civil war in Cambodia during the 1960s and 1970s weakened an already fragile sense of national identity. Following the collapse of the pro-American Lon Nol government in 1975, the Khmer Rouge caused the death of about one quarter of the Cambodian population. As a result, Cambodian refugees attribute their suffering to members of their own ethnic group rather than to the U.S. state, despite its military intervention in the civil war.

Arriving in the United States deeply traumatized by co-ethnic revolutionaries, and with a history of cultural amalgamation and loose kinship norms, Khmer Buddhists bring a worldview that minimizes the salience of ethnic boundaries. They tend to stress individuality over conformity and think that ethnic identities do not require strict allegiance, since group differences are easily bridged. Thus, Cambodians add much more to American diversity than simply increasing the number of "Asians" or obliging the U.S. Bureau of the Census to add a new ancestry and linguistic category. They change the very meaning of American diversity, however modestly, through the history, politics, and culture of their ethnic origins.

Chapter 4

Hmong

Only 350 miles separate Angkor Wat from the Plain of Jars, the area of Laos where the Hmong once claimed autonomy (see figure 3.1). Yet the Hmong and the Khmer have opposite ethnic origins. A well-known story about Hmong origins illustrates this difference. A brother and sister become the only humans to survive a devastating flood (Dang 1993; Livo and Cha 1991). To maintain the species they are forced to mate, but this union produces a gourd-shaped egg rather than a child. The siblings cut the egg into pieces and plant them in different parts of their farm. This gardening yields the eighteen clans from which all Hmong are descended, each one named after an agricultural feature of a rural village. Where the Khmer origin story about an Indian prince marrying a local princess in a far-away land emphasizes exogamy and hybridity, the Hmong story emphasizes endogamy and lineage. Four components of Hmong ethnic origins shaped and amplified this worldview: their diaspora from China, being a highland minority without their own nation-state, having highly structured kinship norms and thus valuing ancestor worship, and experiencing inter-ethnic political conflict with the Pathet Lao and North Vietnam during the twentieth-century wars in Southeast Asia.

Diaspora from China

Approximately 2 million Hmong live in the mountainous region of southern China (Culas and Michaud 2004). At one point in their history the Hmong inhabited the lowlands, but conflict with the central government during the 1600s forced them to migrate (Quincy 1988, 27):

> The Chinese . . . demanded integration into the Chinese way of life as a precondition for decent treatment. The refusal of the Hmong to assimilate cost them much. Eventually they were forced to retreat to the mountain tops, where the freedom to live as they pleased became the prime consolation for the hard life of the montagnard.

Moving to the highlands, however, did not end persecution by the Chinese government, and subsequent population growth created

60

additional motives for migration (Chan 1994; Yang 1975/1993). As a result, many Hmong moved from China to Vietnam and eventually to Laos and Thailand. The first Hmong probably entered Southeast Asia in the mid-1700s. The largest migration occurred in the mid-1800s, following persecution by the Qing state and a subsequent Hmong rebellion (Culas and Michaud 2004). By the 1960s the Hmong population in Laos numbered about 300,000 people.

Groups such as the Hmong, which have experienced a diaspora, develop a very distinctive ethnic identity (Brubaker 2005; Cohen 1997; Safran 1991; Smith 1986). One of the most common features of such groups is a strong ethnic boundary that clearly distinguishes the in-group from out-groups. According to Fungchatou Lo (2001, 25), "The Hmong view the world as 'us and them.' This means that from the larger perspective, 'us' represents the Hmong and 'them' represents the non-Hmong." There are several linguistic examples of this attitude. The Hmong word "qhua" has the multiple meaning of "person from another clan," "outsider," and "anyone other than a member of the Mong/Hmong group" (Lyman 2004, 176). The Hmong word for "Chinese" ("suav") is also a generic term for foreigners or non-Hmong (Hassoun 1997). Similarly, "luag" means "others" or "them" and is used in contrast to "peb hmoob," or "we the Hmong." Jacques Lemoine (1972, 23) describes this worldview, which is based on his fieldwork in a Hmong village in Laos (author's translation from French):

> A fierce ethnocentrism precludes any reception other than a courteous but firm distancing from other ethnic groups with which the Hmong are able to be in contact. The first historical neighbors, the Chinese (*suav*) have left in the collective memory an indelible mark accompanied by an aura of marked fear and animosity.

Cultural conflict with the Chinese is a theme in many contemporary Hmong folk stories (Livo and Cha 1991). One story entitled "Why the Hmong Live in Mountains" describes a dispute between the Hmong and their neighbors, which causes the Hmong to undertake a trek. At daybreak they find themselves in high mountains, where they remain. In another story the breastfeeding habits of Chinese and Lao women are contrasted with those of Hmong women. Several other stories have as their theme land conflict with the Chinese, the latter often resorting to deception to obtain grave sites and other valued property from the Hmong. According to Nicholas Tapp's (1992) analysis of these stories, their themes symbolize sovereignty and rebellion.

One mechanism that maintains a diasporic identity for the Hmong and similar groups is an idealized conception of a golden age prior to forced migration. A Hmong legend in contemporary China concerns "the lost books" and explains how persecution deprived the Hmong of their alphabet. The main themes in this legend are "the original possession of a form of writing, its loss while crossing waters pursued by oppressors who were Chinese, and the moral or conclusion . . . that the Miao [the Chinese name for the Hmong] are now clever in their hearts" (Tapp 1989b, 77).

Diasporic groups oriented toward a mythic past often evince a strong drive for self-determination and sometimes even create a culture of deliverance. Hmong history reveals a number of messianic movements with charismatic leaders that seek to unify the Hmong and conquer enemies; there has been, on average, one such movement "every twenty-five or thirty years over [the past] 150 years" (Culas 2004, 119). The roots of messianism are revealed in Hmong legends about a character named Tswb Tchoj, "the culture hero who periodically arises to unify the clans and establish hegemony over the land" (Tapp 1986a, 91). Timothy Dunnigan (1986, 42) goes so far as to call such efforts "revitalization movements led by Hmong prophets." The most contemporary example is the Chao Fa guerrillas, whose leader claimed supernatural powers in his fight against the post-1975 Communist government in Laos and its Vietnamese allies (Lee 2004).

A final feature of ethnic groups marked by a diaspora is a collective memory of dispersal from an original homeland that sensitizes each new generation to the importance of the past. According to Louisa Schein (2004, 273), "Everywhere the Hmong reside they refer to China as a homeland"; this collective memory of the diaspora is particularly evident in their oral history (Schein 1998). A reporter who traveled with an extended Hmong family from a refugee camp in Thailand to their new home in Mishicot, Wisconsin, recorded their observations en route, including that of the grandfather when the plane neared Hong Kong: "From childhood I've listened to fables of our ancestors in China. But I never believed I'd see the homeland myself" (Everingham 1980, 652). Similarly, in her autobiography, Houa Moua recounts a conversation with her mother about the Hmong migration from China. The two women are in a Thai refugee camp and as they contemplate resettlement abroad Houa's mother recalls a similar conversation many years earlier: "You and your father were talking about his grandparents, about the time they were forced to leave China. He said that they were seed, Hmong seed. That they had to go to a new land and settle there in the earth and grow. It looks like we're the seed now" (Rolland and Moua 1994, 320).

The historic Hmong migration from China is also a landmark for Jou Yee Xiong, a clan leader and elder respected for his knowledge of the Hmong. He begins his life story this way: "My name is Jou Yee Xiong and I am sixty-six years old. More than a hundred years before I was born, the Hmong people had migrated from China into Laos and other places in Southeast Asia" (Chan 1994, 63). References to China are prominent in other oral histories given by Hmong refugees in the United States (Chan 1994, 101 and 210; Faruque 2002, 81; Tenhula 1991, 97). For example, a mother begins recounting her oral history to her son by stating: "My ancestors originally came from China" (Chan 1994, 216). Her son then begins his own autobiographical statement by stating: "According to my great-grandparents, the surname Moua originated in Mongolia during the sixteenth century. Moua means 'to conquer.' It was a popular and well-known name. It is said that many of the powerful leaders in Mongolia were named Moua" (224).

These quotations indicate that the diaspora from China is a salient element in Hmong ethnic origins, one that shapes their sense of ethnicity even after resettlement in the United States. When a group of Hungarian Roma (often inappropriately called Gypsies) visited St. Paul courtesy of the U.S. International Visitor Leadership Program, they requested a meeting with Hmong leaders because, as their host noted, "The comparisons between the Hmong and the Roma are striking since both are diasporas and have been systematically persecuted wherever they've gone."[1]

Hill and Valley in the Lao Nation-State

Laos contains at least sixty distinct ethnic groups, making it one of the most culturally diverse countries in the world (Yang 1975/1993). By the mid-1970s the Hmong in Laos numbered about 300,000 but constituted only 10 percent of the population. Other small highland groups, such as the Iu Mien, accounted for another 20 percent. The Lao-Theung, the original inhabitants of Laos, were pushed from the lowlands to the low hills by the in-migration of a different group, now known as the ethnic Lao or the lowland Lao. The Lao-Theung represented about 20 percent of the population. The lowland Lao lived in the valleys and plains and accounted for 50 percent of the country's population. But the lowland Lao's residence in urban areas and control of the government gave them a position of dominance far beyond their numbers.

The Lao nation-state typifies the "hill-valley" social order in Southeast Asia, in which elevation creates ethnic boundaries (Izikowitz 1969). The lowland groups, such as the Lao, operate the national state and school system, control the markets, have centralized religious institutions, and generally view the highland peoples as uncivilized. The highland people, such as the Hmong, seek political autonomy, economic self-sufficiency, and cultural preservation in their mountain redoubts. A Hmong man succinctly summarized this pattern during an oral history interview

(D. C. Everest Area Schools 2000, 107). He was asked by a Hmong high school student, "How come we went to live in the mountains?" and answered: "One [reason] is because we Hmong like to live in peace. We didn't want to bother anyone or have anyone bother us. Second, we Hmong don't really like government control because we like to be our own government. That's why we lived in the mountains."

A goal of the Hmong migration from China had been to achieve greater autonomy from a dominant group, and this issue reemerged for them in Laos. The Lao maintained political dominance over the Hmong by controlling the institutions of government. In fact, French colonization increased this power (Chan 1994). Colonial administrators used Lao chiefs to collect taxes from the Hmong, often by threatening the deployment of colonial troops if the Hmong did not pay. According to Keith Quincy (1988, 67–68), because the Hmong were "denied political representation, they were regularly exploited by Laotian officials. . . . Because of their isolation and distance from the centers of power, the hill tribes had no effective means to protest unjust treatment by local authorities."

In part because of this administrative exploitation, it was highland groups, not the Lao, who displayed the greatest resistance to French colonization (Chan 1994). Highland groups rebelled in 1896 and again two decades later (Yang 1975/1993). The largest Hmong revolt against the French occurred from 1919 to 1921, and one of its aims was to secure an independent Hmong kingdom. The revolt failed but the colonial government nonetheless granted a greater degree of autonomy to the Hmong in the province of Xieng Khouang, which had the largest Hmong population. At first the Hmong were only able to hold office at the subdistrict level; not until after World War II did Hmong leaders replace Lao officials in Xieng Khouang at the district and provincial level. Democratization proceeded much more slowly in other provinces where the Hmong lived.

As a result of Lao political dominance, one of the most serious inequalities experienced by the Hmong was lack of access to Lao schools and poor treatment in them. The absence of a written Hmong language until the 1950s, and thus limited literacy, historically differentiated the Hmong from other ethnic groups (Tapp 1989b). The Lao government exacerbated this inequality because it tended to build schools only in areas populated by the Lao. The first school in Xieng Khouang province was not established until 1939 and there were only 20 village schools by 1960 (Yang 1975/1993). If Hmong parents wished their children to have a formal education they had to send their children into areas controlled by the Lao. During an oral history a Hmong mother in the United States told her son: "We would have done anything to let you children get an education. Paying the school fees would have been a problem, but not as big a problem as getting you accepted into school because the Lao education system favored Lao over Hmong students. This was especially true at the college level" (Chan 1994, 147).

Other Hmong were averse to Lao schools because they believed that living in the lowlands would expose them to disease or Lao witchcraft. One Hmong elder reports: "At the time I was still small, we Hmong could not go down into the low country. If we did, we would die. Therefore, we Hmong could not send our children down to the low country for schooling" (Mattison, Lo, and Scarseth 1994, 65). Even when the Hmong did attend a Lao school they resisted assimilation into the dominant culture. According to G. Linwood Barney (1957, 35), who used the dated and pejorative name Meo for the Hmong, "Learning Laotian is considered by the Meo as a necessary evil in order to gain prestige and advancement." Similarly, contemporary Hmong youth in Thailand who stay at Buddhist monasteries have little interest in Buddhism and give as a reason for their presence there the desire to become literate (Tapp 1986b).

Although politically and educationally unequal to the Lao, the Hmong could claim economic independence. They practiced an ancient form of agriculture called swidden, or slash-and-burn, horticulture, in which farmers raze a portion of forest to create arable land. In five to ten years the farmers exhaust the nutrients in the soil and then move to a new area. The Hmong further achieved self-sufficiency by raising animals, hunting, and gathering wild plants. These activities enabled the Hmong to meet their subsistence needs with minimal reliance on outsiders.

Yet the Hmong did perform a distinct and lucrative function in the Lao economy through their cultivation of poppies and production of raw opium. As Yang Dao (Yang 1975/1993, 79) summarizes: "Opium helps give the Hmong a strong position in the hierarchy of ethnic minorities in Laos." The typical Hmong family kept only 37 percent of the opium they produced, generally for use as a painkiller. The family would immediately sell or barter 50 percent of their opium—a high proportion, considering that they traded only between 5 and 10 percent of their livestock.

The Hmong had produced opium even while living in China (Chan 1994). In Laos, French colonization increased opium production by requiring that taxes be paid in French coins. Since the Hmong existed outside of the market economy the primary way they could obtain hard currency was by selling their one cash crop. But Lao and Chinese merchants also directly purchased opium from the Hmong on behalf of the French colonial administration, which in effect operated an international drug cartel (opium is the raw ingredient for heroin). In return, these merchants sold or traded tools, silver, textiles, and other products the Hmong could not make for themselves.

Economic self-sufficiency through horticulture and opium production did give the Hmong a degree of freedom but it also solidified the
ethnic boundary separating them from the Lao. Their close relationship
with nature, while economically valuable, reinforced the Lao view that
they were primitive "country bumpkins" (Scott 1986, 116). Donald
Whitaker (1979, 55) observes that the Hmong "have had to face considerable Lao condescension and discrimination," while Quincy (1988, 67)
states that they are "viewed as barbarians" by the Lao.

Some Hmong internalized these stereotypes. The Lao represented a
higher social class and the Hmong used the Lao as a reference group to
judge their own material status. One Hmong man in the United States
recalls: "Our harvests were very good and we had an abundance of rice
in storage. . . . We prospered and our standard of living reached that of
the lowland Lao" (Chan 1994, 68). Schooling, and with it a more modern lifestyle, is another basis of invidious comparison, according to the
same informant: "We lacked education, but we did learn bit by bit from
lowland Lao merchants who came to our villages to sell us sugarcane in
exchange for opium" (Chan 1994, 66).

Religious practices further strengthened the ethnic boundary separating the Lao and Hmong. Described both as animist and pantheist,
Hmong religion rests on the belief in a highly complex typology of animal, plant, human, and supernatural spirits (Chindarsi 1976; Tapp
1989a). These spirits are interrelated so that one form not only affects the
other forms but through reincarnation can transform from one type to
another. One of the Hmong's main spiritual concerns is the relationship
between living humans and ancestral spirits. In this cosmology, ordinary people as well as skilled shamans seek to influence the natural and
the supernatural to achieve the proper balance that maintains such
desirable states as good health and abundant crops. Hmong religion
therefore differs from Theravada Buddhism, the religion of the Lao and
Khmer, in several important ways.

Animism is organized around invariant taboos concerning behavior,
such as actions that will displease ancestors. Conversely, Theravada
Buddhism focuses on ethical abstractions like good and evil, which
require interpretation in different contexts. The two religions also differ
in their institutional structure. Animism is based on oral transmission,
and shamans, who function much like doctors in Western societies, conduct their practices independent of each other. Central features of
Theravada Buddhism, by contrast, are texts, temples, and a segregated
clergy. Finally, Theravada Buddhists view killing as sinful, whereas
sacrificing chickens, pigs, or cows is common in Hmong funerals and
rituals, which seek to establish communication with spirits. During an
oral history a Hmong man summarized how such religious differences

contributed to the hill-valley social order in Laos: "We are what is called highland people, or Hmong tribespeople. We are very different from the lowland people, mostly because they are Buddhist and we believe in spirits" (Tenhula 1991, 97).

Hmong animists are similar to Lao and Khmer Theravada Buddhists in that they attempt to intercede on behalf of the spirits of deceased ancestors. At the Phchum Ben ceremony in September, Khmer families make food offerings to their ancestors during temple ceremonies and this ritual can be enacted at home at other times of the year. But the Hmong have a much more elaborate conception of spirits than do most Khmer. Tapp summarizes the Hmong belief system (1989a, 92) this way:

> The religious world of the Hmong is thus clearly and logically ordered according to a series of oppositions between life and death, men and spirits, this world and the other world, the wild and the tame. These oppositions interact with each other to form new categories of the natural and supernatural.

A Hmong folktale amply illustrates these beliefs. It tells the story of a Hmong man who dies and is reincarnated as a tiger that steals into a Yunnanese village, a province in southwestern China where the Hmong still live. As the tiger attempts to kill a pig he is caught in a trap. Using the term Miao for the Hmong, Nusit Chindarsi (1976, 193) recounts the rest of the plot:

> When the tiger saw a Hmong boy, who was working for the Yunnanese, coming to look at him, he said: "This boy is a Miao boy." The boy was very puzzled that the tiger could speak the Hmong language, so he asked the tiger, "How is it that you can speak Miao?" The tiger answered: "I used to be Hmong; it was not until after I died that I became a tiger."

As conveyed in this tale, Hmong ethnicity is so strong that it continues to differentiate one group from another even after death. Hmong kinship norms further reinforce this hermetic ethnic boundary and polarized ethnic identity.

Clan Kinship and Ancestor Worship

In Hmong culture, individuals sharing a surname, such as Moua, Vang, or Xiong, belong to the same clan because they are descended from a common ancestor. There are eighteen clans, thirteen of which are significantly larger than the others (Chan 1994). Clan members think of one another as kin related by blood and have a leader who conducts ancestral rituals and mediates conflicts among clan members and with other clans. Hmong men remain members of their birth clan for life, but Hmong women join their husband's clan after marriage. The Hmong of Laos also make regional distinctions among Blue, White, or Striped Hmong, largely on the basis of clothing style and dialect.

In daily life the Hmong organize kin relations primarily through sub-clans and direct lineage descent groups (Lee 1994–95). But at the group level the most important function of clan kinship is defining ethnic identity. One way in which a Hmong person could ask another his or her clan ("xeem") is by the literal question: "You are Hmong what kind?" (Yang 2004, 197). Dunnigan et al. (1997) therefore consider clan membership to be one of the four key elements of Hmong ethnicity. Similarly, Sucheng Chan (1994, 58) concludes that "expressing paramount loyalty to the clan and respect for [clan] elders" is one of the core "ethnic markers" for the Hmong. Thus kinship norms shape Hmong conceptions of ethnic boundaries by emphasizing "the ascendancy of group over individual" (Scott 1986, 167) rather than, as for Khmer kinship, a balance of individual choice and loose group commitments.

Although clan kinship serves to unite families sharing the same surname, it is such a powerful basis of social differentiation within Hmong society that it can become a source of tension. An ethnography of the Hmong community in Wausau, Wisconsin, disclosed (Koltyk 1998, 61):

> Even in public places the Hmong tend to segregate by lineage and clans. Marathon County Park in the summertime, with a crowd of Hmong socializing in the back area, may appear to outsiders as a large family get-together. What we find within the large group of Hmong, however, are pockets of families; the Yang in one area, the Vang, Thao, and Her in another area, with little interaction between the groups.

A well-known episode in Hmong history illustrates interclan tensions and concerns a conflict between the Lo and Ly clans during the colonial period (Chan 1994). Beginning in the 1920s, these two large clans in Xieng Khouang province began feuding over political control. This conflict was reproduced for decades, with the Ly clan backing the French and then the Americans, and the Lo clan allying itself with nationalist independence forces, Japan, and then the Pathet Lao. Following the collapse of the U.S.-backed government in Laos in 1975, a leader of the Lo clan assumed a prominent position in the newly created Lao People's Democratic Republic. The Ly-Lo feud is a significant illustration of the power of groups in Hmong culture, but it is not representative of the common intragroup conflicts experienced by the Hmong.

Much more important for families and individuals is the practice of paying bride wealth, whereby a groom compensates the bride's parents for the loss of their daughter's labor and progeny. Since clans practice exogamy, the groom's family must negotiate a bride price with representatives from a different clan. A frequent source of friction occurs when the bride's clan holds out for more than the groom's clan thinks is reasonable. For example, a woman from the Moua clan who married a man from the Vang clan reports in an oral history (Chan 1994, 132):

> Members of the Moua clan . . . demanded more money from the groom and insisted that his family serve everyone corn whiskey at the wedding ceremony. When we got home after the wedding, the elder of my husband's clan was really angry. He never forgot what the Moua clan did. But all the money they made my husband's family pay for me did not hurt as much as the bad words they said about us.

A similar incident is reported by a man from the Moua clan when he married a woman from the Yang clan: "I married my beautiful wife, Yang Pang, in 1952. I remember our wedding quite well. The Yang clan was cruel and harsh. They made my Moua clan pay a lot of money and animals for her. Two pigs and a cow were slaughtered for the wedding feast" (Chan 1994, 212).

Hmong women disproportionately bear the stress of clan conflict because of the norm of patrilocal residence, or residing with or near the husband's parents after marriage. While some marriages in Laos occurred between clans living in the same village or nearby, patrilocality often required a newly married woman to move to a distant village to join her husband. Thus, some Hmong villages had men from the same clan but wives originally from different clans. In an oral history one woman describes some of these hardships: "I was the only Xiong to be married into the Fang [Vang] clan, which made life very difficult for me. Hard as I worked, some people still spread rumors that I was not hardworking. Such a rumor is what a Hmong wife fears most" (Chan 1994, 144).

While clan membership can lead to conflict between Hmong, its most important contribution to Hmong ethnicity is fostering group unity as a value. This value is well expressed in Hmong proverbs (Lyman 1990, 342) such as "One person can't be a household. One household can't be a village. One village can't be a city." Clan kinship also reinforces the collective nature of social relations through religious beliefs. One animist value is the need to placate the spirits of one's ancestors. Illness is usually attributed to "an ill-advised or inopportune disturbance of a spirit's abode, or the wrathful punishment of an ancestral soul for some social impropriety" (Scott 1987, 34). Another value is the desire for ancestral spirits to reincarnate back into human form. For the Hmong the most desired pattern of reincarnation is to have the ancestral spirit reborn in the same clan and especially the same lineage. According to Gary Lee (1994–95, n.p.):

> The ancestral cult not only unites the living under one roof or in one settlement through their common ancestors, but also establishes a mutual dependence between the dead and the living descendants through the bond of blood relationships across the generations. The living members of a lineage are to follow the same ancestral rituals without deviating from the group's norms, and to provide mutual help by virtue of their kinship bonds.

Thus clan membership is so powerful for the Hmong that it transcends death. This conception of kinship establishes a profoundly group-oriented worldview in which a hermetic boundary separates insiders from outsiders.

Inter-Ethnic Political Conflict and the U.S. State

The history of U.S. military intervention in Laos during the 1960s and 1970s is well documented and leads to one inescapable conclusion: the United States brought the Hmong into the war and then abandoned them when it lost (Chan 1994; Hamilton-Merritt 1993; Quincy 2000; Warner 1996). U.S. Special Forces first contacted the Hmong in 1959 and the U.S. CIA began forming a Hmong army in early 1961 with the direct approval of President Eisenhower during his final days in office. The CIA called the Hmong troops the Special Guerrilla Unit.

The Hmong attracted the attention of the U.S. military for several reasons. They already had a skillful military leader named Vang Pao, a lieutenant colonel in the Royal Lao Army who had extensive combat experience. In addition, many Hmong lived around the Plain of Jars, a plateau of immense strategic value to any army defending or invading Laos. They also had a reputation for being hardy mountain folk and Hmong men were renowned for their marksmanship with rifles and cross-bows; as teenagers they used and honed their skills primarily for hunting. According to a study by the U.S. Department of the Army (1970, 573) undertaken to assess the "paramilitary capabilities" of the Hmong in Thailand, "They are rated as excellent jungle fighters and brave soldiers."

During the war in Southeast Asia the U.S. military used the newly created Hmong army to combat Pathet Lao and North Vietnamese troops and to interdict North Vietnamese soldiers and supplies sent to South Vietnam through Laos (Dommen 2001). Hmong soldiers also rescued downed American pilots and guarded a strategic U.S. radar installation in Laos. Vang Pao, now a general, led the Hmong army and hoped that his alliance with the United States would lead to greater autonomy for the Hmong after the successful conclusion of the war (Scott 1990). By the late 1960s his army numbered more than 30,000 soldiers, although many of these recruits were young teenagers. A special CIA airline supplied the Hmong army and the U.S. Air Force provided direct air support.

In 1973 the United States ended combat operations in Southeast Asia. Approximately 17,000 Hmong soldiers had died and more than 50,000 Hmong civilians had perished from attacks by Pathet Lao and North Vietnamese troops (Dommen 2001). But the war was far from over for the Hmong. The Pathet Lao had a particularly strong hatred for these "American mercenaries," yet the U.S. government failed to implement any of the contingency plans designed to protect the Hmong, such as evacuating them to safer parts of Laos. When the second coalition government in Laos finally collapsed in May 1975, the U.S. military only evacuated about 2,000 Hmong, leaving tens of thousands to their fate. In an oral history (Chan 1994, 118), a young Hmong woman in the United States describes this situation:

> After Laos became a Communist country in 1975, my family along with many others, fled in fear of persecution. Because my father had served as a commanding officer for eleven years with the American Central Intelligence Agency in what is known to the American public as the "Secret War," my family had no choice but to leave immediately. My father's life was in danger, along with those of thousands of others.

This brief review of Hmong political history in the 1960s and mid-1970s indicates several differences from Cambodians' experiences in the same period. First, where Cambodians fought each other and then committed atrocities on their own people, the Hmong fought the Lao and Vietnamese and were then persecuted by them after 1975. An exchange between a Hmong wife and husband reported in an autobiography (Rolland and Moua 1994, 13) illustrates the inter-ethnic quality of the war. The conversation followed a raid on the couple's home by a Pathet Lao patrol led by a North Vietnamese officer, in which the family's pigs and pet dog were taken for food:

> Wife: Why did they do this to us? Who do they think they are? . . . It's not bad enough that we have to put up with all the planes and the noise of the guns! This is between the Lao government and the Pathet Lao and the Red Vietnamese. It has nothing to do with the Hmong.

> Husband: Stop it! You know better than that! My brothers and all the rest of the Hmong soldiers are out there in the jungle.

The prominent role played by the United States is a second difference between the Hmong and Cambodian experiences during the war in Southeast Asia. A CIA agent promised Vang Pao and other Hmong leaders assistance in the unlikely event of a military defeat (see Dommen 2001, 443; Hamilton-Merritt 1993, 92). Oral histories with former Hmong military personnel knowledgeable about events in Laos provide first-person accounts of "the promise." A former Hmong employee of the U.S. Agency for International Development (Rolland and Moua 1994, 320), which assisted the Hmong displaced by the war, stated:

> I have talked with men who were present when General Vang Pao and the Americans made their agreement: If we help them, they would help us. And when General Vang Pao asked them what would happen if the Americans didn't win the war, they all heard the answer: If the Americans do not win the war and the Communists take over Laos, we will take care of you—we will get you out of there. They shook hands, the Americans and the Hmong, and it was promised.

Unfortunately, the United States did almost nothing to assist the Hmong in Laos after 1975. A former general in the Hmong army explains (Tenhula 1991, 38) that he holds no grudge against the United States for proving disloyal. What troubles him, however, is the lack of awareness among the American public about the sacrifices the Hmong made to further U.S. military objectives:

> I am not bitter about the war, all of that is over with. But to say that I can start again fresh is simply not true. I never knew how strange our rela-tionship was—I mean Laos and the United States—until I came here to live. Strange in the sense that few people knew or cared about Laos, even as it related to the war effort and all of those events. This was the hardest thing for me to get over.

As this quotation indicates, some Hmong attribute their refugee sta-tus directly or indirectly to the U.S. state, in sharp contrast to Cambodians, who attribute their refugee status almost exclusively to the Khmer Rouge. Such sentiments can even be found among the younger generation of Hmong Americans. Nineteen-year-old Hlee Xiong, Miss Hmong Wisconsin 2004, believes that "it's very important that we bring awareness to the young people about what is going on in Laos—bombs being dropped, children killed and a lot of gruesome things you wouldn't imagine happening. . . . There are thousands of veteran families trapped there without food and supplies hiding in the jungles" (quoted in Ritchie 2005, 10). Similarly, Tou Vang, a Hmong first-year student at the University of Minnesota, wrote an editorial in a local newspaper objecting

to the United States' invasion of Iraq in early 2003. Rather than emphasize the role of oil in the war and casualties among Iraqi civilians (as
many other protesters did) he drew a lesson from recent Hmong history:

> The Bush administration wants an Iraqi fighting force to help in this war,
> and the Kurds are the only opposition group inside Iraq with military
> forces. In America's history, we have become experts at selling out groups
> that have been our allies. . . . A war on Iraq could devastate the Kurds
> because they would suffer the same fate as the Hmong.[2]

The Hmong's conviction that the American government shares cul-
pability for their hardships has motivated many to seek some form of
redress. Although they have not sought any financial reparations, they
diligently lobbied the U.S. Congress to modify the requirements for
obtaining U.S. citizenship in ways that would benefit Hmong veterans
and their spouses (including widows). Due to their advanced age and
limited education, the veterans wanted an exemption from demonstrating English proficiency and to be tested on only twenty-five rather
than one hundred questions about U.S. history and civics. After several years of activism by the Lao Veterans of America Inc. and other
Hmong community organizations, the U.S. Congress took up the Hmong
Veterans Naturalization Act (HVNA) in May 2000. Prior to the vote,
nearly 2,000 Hmong, including hundreds of Hmong veterans wearing
military fatigues, participated in a rally in Washington D.C. in a final
show of support for the legislation.[3]
    Many in the U.S. Congress recognized that passage of the HVNA
would be more than a technical revision of the country's naturalization
policy. They knew that the law would be a highly symbolic statement
about American society's historic responsibility to Hmong refugees.
Representative Bruce Vento, one of the earliest sponsors of the bill,
stated (U.S. House of Representatives 2000, n.p.):

> While the Vietnam War is over for all America, the plight of our friends
> within this region and Laos must be remembered. The Lao-Hmong sol-
> diers, as young as 10 years old, were recruited and fought and died along-
> side 58,000 U.S. soldiers, sailors, and airmen in Vietnam. As a result of
> their contributions, bravery and loyalty to the United States, the Lao-
> Hmong were tragically overrun by the Communist forces and lost their
> homeland and status in Laos after the Vietnam War. Between 10,000 and
> 20,000 Lao-Hmong were killed in combat-related incidents, and over
> 100,000 had to flee to refugee camps and other nations to survive.

With bipartisan support, the HVNA passed overwhelmingly in both
the U.S. House of Representatives and the U.S. Senate and was signed

into law by President Clinton. It was a significant political victory for the Hmong in the United States, as was House passage of a resolution in November 2001, proclaiming July 22 as Lao-Hmong Recognition Day to honor their sacrifices during the war in Southeast Asia (U.S. House of Representatives 2001). But the passage of the HVNA and the declaration of a day of honor occurred twenty-five years after the start of the refugees' resettlement, certainly too late to alter the influence of the war on the Hmong's view of the U.S. government. In fact, this legislation did not result from a sudden sense of accountability in the U.S. Congress for the nation's unfulfilled obligations to the Hmong. Instead, the existence of the HVNA and the Lao-Hmong Recognition Day are in themselves evidence of the Hmong's strong ethnic solidarity and thus their ability to mobilize their community and sustain an aggressive lobbying campaign.

Despite their symbolic significance, the HVNA and Lao-Hmong Recognition Day have not brought political closure to the Hmong. Since the victory of the Pathet Lao in 1975, the Hmong have maintained an active guerrilla campaign against the Communist government, although it shows signs of waning (Yang 2003). A fact-finding team led by a Hmong American estimated that in 2001 more than 17,000 Hmong veterans and their family members still resided in Laos and frequently suffered persecution by the Lao government.[4]

In 2003 two European journalists and a Hmong-American interpreter entered Laos and managed to locate a band of about 600 Hmong soldiers and their families who were in hiding from the Laotian army. According to Thierry Falise, a Belgian reporter, the group had only forty rifles and no ammunition and survived by foraging for plants in the jungle where they hid. His most startling discovery, however, concerned the Hmong's view of the United States: "A lot of them are still waiting for the Americans to come back. It's like a myth, even though most of them were not alive when the Americans were there almost thirty years ago."[5] Lacking the will to help the jungle resistance groups, in 2004 the U.S. State Department once again responded to the legacy of the Vietnam War with refugee resettlement. It authorized the admission of 15,000 Hmong refugees from the Wat Tham Krabok camp in Thailand, the majority of whom were children.

Conclusion

Global diversity in history, politics, and culture means that immigrants arrive in the United States with different ways of conceptualizing ethnic boundaries and identities. Hmong refugees from Laos and Khmer refugees from Cambodia illustrate this variation in ethnic origins.

The Hmong's status as an ethnic minority lacking a nation-state of their own fostered a distinctive worldview based on the need for survival in an adversarial environment and a consequent need for self-reliance. As a result, their ethnic boundary strongly emphasizes differences between members and nonmembers. Cambodians' worldview is based on a history of cultural hybridization through the blending of Hinduism, Theravada Buddhism, and local animism, as well as through balancing the influences of Thailand, China, Vietnam, and French colonization. It is thus not surprising that the Hmong and the Khmer have very different understandings of what it means to belong to a people.

In addition to these distinct experiences with nation-state formation, the ethnic origins of the Hmong and the Khmer are distinguished by nearly opposite kinship norms and religious values. Hmong kinship is based on patrilineal clans that practice exogamy, which reinforces a worldview where group differences are highly significant and not subject to individual preferences. Khmer kinship norms balance group obligations and individual choice. Thus Cambodians rely much more for support on the nuclear family and sometimes even on fictive kin. Similarly, Hmong animism and ancestor worship require adherence to strict rules and taboos, whereas Buddhism as practiced by the Khmer is a personal philosophy concerning ethical conduct in everyday life.

Political cleavages during the 1960s and 1970s augmented these distinctive ethnic origins even further. Where Cambodians fought each other, the Hmong fought the Pathet Lao and North Vietnamese and were persecuted by them following the collapse of anti-Communist U.S. foreign policy in the region in 1975. More significant, many Hmong refugees hold the U.S. state accountable for abandoning them despite their being loyal allies. Hmong veterans wearing military uniforms frequently participate in memorials and political rallies organized by Hmong in the United States. Such public displays of militarism are nonexistent among Cambodians. The politics of U.S. military intervention and its consequences drives Cambodians apart, whereas it pulls the Hmong together.

Because of this variation in histories, politics, and cultures the Khmer and the Hmong have profoundly different ethnic origins. The Khmer ethnic boundary is porous, and as a result, Khmer ethnicity is fluid and amalgamates differences. The Hmong ethnic boundary is hermetic and therefore Hmong ethnicity has a preservationist orientation that polarizes insiders and outsiders. As these refugees settled in large and small cities in the American Midwest they created a natural experiment on the effects of ethnic origins for racial and ethnic adaptation.

Part III

Places

═ Chapter 5 ═

Small-Town Hospitality
and Hate

W hites accounted for nearly 100 percent of residents in Eau Claire and Rochester when refugees from Vietnam, Laos, and Cambodia began arriving in the mid-1970s. The first arrivals came directly from Southeast Asia via the federal resettlement program organized by the U.S. State Department and the U.S. Department of Health and Human Services. At the migration's peak, two hundred to three hundred refugees flew into the small regional airports over the course of a year. Others moved to Eau Claire and Rochester after initially settling in another part of the United States, pushed by unfavorable conditions in large urban areas and pulled by the presence of kin. Birth rates that are high by U.S. standards further contributed to the growth of Southeast Asian populations in places where few nonwhites lived. Thus, within fifteen years of the migration's start in 1975, more than 1,400 Cambodians lived in Rochester and about 1,900 Hmong lived in Eau Claire.

The ways native-born people in these places reacted to Southeast Asian refugees reveal a pattern of American race and ethnic relations that can be termed "small-town hospitality and hate." Some whites wanted their community to live up to ideals about social solidarity and neighbors helping neighbors, but others viewed the refugees as unwelcome strangers who threatened the established social order. This duality is aptly conveyed in a volunteer's explanation for why she began assisting the Hmong in Eau Claire: "I was . . . concerned about the lack of communication that existed on a city-wide basis which caused the Hmong to be recipients of hostility and abuse, especially among the young school children and teenagers. I was committed to becoming better informed about them so that I could help members of my church and community relate to them in a more positive way" (Gonlag 1985, 124).

Hospitality

The absence of racial and ethnic diversity in Eau Claire and Rochester did not mean that arriving refugees landed in a hostile environment.

Many Americans enthusiastically assisted the Hmong and Cambodians, facilitating the formation of Asian American communities in the most unlikely of places. A small-town ethos of volunteerism and civic pride motivated some local people, such as the Rochester 4-H club, which picked an unprecedented annual community project: co-sponsoring an extended Cambodian family of twelve.[1] In keeping with the organization's agricultural mission, club members farmed a garden plot with the family and submitted a scrapbook of their work to a county competition (and won second place). In Eau Claire, the special-needs coordinator at the Chippewa Valley Technical College helped organize the first Hmong New Year celebration in 1980 and became the chairperson of the Eau Claire Advisory Refugee Committee.[2] The twenty members of the committee coordinated the work of over eighty volunteers who helped the Hmong with problems ranging from clothing and furniture to shopping and employment.[3]

Religious faith, however, provided the primary inspiration for beneficent midwesterners and explains why Southeast Asian refugees came to Wisconsin and Minnesota in the first place. In July 1975, the Gloria Dei Lutheran Church sponsored the first of the refugees to come to Rochester, a former South Vietnamese Army pharmacist and his wife.[4] Three Vietnamese orphans became the first refugees in the Eau Claire area when a family in adjacent Altoona adopted them in April 1975. Their father explained the adoption decision this way: "The lord has blessed us, we want to pass that on to these children, and we'll be blessed again."[5] By 1989 Lutheran Immigration and Refugee Services had sponsored 299 Hmong refugees in Eau Claire and the U.S. Catholic Conference had brought in another 244 (Miyares 1998).

The church-congregation sponsorship model typified the initial resettlement of Southeast Asian refugees across the United States and produced some of the most intimate interactions with local people that the refugees would ever experience (Fein 1987). In Rochester thirty members of the First Church of the Nazarene assisted Cambodian refugees. They became sponsors, greeting new arrivals at the airport, and subsequently helped the refugees obtain basic necessities, learn English, and find jobs. But according to one volunteer, their work with Cambodians went well beyond material survival: "The government can offer money and food stamps but it cannot offer friendship and moral support."[6]

Religion not only provided the infrastructure for refugee resettlement in small midwestern cities but also the moral imperative for assisting those in need. In 1985 Joan Hill, an Episcopal deacon, visited Our Savior's Lutheran Church in Rochester to encourage congregants to sponsor refugees. She showed slides of Hmong, Lao, and Cambodians in the Thai refugee camps and told her audience, "Churches will have to plan resettlement as part of their ongoing ministry, alleviating suffering one family at a time."[7] A series published in the *Rochester Post-Bulletin* the next year explicitly framed the refugees' situation within Christian theology.[8] In the days preceding Christmas, headlines in the series included "Exiles, like Holy Family, Flee from Threats" and "Refugees Overcome Agony, as Christ Did."

The arrival of refugees also revealed the depth of Christian humanitarianism in the Eau Claire area. Dona Krienke uses almost sacred terms to describe the first time she meet Hmong refugees, in 1983. She spent many years aiding them, including selling "paj ntaub"—ornate embroidery sewn by Hmong women—in her arts and crafts store. Krienke recalls that her initial encounter with the Hmong occurred at night after a meeting of members of the American Lutheran Church Women in Osseo:

> I will never forget the feeling that came over me right then. I looked at the eyes of those beautiful children dressed in clothes several sizes too big for them, the proud smiles of their parents and the tired look of the older women. My heart went out to them like you wouldn't believe. I just loved them. They needed someone to speak for them.[9]

Other good Samaritans in the Eau Claire area give remarkably similar descriptions of their faith leading them to aid arriving refugees. Ruth Gonlag assisted the Hmong for several years during the early and mid-1980s, including tutoring English and organizing a farming project. Reflecting on her volunteerism she concluded: "I have great respect for these dear people who are satisfied with so little of material value by our standards. They continue to teach me much about what it means to be a Christian" (Gonlag 1985, 126). Another volunteer who helped a Hmong family sponsored by a Lutheran church in Menomonie commented: "It's what Christ tells us to do. It's been a marvelous experience for all of us. We are looking at our blessings with new eyes."[10] A sponsor in Stanley also invoked religion to convey his feelings toward a newly arrived Lao family: "We've been blessed with a lot and for us it's kind of a payback. We feel this is something we ought to do."[11]

By the mid-1980s a network of churches, nonprofit organizations, and volunteers operated a highly efficient resettlement system in the small cities of the upper Midwest. In Eau Claire an arriving Hmong family could expect to receive clothes, furniture, and household items from Lutheran Social Services or the Catholic diocese.[12] One of these organizations would also find an American family or individual to assist them. Some volunteers became "sponsors" (complete with a written contract detailing their new responsibilities), while others chose the less formalized role of "mentor," agreeing simply to help the refugees learn "coping skills." The Hmong Mutual Assistance Association aided newcomers with problems ranging from food to family conflicts. County and city government agencies registered most of the arriving refugees for public assistance but found jobs for those with the requisite skills. The Chippewa Valley Technical College provided English-language classes, as did volunteers working in a special program sponsored by the Eau Claire Parks and Recreation Department. Resettlement operations were so successful that federal refugee policy actually encouraged the Hmong to relocate to Eau Claire and several other cities in Wisconsin if they were dissatisfied with life in large urban areas (Coffey, Zimmerman, and Associates 1985).

In Rochester no less than six organizations sponsored and provided assistance to refugees: Lutheran Immigration and Refugee Services, U.S. Catholic Charities, Church World Service (a multidenominational Protestant organization), World Relief (representing evangelical Protestants), the Presiding Bishops Fund (an Episcopal organization), and the Intercultural Mutual Assistance Association. Civic groups supplemented the work of these agencies. Both the Rochester Human Rights Commission and the Rochester International Association quickly brought the refugees within their purview.[13] So did the Citizens Advisory Council for Community Education, which spent $5,000 to teach health and safety practices to at-home Southeast Asian women.[14]

Refugee resettlement clearly brought out the best in Rochester and Eau Claire, revealing a group of whites who celebrated the new diversity and became models of compassion. In Rochester, Sister Chrishelle worked as a case manager for U.S. Catholic Charities, collected clothes in her home for refugees to take as needed, and helped create the Refugee Volunteer Assistance Council. Marie Alexander is another one of these extraordinary altruists. The *Rochester Post-Bulletin* described her as "the matron of refugee sponsorship in Rochester" because she had worked with more than eight hundred refugees since 1975, spending thousands of dollars of her own money in the process.[15] In 1995, Cambodians in the city held a ceremony to honor Ms. Alexander and nine other "unsung heroes" who were accurately described as "the ones who quilted blankets, collected food and furniture, found apartments and taught English to Cambodian refugees who settled in Rochester. Many donated hundreds of hours without receiving a cent. Together, they helped establish Rochester's Cambodian community."[16]

Eau Claire also had heroes and heroines. Hmong people dubbed Maureen Homstad "the mother of the Hmong in Eau Claire" because of the selfless assistance she gave them beginning in 1976. For example, in 1980 a Hmong woman called to ask for help when relatives arrived from a refugee camp in Southeast Asia. Homstad agreed and then learned that they would be at the airport in forty-five minutes. The new family exited the plane barefoot in late winter with all their possessions in four boxes. It was Ash Wednesday and Homstad asked her pastor to announce the family's dire need to the church congregation: "By Friday noon, we had all the basic necessities to make them comfortable. It was like the heavens opened up and it all fell in."[17] By 1987 Ms. Homstad was the godmother of twenty-one Hmong children.

The many devoted volunteers and church congregants who aided Cambodian and Hmong refugees show that some residents of Eau Claire and Rochester responded positively to international migration from Asia. But others saw this new diversity as a threat.

Hate

Despite the best efforts of those locals with faith and civic pride, Asian Americans in small midwestern cities would never quite be free of the stigma that they were, as Mia Tuan (1999) put it, "forever foreigners." Public discourse about Southeast Asian refugees took it for granted that they were out of place. In Wausau, a small city about 100 miles from Eau Claire, a reporter described how the Hmong migration introduced diversity to a previously all-white population so that now "Oriental faces are frequently seen on the streets."[18] A *Rochester Post-Bulletin* reporter, perhaps short on synonyms for refugee, referred to Cambodians as "the foreign people."[19] In an otherwise thoughtful series on Southeast Asians, another one of the newspaper's reporters described the northwest neighborhood where many refugees lived as "the center of an alien culture."[20] One white resident of this neighborhood actually gave her name to a reporter and stated: "I don't think anybody likes them around here. It's a pretty nice neighborhood otherwise."[21]

Such prejudice is common in small midwestern cities. To verify its prevalence, Building Equality Together, an antiracism group in Rochester, commissioned a professional polling organization to conduct a survey of whites in Olmsted County, where Rochester is located.[22] The survey found that "a significant number have distorted attitudes" about minorities. For example, 40 percent believed that Southeast Asians did not maintain their property as well as whites, and "many [of the respondents] would prefer limited casual contact between whites and minorities."

A random-sample survey in La Crosse, Wisconsin, about 70 miles from Rochester and 120 miles from Eau Claire, also revealed the prevalence of prejudice toward Southeast Asians (Ruefle, Ross, and Mandell 1992). It found that 43 percent of respondents opposed or strongly opposed the arrival of more Hmong refugees. Many explained their opposition by stating that there are "enough here already," "they cost too much

[in] welfare," and they "take our jobs and contribute to unemployment." Such attitudes must also have been common in Minnesota since in 1986 U.S. Senator David Durenberger asked the U.S. State Department to curtail refugee resettlement in his state, arguing that refugees "have proved economically difficult to assimilate."[23]

A survey in Wausau disclosed similar sentiments: 47 percent of residents felt the area's quality of life had declined as a result of the arrival of Hmong refugees. One outspoken white man gave his name to a reporter writing about the survey findings and stated, "It's the general consensus in this town: If they want to be accepted, they have to start living like Americans and stop living off other people in society."[24] Another resident had the same view: "I've paid taxes for years and people who never worked a day are living off me and don't even say thanks."

Although surveys have never been done to measure the extent of prejudice in Eau Claire, there is no doubt that it is widespread. For example, in 1991 the Eau Claire city manager received an anonymous postcard that read: "Please don't saturate our area with a flock of Orientals and goof up our quality of life. You got us supporting enough gooks as it is."[25] The pernicious rumor that the Hmong ate dogs was a particularly virulent and well-documented stereotype among whites. Utterly false in both Laos and the United States, the Hmong knew of the tale's prevalence among Americans. According to Sy Moua, a prominent Hmong community leader, "We are very concerned about this rumor. It angers us because never in the Hmong history have we eaten dogs."[26] Yet so many Americans called the Eau Claire Police Department to report this alleged violation of an American taboo that Chief James McFarlane was forced to issue a public repudiation: "We found no evidence whatsoever of anyone, particularly the Hmong people, eating any domestic animals in Eau Claire."[27]

Despite this pronouncement, a segment of the white population remained vociferous advocates of the stereotype that the Hmong ate dogs. An anthropologist at the local university collected these rumors to demonstrate their parallel structure with the much older urban legend that Chinese restaurants serve dog meat (Mitchell 1987). He conducted interviews with a wide range of native-born residents who had been told that the Hmong ate dogs, such as a woman who reported (14):

The story I've been hearing is about the Hmong stealing a dog from a car. This happened on the Randall parking lot. A woman had gone in to shop and she left her dog in the car. It was a Pekinese or a poodle—one of those fancy little dogs. So the window was down a little to give it some air. Some guys saw these Hmong come running up. They reached in through the window and opened the door. They grabbed the mutt and ran.

Some whites kept their negative attitudes to themselves, but others acted out their prejudices. The first public account of discrimination against the Hmong in Eau Claire was given by a public school teacher and merited a newspaper article headlined "Hmong Often Treated Badly in New Home."[28] The teacher reported that the Hmong "have been accused of eating dogs and have received obscene and threatening phone calls. Their children have been harassed and even beaten."

Cambodians in Rochester sustained a similar level of abuse. In a detailed series on Southeast Asians, two reporters found that the refugees "ask how long they will be labeled 'chinks' and when people will stop telling them to go home."[29] One front-page story in the series was headlined "Refugees Encounter Some Bias." The reporter noted that the refugees experience name calling, anonymous phone calls, and (according to an employment counselor) reluctance on the part of about one-quarter of employers to hire them.[30] Another series two years later noted: "At times the abuse can be as subtle as whispered remarks or rude treatment. At other times it can involve a 'rip off,' usually by taking advantage of a refugee not familiar with the English language or [U.S.] currency."[31]

One place where refugees were exploited on a large scale was a mobile-home park north of Rochester. The ill-named Zumbro Hill Estates was a pocket of poverty, but Cambodian families perceived it as an improvement over renting and as a tentative step toward home ownership. They could purchase a mobile home for about $4,000 and the park's rent was only $175 a month, far less than an apartment or duplex in Rochester. Many mobile homes passed from one Cambodian family to another as the former residents moved on after accumulating enough savings to qualify for a home mortgage and purchase a house. By 1996, Asian families, mostly Cambodians, occupied about sixty of the hundred twenty homes in the park.[32]

But in 1998 the park owners appointed new managers, who immediately issued citations to one hundred tenants for poorly maintained property. They gave each one a detailed list of mandatory repairs and even specified the color of paint to be applied. Some projects would have cost more than $1,000 to complete, a sum far beyond the means of the low-income families that lived there. Within a few months the managers evicted five families. Others left on their own, forced to abandon their so-called mobile home because they could not afford the repairs nor the more than $1,000 it would have cost to relocate their dwelling to another park. One Cambodian man living in the Zumbro

Hill Estates bluntly stated, "The new managers are trying to push minorities out by forcing them to make expensive and unnecessary repairs."[33]

Housing discrimination against the Hmong is also well documented in Eau Claire. A staff person at one rental agency actually stated to a sponsor looking for housing, "We don't rent to Hmong people."[34] An exposé by the *Eau Claire Leader-Telegram* demonstrated the prevalence of such practices. Hmong and Americans posing as prospective tenants but actually working for the paper made one hundred calls to the same landlords and realtors to test how frequently the Hmong caller received inferior treatment. This investigation concluded, "When inquiring about apartments, Hmong callers routinely are hung up on, put off or lied to about a unit's availability."[35] Hmong and white testers in Appleton and Oshkosh, Wisconsin, also proved the existence of rental discrimination, leading to an investigation by the U.S. Department of Justice and subsequently the largest housing discrimination settlement in state history.[36] A similar problem prevailed in Rochester, where a landlord openly stated to a reporter, "We don't rent to Vietnamese. I just don't rent to that kind of people."[37]

Blatant racist violence compounded the inequality experienced by Southeast Asians in small midwestern cities. In Rochester, white high school students in three cars forced off a road a car with a Southeast Asian driver and five children.[38] When police searched the perpetrators they found baseball bats and knives in their possession. That same year two white men driving a car purposefully knocked a Southeast Asian man off his bike and yelled at him to go back to his country.[39] In Eau Claire, three white men harassed several Hmong women and children in a parked car by pulling at the locked doors, punching the windows, and threatening to rape and kill them.[40] In 1996, unknown assailants burned a ten-foot-tall cross labeled with a swastika in an Eau Claire park next to a neighborhood where many Hmong families lived.[41] The Hmong even suffered harassment in their homes: "In Eau Claire, Hmong names stand out in the telephone directory, and they get hostile phone calls. Angry voices tell them: 'Go back to your country.' 'You eat dog.' 'I'm coming to kill you!' " (Takaki 1989, 463).

The overt racism of a few whites badly tarnished the self-image of Rochester and Eau Claire. But many more whites gradually became swept up in a racially tinged moral panic: an episode of collective fear when people perceive a threat to their fundamental values and norms. This insidious conflict took different forms in each city. Hmong marriage practices raised alarm in Eau Claire, whereas in Rochester, native-born residents feared that Cambodian gangs and youth violence created big-city problems.

"Gang Problem"

Rochester conducted refugee resettlement with great efficiency in the late 1970s and early 1980s. But by the early 1990s some residents and civic leaders sensed that Southeast Asians jeopardized the city's quality of life. Rochester basked in the recognition it received in 1993 when *Money* magazine ranked it number one among the ten best American cities to live in. Road signs still advertise the award at the city limits. Bob Jones, resettlement director for the local office of U.S. Catholic Charities, presciently described how the refugees might threaten this distinction:

> There are many prominent people in Rochester who see the community as a kind of oasis, as one of the last remaining communities where there are good conditions for raising a family. As long as they see the refugees as contributing to the community, the saturation point is going to remain fairly high. But if the community perceives we are bringing in people who are going to be problems, that could change dramatically.[42]

Just such a development began in the late 1980s. Several robberies and assaults involving Southeast Asians led to a *Rochester Post-Bulletin* story entitled "Asian Gangs Using Strong-Arm Tactics May Be in Rochester."[43] A reporter asked Jones to comment on these crimes and he perceptively remarked that "the greatest threat of all to the Rochester refugees as a result of the activities of the small group is the loss of acceptance and support from the American community."[44] The early and middle 1990s continued to be punctuated by events that enabled locals to equate diversity with the arrival of big-city problems. In 1992, a member of the Royal Cambodian Bloods gang shot an African American member of the Gangster Disciples. The Cambodian gangster was only twelve years old. A headline that year proclaimed "Rochester Citizens Confront Gang Problem."[45]

By 1993 the Rochester police identified seven gangs in the city and warned adjacent small towns to prepare for their arrival. Occasional assaults, robberies, and even drive-by shootings involving Cambodians continued to be reported during the mid-1990s. Police frequently called the suspects "gang affiliated" and explained the violence as an effort to gain prestige within or between gangs. Whatever its cause, the violence led to a public image of Cambodians as menacing criminals. After eleven- and twelve-year-old white boys were robbed they described their assailants as "Cambodian, 18 to 21 years old, 5-feet-10 inches to 6-feet tall, wearing black baggy pants."[46] It is doubtful that the youths actually knew the ethnicity of the robbers and extremely unlikely that one or more of these Asians was six feet tall, yet the local newspaper published this account. One Cambodian youth expresses how much pain the "gang member" stereotype causes: "It is hard for me, sometimes people act afraid of me. I want to say I am not in a gang. I do not belong to a gang. I wish people would look at everyone as individuals."[47]

Social conflict between locals and the refugees intensified when inter-ethnic violence occurred in schools. Headlines such as "Gangs a Part of Everyday Life in Junior High School"[48] exacerbated the community's moral panic. According to David Brown, a youth programs coordinator, gang violence was escalating among adolescents: "At one point it was fistfights, then it turned to flashing a gun, now the thing is to pop off a few rounds into the air or at a passing car."[49] Intra-ethnic crime could be dismissed by sympathetic whites as the work of a few or by less tolerant whites as "their problem." But the issue of school safety touched an insti-tution essential to the city's quality of life.

Often the interracial violence in the schools flared up when Asian stu-dents retaliated against bullying by white students. Among 203 Asian junior high and high school students who completed a questionnaire in 1984, 57 percent reported being harassed at least one time in school.[50] A task force of teachers investigating this problem concluded that typi-cal cases of harassment "involved name-calling, pushing and shoving, and 'wolf-packing' in which a group of whites will attempt to intimidate and frighten a single Asian student."[51]

Small fights involving a few students continued into the late 1980s and throughout the 1990s, and at times the confrontations erupted on a massive scale. A 1989 melee involving one hundred Southeast Asian and white students at a mall was only quelled by the arrival of sixteen city, county, and state police cars.[52] Two years later about one hundred fifty white students walked out of classes at one high school to protest the lack of support for the white victim of an interracial fight.[53] Although police arrived to patrol the school, the superintendent of schools felt that the situation remained explosive. He requested intervention by officials from the U.S. Department of Justice's Community Relations Service, an office established during the 1960s to mediate local racial conflicts.

In light of these events it is not surprising that a questionnaire com-pleted by 5,500 students of all backgrounds in 1991 found widespread distrust, anger, and prevalent racial stereotyping.[54] A white high school student participating in a forum on racial problems that year reported an ordinary occurrence:

> I was walking down the hall when a white student started to call a Southeast Asian names and make fun of them by trying to talk like them and such. I guess it made me feel really bad for they came to our country to be free and have a chance and look what they get for wanting one, it just

doesn't seem fair. They are already having a hard time adjusting and we aren't making it any easier.[55]

This incident is remarkably similar to the first reported case of harassment in a Rochester school. In 1976 a teacher's aid overheard American children mimicking the way Vietnamese children spoke their native language. She naïvely concluded that it merely reflected "the natural tendency of children to poke fun of things that are strange."[56]

"Girl Kidnapped for Marriage"

Natives in Eau Claire never came to perceive Hmong gangs as a serious threat and in the mid-1990s public school principals disavowed the existence of Hmong gangs. The police officer specializing in juvenile delinquency disagreed. His proof: "a drawing, submitted by a middle school student as a class assignment, showing gang symbols and listing the names of 10 gangs."[57] Evidence of Hmong gang activity remained circumstantial for the rest of the decade, despite a nonfatal gang-related shooting at the 1994 Hmong New Year in adjacent Altoona (both the perpetrator and the victim were from Minnesota). Nonetheless, the local newspaper published an article inaccurately titled "Gang Activities Spark Concern."[58] The so-called evidence included truancy, graffiti, and an inter-ethnic fight in a high school lunchroom in 1998. Yet according to police estimates cited in the article there were only about one hundred ten Hmong gang members in the city, and 80 percent were "gang associates" who joined for social reasons and did not engage in crime.

The moral panic in Eau Claire did not focus on fear for the town's quality of life but instead featured a public discourse portraying aspects of Hmong marriage practices and family life as deviant or even illegal. One perceived violation of the moral order concerned Hmong girls whose parents pressured them into marriage. In Laos, as in other parts of Asia, it is common for parents to arrange a marriage for a teenage daughter. But the cultural meaning of "pressure"—admonishment or actual coercion—becomes ambiguous when this norm is transplanted to the United States. Sensationalized cases of "marriage by capture" further contributed to the moral panic. Rare even in Laos, this ritualized elopement involved a bachelor taking an unmarried woman (often his girlfriend) from her home in order to force her parents to consent to their marriage (see Ly 2001 and Scott 1988 for an objective analysis of the Hmong bride theft custom). Once in the United States, some Hmong men misused this practice and the custom's patriarchal bias became objectionable to Hmong women as they took on more egalitarian gender roles. In combination, the symbolic and legal issues surrounding

Hmong marriage traditions fueled a moral panic among the civic leaders in Eau Claire, who in other contexts were among the strongest supporters of the Hmong.

The first moral panic in the city began in January 1987, following the local newspaper's story, picked from the Associated Press, of a "marriage-by-theft" case in La Crosse.[59] The article reported that a Hmong man had "abducted" and "impregnated" a Hmong woman against her will after obtaining her parents' permission to marry her. Following publication of this story a white volunteer in Eau Claire who worked with the Hmong confirmed that several Hmong girls in the city had been "kidnapped" in a similar manner.[60] Other girls also told her they feared parental pressure would force them into early marriage and thus failure to complete high school. A professor at the local university who was active in resettlement efforts corroborated this report. Two Hmong women refuted these allegations, as did the male director of the Hmong Mutual Assistance Association. Nonetheless, local authorities organized a meeting in the Eau Claire Public Library to discuss what the newspaper called "Conflicting Customs, Laws."[61]

One need not be an adherent of postmodernism to appreciate the symbolism of this event: a dominant group constructing a discourse through which to control a subordinate group perceived as a threat to the moral order. A district attorney and a pediatrician—representatives from the twin canons of Western rationality, law and science—lectured a people with an oral history inside a shrine of Western recorded knowledge. These authorities informed an audience of about fifty Hmong men, women, and teenagers of U.S. laws regarding marriage and statutory rape of minors. They advised young women to report their parents to a teacher, the municipal Human Services Department, or the police if they felt pressured to marry.[62]

The discourse was not entirely one-sided. Some Hmong participants complained of biased reporting. A Hmong girl stated that she thought the U.S. Constitution protected the customs of ethnic groups. A Hmong man said sex education in American schools was the real problem because it led to early pregnancy, thus forcing Hmong parents to arrange marriages. Another Hmong man argued that the ages of some Hmong youths had been inaccurately recorded on official documents in the Thai refugee camps and were still in use, with the result that the youths were actually older than their ages on paper. The Hmong traditionally permit first cousins to marry and soon the topic of incest was raised, to which "The Hmong protested that incest was non-existent or very rare in their culture."[63] As these responses suggest, some Hmong in Eau Claire viewed the emerging public discourse on their marriage and family practices as a serious threat.

Other Hmong contested the public representation of their culture as deviant by sending a letter to the local newspaper, which it published under the headline "Hmong Try to Keep Customs."[64] The authors, "members of the Hmong student associations of UW-Barron County Center, Rice Lake, UW-Eau Claire and the Hmong community in Eau Claire," objected to the paper's use of the terms "kidnap" and "force" in discussing Hmong marriage practices. In an articulate and well-reasoned rebuttal the students and their supporters sought to clarify some of the pertinent differences between Hmong and American culture. After presenting their anthropological synopsis the authors directly challenged the authority of a dominant group to coerce their assimilation:

> We know that the American-type family has many weaknesses of its own. We doubt the wisdom of adapting a new family structure when we have yet so much to learn. We have read that the Japanese and Chinese Americans made a successful adaptation to America by maintaining a strong and traditional family. We would like the opportunity to do the same. We are not asking for conflict with the laws and values of the descendants of the earlier immigrants. But we fear that the hasty destruction of our traditional Hmong family structure could condemn us to a future as just another dependent minority caught in poverty and illiteracy.

There is no need to deconstruct the meanings of this eloquent passage beyond listing its themes: high U.S. divorce rates; Asians as a model minority; a nation of immigrants; and welfare dependency among poor inner-city single parents. The Hmong authors were clearly cognizant of their role in a contested discourse to define their social problems and progress toward cultural adjustment.

Despite its skillful rhetoric the Hmong rebuttal did not change the views of locals nor even the newspaper's vocabulary for describing cases of cross-cultural conflict. In 1989 the *Eau Claire Leader-Telegram* reported that a Hmong girl in Eau Claire had been "kidnapped" and taken to St. Paul.[65] The reporter cited anonymous Hmong sources who stated that Hmong girls from the ages of fourteen to seventeen were routinely pressured into marriage and that several other kidnappings of girls had occurred in Eau Claire, one of which involved a thirteen-year-old. Officials at North High School, which had the largest number of Hmong students, claimed that one or more cases of bride kidnapping was an annual occurrence. The following year the newspaper ran an article entitled "Hmong Custom of Marrying Young Hinders Girls,"[66] which reported that twenty of the thirty-two Hmong girls at North High School were married and had thirty-seven children among them. Often the problem with such reporting was not the facts but the headlines' allusions to stereotypes about sexual perversion, which Edward Said

(1978, 188) called "a remarkably persistent motif in Western attitudes to the Orient." For example, an article on events in Eau Claire was entitled "Girl Says Asian Ritual Forced Marriage."[67]

Throughout the 1990s Hmong marriage practices remained, in the view of the white residents of the area, a public litmus test of their willingness to assimilate. In 1994 more than forty Hmong organized and attended a meeting with the four candidates for the Eau Claire County Circuit Court "seeking assurances that their cultural traditions will be respected under American law."[68] But by then a new and more serious issue, domestic violence, threatened their standing in the community. In 1991 police arrested a Hmong man for strangling to death his divorced wife, the mother of eight children, outside a motel where he believed she was meeting a boyfriend. In 1992 police arrested a Hmong mother for taking her four children ages under one to six years old to the city's central river and attempting to drown herself and them following a fight with her husband (all five were rescued by two passersby). In 1994 a single Hmong woman drowned herself when a romantic relationship ended. In 1998 police arrested a Hmong man for killing his wife and three of their five children over an argument about one of the daughter's marriage plans. Then came a case of infanticide later in the year. A thirteen-year-old Hmong girl, who was subsequently determined to have been raped by a twelve-year-old Hmong boy, gave birth in a YMCA bathroom, panicked, and then allegedly suffocated the infant. This incident soon affected the Hmong community in Minneapolis–St. Paul. A talk-radio host there used the tragedy to ridicule the Hmong for failing to assimilate. During the ensuing public controversy over his hostile remark, many listeners actually called in to support the host (Rockler 2003).

Unlike the issue of marriage, the Hmong could not easily contest the portrayal of their families as suffering from domestic violence. Indeed, some Hmong wanted to ameliorate the patriarchal aspects of their culture, such as the male prerogatives that went with the custom of paying "bride wealth." A female community liaison officer with the Eau Claire Police Department, Ma Chang, stated, "I still go to some domestic abuse cases where the man will say, 'I bought my wife, so you can't tell me not to hit her.' "[69] Pacyinz Lyfoung, the director of Asian Women United of Minnesota, commented on the infanticide case: "In the Hmong culture, men who took advantage of a woman knew that he would have to pay a penalty or marry the girl. But now they're more American, and they don't have to take responsibility. The Hmong traditions have gone out the window."[70] As these comments suggest, Hmong women often experience serious gender inequality that is not a media fabrication.

Yet the Hmong, like other racial and ethnic minorities in the United States, are subject to a double standard concerning social problems.

Whites also participate in a patriarchal culture punctuated by male violence that for some reason the media deems unworthy of coverage. When white violence is reported the focus is on the actions of an individual. In October 2005, a brief story buried in the back pages of the *Eau Claire Leader-Telegram* tersely described how a man with a gun "kidnapped" his former girlfriend and her five-month-old child and drove them to Minnesota.[71] The paper did not identify the man's race, presumably deeming it not newsworthy because he was white, and following his arrest the police did not file charges against him.

In contrast, media stories about the Hmong and other minorities portray violent incidents as symptoms of a communal pathology that apparently warrant more prominent coverage. For example, a 1993 story that began on the front page of the city/region section of the *Eau Claire Leader-Telegram* was entitled, "Cultures Define Crime, Attitude Toward Officers."[72] It stated: "The immense differences between the culture of Hmong people and Americans can lead to great difficulties for the Laotian refugees, many of whom don't speak English or understand the complex ways of American culture." The reporter then listed each "troubling aspect of Hmong culture that interferes with police work," including the following:

> Hmong men in Laos often kidnap their prospective wives, some as young as 13, and take them to their homes where they force them into marriage.
>
> In Laos, men are allowed to physically beat their wives because the man is considered the master of the household. At times, women could even legally be killed by a husband who could prove she had caused him significant pain or hardship.

This grossly inaccurate representation of Hmong culture influenced far more Americans and affected more Hmong negatively than did occasional racist aggression. For some Americans, reports of "kidnappings" validated stereotypes of the Hmong as primitive and violent. The Hmong found such reports galling because they came from local notables, not the uneducated crowd who passed on rumors of dog eating. Given their strong sense of ethnic solidarity and pride, the Hmong were very concerned with the reputation of their community among authority figures as portrayed in the local newspaper and as viewed by schools, social service agencies, and the criminal justice system. Christopher Thao, a Hmong lawyer in St. Paul, aptly describes this sensitivity to their public image by stating that in small cities, "If one [Hmong] person causes a problem it has a devastating effect on the whole [Hmong] community, while in a bigger city, it doesn't have as much effect."[73]

For more than two decades following their arrival in Eau Claire, the Hmong community was engaged in just such a struggle to solve its adjustment problems, ever cognizant of the delicate relationship with the larger community that sought both to assist and manage them. Paraphrasing the words of a police captain, a newspaper article on Hmong culture and crime concluded, "But amid all this cultural confusion, order has been maintained, and the Hmong in Eau Claire have contributed very little to the city's crime rate."[74] Few readers would miss the moral of the story: Hmong culture caused disorder but could not undermine the efficient social control of the dominant group.

A recurrence of moral panic began in November 2004, when a middle-aged Hmong man, Chai Vang, shot eight white hunters in some woods about fifty miles north of Eau Claire.[75] Vang had lived in the United States for twenty-two years, was a U.S. citizen, spoke English well, and had served six years in the California National Guard before moving to St. Paul. Like other residents of the upper Midwest he was also an avid deer hunter. Unfortunately, while searching for deer Vang strayed on to private land that was not marked with "No Trespassing" signs. A party of eight white hunters, two of whom owned the land, confronted him. The ensuing argument escalated into a shootout that left six white hunters dead.

Like the moral panic in 1987 over "bride kidnapping," the hunting tragedy led to a meeting at the Eau Claire Public Library to provide a forum for community views.[76] Some whites expressed the hope that the incident would not mar local race relations. Then, a white representative from a local hunting group claimed the Hmong frequently trespassed on private land because they had depleted the deer population on public land by "hunting for the clan." Even some sympathetic whites felt that the Hmong needed more hunter education in order to learn about American conceptions of private property. Intensive media coverage further distorted the tragedy as newspapers searched for a master narrative to explain what seemed inexplicable. Invoking the cultural-aliens stereotype that had plagued the Hmong since the late 1980s, a front-page article in the *New York Times* proclaimed, "A Hunt Turns Tragic, and Two Cultures Collide."[77] In September 2005 an all-white jury convicted Vang on six counts of premeditated first degree murder, dismissing his testimony that the white hunters racially harassed him and fired the first shot.[78]

Hmong Community Formation in Eau Claire

Despite the often adversarial social environment, a strong sense of collective initiative enabled the Hmong in Eau Claire not just to survive but to thrive in a place that superficially appeared a most unlikely site for an Asian American community. In local politics the Hmong of Eau Claire demonstrated a level of involvement that refutes the stereotype held by some of Asian Americans as acquiescent and passive.[79] Charles Vue, the first Hmong graduate from the University of Wisconsin–Eau Claire, also became the first Hmong person to seek political office in the city, running for a seat on the Eau Claire School Board in 1993. Three years later Joe Bee Xiong won a seat on the city council, placing third in a field of seven candidates, which made him among the first elected Hmong officials in U.S. history (the first won a seat on the St. Paul school board in 1992). Xiong easily won reelection two years later. When Xiong declined to run for a third term in 2000 he coached Neng Lee, a case worker at the Hmong Mutual Assistance Association, to be his replacement on the council. Lee came in fourth out of seven candidates and beat two native white incumbents. That same year Chong Chang Her ran for a seat on the Eau Claire School Board. He was not elected, but in 2001 the Hmong in Eau Claire scored a significant educational achievement when Kaying Xiong became the first Hmong principal of a Wisconsin public school. After Lee declined to seek reelection to the City Council in 2002, Saidang Xiong, the owner of a grocery store, competed in a field of eight candidates and came in second. To win these at-large seats the Hmong candidates had to reach out effectively to native-born voters, since the number of Hmong who were eligible to vote was insufficient to ensure their electoral victory.

Not content simply to participate in local politics, the Hmong in Eau Claire mobilized to advance their national and international interests as well. In 1997, for example, Hmong National Development Inc., a Washington-based Hmong interest group, chose Eau Claire as the site for a three-day conference on economic, cultural, and political issues that drew about 1,500 Hmong people from across the country.[80] Topics of discussion included the impact of recent federal cuts in public and medical assistance to legal immigrants who were not yet U.S. citizens.

In fact, international politics had long been a concern for the Hmong in Eau Claire, and many kept themselves informed by listening to a Hmong-operated radio program that broadcast six days a week, from 1989 until its demise in 2002.[81] The Eau Claire Hmong community had been sending money to Hmong resistance fighters in Laos since 1981, the year in which General Vang Pao made the first of several visits to this community. In 1990, one hundred Hmong from the city traveled to Milwaukee for a statewide Hmong protest against the Laotian Army's killing of Hmong civilians.[82] To give the movement greater stability, Vang Pobzeb, an Eau Claire resident, organized the Lao Human Rights Council in 1993. Its mission is publicizing the Lao government's continued persecution of the Hmong. During its first year the organization held a conference on the forced repatriation to Laos of Hmong refugees in Thailand. Over one hundred Hmong from western Wisconsin and St. Paul attended the event, as did U.S. Representative Steve Gunderson.[83]

The Hmong in Eau Claire displayed a similar level of organizational zeal in religious and cultural pursuits. Only three hundred Hmong lived in the city in 1980, but this nascent ethnic community still managed to organize its first New Year celebration. Virtually all the Hmong in the city attended as did 100 native well wishers.[84] The Hmong New Year, the most important annual communal event, is held in November or December (the date is determined by the lunar calendar). In Laos the date marked the end of the harvest season, and kin would gather in a central location for weeks of ritual, socializing, and entertainment. Traditionally, unmarried male and female youth dress in their best clothes and engage in various games and songs in order to attract a potential spouse.

The year 1980 also marked the first Christian church service in the Hmong language, which was led by a Hmong assistant pastor at the Eau Claire Wesleyan Church.[85] By 1986 the congregation numbered 275 individuals and had organized itself as a branch of the Christian and Missionary Alliance, an evangelical church that rapidly recruited Hmong members by appealing to their familial and patriarchal values.[86] Four years later, the church claimed 350 members in Eau Claire, one of 65 Hmong Christian Alliance congregations in the United States.[87]

Hmong interest in Christianity was so great that even the large and well-organized Hmong Christian Alliance Church could not contain all the new converts. Hmong congregations or Bible study groups also formed at the Church of Christ, the Evangel Assembly of God, and the Lutheran Church of St. Matthew.[88] The rate of religious conversion for the Hmong in Eau Claire has never been determined, although my nonrandom sample found that 23 percent exclusively identified themselves as Christian and another 6 percent identified themselves as both Christians and animists. In Wausau, a city quite comparable to Eau Claire, a knowledgeable priest estimates that 30 percent of the Hmong are Protestant and another 13 percent are Catholic (D. C. Everest Area Schools 2000).

The activity of the Hmong in churches and politics was only the most visible sign of their communal organization. In addition, clan kinship—rarely discussed publicly—provided a sub-rosa social order for the Hmong in Eau Claire.[89] Each of the thirteen clans in the city pick a leader to promote its well-being, and individual clans often encourage clan members in other parts of the United States to move to Eau Claire (Pfaff 1995). Clan leaders also resolve problems within the clan, such as fights between youth, and raise money for funerals, which are usually quite costly owing to the need to provide for public veneration of the corpse for several days in a funeral home and the sacrifice of cows (off premises) equal in number to the deceased's social status. In addition, they are called upon to mediate tensions between clans, such as divorces and other economic transactions subsequently deemed by one party to be unjust. Hmong clans even pick state and regional leaders. By 2002, Yong Kay Moua, among the first Hmong to settle in Eau Claire in 1976, was the leader for the Moua clan in the midwest. He was a 1990 recipient of a volunteerism award from President George H. W. Bush.

Cambodian Community Formation in Rochester

Like the Hmong in Eau Claire, Cambodians found Rochester a good place to live, despite the intolerance they faced. During the 1980s the Cambodian population steadily grew from less than 100 to over 1,700. From this small demographic base Cambodians created a thriving ethnic community that achieved a degree of cohesion and institutional development far beyond its numbers.

Cambodians in Rochester held their first New Year celebration in April 1982—although they numbered less than five hundred—and they have done so ever since.[90] The Cambodian New Year combines religious devotion and a festive rejoicing at the traditional end of the harvest season. It is one of the two most important holidays celebrated by Cambodians in the United States, the other being Phchum Ben (Ancestor Day) in September. The Cambodian New Year celebration involves prayers and food offerings to monks, a collective meal by participants, and an evening party with music and dancing. By 1999 the Cambodian New Year in Rochester was such a significant event that it featured three dignitaries from the Cambodian embassy in Washington, D.C.[91]

The Cambodian community also demonstrated its cohesiveness through ethnic music and ethnic media. In 1988 the Olmsted County fair included for the first time a performance by a Cambodian band, which played contemporary music.[92] Cambodian bands regularly attended public celebrations during the 1990s, giving the larger community an opportunity to view Cambodians as equals rather than as refugees needing assistance or criminals needing to be controlled. The bands served an important function within the Cambodian community as well. Cambodian wedding celebrations typically include a party at a restaurant at which guests give monetary gifts that help defray the costs of the party and with which guests reciprocate for gifts given to them or their relatives at a previous wedding. The evening portion of the wedding celebration would be incomplete—if not impossible to hold—without a Cambodian band performing a hybrid of Western and Khmer dance music.

Such was the extent of community organizing among Rochester's Cambodians that they could even attract international-level talent. Beginning in the mid-1990s, movie stars, comedians, and singers from Cambodia performed in the city, although their primary venues were Long Beach, California, and other Cambodian enclaves in the United States.[93] They had been lured to Rochester by Yannara Ou, a prominent member of the Cambodian community, who beginning in 1994 hosted a biweekly Cambodian program on the cable television's public-access channel. Two years later he started a talk-radio program to broadcast local and homeland news in Khmer. By then Ou was the proprietor of Apsara Jewelry and Video Store, and his parents and other relatives owned three more small businesses that catered to Cambodians.[94] His success and contributions to the Cambodian community could hardly have been predicted when he arrived as a teenager in 1980. Ou entered Rochester in an ambulance on his way to the Mayo Clinic, having been flown from a refugee camp in Thailand to the Minneapolis airport because of a potentially fatal heart problem.[95]

Sports became another way for Cambodians to express their communal ties. By 1985 the community was sufficiently rooted to hold a picnic and a soccer game that was attended by two hundred Cambodians from Rochester and Minneapolis–St. Paul.[96] In the summer of 1987, seven hundred Cambodians, including some from Chicago, gathered to picnic, listen to Cambodian bands, and play soccer in one of the city's parks.[97] In the early 1990s, Cambodians in Rochester formed their own soccer team within a midwest league that featured Hmong, Lao, Hispanic, and other ethnic-based teams. Called the Cambodian Cobras, the team's name symbolized much more than the deadly Asian snake. In Cambodia the snake is a mystical animal that figures prominently in stories about the Buddha's enlightenment and in Hindu-inspired statues in Angkor Wat. Soccer was so popular among Cambodian males in Rochester that the team always had more applicants than available positions. In 1998 the Cambodian Cobras won second place in the league's regional competition.

The New Year, media, and cultural and sporting events connected Cambodians in Rochester while simultaneously expressing their ethnicity. At the same time, many Cambodians relied on Christianity to develop a sense of solidarity. The Rochester First Church of the Nazarene had sponsored refugees since the early 1980s and by the early 1990s it held Khmer-language services conducted by Pastor Sarasarith

Chhum.[98] In 1996 Pastor Chhum invited Som Chan Both, a member of Cambodia's newly elected parliament, to speak at the church and solicit donations for school construction in the homeland.[99] In 1997 the church held a conference, the Fourteenth Annual Cambodian Ministries for Christ, which was attended by about twenty Cambodian pastors from around the country.[100]

As these developments indicate, the refugees had moved from being a component of the First Church of the Nazarene's outreach efforts to being full members of the institution. Indeed, by the end of the 1990s the church was evenly divided between Cambodians and local residents. The English-speaking congregation had dwindled from over 300 when the refugees first arrived to only 80 members. Conversely, there were 75 members of the Khmer-speaking congregation and their numbers had held steady during the decade.[101]

Although some Cambodians in Rochester used American institutions to organize their ethnicity, the core of any Cambodian community in the United States remains the "Wat Khmer," the Cambodian Buddhist temple. Recreating this institution requires a high degree of communal involvement and resource mobilization. A house must be purchased or a new building constructed. One or more monks must be recruited among those already in the United States or brought from a temple in Cambodia. Lay men and women must give their time to continuously organize temple activities (a function not performed by the monks) and raise money and manage a bank account to support the monks (who traditionally are barred from touching money). Typically a nonprofit religious organization is formed to accomplish these goals and to ensure that the temple receives tax-exempt status. Other lay workers, usually older women, live at the temple to cook and keep house for the monks.

Cambodians in Rochester managed to meet all of these requirements by 1987. That year the first permanent monk arrived from Providence, Rhode Island, and settled in an old house that community members had purchased and converted into a temple.[102] Reth Oum, the leader of the Buddhist Support Society, gathered more than one hundred fifty Cambodians at the airport to greet the monk, despite a severe winter storm.[103] By the late 1990s, two monks had come from Cambodia to serve in the Rochester temple. By 2000 the Cambodian community had raised sufficient funds to purchase land outside the city and to commission plans for an architecturally authentic Buddhist temple. The first building was consecrated in 2003 at a ceremony attended by the city's mayor, other local notables, and several hundred Cambodians.

Conclusion

Until Southeast Asian refugees began arriving in 1975, diversity in Eau
Claire and Rochester meant being Catholic or Lutheran, having
German or Norwegian ancestry. Those unfamiliar with midwestern
towns might assume that such homogeneity would ensure that
Cambodians and the Hmong encountered only antipathy, but they
would be mistaken. Many natives in Eau Claire and Rochester wel-
comed the refugees and greatly facilitated their initial adaptation. Some
were motivated by a volunteer ethos rooted in a sense of midwestern
communitarianism. Religious faith and membership in active church
congregations inspired many to become sponsors and volunteers.
Others simply saw refugee resettlement as an issue of civic pride, an
opportunity to demonstrate that a small but well-run city could effi-
ciently take care of whatever business the world sent its way. This
largely undocumented resettlement saga was repeated across the United
States and involved tens of thousands of Southeast Asian refugees and
Americans during the 1970s and 1980s (Burton 1983; Fein 1987; Gonlag
1985; Rose 1983; Tillema 1981). It surely ranks as one of the most positive interracial exchanges in U.S. history.

Yet both Eau Claire and Rochester contained whites with extreme
racial prejudice. As the Hmong and Cambodians became a visible presence, predictable acts of aggression occurred. From harassment in
school and rude treatment in public to discrimination when they tried
to rent an apartment or get a job, Cambodians and the Hmong encountered all the inequalities known to contemporary African Americans.

A second conflict developed when hospitable whites came to see
Cambodians and the Hmong as a threat. Whether the flashpoint was
gangs and quality of life in Rochester, or teen marriage and the moral
order in Eau Claire, real problems morphed into stereotypes as the
media and civic leaders framed the refugees in a narrative of big-city
problems reaching pristine towns. These racialized moral panics were
often more painful for Cambodians and the Hmong than the harsh acts
perpetrated by racists. On issues concerning crime, schools, and the
family, some of the refugees' critics were the same local notables who
had been so helpful to them when they first arrived. The upper
Midwest was not a bleak hinterland of intolerance, but the Hmong in
Eau Claire and the Cambodians in Rochester discovered racial and
ethnic inequalities they had never imagined could exist in the land of
asylum.

= Chapter 6 =

Ethnic Succession in the Urban Pecking Order

In small midwestern cities Southeast Asian refugees brought a new kind of diversity, but in Chicago and Milwaukee they were just the latest installment in a century of ethnic succession. Southern blacks began arriving in Chicago and Milwaukee during World War I, followed by Mexicanos, Chicanos, and Puerto Ricans during the 1940s and 1950s, and then more African Americans in the 1950s and 1960s. The proportion of racial and ethnic minorities in both cities expanded as white residents left for the suburbs during the 1970s. Their departure coincided with the new immigration from Asia and Latin America as well as economic distress brought on by deindustrialization. How established residents in Chicago and Milwaukee reacted to newcomers from Southeast Asia reveals a pattern of American race and ethnic relations that can be termed "the urban pecking order." The Cambodian Association of Illinois (2000, 2), originally located in Chicago's Uptown, poignantly describes what the refugees experienced there: "Negotiating their way amidst gangs, drugs, urban violence, inadequate housing, and poor schools, many felt they had been transported from one war zone to another."

Ethnic Succession in Chicago

Between 1975 and 1978 about 1,200 Southeast Asian refugees resettled in Chicago, and they quickly congregated in Uptown, an area in northern Chicago on the shore of Lake Michigan (see figure 6.1). The 1980 census found that blacks accounted for 15 percent of the area's population, Hispanics 28 percent, American Indians 3 percent, and Asians 23 percent (Brune and Comacho 1983). By 1981 more than 4,000 Southeast Asian refugees lived in Uptown.[1] Direct resettlement from refugee camps in Southeast Asia peaked during 1982 and 1983, when about 900 Lao and Hmong, 1,000 Cambodians, and 2,500 Vietnamese came to Chicago (Asian American Services of Chicago 1986). The migration continued at a slower pace during the mid- and late 1980s. Community

Figure 6.1   Northern Chicago

Source: Graphics Division, Learning and Technology Services, University of Wisconsin–Eau Claire.

leaders estimated that by the early 1990s approximately 8,000 Vietnamese, 4,000 Cambodians, and 1,000 Lao lived in Uptown. Almost all of the Hmong, however, had left for Wisconsin and other states (Hansen and Hong 1991). The coordinator of the Illinois Refugee Resettlement Program provides a succinct assessment of the neighborhood's role in the city: "Uptown is the Ellis Island of Chicago" (Immigration and Refugee Services of America 1986b, 9).

Southeast Asian refugees joined a long list of ethnic groups that called the Uptown area home. Germans, Swedes, and Irish first settled the area during the early 1900s, moving north as more recent immigrants from southern and eastern Europe moved into their neighborhoods in the southern part of the city (Cutler 1982). Development in Uptown subsided during the 1920s, and for the next two decades the area became synonymous with affluent leisure and recreation in cafes, nightclubs, and auditoriums (Lyden and Jakus 1980).

After World War II a new series of displaced people began moving into Uptown, attracted by low-cost housing and an increasing number of single-room occupancy hotels that catered to transient populations. Japanese Americans were the first of the new groups to settle in Uptown in 1944 and 1945, when the U.S. government released them from the internment camps. About 30,000 of the more than 110,000 Japanese Americans leaving the camps in remote regions of western states came to Chicago and about one-half of these settled in Uptown (Yoshino 1996). Many Japanese Americans subsequently left the city to return to their native state of California. Nonetheless, in 1990 Uptown had a Japanese American population numbering approximately five hundred. The Japanese American Service Center was still in operation when Southeast Asian refugees began arriving, as was a Japanese Buddhist temple.

From the mid-1950s to the mid-1960s a second wave of newcomers arrived in Uptown: poor whites from the Appalachian Mountains of Kentucky and West Virginia.[2] The mechanization of coal mining and the closing of some mines altogether uprooted many Appalachians and they sought jobs in urban areas such as Chicago. Sister Evelyn, a Catholic nun who lived in the neighborhood, provides an eloquent description of the migrants' transition from rural to urban life that is remarkably applicable to the experience of Southeast Asian refugees two decades later (Terkel 1967, 114–15):

> The initial reaction of an Appalachian in this big city is one of fear and frustration. It intensifies the normal isolation that a new group would have coming in. I think the city of Chicago is a big unanswered question. This is in the mind of many Appalachians. The complex network of relationships, which those of us who have grown up in a large city take as part of the way the world turns, is a new experience for the Appalachian people.

The migration of rural southern whites into Uptown coincided with the arrival of Native Americans due to a change in federal policy at the Bureau of Indian Affairs. One component of the new policy involved moving people from their reservations to urban areas, ostensibly for improved employment opportunities. Chicago was one of six cities in this program, and many Native Americans in the Midwest came to Uptown in the 1950s and early 1960s (Beck 1996). The All-Tribes American Indian Center in Uptown, founded in 1953, was the first urban community center created by Native Americans. According to Benny Bearskin, a Winnebago from Nebraska, the purpose of the center was "to preserve and foster the cultural values of the American Indian, at the same time helping him to make an adjustment to an urban society" (Terkel 1967, 104). The Vietnamese, Cambodian, and Hmong mutual assistance associations that eventually opened offices only a few blocks away from the All-Tribes Center would articulate the same goals, using almost identical terms. The All-Tribes Center was still in operation during the 1990s, although Uptown's Native American population had fallen to about 850.

Uptown continued to attract the dispossessed during the 1960s, when alcohol rehabilitation centers opened there. By the middle of the decade the Uptown population was thought to have the highest rate of alcoholism in the country.[3] At the same time the Illinois Department of Mental Health moved people with mental health problems into the area as a result of a new deinstitutionalization policy.[4] Some of these former inmates eventually became homeless and took to living on the streets.

Failed real estate speculation during the early 1970s added to Uptown's turmoil. It undercut property values and left many buildings abandoned and storefronts shuttered.[5] One such project began in 1974, when an investment association from the South Side Chinatown made elaborate plans to remodel a three-block section of Argyle Street, in Uptown, to create a North Side Chinatown. It purchased nearly 60 percent of the commercial and mixed commercial-residential buildings on the street, but abruptly canceled its plans.[6] By 1976 the buildings along Argyle Street were rapidly being sold or abandoned and 28 percent of the apartments in Uptown were vacant (Immigration and Refugee Services of America 1986b).

Uptown was reaching its twentieth-century nadir just as refugees from Southeast Asia began arriving in 1975. Argyle Street, the area's main thoroughfare, was "a ghost town after dark. Its commercial life was dominated by pimps, prostitutes and drug pushers who assembled on unlit, crumbling sidewalks to ply their trades."[7] The area also had many other social problems, of which one of the most severe was the housing conditions. The photographer-journalist team of Marty Hansen and Sam Hong (1991), who produced an exquisite book on the many ethnic groups living in the neighborhood, accurately describe one building where Cambodians constitute the majority of residents (50):

> During bitterly cold Chicago winters drug addicts and the homeless seek shelter inside the building's lobbies and landings. Empty liquor bottles and discarded hypodermic needles are routinely found in common hallways where barefoot children and an occasional rat scurry about . . . [C]hildren from age 2 on up play around the garbage dumpsters and a hopelessly disabled vehicle parked in the rear alley.

Despite these harsh conditions, Southeast Asians as consumers, entrepreneurs, and families dramatically improved the area. Only three Chinese restaurants and one Chinese bakery—the remnants of the failed North Side Chinatown project—existed on Argyle Street in 1977 (Immigration and Refugee Services of America 1986b). That year two Vietnamese restaurants and two Vietnamese grocery stores opened for business. By the early 1980s, more than forty Southeast Asian restaurants, boutiques, grocery stores, hair salons, and jewelry shops lined Argyle Street and more businesses had spread into side streets. The refugees' transformation of the neighborhood led newspapers to proclaim "Vietnamese Reviving Chicago Slum"[8] and "How They Saved a Neighborhood" (Santoli 1988b). By 1992 the area was estimated to annually generate $77 million worth of business.[9] At a time when many low- and moderate-income neighborhoods in Chicago lost their small retail stores to competition with large malls, Uptown experienced dramatic entrepreneurial growth.

By the mid-1990s, middle-class outsiders called the area Little Saigon. To them it represented ethnic food, a place where "one could spend a gratifying day just opening each restaurant's door and sampling the aroma."[10] Such was the new appeal of Uptown that it became one of the ethnic attractions touted by the tourism industry: Passport Books' *Guide to Ethnic Chicago* (1993) and Fodor's *Chicago* (1995) encouraged visitors to explore the area's Vietnamese shops and restaurants. According to Fodor's *Chicago*: "If you've never been to Southeast Asia, a walk down Argyle Street is the next best thing" (99).

Despite its attractions for entrepreneurs and tourists, many Cambodians considered Uptown a way station and eventually achieved enough acculturation and saved sufficient resources to move out. As they began departing in the early 1990s, refugees from the ethnic cleansing in Bosnia were moving in, sometimes occupying apartments whose last refugee residents were from Cambodia.

Cambodians who left Uptown often moved only fifteen blocks west, to a community area called Albany Park, where they entered an equally complex pattern of ethnic succession (see figure 6.1). Albany Park had been a predominantly Jewish neighborhood since the 1930s. The number of Jews increased rapidly during the 1950s, when families and businesses left the West Side of Chicago as African Americans moved in (Cutler 1982). But during the 1960s and 1970s the younger generation moved north to more affluent neighborhoods in the city or to suburbs such as Skokie, and the Jewish population in Albany Park aged and declined (Jaret 1979).

At the time of the Cambodian influx, circa 1990, the area was already called "Korea Town" because of the large number of Korean shops on Lawrence Avenue (VanGeest and Royer 1995). That year, Asians made up 24 percent of the Albany Park population and 47 percent of all inhabitants were foreign-born. Cambodians who moved from Uptown to Albany Park thus found a comparable level of ethnic and racial diversity. Blacks, Hispanics, and Asians together accounted for about 60 percent of each area.

Although migration to Albany Park represented economic advancement for many Cambodians, the neighborhood also had typical urban problems. The malodorous north branch of the Chicago River ran along the eastern and northern boundary of the area. Cambodians called it "luu tik sa'oy"—stinking pipe water—a name they used for the entire neighborhood. Two apartment complexes bordering the river had so many blatant building-code violations that a county judge considered ordering residents to vacate their dwelling.[11] Conditions were even worse in a building one-half block away (Conquergood 1992). Its Mexican, Hmong, Cambodian, and Syrian families often lived in one-bedroom apartments. Toilets overflowed, ceilings collapsed, and cockroaches lived in refrigerators. The landlord collected rent in person once a month and did not object to the presence of a basement sweatshop—run by one of the more entrepreneurial families in the building—that manufactured surgical suits for hospitals.

What attracted Cambodians to Albany Park during the 1990s was the chance to own a home.[12] Owners occupied one-third of housing units in Albany Park, compared to a mere 15 percent in Uptown, according to the 1990 U.S. census. Cambodian families with multiple wage earners were able to accumulate enough money to purchase two- and three-story apartment buildings. To save more money they lived with relatives and to earn money they sometimes rented an apartment or just one room to other Cambodian families. As if to proclaim the area the new center of the Cambodian community, in 1999 the Cambodian Association of Illinois moved its offices from Uptown to Albany Park.

Ethnic Succession in Milwaukee

Between 1975 and 1980 about 2,000 Southeast Asian refugees, mostly from Vietnam, resettled in the Milwaukee area.[13] The first Hmong arrived in 1976, but three years later only nine Hmong families lived in the city.[14] By then the Vietnamese had already begun leaving due to the cold climate, lack of job opportunities, and presence of relatives in other states. The U.S. census, however, found that Hmong population in the city increased from about 550 in 1980 to over 3,000 by 1990 and to 10,000 by 2000. Only about 40 percent of Milwaukee's Hmong refugees arrived directly from Southeast Asia (Miyares 1998). About 60 percent moved there after first resettling elsewhere in the United States, giving Milwaukee the distinction of being one of the few big cities where the Hmong chose to live. According to Susan Levy, the director of Wisconsin's resettlement assistance office, the Hmong "have taken a liking to the upper Midwest."[15]

As the Hmong community took root and grew it became enmeshed in two distinct patterns of ethnic succession. Since the early twentieth century, Milwaukee's social geography could be summarized by what the historian John Gurda (1999, 362) terms "the old ethnic short hand": "Germans on the North Side, Poles on the South Side." Yet much had changed by the time the Hmong arrived, and they settled in both areas (see figure 6.2). On the Near North Side they moved into the Merrill Park neighborhood and the adjacent southern section of Midtown, the area of Milwaukee with the largest African American population. On the Near South Side the Hmong straddled the community areas of Clark Square and Walker's Point, the home of many Hispanic Americans. The dynamics of these population shifts—Germans and Poles moving out, and blacks and Hispanics moving in—shaped the trajectory of Hmong refugees' insertion into the urban pecking order.

Figure 6.2   Central Milwaukee

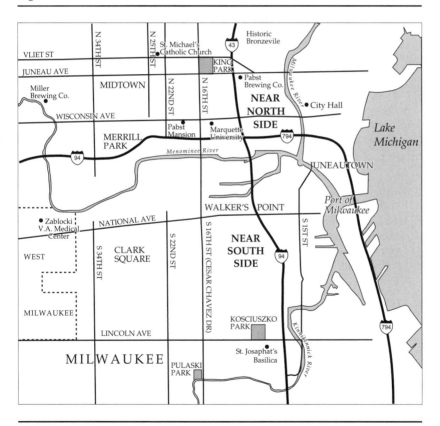

Source: Graphics Division, Learning and Technology Services, University of Wisconsin–Eau Claire.

Between 1960 and 1970 the Near North Side changed from predominantly white to black, as the number of African American residents increased from 21,000 in 1950 to more than 100,000 in 1970 (Gurda 1999). The geographic expansion of Bronzeville, the traditional area of black settlement in the center of the city, was not atypical: "Germans and other Milwaukeeans of European lineage had been moving steadily north and west from the heart of town for decades, and African Americans followed precisely the same routes as their numbers grew" (Gurda 1999, 387). Yet the social context of these black and white residential moves was very different. Discriminatory housing practices in the suburbs confined blacks within the city and in neighborhoods far from job growth (Massey and Denton 1993). Since the 1940s, Milwaukee has had levels of racial segregation above the average for northern cities and nearly the lowest level of black presence in suburban communities. In the mid 1970s Milwaukee's mayor, Henry Maier, termed this pattern "urban apartheid."

The experiences of Sam and Stella Davis exemplify these neighborhood dynamics on Milwaukee's Near North Side (Gurda 1999). They left Tennessee in 1957 and settled into 2021 North Twenty-Second Street after John and Florence Bruno, the white family who had occupied this house, moved to a bucolic neighborhood in the northwest corner of the city. Sam worked as a laborer in an auto-body plant and Stella as a maid. They were among the first African Americans to live in this part of Midtown, a neighborhood that eventually became synonymous with urban problems (Gurda 1999, 320):

> During her long reign as the matriarch of the block, Stella witnessed dramatic change, all for the worse. Although she and a handful of neighbors took meticulous care of their properties, blight ultimately claimed nearly a third of the homes on the street. As the houses came down, poverty rates went up; unemployment and underemployment were distressingly familiar problems. Crime rates rose at the same time; wire mesh eventually hid the white curtains on Stella's windows.

Stella lived in the infamous census tract 100, the focus of a *Milwaukee Journal Sentinel* exposé on the area of the city having the highest crime rate.[16] The number of violent crimes committed in these twenty-eight square blocks rose from forty-nine in 1981 to ninety-eight in 1992, and included almost one murder each year, a result primarily of gang conflict over the drug trade. Poverty was rampant among the 1,400 residents of census tract 100. Only 16 percent of children lived in a two-parent family, 40 percent of the population over the age of sixteen was unemployed, and 60 percent of households earned less than $10,000 a year. According to Bettie Dear, another longtime resident of tract 100, "Just living in this neighborhood, it's been kind of rough. Oh, its much different now, it has gotten worse. When I'm in bed at night I wake up hearing gunshots."[17] Hmong refugees fleeing political violence in Laos during the 1980s resettled only a few blocks away from Bettie and Stella.

As the Near North Side changed from white to black in the decade prior to the Southeast Asian refugees' arrival, the Near South Side entered the late stages of another process of ethnic succession (Beverstock and Stuckert 1972; Gurda 1976, 1999; Milwaukee Department of City Development 1984b). Predominately Polish at the end of the nineteenth century, its diversification began during the 1920s, when Pfister & Vogel Tannery, International Harvester, and Illinois Steel recruited Mexican workers, initially from Michoacan and then from Texas. The first institution in the nascent Mexican American community was the Mission of Our Lady of Guadalupe, established in 1926 only a few blocks from the factory district. Four years later the community celebrated Mexican Independence Day for the first time; it has done so ever since.

Continued migration from Mexico and Texas during the 1950s, as well as the arrival of Puerto Ricans, increased the Hispanic population on the Near South Side (Gurda 1976). It also accelerated the transformation of some local institutions, particularly since by the middle of the twentieth century, many of the new arrivals were families rather than single men looking for temporary work. Indicative of this change was the creation in 1965 of the Guadalupe Center Head Start Program for pre-school-age children. In 1967 the Guadalupe Mission merged with Holy Trinity Catholic Church, which had been founded in 1850 as a German parish. St. Patrick's Catholic Church held an annual commemoration of Latin American martyrs during the 1970s (Pokorny 1991). A local Anglo pastor quaintly summarized this demographic transition by stating, "My funerals are all Anglo, and my weddings and baptisms are all Latin" (quoted in Gurda 1976, 27). Local elections also reflected this process of ethnic succession, such as the 1992 race between Emilio Lopez and Jim Witkowiak for the position of alderman. By then, diversity in the area meant much more than being Hispanic or Polish: both candidates required Hmong and Lao interpreters at some of their neighborhood forums.[18]

When the first Southeast Asian refugees arrived in 1975, the Hispanic population on the Near South Side already numbered about 9,000 but had not made much economic progress from its original type of employment in the city, factory work (Gurda 1976). More than 70 percent of Near South Side Latino men had blue-collar jobs (compared to only 40 percent of all men in the city), and almost 20 percent of Latino families had incomes below the poverty level (in contrast to 11 percent for the city as a whole).

By the 1970s Walker's Point was deemed "a deteriorating area" because "Surveys by the city indicate that it has the second highest concentration of blight in Milwaukee" (Beverstock and Stuckert 1972, 268). Terms like "aging" and "deteriorated" were also used to describe the Muskego Avenue and Clark Square neighborhoods to the west. These problems were in part attributed to "a new influx of persons from Walker's Point and Juneautown" (200), a statement that could easily be taken to imply prejudice toward the Puerto Ricans and Mexicans who lived there.

In fact, Gurda (1976, 24) believed that "Virtually every Latin on the South Side has heard the word 'spic' often enough to know what it means." The social distance between Anglos and Hispanics did not diminish with the passage of time. In the mid-1990s an Anglo resident who enjoyed the neighborhood's diversity ruefully noted that her sentiments were uncommon: "People will dance the Macarena and eat a taco, but they won't have anything to do with their Hispanic neighbors."[19]

If some Near South Side residents felt threatened by the growth of the Hispanic population, then they were totally unprepared for the activism of the black civil rights movement during the late 1960s. A few weeks after the historic Near North Side riot in late July 1967, Father James Groppi led two hundred members of the NAACP in a march to protest segregation in housing (Gurda 1999; Zeidler 1991). When the activists crossed the Sixteenth Street viaduct, spanning the Menomonee River Valley, and entered the Near South Side, they found 5,000 rowdy white counter-demonstrators lining the march route and holding "white power" signs and an effigy of Father Groppi. Some even threw bottles and bricks at the marchers. Undeterred by the hostility and violence, Father Groppi stated, "We're going to keep marching here until we get fair housing, so we can move in here with these white bigots or wherever we want" (Gurda 1999, 374).

Had the protesters and counter-demonstrators returned to the march route in the mid-1980s they would have been stunned by the new cultural pluralism. On the 1200 block of South Sixteenth Street, trumpeted a poster of the Walker's Point area put out by the Milwaukee Department of City Development (1984b), "You can find an Arab food store, an Italian restaurant, a Vietnamese department store, and a Mexican restaurant." In fact, South Sixteenth Street was renamed Cesar Chavez Drive during the mid-1990s to honor the famous Chicano labor leader. By then, six census tracts east and west of the thoroughfare were home to more than 1,000 Hmong residents as well as about two hundred fifty Lao and one hundred fifty Vietnamese. Ultimately, international migration did more than marches to diversify the Near South Side. Of course, the newest refugees in Milwaukee still had to adapt to the urban pecking order, as did those in Chicago.

"There Has Always Been a Pecking Order"

Although many groups had passed through Chicago's Uptown, established residents regarded it as their turf. Neighborhood associations initially opposed the settlement of Southeast Asian refugees, viewing them as another needy population dumped in the area by social welfare organizations. Housing became a particularly significant source of conflict. At a community meeting held in December 1981 to allay concerns, officials from several resettlement agencies admitted placing newly arrived refugees in dilapidated apartment buildings because they lacked the funding to pay for better accommodations.[20] Unfortunately, by accepting substandard housing for the refugees these agencies unintentionally undermined the efforts of tenants already living in the neighborhood to force landlords to improve conditions. Refugees fleeing Socialism thus became enmeshed in American class conflict exacerbated by racial differences. A Vietnamese refugee who lived in Uptown from 1976 to 1980 explained (Santoli 1988a, 105–6):

> In Uptown, we felt like we were thrust from one war zone to another. Local community organizations strongly opposed the refugees. People talked about a "Yellow Horde Invasion." They started a lawsuit campaign against the city for bringing Indochinese into their area. They said, "Because the refugees are moving in, rents are going higher." The absentee landlords in the neighborhood were horrible. The organizations had started a boycott against them before the refugees arrived. This created a lot of vacancies in some run-down buildings. The voluntary agencies who sponsored the refugees saw the cheap rents and placed refugee families in those apartments. That allowed the slumlords to stay in business.

The same pattern of conflict between established residents and newcomers was repeated when the Hmong settled in Milwaukee. Kelly, a Hmong informant I interviewed on the Near South Side, reported what happened when she went into a store one day:

> I went shopping on National [Avenue], at this store where you can negotiate to lower the price. And when I tried that this white guy said, "Go to your country, go back" instead of just saying, "Buy it or leave." He was so angry he almost spit in my face. It seemed he was about to give me a punch on the nose. That was just one experience.

A more prevalent problem, according to my Hmong survey respondents and informants, was frequently being called Chinese in a sneering, derogatory way, an instance of a legitimate ethnic name becoming a slur (Allen 1993). In a revealing example of how the definition of newcomer is relative, a Hmong survey respondent, when asked about unfair treatment she had experienced, described the following incident:

> I was driving on one of the South Side streets and three Mexican men around thirty or forty years old yelled at me and said "Chinese! Go back to your own country!" I was very angered by this and I said to them, "Taco Bells! Go back to the border!" They stopped and didn't say anything else.

It is worth noting that this incident occurred in 1997, more than a decade after the Hmong began settling on the Near South Side. In fact, inter-ethnic conflict between Hmong and Hispanics began much earlier. In 1986 a judge approved a two-year restraining order against a Hispanic man for repeatedly harassing three Hmong families. Such experiences were apparently so common that the Hmong usually accepted them as inevitable. Vang Cheng, the director of Lao Family Inc., a self-help organization on the Near South Side, commented on this case, "There is some harassment, but it's not a very big problem. It's normal for newcomers to come in and be harassed—it has happened throughout American history."[21] Ricardo Diaz, executive director of the United Community Center, agreed: "Historically, there has always been a pecking order. The minority above pecks on the minority below."[22]

On Milwaukee's Near North Side blacks were the established residents. Ying, an informant and owner of a grocery store in the area, reported that the Hmong living there received much abuse from them. He described the behavior of some unhappy customers:

> Ying: They say, "Hey Chink, go back to your country." Even people who come here [to shop] every day call this the "Chinese store."

> Author: Have you ever talked with African Americans about their experiences in the United States?

> Ying: When I first opened this store, almost every black person who came in stole. I hired a black security guard. One time I said to him, "Why are people with different skin color doing bad things?"

> Author: You meant black people.

> Ying [answering defensively, indicating he was trying to avoid sounding prejudiced]: I didn't say black people. I said "people with different skin color." I said, "Why do people with different color skin think we are Chinese?" We do good things, better education, establish business in the inner city. We help build businesses even though whites, whites move to

the suburbs. Today Asian Americans do it but they [blacks] are still stealing. That disturbs me. He [the black security guard] said, "These people don't care. Before you came here there was slavery. They got so angry during their slavery." I read the history about slavery but I said, "How many generations and it's still not getting better? You still feel that about slavery?"

Ying had discovered how social inequality in the United States creates an urban pecking order in which the dispossessed hoard their meager resources and often exploit those more vulnerable than themselves. Sy, another Hmong informant who lives and works on the Near North Side, provides an eloquent description of this conflict:

> There is prejudice against Asians and it's not just whites but the other groups, too. African American. Hispanic. Other races do have the same barriers and they are the ones that compete with Asians. With that, being Asian means being picked on not just by whites but by other groups because of race. We are a minority just like the others. We cannot pick on whites so we pick on each other.

"They're Easy Pickings"

Southeast Asian refugees ranked near the bottom of Chicago's and Milwaukee's pecking orders, and street-savvy residents took advantage of their vulnerability. Sarah Raber, the United Methodist district coordinator for Hmong Ministry, worked closely with Hmong families on Milwaukee's Near South Side. She reported that they commonly became victims of crime since "an awful lot of people think that because the Hmong are inexperienced and unknowledgeable, the wool can be pulled over their eyes. They're easy pickings for someone who wants to take advantage of them."[23] Sister Alice Thepouthay, a Catholic nun from Laos, reported similar problems on the city's Near North Side among the congregants of St. Michael's Church, one-third of them Hmong and one-quarter Lao.[24] Herself a crime victim on several occasions, Sister Alice described conditions in the neighborhood:

> People come in their homes and steal right in front of them. They kick the door, they come in. [On the street] they just steal the purse from you. I'm used to struggle, but [Lao and Hmong] people never have this kind of fear. People [are] afraid to go out. People have flashbacks from the war. They even smell the blood.[25]

According to Hmong survey respondents, conditions were particularly severe on the Near North Side; here, the Hmong refugees suffered badly at the hands of some black youths. A Hmong woman reported on the survey:

> Black kids throw rocks at us. One rock hit Grandma on the head. Blood was everywhere. We called the police and the policemen were black or one was white and the other black. They came and looked around and said a couple of things and left. It didn't seem to help and I didn't feel safe after they left.

Apparently it was so common for rocks to be thrown at cars and homes in the area that the verb "bricked" became a street-slang coinage for describing this type of attack. After a particularly serious incident on the 1400 block of North Thirty-Fourth Street in which gun shots were exchanged, a fourteen-year-old Hmong girl told reporters that young blacks frequently harassed her family: "Right now we are just hiding. They throw rocks and tease us. They are treating us like they used to be treated. They just want to get rid of us."[26]

Yet the Hmong proved incredibly resilient in the face of such treatment, according to John Worm, a housing specialist with Milwaukee's Department of City Development:

> I wouldn't call the experience of home ownership in a violent neighborhood the American dream, but I guess you have to look at what they had before. They buy here, pay less per month [in mortgage payments than they would pay in rent], can fix the place up and control their own household better. Violence just kind of nicks them. Car windows busted, rocks thrown, things stolen from their yards. But they haven't had anyone, that I know of, killed or assaulted, though one woman was thrown aside in a carjacking and they ran over her leg.[27]

In fact, deadly assaults did occur. A Hmong man was shot to death in a robbery attempt while loading groceries into a car after shopping at a Near North Side store. His cousin commented: "The Hmong people worked with the Americans in Laos. After 1975, the Communists made life very bad for us. It was very hard work to come here. Thousands died along the Mekong River and in the forests. But that was war, the fight for power. This was crime. It's different."[28] Such crimes, however, pale in comparison to those committed on Milwaukee's Near North Side by Jeffrey Dahmer. One of the twentieth century's most gruesome serial killers, Dahmer murdered seventeen young males, often dismembering their corpses and engaging in cannibalism and necrophilia. One of his eleven victims at his apartment on 924 North Twenty-Fifth Street was fourteen-year-old Konerak Sinthasomphone, whose family had fled from Laos. A subsequent investigation revealed that the drugged, naked, and bleeding teenager had actually escaped from the killer's apartment, only to be returned there by two white police officers. During the officers' approximately fifteen minutes on the scene, Dahmer, who was also white, convinced them that the boy was his adult lover named "John Hmong." The officers ignored protests to the contrary by the black woman who had called them.[29]

The hideous nature of Dahmer's crimes should not obscure the fact that much of the violence in Milwaukee's urban pecking order reflected almost random aggression. During the 1990s a prevalent urban legend purported that crime was so rampant that youths could be robbed of their expensive name-brand sneakers. In fact, this did occur at least one time on the Near South Side: four men attacked a seventeen-year-old boy and stole his shoes.[30] A Hmong man who lived in the area and participated in the survey described a more serious incident of random violence:

> In 1988 my wife was gardening on the corner of Orchard Street and South 22nd. While she was walking home, a boy about 12 or 13 shot her. We know that the shot was intentional but the police insisted that it had been accidental. She was taken to St. Luke's Medical Center and a doctor indicated that the bullet did not penetrate into her body. She was released. At the time she was in her late pregnancy. This is an example of the extremely poor services provided to the Hmong by the police.

Urban aggression was also part of Cambodians' experiences in Chicago's Uptown. A Vietnamese social worker who lived in the area described conditions in the neighborhood during the late 1970s (Santoli 1988a, 116):

> Crime threatened everyone's daily life. Muggers robbed refugees on the street, in the lobby of apartment buildings, in the elevators, in the stairwells, everywhere. In Vietnam, people seldom had locks on their doors. We had to teach them to bolt the door or hook the chain on the lock. Whenever an incident happened, the refugees would call my office. One day there were more than thirty robberies.

In the summer of 1986 a Vietnamese refugee was killed during a robbery, prompting other refugees, social service agencies, and business owners to hold a community meeting with the police and local politicians. Soon after, a delegation met with Mayor Harold Washington, the first black mayor of Chicago, to express their concerns (Immigration and Refugee Services of America 1986a). According to police and city officials, would-be robbers perceived Southeast Asian refugees as easy targets because of their generally small stature and their reputation for keeping their savings at home or wearing it in the form of jewelry (Fu 1986). Language barriers and distrust of the police also prevented the refugees from reporting crimes.

My Cambodian survey respondents in Chicago often described "a lot of crime, especially at night" in Uptown during the 1980s and 1990s. They cited instances of robbery, drug dealing, prostitution, and rape. For example, a widow and mother of two children reported: "Sometimes when I take my son to school or when I go to the store, black teenagers say bad words or try to rob me. I yell back at them." Another middle-aged woman living in Uptown reported particularly strong feelings of vulnerability because of victimization during the mid-1980s:

> The first couple of years after I got here, I always answered yes [because I didn't speak English]. I encountered bad incidents by answering yes. The first time I almost got raped. The second time I got robbed at home. I still don't speak English and so I have difficulty communicating. Wherever I go or what ever I do, I always feel afraid. I am afraid of crime in my neighborhood.

"Walking to the Wrong Place"

Learning about claims to urban space is one of the most essential requirements for negotiating the urban pecking order. Becoming streetwise means knowing which places are safe and which are dangerous, being able to detect the difference between serious and inconsequential threats, and regulating one's flight or fight response when danger cannot be avoided.

Aggressive harassment by street people was a particular problem in Uptown, according to Cambodian survey respondents. A middle-aged man reported an incident that occurred in Uptown in 1983, one year after his arrival in the United States: "When I was walking from school I was asked by three black men for money. I gave them some quarters. But they wanted three dollars and I didn't give it to them. So they wanted to rob me but my friend and I beat them up." Another man reported a similar incident in Uptown in the late 1980s: "Someone asked me for a cigarette and I refused to give it to him. Then he took his knife to threaten me. I didn't retaliate and I walked away. He looked drunk."

Of the many threats in the urban pecking order, gang claims to turf proved among the most intractable for Southeast Asian refugees. According to the police, social networks connect Southeast Asian gangs in different cities and even states, making them less territorial than other groups who engage in crime and delinquency.[31] Nonetheless, gang violence remains a problem for the refugees in urban neighborhoods. In March 1993, a nineteen-year-old Vietnamese member of the Latin Kings shot three students outside a middle school on Milwaukee's Near South Side, in retaliation for an earlier attack by members of the Black Gangster Disciples.[32]

When community organizers on Milwaukee's Near South Side surveyed one hundred fifty Hmong youths, they found drugs to be the top problem, followed by violence and gangs.[33] Hmong parents and community leaders noticed a pattern in this delinquency. Ge Xiong, the director of Hmong Educational Advancements, a mutual assistance association, believed that these problems among Hmong youth had increased over time, stating: "The truancy rate has gone up and also the disciplinary problems and suspensions are increasing among Asian students. The number of Asian students qualifying for advanced math has gone down, and the drop-out rate has gone up."[34] Xiong is clearly describing the process of segmented assimilation (Portes and Rumbaut 2001; Portes and Zhou 1993), and the formation of Hmong gangs was a particularly serious consequence. According to Gary Graika, coordinator of the Youth Diversion Program at the Social Development Commission:

> When Lao and Hmong families began settling in Milwaukee, the high school honor rolls consistently listed a number of Southeast Asian surnames. They were the best students and the best behaved, then they began to hang out with the wrong crowd. I think these kids are becoming Americanized. They're turning to the same fashions and activities and music that is the subculture of teenagers. Along with that goes gangs.[35]

Cambodians in Chicago had similar troubles with gangs, involving both Cambodian youths and other ethnic groups. Gangs existed in Uptown before the refugees moved in. Two years after his arrival in the mid-1980s, a young Cambodian survey respondent learned that local gangs in Uptown had already laid claim to distinct territories: "When I was walking with my friends we were harassed by blacks and Hispanics, especially when walking to the wrong place. They called us names and said why were we here in the States." Unfortunately, some Southeast Asian youths eventually engaged in this form of delinquency as well, as described by the photographer-journalist team of Hansen and Hong (1991, 51): "Cambodian boys have vivid memories of being beaten up by gangs of black youth during their first week in public school. They began to fight back in self-defense, which has fueled a vicious cycle of violence. Corners like Leland and Winthrop have seen many pitched battles between Southeast Asian and African-American gangs."

Hansen and Hong were not exaggerating. Some Cambodian survey respondents did have "vivid memories" of mistreatment. One male in his early twenties described a common incident that occurred during the late 1980s and early 1990s: "From school I was chased and beat up by blacks. Black gang members (six of them) beat me up. I was beat up by them three times."

Not only did gangs in Uptown and Albany Park cause problems for Cambodian youths, their parents, and community leaders, but police efforts to control gang violence could itself become a source of insecurity. A young Cambodian woman reported the following incident on the survey:

> In 1993 my friend who is white and I were standing on the sidewalk along with other Cambodians. Then an American family called the police and the police arrested all of us Cambodians except the white person. I was shocked when the police said to my friend, "If you don't want to be arrested you better leave." Then I felt the pressure of racism.

Another Cambodian survey respondent described similar but more serious occurrences when he was a teenager: "I got beat up by the police many times. I got arrested by the police when walking in a group [of Cambodians]. I always felt very sad and bad." Cambodians in Uptown interviewed by Hansen and Hong (1991, 51) also told of excessive use of force by police officers. Some residents of one decrepit apartment building reported:

> The police came to the tenement searching for illegal guns. They also suspected that some of the boys were gang affiliated. In the course of their visit they allegedly kicked and beat a 16-year-old boy (orphaned by the Khmer Rouge) and ransacked a neighbor's bedroom.

The urban pecking order thus included not only conflict among minorities but also with those charged with its social control.

Cambodian Community Formation in Chicago

Life in an urban pecking order was an unanticipated ordeal for Cambodians in Chicago and the Hmong in Milwaukee, but through communal efforts both groups managed to make some of the urban space their own. In Chicago's Uptown Cambodians developed a cognitive map of physical and social space that differed substantially from that of outsiders, who usually defined the area by its entrepreneurship and chic ethnic cuisine. Cambodians did appreciate Southeast Asian grocery stores for their produce, and a shopping trip invariably meant running into friends, former neighbors, and occasionally acquaintances from the Thai refugee camps. Although they rarely "ate out," Cambodians valued Argyle Street's restaurants as venues to hold wedding celebrations. More common destinations were jewelry stores, which sold items on credit and repurchased unwanted gold bracelets and necklaces, and video shops with Khmer language films and music. By the late 1980s, Cambodians owned fourteen businesses in the area (North and Sok 1989).

The offices of the Cambodian Association of Illinois (CAI), near Argyle Street, became another landmark on Cambodians' cognitive map (Cambodian Association of Illinois 2000). It was founded in 1976 by some of the first Cambodian refugees in the United States, including Kompha Seth, a former monk with a B.A. in theology and Khmer literature from the Buddhist University of Phnom Penh. The organization employed Cambodian social workers, who assisted new arrivals with problems ranging from the paper work for public aid and citizenship to family crises and employment. The CAI also held weekend classes to teach Cambodian children about Khmer culture and to read and write the Khmer language. In 1999 it began an ambitious $1 million fund-raising campaign and succeeded in recruiting Mayor Richard M. Daley as a co-chair of its honorary committee. With a portion of the funds the CAI created a Killing Fields Memorial, including a wall of remembrance listing the names of community members' relatives who perished during the Khmer Rouge revolution.

The CAI's earliest achievement for the community occurred in the mid-1980s, when it sponsored the immigration of several Buddhist monks from Cambodia and purchased a house to serve as a temple (Hein 1995). At this time Cambodians were unknown and impoverished newcomers who could not avail themselves of mainstream philanthropy. Through community donations the CAI raised $60,000 to purchase a house on Argyle Street. Volunteers created a prayer room containing a life-sized statue of the Buddha and refurbished bedrooms for several Buddhist monks. Following the house's consecration as a temple, activities included services on the site for Buddhist holidays and at the request of Cambodians, such as earning merit for a deceased relative by donating money and goods to the temple. The monks also performed rituals in people's homes and apartments, including wedding ceremonies and the blessing of a new house when a family moved in. By far the most important events over which the monks presided were the celebrations for the New Year and Phchum Ben holidays, held in the gym of the local high school or the recreation room of the community college.

A few years after the temple's founding, a dispute arose between younger and older monks over adapting monastic etiquette to conditions in the United States (Hein 1995). Congregants began taking sides, which created serious conflict. To minimize damage to the community, the CAI facilitated the establishment of another temple, even organizing the ritual transporting of a large bronze Buddha to the new site. About one hundred brightly clad, chanting Cambodians marched in procession through Uptown, playing gongs and drums. Street people and drifters looked on in disbelief. Dubbed the Old Temple and the New Temple, they organized separate holiday celebrations and competed for community donations. In 2003 accusations of impropriety against two monks who came from Cambodia to serve in the New Temple caused them to leave and form a third temple. Such factionalism has plagued Khmer communities in other parts of the United States (Chan 2003).

In addition to the stores, the mutual assistance association, and temples, among the most salient features on Cambodians' cognitive map of their community were the apartment buildings in which they constituted the plurality or even the majority of tenants. In these dwellings Cambodian neighbors routinely shared food, looked after each other's children, and watched rented videos together. Neighbors were often classmates, and they walked to English-language courses at Truman College. Most important, earlier arrivals provided newcomers with invaluable information about living conditions in the United States. One reporter was greatly impressed by the dense social networks he found in one building where many refugees from Southeast Asia lived. He concluded that "several clans of Hmong have vertically reconstructed the villages of their native Laos" (Burstein 1983, 1). This image is an exaggeration, but it is certainly true that some apartment buildings in Uptown and Albany Park developed a distinctive social life as a result of their ethnic density. During the mid-1980s, the mere number of a well-known address—"I live at 5054 [Winthrop]" or "I live at 5050 [Sheridan]"—told a Cambodian a great deal about another person and sufficed to convey knowledge of his or her social life in the building and probably one or more friends or relatives who resided there. Although such buildings had a high turnover rate, Cambodians formed life-long friendships in them as they collectively coped with the urban pecking order in Chicago.

Hmong Community Formation in Milwaukee

The Hmong in Milwaukee faced the same daunting task as Cambodians did in Chicago: staking out some very inhospitable urban space. Two of the endeavors that required the most courage were buying homes and starting businesses in poor and crime-plagued areas. Between 1988 and

1999 the number of Hmong-owned businesses in the city increased from two grocery stores to forty-two businesses, including daycare, insurance, job placement, and of course—more groceries (Lo 2001; Yang and North 1988). The Hmong also showed a strong interest in home-ownership programs for low-income families.[36] The city's Urban Homesteading Program enabled residents to buy abandoned and badly damaged houses for $1 if they signed a contract to rehabilitate the dwelling. The city supplied low-interest loans to encourage this rehabbing.

Perhaps the most effective housing program was created by an unlikely entity: the Near North Side's St. Michael's Catholic Church.[37] In 1992 Father Dennis Lewis organized St. Michael's Landmark Housing with the cooperation of the city and the Hmong American Friendship Association. These organizations helped poor families buy homes on the Near North Side by matching elderly residents who wished to sell with families who wanted to buy but could not obtain loans from banks because of a lack of knowledge of the mortgage process. By 1996 more than two hundred Lao and Hmong families had purchased homes within a four-block radius of the church.[38]

Like Cambodians in Chicago, the Hmong in Milwaukee poured much of their communal energy into religion. Unlike Cambodians, many Hmong had become Christian. Some of the refugees had converted in the Thai refugee camps or even in Laos prior to emigrating (Chan 1994; Faruque 2002), but the process accelerated dramatically after their resettlement in the United States. Estimates for the proportion of Hmong in Milwaukee who are Christian range from 28 percent (Lo 2001) to 70 percent (Lucke 1995). The truth is probably somewhere in between, since about 40 percent of the Hmong in St. Paul are Christians.[39] The precise extent of Hmong conversion remains to be determined, but it is certain that Christianity became a fundamental building block of the Hmong community in Milwaukee. Particularly noteworthy is the fact that the Hmong embraced the full spectrum of American Christian denominations, including Catholic, Lutheran, Methodist, Baptist, and several evangelical churches.

St. Michael's Catholic Church on the Near North Side was the primary place of worship for Hmong Catholics, although some also attended services at St. Anthony's Catholic Church on the Near South Side. St. Michael's provided a model of how a Catholic church could adapt to the new urban diversity.[40] Through the ministry of Deacon Blong Yang, St. Michael's organized an annual baptism for the Hmong starting in the mid-1980s, and sometimes as many as one hundred converts took part in the ceremony (Lucke 1995). Sister Alice Thepouthay, a refugee from Laos, was also instrumental in recruiting co-ethnics to the church. By 1996 the Hmong constituted 33 percent of the congregation (the largest ethnic group) and the Lao accounted for another 25 percent.[41] Reverend Denis Weis, the senior pastor, was particularly proud of his congregation's diversity: "We've tried hard not to be the melting pot. We hold hands and say the Lord's Prayer in four languages—English, Spanish, German, and Hmong—all at the same time. People have been known to cry" (Milwaukee Department of City Development 1984a).

Protestants, however, substantially outnumbered Catholics in the Hmong community by about ten to one (Lo 2001), reversing the pattern in Southeast Asia, where Hmong converts to Catholicism were more numerous (Tapp 1989b). Hope Lutheran Church on the Near North Side had a Hmong pastor, a large Hmong congregation, and a Hmong choir. The Walker's Point and Clark Square neighborhoods on the Near South Side were home to several Hmong Protestant congregations, including those of the Hmong Christian Missionary Alliance Church (the largest), the Hmong Christian Community United Methodist Church, Ascension Lutheran Church, Assembly of God, and the Hmong First (Southern) Baptist Church. Some of these groups were independent Hmong churches with their own buildings. Others were preexisting congregations where the Hmong used church premises to conduct their own Hmong-language services and educational activities.

The Hmong community in Milwaukee also exhibited a high degree of political activism, at least as measured against the common misconception of Asian Americans as politically passive and acquiescent. In 1991 the Hmong community was quite vocal in protesting the handling of the Dahmer investigation by the city police. At a candlelight nighttime vigil, Thai Lee, of the Hmong American Friendship Association, stated, "Just because we are not American-born, just because English is not our first language, just because we do not understand your justice system, please do not think we are totally ignorant. Police need to learn to listen to all minority witnesses and victims, even if they are upset and even if English is not their first language."[42]

Hmong political activism continued during the rest of the 1990s. The community protested consideration of a bill to make English the official language of Wisconsin[43] and another to cut public assistance.[44] U.S. foreign policy and human rights in Laos, however, remained the most galvanizing issues for the Hmong in Milwaukee. In 1990 the Lao government's use of chemical weapons against civilians led more than 1,000 Hmong from throughout the state to rally in downtown Milwaukee for a six-hour demonstration.[45]

Taking seriously their in-group solidarity, many Hmong in Milwaukee worked to provide badly needed educational, employment, and family services to compatriots. Lao Family Inc., a chapter of the national organization of the same name founded by General Vang Pao (Lucke 1995), was the first Hmong social-service agency in the city when it was created in 1981 on the Near South Side. Other nonprofit organizations formed on the Near North Side, including the Hmong American Friendship Association (founded in 1983), Hmong Educational Advancements (founded in 1991), and the Hmong American Women's Association (founded in 1997). So neatly did the self-help initiatives of the Hmong fit within those among established residents that at various times each of these organizations had its office in the community center in Martin Luther King Jr. Park.

The Hmong didn't plow all of their communal energy into self-help initiatives—they still found time for revelry. The Hmong New Year has been celebrated in the city since at least 1985, but for many years political and religious conflict in the community led different organizations to hold separate events. In 1991 the community achieved a partial rapprochement when Lao Family Inc., Hmong American Friendship Association, and Shee Yee Community (an organization founded in 1987 to promote traditional religious practices) held a joint New Year celebration for the first time (Lucke 1995). Event organizers estimated that about 4,000 Hmong from Wisconsin and other states attended.

The 1991 New Year marked an important milestone for the Hmong in Milwaukee, according to Ge Xiong, a member of the planning committee, who stated, "We are beginning to have more organized events, more opportunity for cohesion in our community."[46] This comment is certainly an understatement. What the Hmong accomplished in Milwaukee is remarkable, given that they arrived traumatized by military defeat and subsequent persecution and possessing only the work skills useful in an agrarian economy. Yet they became successful urban pioneers in the toughest neighborhoods and thus contributed to the making of Milwaukee at the end of the twentieth century.

Conclusion

When Cambodian and Hmong refugees settled in Chicago and Milwaukee, they entered a harsh urban pecking order, one with a pattern of race and ethnic relations substantially different from what prevailed for their compatriots in Rochester and Eau Claire. In small cities the refugees initially received a generous reception from many local residents, whereas in big cities, this kind of local congregational and family sponsorship were much less prevalent. In big cities the numbers of refugees usually exceeded the supply of natives willing to help, and sponsors tended to live in the suburbs, where the cost of housing made it impossible to resettle poor families.

In Chicago and Milwaukee, the refugees—while often missing the welcome wagon—were free from feeling like foreigners and could create enclaves by reclaiming urban space for their ethnic group. The transformation of Chicago's Uptown was so dramatic that refugee advocates cited it when they met with federal officials in 2003 to plead for increased refugee admissions to the United States, which were reduced following the terrorist attacks on September 11, 2001: "One particular neighborhood in Chicago changed from a dangerous stretch of vacant storefronts to a bustling and vibrant economic engine for the whole community" (Immigration and Refugee Services of America 2003, 7). The Hmong also had a beneficial impact on Milwaukee, particularly on the Near North Side. They started businesses, revitalized church congregations that had dwindled with the out-migration of whites, and purchased homes through city programs designed to rehabilitate distressed neighborhoods. John Worm, a Milwaukee urban planner, concluded, "They are a tremendous asset to our central city."[47]

To make these contributions, Cambodian refugees in Chicago and Hmong refugees in Milwaukee endured the traumas of urban ethnic succession. In small cities the refugees faced overt racism because they were the first nonwhite populations to live there in significant numbers. Some initially sympathetic whites eventually stigmatized them when gangs and familial conflict appeared to threaten the preexisting social order. In big cities the refugees experienced aggression because they were vulnerable newcomers arriving on the turf of more established residents already stressed by social inequality. Often the aggressors were African and Hispanic Americans, but whites in positions of power, such as the police, also mistreated the refugees on some occasions. The urban pecking order and small-town hospitality and hate are tests of how two refugee groups arriving with dramatically different ethnic origins respond to new identities and inequalities in various social environments.

= Part IV =

Identities

= Chapter 7 =

Asian American

"ASIAN" is commonly used by government officials, the media, and social scientists to name people. It appears on all documents that ask about a person's race, from birth certificates and college admission forms to surveys by the U.S. Bureau of the Census and sociologists. "Asian" is thus a fundamental element of American diversity and a central identity in the racial and ethnic adaptation of immigrants from places such as China, India, Korea, and Southeast Asia.

Yet Asian Americans are an extremely diverse population (Espiritu 2004). The largest ethnic group, the Chinese, accounts for only about one-quarter of all Asian Americans. In addition to differences in ethnicity, Asian Americans also vary in the degree of U.S. intervention in their homeland, depth of historical roots in the United States, level of acculturation, and socioeconomic status. The diversity of the Asian American population is self-evident, yet aggregating all Asian Americans is a ubiquitous practice in public policy, media reporting, and social-science research. In many instances this generic label is used for the convenience of the observer.

Nevertheless, the aggregate name "Asian American" has some relevance. Social scientists recognize that several social processes may lead immigrants and their descendants to develop an affiliation with pan-ethnicity—identities that emphasize cultural ties and social similarities with other groups. First, assimilation and the demise of immigrant ancestors' culture can dissolve ethnic boundaries and lead groups to emphasize what they have in common (Alba 1990; Jones-Correa and Leal 1996). Ethnic conflict can also shape choice of identity. Immigrant youths who select a pan-ethnic identity such as Hispanic are more likely to report having experienced discrimination than those who choose "plain American" as their identity (Portes and Rumbaut 2001). Finally, adopting a more encompassing ethnic identity can be a symbolic response to unfamiliar ethnic boundaries following migration. Puerto Rican women on the U.S. mainland often use Hispanic and Latina as their racial identity rather than accept the black-white dichotomy prevalent in American society but not their island (Landale and Oropesa 2002).

Among Asian Americans, events that heighten awareness of social inequality, such as the 1982 hate-crime murder of Vincent Chin in Detroit (Espiritu 1992), provide an especially powerful incentive for the formation of a pan-ethnic identity. Activists often promote pan-ethnicity to augment their political power, particularly when their respective ethnic-group members are too few in number to make their voices heard. The State Council on Asian-Pacific Minnesotans (2004, 6) includes representatives from fourteen different ethnic groups and proclaims as one of its four goals, "We believe in and will work towards an Asian-Pacific American identity." In fact, feelings of pan-ethnicity among Asian Americans increase with political activism (Lien, Conway, and Wong 2003), particularly participation in social movements (Geron et al. 2001) and exposure to anti-Asian prejudices (Kibria 2000; Tuan 1999). Given these patterns, some social scientists conclude that the identity "Asian American" has become a name for another racial interest group (Kibria 1998). But common cultural values, and not just political conflict, also promote pan-ethnicity among Asians (Kibria 1997, 1999; Lee 1996; Lien, Conway, and Wong 2003), as do structural factors such as housing and occupational segregation (Lopez and Espiritu 1990; Okamoto 2003; Shinagawa and Pang 1996).

These findings on pan-ethnicity are important but also inconclusive. One anomaly concerns the unexplained variation by national origin in the likelihood of pan-ethnic identification among Hispanics (Bobo and Johnson 2000; Jones-Correa and Leal 1996; Portes and MacLeod 1996) and Asians (Bobo and Johnson 2000; Lee 1996; Lien, Conway, and Wong 2003). I infer that immigrants' ethnic origins shape their receptivity to pan-ethnic identities.

Similarities and Differences

Cambodians and the Hmong consider physical features, typically skin and hair color, their primary similarity with other Asian Americans (see table 7.1). Surprisingly, they rank eye shape last as a shared physical trait, even though many whites use this feature to identify the "Asian" race. Several respondents specify that eye color (brown) rather than eye shape is an important physical feature shared by Asians. Conversely, six Cambodians and two Hmong (5 percent of the sample) list eye shape as a feature that differentiates them from other Asians. One Hmong woman in Eau Claire states that the Hmong have "smaller eyes" than other Asians. This discrepancy in how whites, Cambodians, and the Hmong construct racial identities confirms the premise of the ethnic-origins hypothesis concerning immigrant resocialization. Obviously, the refugees have their own notions about what constitutes a prominent or minor phenotypic feature.

Table 7.1   Responses to the Question "What Makes Cambodians/the Hmong Similar to Other Asian Americans?" (Percentages for Responses Given by 10 Percent or More of Sample; Multiple Responses Accepted)[a]

Physical		Cultural		Social	
Skin	53%	Food	24%	Social[c]	16%
Hair	49%	Clothing	16%		
Size	23%	Religion	15%		
Appearance	20%	Cultural trait[b]	14%		
Nose	19%				
Eyes	18%				

Source: Author's compilation.
Note: N = 179
[a]Responses were assigned to one or more categories based on content analysis.
[b]"Cultural trait" is a residual category comprising diverse responses about norms and values, such as "looking after parents when they are old" and "respect for authority."
[c]"Social" is a residual category comprising diverse responses contrasting Asian Americans with other people in United States, such as speaking a language other than English and experiencing discrimination.

Cambodians and the Hmong see physical features as their most important similarity with other Asian Americans, and point to culture when discussing important differences (see table 7.2). Less than half of the entire sample, 46 percent, cited one or more points of cultural similarity with other Asian Americans, whereas almost all respondents

Table 7.2   Responses to the Question "What Makes Cambodians/the Hmong Different from Other Asian Americans?" (Percentages for Responses Given by 10 Percent or More of Sample; Multiple Responses Accepted)[a]

Physical		Cultural		Social		Class	
Skin	13%	Language	81%	Social	10%	Education	11%
		Culture	36%			Jobs and	
		Cultural trait	31%			income	11%
		Customs	22%				
		Clothing	19%				
		Food	17%				
		Religion	17%				
		Family and					
		kinship	16%				

Source: Author's compilation.
Note: N = 179
[a]Responses were assigned to one or more categories based on content analysis.

(97 percent) listed at least one cultural characteristic that distinguishes them from other Asians, typically language and the specific words "culture" or "customs."

The area in which Cambodians and the Hmong are most likely to note how they differ from other Asians in the United States is class, as reflected in educational and professional achievements. Only 1 percent of the entire sample point to an economic similarity among Asian Americans (such as being self-employed), but 14 percent list at least one difference among Asian Americans in educational achievement, the types of work done (professional or unskilled), or income. Some Cambodians and Hmong clearly feel that Asian Americans are stratified by socioeconomic status.

As these data indicate, Cambodian and Hmong refugees evaluate a very wide range of characteristics in determining the degree to which they identify with the name "Asian American." This social-psychological dimension of racial and ethnic adaptation is primarily determined by ethnic origins rather than experiences with the urban pecking order or small-town hospitality and hate (see table 7.3). Regardless of where they live, the Hmong are more likely than Cambodians to cite a physical feature as a similarity with other Asian Americans. Cambodians in both Rochester and Chicago, on the other hand, emphasize cultural similarities with other Asian Americans—typically food, clothing, religion, and cultural traits such as "attitude toward work" and "same values and goals."

Ethnic origin is also the main source of variation in what respondents think differentiates them from other Asian American groups (see table 7.4). A significant proportion of the Hmong think that Asian Americans vary by class, and they also emphasize social differences

Table 7.3   Characteristics Shared with Other Asian Americans, by Ethnicity and City (Percentage of Respondents Listing at Least One Characteristic; Multiple Responses Accepted)

	Hmong in Eau Claire	Cambodians in Rochester[a]	Hmong in Milwaukee	Cambodians in Chicago[a]
Physical	98	78*	81	69
Cultural	19	59**	36	67**
Social	19	16	19	10

Source: Author's compilation.
Note: N = 48 in Eau Claire, 49 in Rochester, 32 in Milwaukee, and 50 in Chicago.
[a]Tests of statistical significance are between the same-sized city for different ethnic groups.
*p < .01; **p < .001

Table 7.4   Characteristics Different from Other Asian Americans, by
Ethnicity and City (Percentage of Respondents Listing at
Least One Characteristic; Multiple Responses Accepted)

	Hmong in Eau Claire	Cambodians in Rochester[a]	Hmong in Milwaukee	Cambodians in Chicago[a]
Physical	4	14	9	36**
Cultural	96	98	94	98
Social	19	4*	16	2*
Class	31	0***	28	2***

Source: Author's Compilation.
Note: N = 48 in Eau Claire, 49 in Rochester, 32 in Milwaukee, and 50 in Chicago.
[a]Tests of statistical significance are between the same-sized city for different ethnic groups.
*$p < .10$; **$p < .01$; *** $p < .001$

more than Cambodians. One Hmong respondent in Eau Claire believes that the "Chinese and Japanese have more money because they have been here for a long time." This perception is intriguing because the Hmong sample has a higher level of U.S. education and income than the Cambodian sample (see appendix A). Yet the Hmong are more likely to make invidious class comparisons, suggesting that the Hmong are more sensitive than Cambodians to group differences in socio-economic status.

Cambodians in Chicago reveal an important anomaly in the refugees' perceptions of pan-ethnicity: they are the most likely of all the groups to note their physical differences from other Asian Americans. In Uptown they often interact with Vietnamese (whom they perceive as having lighter skin), and in Albany Park they often interact with Koreans (whom they also perceive as having lighter skin). This pattern is an important reminder that urban setting can be very influential in shaping pan-ethnic affiliation among Asian Americans.

Overall, however, the Hmong express a weaker sense of pan-Asian ethnicity than do Cambodians. Not only do the Hmong emphasize class and social differences more, but they also consider physical features as their primary similarity with other Asian Americans, whereas Cambodians emphasize shared cultural characteristics. This difference is significant because culture provides a stronger foundation for pan-ethnicity than does the body. Hair and skin color are merely external markers often emphasized by a dominant group. Food, religion, clothing, and values characterize a way of life and facilitate interaction among insiders. The ethnic origins of Cambodians and the Hmong explain why they have such different responses to a pan-Asian identity in the United States.

Ethnic Solidarity Precludes
Pan-Ethnic Solidarity

I used follow-up interviews to learn more about informants' feelings toward other Asians at the micro-level of interpersonal relations. I asked them whether they would feel closer to an Asian American who was not from their ethnic group than to a white person, assuming that they did not know either one. I provided a specific setting for this hypothetical interaction, depending on my informant's current activity, such as a workplace meeting, a professional conference, or a classroom. I also named a Japanese American as the only other Asian person in that setting in order to elicit respondents' feelings toward an Asian American group that is more assimilated and whose members generally have a higher socioeconomic status than is typical for Cambodians and the Hmong.

Hmong and Cambodian informants responded to this question about micro-level pan-Asian solidarity in ways that corroborate the patterns shown in tables 7.1 through 7.4. All but one of the Hmong informants explained that she or he would not automatically feel closer to an Asian person in a group of whites when all of them were strangers. In Eau Claire, Chou provided a concise statement of this view: "No, I would treat her or him as equal. I wouldn't feel more comfortable. If they are white or Japanese, they don't know my language, don't know about the Hmong."

Although brief, Chou's comment nonetheless points to the primary reason why Hmong informants express a weaker sense of pan-Asian ethnic solidarity compared to Cambodians: they tend to view ethnicity as a dichotomy between Hmong and non-Hmong. In Chou's remarks this distinction is made on the basis of language but then augmented by her phrase "don't know about the Hmong." Hmong ethnicity is so powerful that the connection Hmong feel to each other makes any feeling of solidarity with other Asians appear trivial. Yer articulated this point better than any other Hmong informant. I asked about his feelings toward Asian and white students in his classes at the University of Wisconsin–Milwaukee, and he replied:

> To me, if they are just Asian, not Hmong, then they are just like any other person. But if that person is Hmong I feel I have a strong connection. Even if I don't know them I automatically feel they are my brothers or sisters. We have a background together. When I was living in Thailand the whole village knew each other. Everywhere you go you'd find friends and relatives. That sort of feeling has been passed down to me. It might be different for other Hmong, but I still feel a stronger connection to Hmong than another Asian.

Yer's telling phrase "just Asian" signifies how generic commonalties such as physical features among an otherwise diverse population fail to generate a feeling of solidarity for him, because relations among the Hmong are so special. In Eau Claire, Nao uses much the same language as Yer to explain how the dichotomy between Hmong and non-Hmong tends to limit feelings of pan-Asian solidarity. When I asked him about social interaction in a hypothetical business meeting with whites and one other Asian he candidly stated: "If that Asian person is Hmong, he's a Hmong, things change. I'm from the Hmong culture so we will have our own opinion of the meeting, we can discuss things. But if that person is from a different ethnic group, then I have to be careful, the same as with the other Caucasians at the table." Robert, another Eau Claire informant, goes even further than Nao in describing how feelings of solidarity with other Hmong are so strong that similarities with other Asian Americans are diminished by comparison. Asked the same question as Nao, he responded:

> You know, if they are Hmong people I know I will feel comfortable right away and would like to sit, talk, have lunch. But if Chinese, Vietnamese, then I'm reluctant. I don't know them. We each have our own culture even though we are the same color, same hair. I would feel reluctant. Pretty much the same as if they were white people. But if I know they are Hmong, that's different. I would feel at ease and want to talk.

Yer, Nao, and Robert clearly describe how the hermetic quality of the Hmong ethnic boundary diminishes the development of a pan-Asian ethnic identity by including other Asians and whites within the out-group. Their views mirror those of Hmong survey respondents since they emphasize that cultural differences far outweigh bonds based on physical similarities. In Eau Claire, Mee also makes this point but focuses on social and class differences. She is aware that Asian Americans vary profoundly in their historical period of arrival and socioeconomic progress. Asked whether she would feel closer to another Asian American than a white person in a workplace setting Mee responded:

> Mee: I don't think it would matter unless they were Hmong. That would make a big difference.
>
> Author: Why would it matter only if that person is Hmong but not another Asian American?
>
> Mee: It really depends on how acculturated they are. It's less likely I would feel anything in common with someone who is more acculturated

than me. I'm not really even the first generation [of Hmong Americans] because I still have roots in Laos. If that person had overcome the same obstacles as I did it might be okay, if it's not high and low. Then both of us would be learning about American culture. We would understand our mistakes.

Mee's succinct phrase "high and low" exquisitely captures what some Hmong briefly describe on the survey by listing social and class traits that differentiate the Hmong from other Asian Americans. Chong, another Eau Claire resident, also thinks the amount of Americanization distinguishes Asian Americans when he notes that "it does not make any difference, Caucasian or Asian. Some of these [Asian] people speak English well so I would have the same problem with them." Thus, even though many Hmong survey respondents note their physical similarities with other Asians, these traits are an insufficient basis for creating feelings of solidarity among minority groups that differ in socioeconomic status and degree of cultural assimilation.

It would be a mistake, however, to conclude that the Hmong feel no affiliation with other Asian Americans. Despite seeing similarities between whites and very acculturated Asian Americans, Chong still expresses a faint sense of pan-Asian identity under some circumstances:

> If you went some place, go to the zoo, and see some group similar to your-self, you have the same feeling, it's not just you coming to this place. But I would not ask them a question "How you doing?" Just the same feeling about the other group. If the majority is Caucasian someplace and there is only one [Asian] family who goes there, then they don't know about us. But if there is more than one [Asian] family, then Caucasian people know we are part of a minority group.

In this observation Chong hints at an incipient pan-Asian solidarity based on the shared experience of vulnerability when being the only Asian in a public place. Thus the Hmong or non-Hmong dichotomy is flexible enough to distinguish between the white dominant group in the United States and other nonwhite minority groups. Nonetheless, only one Cambodian informant among the fourteen that I interviewed expressed the view that ethnic group solidarity precludes pan-Asian solidarity. This one exception, Elizabeth in Rochester, responded to my question about being more comfortable with another Asian American in a group of whites by stating: "If they're from a different group than Cambodian I probably would feel that it doesn't matter. If Cambodian then I feel more comfortable. They understand who I am. How to explain. . . . Just not from the same group, so I don't know much about their background and they might not know me."

Elizabeth is clearly describing a hermetic ethnic boundary in the same way as the Hmong informants. Like Chou, she cites culture ("their background") as the basis for drawing a sharp distinction between Cambodians and other Asians. Yet Elizabeth's views are atypical. All the other Cambodians whom I interviewed feel close to other Asian Americans in social settings or stated that race and ethnicity as a whole do not shape their group affiliations.

"Asian Like I Am"

Where Hmong informants repeatedly indicate how ethnic solidarity precludes pan-Asian solidarity, Cambodian informants reveal just the opposite. Rather than viewing ethnic relations as a distinction between Cambodians and non-Cambodians, Khmer ethnic origins involve porous boundaries and liminal identities and thus promote pan-Asian ethnic identity. In Chicago, Roun provides the most direct example of this pattern. When I asked her about feeling closer to another Asian than a white person she answered, "I would feel closer to them. They are Asian like I am. I share with them. I had a Vietnamese friend in Mason [Michigan]. She gave me her trust. I always asked her when I had questions. She helped me with the language, told me what food to eat. We both liked Asian food."

Roun's simple phrase "Asian like I am" would be unremarkable except for its absence from so many statements made by Hmong informants about their interpersonal interactions with other Asians. She cites food, as do many Cambodian respondents in the survey, as the most obvious basis for this feeling. Yet Roun also alludes to a more general affiliation in her phrase "I share with them."

Heng, another Chicago resident, is an even better example of how Khmer ethnic origins foster a sense of cultural affiliation with other Asian Americans. When asked whether he would feel something in common with a Japanese American in a group of Caucasians he answered:

> Yes. We are both Asian. We look similar. We are just Asians. Not the same but the same category. Similar culture. If I walk into an Asian group I feel more normal. With Hispanics, blacks, and whites we have to be like them but we are not. Living in the U.S. you have to be like them. If I work with blacks, be like them, otherwise we will not get along. With other groups you have to be like them.

For Heng, Asians in the United States share not only similar physical features but also a similar culture, which is the pattern evident among the majority of Cambodian survey respondents in both Rochester and Chicago. While acknowledging that Asians of different backgrounds are not identical, he perceives a balance of cultural similarities and differences that leads to a feeling of pan-ethnicity ("the same category").

Cambodians are so sensitive to the cultural similarities among Asian Americans that some even specify which ethnic groups have the most in common with Khmer culture. Referring to the Japanese American in my question, Buon, an informant in Chicago, stated:

> Buon: Not Japanese, I don't know anything about them. If another group like Lao, Thai, or Filipino, then I would feel closer. They are like me, understand me more than Americans. We have some of the same things to eat. Lao, Thai, how they live is the same as in our country.

> Author: So it's more than physical appearance that would make you feel something in common with them?

> Buon: It's not just physical appearance. I would feel closer because they could understand me more than Americans. They feel that way about me too. They talk to me. It's not just looking similar.

Buon's statement is important as it illustrates a sense of pan-Asian ethnicity as well as how this bond ("understand me more") leads to communication ("they talk to me"). Pan-Asian ethnic identity can be abstract ("the same category" to use Heng's phrase). But as Buon indicates, it also can be a basis for micro-level interaction. This interpersonal dimension of pan-Asian identity is central to Carl's view of other Asians in the United States. During the interview in Rochester I asked if he would feel closer to an Asian American he did not know in a group of whites who were also strangers. Carl answered:

> It does happen. You tend to affiliate more with people you have something in common with. People categorize you as Asian. So it's something more in common. People want a sense of belonging to a certain group, it's easier for them. In terms of me, I'm fine with that. In all situations it's just a tad easier to communicate with other Asians. You feel like you have something in common, maybe the geographic area where you came from or being a minority here. I don't know, it's hard to explain. It has to do with the majority or minority. Even if you are not the same type of Asian you still have something in common. They know where you are coming from. Caucasians may not experience what you have experienced.

Despite his disclaimer that "it's hard to explain," Carl's insightful statement itemizes all of the factors that lead many Cambodians to have a strong identification with other Asian Americans. He begins with a basic sociological insight—"People want a sense of belonging to a certain group"—and then explains why Asian is one of the groups in which he feels membership. In addition to common geographic origins Carl cites being "a minority" in contrast to whites. He emphasizes that these characteristics are important because they make it "easier to communicate." This description of a porous ethnic boundary is what most distinguishes how Cambodians view pan-Asian ethnicity in contrast to how the Hmong view it. Where the Hmong start from the premise that Hmong solidarity is unique, Cambodians assume that ethnic differences can be easily outweighed by similarities.

Other Cambodians' views on their pan-Asian ethnic identity amplify one or more of the points found in Carl's encapsulating statement. In Rochester, Rebecca provided an affirmative response to my question and emphasized feeling at ease when interacting with another Asian:

> Rebecca: That's true. It's sad to say that but it's true. I feel more comfortable with the Asian race. It's easier to approach them, know how to react to them, to start a conversation. It's just a feeling. I can make friends with Americans but when I sit down to start a conversation I don't know what to ask about.
>
> Author: What is it that makes you feel something in common with other Asians?
>
> Rebecca: That instinct feeling. It feels like we have the same aspect of our culture, a similar background. They understand you more, where you come from. It's a similar culture, the same living style like food, whatever.

Rebecca's poetic phrase "instinct feeling" puts into two words what is clumsily expressed in a more sociological statement: Cambodians often seek to bridge ethnic differences because their ethnic origins are characterized by a porous boundary and a liminal identity. Unlike Hmong informants who emphasize the distinctiveness of Hmong ethnicity from that of other Asians, Rebecca actually states the reverse about Asians: "It's a similar culture." In fact, she uses the same phrase as Carl ("know where you are coming from") to explain why she feels an inherent ease in talking with other Asians but not with whites, even after they have become friends.

Like Carl and Rebecca, Sombat focuses on communication to explain his pan-Asian identity. Interviewed in Chicago, he swiftly responded to my question on feelings toward other Asians and then elaborated on his reasoning:

> Sombat: Interesting question. Definitely. I would trust them better than an American white. Even Vietnamese and Chinese [with whom Cambodians experienced political and economic conflicts in Cambodia]. I would trust

them better than other Americans. We relate in the same way, understand each other better as Asian people. I feel they understand me better because we are Asian, despite sometimes hating each other [in Cambodia]. We would have a more honest, more true friendship, more commitment to it.

Author: Can you give me an example of that happening to you?

Sombat: The first bond is the conversation. Introducing happens by itself just by asking "Where are you from? What are things like there?" We get to know each other that way. If the person is white and I don't know where they come from the only thing we have to talk about is their state, their city [said in a monotone, indicating how boring these topics are]. Talking with other Asians is more interesting. We show our feelings.

Sombat provides the most detailed explanation of any Cambodian informant as to how the group's ethnic origins foster a sense of pan-Asian ethnicity by facilitating inter-ethnic communication. The substance of this communication is clearly not what is most important, such as knowing the answer to the question "Where are you from?" What matters to Sombat and other Cambodians is the "instinct feeling" that it is easy to start talking with another Asian person. Sombat describes this predisposition toward pan-ethnic solidarity as "introducing happens by itself."

By contrast, only one Hmong informant conveyed an immediate sense of pan-ethnic solidarity with other Asians. In Eau Claire, Teng discussed the same themes as the Cambodians who displayed a strong pan-Asian ethnicity: an inherent sense of similarity that promotes inter-action. Since he works in a factory I asked Teng whether he would feel different about another Asian who was not Hmong in a group of white workers. He answered:

I think, for myself, if there is one Asian person, it wouldn't matter if they are Vietnamese, Chinese, Lao, I would feel better. For example, if I see someone from an Asian group, he and me are similar. We could have a conversation and I would feel better. I've been working since eight years ago to the present. I feel about Asian people, if we are working together, if he and me are new employees and if I cannot understand some equipment, he can tell me what job to do. Americans, their culture, my culture is different. American culture is not like. . . . They would just say do this, do this [motions with hands]. My people, we like to help each other, explain. We help explain how we can do something safely.

Teng obviously has a strong sense of pan-Asian identity, since he goes so far as to contrast "Asian people" with Americans. This bond ("he and me are similar") forms the basis for something important in his workplace: advice about how to handle equipment. It is communication, not simply an abstract sense of shared interests, that makes pan-Asian ethnicity at the micro-level important to Teng and the Cambodians discussed in this section.

"I Don't Classify Who Is Who"

Some Cambodians do have a strong sense of pan-Asian ethnic identity because they find it easy to communicate with other Asians. Other Cambodians, however, emphasize the importance of interpersonal interaction to the point where they disavow any interest in group identities. According to these Cambodians, thinking about race or ethnicity interferes with getting to know people. For example, I asked Samnang, in Chicago, whether she would feel closer to a Japanese American in a group if everyone else were white:

> Samnang: It wouldn't really make a major difference. It depends how you approach a person. Some personalities might prefer an Asian. It depends on how you talk to people. My experience isn't like that, it doesn't make much difference. I don't classify who is who. Some of my friends feel more comfortable with Asians.

> Author: But you don't?

> Samnang: I even might feel less comfortable if there were other Cambodians in a group of whites. I couldn't say what I really want to. There is a limit, a certain point you reach, where I don't feel free. If I said what I wanted to, the Cambodians might say, "What kind of lady is she?" Like relationships, dating. It's easier to talk to Americans about that. It's harder to carry on a conversation about that in an Asian group. With Asians you have to behave a certain way or they will say, "She is acting too American."

Samnang's insightful response indicates several facets of Cambodians' highly individualistic approach to race and ethnic relations. Her phrase "I don't classify who is who" is a perfect shorthand for the more cumbersome sociological conclusion: members of an ethnic group with a porous boundary and a liminal identity often de-emphasize group differences so much that ethnicity is seen as a dogmatic distinction. Rather than group people, Samnang thinks of them as "personalities." In fact, she goes so far as to admit that in some situations she feels more comfortable with Americans than with other Cambodians. Phen in Rochester has a surprisingly similar view of other Cambodians:

> Maybe it's something bad about myself, but when I see Cambodians hanging around outside a store, I don't think I have anything in common with them. Like outside a Cambodian market, I see them drinking and

smoking, especially smoking, and I don't smoke. They get together because they all work at a restaurant and they don't start work until late in the morning. I don't feel involved with them. It's the same with the two new residents at the clinic. One is Thai, one is Japanese. I don't feel anything in common with them.

Phen's expression of estrangement from members of his own ethnic group is nearly impossible to imagine coming from a Hmong person. The distinction smoker versus nonsmoker provides a stronger identity for him in one context than being Cambodian, and it's not surprising that he also disavows any sense of solidarity with other Asians. In this respect he is like my Hmong informants but his motivation is different. Phen explains why race and ethnicity hold so little meaning for him: "I pretty much respect everybody, black, white, blue. It doesn't matter to me. I can always talk to anybody." He suggests that feeling something in common with Asian Americans implies disrespect for other groups. Phen therefore provides one explanation for why some Cambodians repudiate feelings of pan-Asian ethnicity in the United States. To them it is a form of prejudice.

In Chicago, Kantal expressed this view even more directly than does Phen. Kantal had worked with people from many ethnic groups during his twenty years in the United States. His workplaces included a hospital, a truck factory, and an Asian American mental health clinic, where he now works. Despite the ethnic affiliation of the clinic, Kantal strongly disavowed having a pan-Asian identity. When asked whether he would feel something in common with a Japanese American among a group of whites he immediately thought of the factory lunchroom:

> At Caterpillar [Corporation], there were some people who would only sit with Americans or only with Mexicans. But for me, I sit where I want to sit, I talk to anyone. If they don't talk back, that's okay, I won't talk to them next time. A lot of people talk to me. I don't know what they think inside, but I know their outside.

Kantal interprets racial or ethnic solidarity as a form of exclusion and gives segregated lunch-time peer groups as an example. He expects members of other ethnic groups to be open to him and feels it would be hypocritical if he were to emphasize group differences by associating only with other Asians. Kantal's phrases "talk outside" and "think inside" are ideal shorthand for conveying one consequence of Cambodians' ethnic origins: individual interaction supersedes group identification. This ideal is prevalent among Cambodians and explains an anomaly in my interview with Suom in Chicago. Several times during our discussion he called himself Asian American and I thus expected him to give an affirmative response to my question on feeling something in common with other Asians. Yet in thinking about my workplace example, Suom said he would experience little solidarity and explained: "I would feel the same if the boss is Japanese American or American. I would feel the same. At work, on the job, it's the same. I have to know those people, make friends with them, say hi, hello."

Cambodians like Samnang, Phen, Kantal, and Suom sound much like my Hmong informants, since both groups disavow any pan-Asian ethnic identity. Yet their reasoning—how each group explains the absence of a special affiliation with other Asian Americans—are in fact quite different. Where the Hmong cite strong feelings of Hmong intra-ethnic solidarity, some Cambodians place a higher value on interpersonal relations than on group identities. In Chicago, Sokorn's succinct answer to my question summarizes this point: "It doesn't matter to me, Japanese or American. What matters is how we work together. Nationality doesn't matter. Some people share, some people don't."

Sokorn's elegant phrase "some people share, some people don't" epitomizes how one set of Cambodians express their group's porous boundaries and liminal identities. Several other informants express this view more elaborately. In Rochester, Kouy stated:

I can get along pretty well with anyone. If I talk and get to know them I can get along. Before, in high school, I always wanted to have at least one Asian in the classroom because it's easier to talk to them. But after college it didn't matter. I can talk to anyone who looks friendly and nice. When I was in college, most classes I took, there were no Asians, all Americans. So I had to learn how to get along with everyone.

The centrality of communication to Kouy's feelings of group affiliation explain the decrease in strength of her sense of pan-Asian ethnic identity over the course of her life. She notes that personality traits ("looks friendly and nice") came to be better indicators of the potential for positive interpersonal relations than race and ethnicity. Even when Cambodians acknowledge the reality of group differences they often prioritize individual interaction over collective identities. Sopot, for example, recognizes differences among ethnic groups but does not find it easier to communicate with other Asian Americans, stating, "I don't think it makes a difference." During our interview in Rochester she explained her approach to meeting someone from another ethnic group:

Sopot: I want to get to know their culture. I want to know how they are the same or different. I've known a lot of different people from different cultures. I like to know what their weddings are like, do they have a Buddhist or regular [church] wedding. I like to know about other cultures, not just mine. It's more interesting. I'd like to learn another language.

Author: Which one?

Sopot: Thai, Hispanic. I've learned a little Somalia. There are a lot of Somalians that work with me. French. It's good to learn a lot of languages.

Sopot's view of language reveals much about the way Khmer ethnic origins influence Cambodian refugees' racial and ethnic adaptation. Her interest in other Asian Americans does not stem from their shared status as a racial minority but from her inclination to view ethnic boundaries as differences to be explored and shared rather than avoided and preserved. In fact, Sopot has an equal interest in learning to speak Thai, Spanish, Somali, and French, and clearly does not prioritize learning a language spoken by other Asian Americans.

The value some Cambodians place on interpersonal interaction over ethnic identity differentiates their non-pan-ethnic views from those of the Hmong. The attitudes toward other Asians expressed by You, a Hmong informant in Eau Claire, contrast sharply with those of the Cambodians quoted in this section:

> I wouldn't feel different toward that person. In a classroom of twenty white kids and two minority kids, Japanese Americans, I would feel more comfortable asking the American kids something because it's their country. I would try to ask, to be friendly, so we can get along. I would feel more comfortable with them than others. I feel that this is their country, I will live with them so we should be friends. If I talk to them, like asking questions or for help, then they will find out about my background, know me too.

You's response begins like those of Cambodians such as Kouy and Sopot, who disavow a feeling of pan-Asian ethnicity at the micro-level. Yet You's explanation is based on a very different reasoning. Rather than emphasize individualism, as many Cambodians do, she emphasizes group differences based on culture ("my background") and nativity ("their country"). Although the Hmong and some Cambodians both have a weak sense of pan-Asian ethnic identity they arrive at this view via different cognitive routes. The Hmong think ethnic group differences are too powerful to be superseded by pan-ethnicity, whereas some Cambodians think that individualism supersedes all group differences, including pan-ethnicity.

Conclusion

There is substantial support for the prediction of the ethnic-origins hypothesis concerning pan-ethnicity: immigrants with a hermetic ethnic boundary and polarized ethnic identity (for example, the Hmong) have a looser sense of affiliation with other Asian groups—a lower pan-ethnicity quotient—than do immigrants with a porous ethnic boundary and a liminal ethnic identity (for example, the Khmer). Regardless of whether they live in an urban pecking order or with small-town hospitality and hate, Cambodians perceive cultural similarities with other Asian Americans more often than the Hmong. The Hmong are much more likely than Cambodians to note their lower socioeconomic status as well as social differences, such as length of time in the United States. When the Hmong do acknowledge being similar to other Asian Americans, it is largely due to physical traits. Thus, on the whole, Cambodians in the Midwest have a more developed sense of Asian pan-ethnicity than do the Hmong.

It would be incorrect, however, to conclude that pan-Asian identity is absent among the Hmong. Some do express a greater feeling of trust toward other Asians than toward whites and report that they gain a sense of security when other Asians are present in public places. Other Hmong describe close personal relationships with Asians who are not Hmong. And, not surprisingly, some Cambodians show few signs of pan-Asian ethnic solidarity and claim that race and ethnicity are irrelevant to their interpersonal interactions with other people. They explain that personality traits and communication styles are important, not the ethnic group a person belongs to. "I don't classify who is who" is how one Cambodian woman in Chicago describes this attitude. The Cambodians who deny feeling an affinity for other Asian Americans sometimes go so far as to call such a preference a form of prejudice. Contrary to the ethnic-origins hypothesis, a porous ethnic boundary and a liminal ethnic identity can sometimes curtail a sense of pan-ethnic identity by reducing the importance of all group identities.

Cambodians' and the Hmong's views of pan-ethnicity reveal that diversity in the United States is more than a demographic process in which immigrants expand preexisting categories such as Asian. International migration from Asia and other parts of the world is causing social identities in the United States to be redefined. These identities are in part shaped by how the host society defines race and ethnicity for immigrants. But they are also shaped by the historically, politically, and culturally embedded understandings of diversity that immigrants bring with them from their homelands.

= Chapter 8 =

American Citizen

Many policy makers think of U.S. citizenship as one of the last identities that can foster a sense of unity in our increasingly diverse society. President Clinton's Advisory Board on Race recommended developing programs "for both immigrants and those born in the United States, that would promote a clear understanding of the rights and duties of citizenship. These types of programs would help to promote national identity and cohesion" (President's Advisory Board on Race 1998, 91). Immigrants have several incentives to naturalize, a peculiar term that means acquiring the same legal status as those born in the country acquire at birth. Some immigrants may feel an increased sense of social membership in American society when they adopt a new nationality. U.S. citizenship also gives immigrants new rights, including voting, eligibility for federal employment and social welfare programs, and priority in sponsoring relatives to come to the United States.

Since becoming a U.S. citizen can be a very significant stage in immigrants' racial and ethnic adaptation, social scientists have sought to determine why some groups of immigrants naturalize more than others (Bueker 2005; Jasso and Rosenzweig 1990; Yang 1994). Immigrants whose homelands are farther from the United States tend to naturalize more often than those who can easily return to their country of origin, such as Mexicans and Canadians. Immigrants from socialist states, such as Cuba, China, and the former Soviet Union, become U.S. citizens at a much greater rate than others, as do immigrants admitted as refugees. Higher levels of homeland education are also associated with higher rates of naturalization.

Although the correlates of naturalization are well established, there remains considerable debate over citizenship's power to sustain national unity (see Bloemraad 2004, Joppke 1998, and Schuck 1999 for reviews of this literature). The transnational perspective argues that immigrants often retain a sense of membership in their native nation-state even after they adopt the citizenship of the host society. The postnational perspective goes further, arguing that immigrants no longer value any form of national citizenship because they do not define themselves by national

144

borders. Proponents of these views can cite credible examples where both dynamics seem to be operative, including the growing number of countries that recognize dual nationality and the European Union with its supranational citizenship. Furthermore, membership in Western societies cannot be described by the simple dichotomy of citizen or noncitizen. There are a range of intermediate statuses, such as guest worker and permanent resident, that confer some of the rights of full citizenship. Finally, it is well known that immigrants maintain ties to their homelands, further eroding the monopoly of host-society citizenship on cultural identity.

Other scholars, however, believe that "national citizenship remains indispensable for integrating immigrants" (Joppke 1999, 632). In fact, applications for U.S. citizenship rose dramatically during the late 1990s, with one-third of all filings during the twentieth century occurring between 1991 and 1998 (Singer 1999). About 45 percent of immigrants admitted during the late 1970s and early 1980s have become U.S. citizens. These new citizens include Cambodian and Hmong refugees. The degree to which their views of U.S. citizenship are shaped by their ethnic origins and the type of city they live in tells us much about what it means to be a full member of American society during this era of globalization.

Rights but Rarely Membership

Upon arrival, legal immigrants such as Cambodian and Hmong refugees are entitled to become permanent residents of the United States and can only be deported if they commit a serious crime. An immigrant is eligible to become a U.S. citizen after five years of residence, and 43 percent of Cambodian and Hmong respondents to my survey had naturalized. Of those who had not naturalized, 98 percent indicated that they want to become U.S. citizens in the future. Obviously, these refugees consider it very important to adopt the nationality of the United States, an attitude that may contradict the postnational perspective of citizenship.

Cambodians and the Hmong tend to think that naturalization conveys a new set of national and international benefits. More than three-quarters of respondents cite as least one legal advantage enjoyed by U.S. citizens but not by permanent residents (see table 8.1). Only about one-quarter associate U.S. citizenship with a greater sense of social integration in American society. In fact, about one-fifth of the refugees describe naturalization in ways that indicate it is not really a choice reflecting feelings about membership. They think naturalization is forced upon them by the impossibility of ever returning to their homeland. These patterns support the postnational perspective, since Cambodians and

Table 8.1　Responses to the Question, "Why Did/Do You Want to Become a U.S. Citizen?" (Percentages, Multiple Responses Accepted)[a]

National Benefit		International Benefit		Social Integration		Exile	
Vote	50	Travel security	36	Integration	28	Exile	19
Equal rights	33	Sponsor relatives	8				
Employment	20						
Public aid	8						

Source: Author's compilation.
Note: N = 179
[a]Responses were assigned to one or more categories based on content analysis.

the Hmong, far from naturalizing due to a new identification with the people and culture of American society, overwhelmingly have an instrumental attitude toward U.S. citizenship.

Although the postnational perspective helps correct an overly sentimental conception of U.S. citizenship, it suggests a universal trend in immigrants' views of naturalization and thus obscures their ethnic origins. Some versions of the theory argue that globalization homogenizes immigrants' views on naturalization, yet this is surely an overstatement, since Cambodians and the Hmong have distinct ideas about what naturalization means (see table 8.2).

Table 8.2　Reasons for Becoming or Wanting to Become a U.S. Citizen, by Ethnicity and City (Percentages, Multiple Responses Accepted)

	Hmong in Eau Claire	Cambodians in Rochester[a]	Hmong in Milwaukee	Cambodians in Chicago[a]
National benefit	72	80	68	76
International benefit	15	52***	29	64**
Social integration	38	35	26	11
Exile	40	9***	23	4*

Source: Author's compilation.
Note: N = 48 in Eau Claire, 49 in Rochester, 32 in Milwaukee, and 50 in Chicago.
[a]Tests of statistical significance are between the same-sized city for different ethnic groups.
* $p < .05$; ** $p < .01$; *** $p < .001$

The Hmong, particularly when they live in a small city, are more likely than Cambodians to feel that they must become citizens because they cannot return to their homeland, a perception that is shaped by their historic diaspora from China. A Hmong proverb states: "Live in their world, you have to follow their rules. Live in their land, you have to obey their ways" (Miyares 1998, 106). Numerous Hmong respondents made comments very much like this proverb to explain why they became or want to become citizens. For example, a Hmong man in Milwaukee simply stated, "No chance of going back. Had to become a citizen." Similarly, a Hmong woman in Eau Claire commented, "I believe we have to live in America so I just want to become a citizen."

Another way that some Hmong express how exile necessitates naturalization is by focusing on the views of their children. Rather than their own feelings of membership in American society, what concerns these parents is that their sons and daughters already think of the United States as their homeland. In Eau Claire, a Hmong mother of five children explained why she wants to naturalize: "My children were born here and I don't see anywhere that we can go. So I have to live here with my children. I know that my children would not go anywhere else because they are used to living here."

Viewing naturalization as an involuntary consequence of forced migration also shapes how the Hmong connect citizenship with social integration. For some, becoming a full member of American society does not entail a new social identity. Instead, a Hmong woman in Eau Claire notes how exile leads to a quasi-compulsory social integration via citizenship: "Because I have no country, I have to live here and I want to be part of the American people. But I can't read and write and it will be difficult [to pass the citizenship test]." A similar view is offered by another Hmong woman in Eau Claire. The mother of six children (born in Laos, Thailand, and the United States), she too uses the phrase "have to" when explaining the connection between U.S. citizenship and social integration: "Since we came to this country we have to live here. Now we are refugees. It seems that we have no country or land [of our own]. So I'd like to become a citizen and become American and live here. Also, become a citizen so American people would respect us."

Unlike the Hmong, who often consider U.S. citizenship to be a necessity because they are refugees, only a few Cambodians cite exile as their motivation to become a citizen. Cambodians are much more likely than the Hmong to associate naturalization with international benefits. In fact, a larger proportion of Cambodians value U.S. citizenship because it facilitates international travel and sponsoring relatives (58 percent) than because it grants them the right to vote (51 percent).

Cambodians explain that it is easier to travel to Cambodia when one is a U.S. citizen. Many feel a greater sense of security knowing that other countries respect the power of the U.S. government to guard its citizens. Others note that using a U.S. passport to leave and return to the United States is far more convenient than using the "permit to reenter," a complex and difficult-to-obtain document required of permanent residents. Cambodians also know that U.S. citizens have priority over permanent residents in sponsoring relatives to come to the United States, such as parents or siblings. In other cases Cambodian men (but also some women) visit Cambodia to find a spouse and then sponsor the bride (or groom) to join them in the United States.

The fact that Cambodians are far more likely than the Hmong to associate U.S. citizenship with international benefits refutes the postnational perspective, which often portrays citizenship as a useless relic for people living in a global village. Laos and Cambodia both have a peripheral position in the world-system. Political conditions, however, still affect how refugees make travel plans for themselves and close relatives who remain in their homeland. Democratization has made progress in Cambodia since the first postwar election in 1993, whereas Laos is one of the last socialist states in the world and the Lao People's Revolutionary Party has instituted fewer reforms since taking power than has the Communist Party in neighboring Vietnam. Although it is common for the Hmong to visit Laos, they face considerable constraints and some risks because of continued government persecution of the Hmong. In 1999, two Hmong men, both U.S. citizens, were arrested upon arrival in Laos and have never been heard from again.[1] Variation in homeland politics can explain immigrants' reasons for naturalizing in the United States.

Similarly, the basic premise of the transnational perspective—that immigrants often retain a sense of membership in their native nation-state even after they adopt the citizenship of the host society—is problematic because it ignores the variety of locales in the host country. Naturalization has different meanings for refugees residing in big and small cities. Cambodians in Rochester are much more likely than those in Chicago to think that citizenship promotes social integration ($p < .01$). The same is true for the Hmong in Eau Claire as compared to those in Milwaukee, although the difference is not statistically significant. Combined, 37 percent of the refugees in small cities associate U.S. citizenship with social integration into American society; only 17 percent of those in big cities make this association ($p < .01$).

One reason for this localized citizenship is that refugees experiencing small-town hospitality and hate feel that naturalization helps them gain social acceptance. In Rochester, a Cambodian woman explained why she became a U.S. citizen simply by stating: "Because I didn't feel very good to be a different nationality." Another Cambodian woman in the city believed that after she naturalized, "No one can say I am a refugee," a term some Americans use pejoratively as a synonym for foreigner. In Eau Claire, a Hmong woman went so far as to assert the benefits of citizenship for the Hmong as a group: "If we become citizens Americans would treat us better."

Refugees in small midwestern cities also think of naturalization as part of the acculturation process. Asked if he felt different after becoming a citizen, a Hmong man in Eau Claire responded, "Of course, I feel more belonging to this country—hometown, home college, and part of [home] ownership." This brief but fascinating quotation from the survey reveals how U.S. citizenship acquires a local meaning in small cities and becomes a rite of passage akin to graduating from the University of Wisconsin–Eau Claire or buying a home for the first time. Given that feeling foreign is a salient aspect of race and ethnic relations in Eau Claire and Rochester, it is not surprising that some refugees consider U.S. citizenship one of several steppingstones toward integration into the community. As a Cambodian woman in Rochester explained, "Being an American citizen to me means I am now a part of the American people and taking part in the American culture and learning to adapt to the American way of life. For example, eating American food, how I dress and my clothing, speaking the language, and adjusting to the environment." Such views are much less common among refugees in the urban pecking order, where they create their own enclaves amidst crime, random violence, and resource competition.

Yet Cambodians and the Hmong in Rochester and Eau Claire agree with those in Chicago and Milwaukee on one point that is central to the debate over postnational and transnational views of citizenship. Followup interviews make it abundantly clear that neither Cambodians nor the Hmong think that U.S. citizenship turns them into Americans, even if it increases their social integration.

Refugee + Citizenship = American?

Legally, naturalization means that an immigrant becomes a U.S. citizen and not an "American" citizen, since "American" refers to culture and ethnicity, while "United States" refers to nationality. But "American citizen" is the common parlance among both Cambodians and the Hmong and I continued this usage in my follow-up interviews. In fact, the inaccurate term "American citizen" created a valuable interview technique for assessing the meaning of citizenship. Even though the phrase "American citizen" has a universally accepted meaning in everyday speech—a citizen of the United States of America—I asked my informants:

Does becoming a citizen mean becoming American? Without exception the answer is some form of no, and informants give two reasons for this response: the salience of racial divisions in American society and the ways citizenship affects their relationships with significant others in the ethnic community.

"I Will Always Look Asian"

Cher, a U.S. citizen in Milwaukee, thinks of naturalization in ways that would greatly please the members of President Clinton's Advisory Board on Race. In response to the survey question on the meaning of citizenship, she stated: the "freedom to be Asian American and it enables me to do what I've dreamed of doing." During the follow-up interview I asked Cher why she held this view of U.S. citizenship and she replied:

> If someone calls me Asian American I feel I belong to America, it's my country too, not just for one people, one ethnic group owns it. If they call me Asian American that means I belong in this society, more home, more wanted. If they call you Hmong then I feel I don't belong in this society. If it's just Hmong then we are only one small group. We all belong in the salad bowl but every time you take a bite you get a different ingredient. You have to add in to make it taste better, so that's what Asian American means. But sometimes it's like a sandwich. If you want a hamburger you don't have to have the mustard. That's the race case. If I don't want mustard I can just have pickles and ketchup.

Among all my informants Cher has the most optimistic view of U.S. citizenship's power to create social cohesion in an ever more diverse society ("we all belong in the salad bowl"). Yet she also mentions "the race case," an allusion to the racial divisions in American society. This issue is a concern for many respondents. In fact, some Cambodians and Hmong were surprised that I would even ask whether being an American citizen did or would make them American. My question seemed absurd because to them it is obvious that race is one of the most important identities a person has in American society, whereas one's citizenship is invisible. Roun, a permanent resident in Chicago who wants to become a citizen, provides the most succinct expression of this perspective. Asked whether becoming a citizen would make her feel more American, she responded: "No, because I will always look Asian. If I go outside people will look at me and still think I'm Asian." In Eau Claire, Teng feels the same way about becoming a U.S. citizen, but expresses it even more directly: "Mostly it was only a change on paper. I feel part of this country but only on paper. Myself, I cannot change my color."

Other Cambodian and Hmong informants have the same view as Roun and Teng. They think that since a person's citizenship cannot be observed in daily life it carries little meaning as a marker of identity and is overshadowed by race. In Eau Claire, Mee stated on the survey that she became a citizen because "I wanted a country that my children and I could finally call our home. I also wanted to have the same rights as a citizen, but most importantly I needed to become one to be a certified nurse some day." Like other Hmong, Mee expresses how exile necessitates citizenship and thus leads to a quasi-compulsory integration. Yet in the follow-up interview, when I asked her if becoming an American citizen made her feel more American, she conveyed how prejudice can void citizenship of its equalizing effect:

> It made me more aware of things like making jokes about Americans and Americans not just being white. As time went by . . . Sometimes I forget I am an American citizen, like it doesn't apply to me. The only things I can really do is vote, get out of this country easier. It still depends on how others treat you. If others don't respond to that change in you then citizenship is just a document. If they don't treat you differently then you're just refugee, Hmong.

Mee spat out the last two words—"refugee, Hmong"—to convey their negative, stereotypical meaning in the mouths of some Americans. She is clearly describing how small-town hate creates a perpetual feeling of being foreign and thus prevents U.S. citizenship from fostering a sense of national identity.

Racism can also drain away citizenship's symbolism in big cities. In Chicago I asked Kantal whether becoming an American citizen made him feel American and he responded, "I never thought about becoming American when I became a citizen. I just did it after six or seven years to take advantage of things, to have things more convenient, like job interviews. Even though I'm not white, not an American-American, being a citizen makes me more legal." In Khmer, repeating an adjective intensifies the meaning, like saying "very" or "really" in English. Kantal applies this grammatical idiom to the term "American" to express his instrumental view of citizenship. He believes that citizenship raises nonwhites' status but can never give them full equality with native-born whites, who, he thinks, view themselves as the "real" Americans.

Sombat, who is also a citizen and lives in Chicago, provides an even more explicit description of how racial divisions devalue citizenship. Some of the rights granted by citizenship are profoundly meaningful to him. Yet he is acutely aware that citizenship does not alter the reality of a racial hierarchy in the United States:

Sombat: The way I perceive it, it's only a piece of paper. If some one says "Are you American?" what am I going to do, say, "Yeah, I have a certificate"? [He makes a mock gesture of taking his wallet from his back pants' pocket as if he were about to display a piece of ID]. It's a racial issue. I'm still Cambodian. Americans still say "flat-nose." That's how they distinguish American from Asian.

Author: So why is citizenship important to you?

Sombat: When I became a citizen I was about to graduate [from high school]. I knew I could not go back to Cambodia. I needed employment, financial support. In order to work I needed citizenship. But voting was my first issue. I went out and voted in November 1996. It was the happiest day of my life. I'm not sure why, it was just having the right to vote, pretending to live the American dream.

Sombat's assessment of naturalization highlights the duality of citizenship for Cambodians and Hmong who have an instrumental view. The exclusionary effects of race reduce citizenship to rights on paper because racial distinctions are observable in daily life while legal status is not. Yet gaining these rights can still be a significant event in a refugee's life course in the United States. Nevertheless, Sombat does not identify himself as an American. Despite participating in a core institutional process like voting, he still only feels he is mimicking full membership in the society.

Sy provides the most detailed and complex expression of how race and ethnic relations in American society combine to make U.S. citizenship a legal status rather than a cohesive identity. A college-educated pastor and U.S. citizen, I expected that his extensive acculturation and high socioeconomic status would lead him to associate naturalization with Americanization. During the follow-up interview in Milwaukee, however, he expressed the opposite view:

Being a citizen, I felt it changed my status to being a legal citizen of the country. But that doesn't change me to become white or American-born. That doesn't change my race as Hmong. It just helps me feel more comfortable that I can do a lot more things than just being an alien, refugee, permanent resident. Because Asians have different skin even though they become citizens. I still feel Asian, not white, because of my skin. Even though we may become Christian, citizen, we are still Asian. We will never be white, have white skin, or a different hair color.

Clearly, Hmong and Cambodians' views of citizenship are heavily influenced by race. The profound racial divisions in American society lead them to view citizenship primarily or exclusively as legal advantages with little or no change in their social identity. Race, however, is not the only reason why some refugees have an instrumental view of citizenship. As Sy suggests by his use of the pronoun "we," compatriots in the ethnic community also shape the meaning of naturalization.

"I'll Do It If You Are"

Citizenship alone cannot turn Cambodians and Hmong into "Americans" because they recognize a basic insight of symbolic interaction theory: social identities are more than individual choices because they develop through socialization with peers, family, and community. Citizenship is conferred by a state on an individual, but individuals define its meaning in the context of their relations with significant others.

Ka lives in Milwaukee, is a permanent resident, and wants to become a U.S. citizen. She responded to my question on becoming a citizen and thus becoming American by stating: "It will be no different to me. I just want to be a citizen so that if I go from place to place it's safer." A follow-up question, "So it won't make you feel more American?," uncovered an important reason for Ka's instrumental reasoning—the social context of naturalization:

Ka: Well, I still think that I belong to here, but still think I belong to Hmong, not that I belong to American or the country.

Author: Why wouldn't becoming a citizen change that?

Ka: If I'm a citizen that won't totally change me to an American. I would follow the rules here, but in my family I still respect them, I wouldn't say to them "I'm American now." It's hard to stay in the middle.

Ka's last statement provides an interactionist explanation for why Cambodians and the Hmong tend to view citizenship as a source of national and international advantages but not of a deeper sense of membership in American society. As a college student Ka is acculturating faster than other family members. Her rapid adaptation colors her views of citizenship, since any additional acculturation would further accentuate the tension she already feels from changing her lifestyle more rapidly than her parents and siblings. For Cambodians and the Hmong, the social significance of citizenship is determined not simply by their own attitudes but by those of their familial reference group as well.

Sopot's perceptions of citizenship amply illustrate how its meaning is defined by multiple actors, not just by the person who naturalizes. In the follow-up interview in Rochester Sopot mentioned that she had become a citizen since completing the survey but also reported that her parents had failed the test for a third time. After congratulating her, I asked if she now felt more American, but she responded: "For me, it's just a piece of paper." Our ensuing dialogue reveals how her parents' attitudes shape her own views about the social insignificance of becoming a U.S. citizen:

Author: Why wouldn't becoming a citizen make you feel more American?

Sopot: I feel in between, but sometimes more Cambodian. I listen to Cambodian music. With my friends, we talk about our culture. So then I think citizenship doesn't make no difference, it's just a piece of paper so you can vote. One thing, you can find better jobs, but there's a lot of people who are racist down here.

Author: So it didn't make you feel more . . .

Sopot: American-American? No, I feel more Cambodian, even though I was raised here. I still follow my culture. My parents and relatives are still full Cambodians. They speak Cambodian. Someday, if I forget my language and culture, I will regret it. If I call myself American Cambodian I would feel uncomfortable. I want to carry my culture. If I dropped my culture it would make me feel uncomfortable. I hope I never forget.

Author: So the culture of your parents is important to how you feel about being Cambodian or American.

Sopot: It does depend on who your parents are. If your parents follow American culture you can be part of it. I've seen some [people] of my culture, their parents are more of American culture and they forget their culture and just be American.

Like Sopot, Yer struggles with intergenerational differences in the meaning of American citizenship. A permanent resident in Milwaukee, he arrived in the United States at the age of seven. On the survey he stated that becoming a citizen meant "knowing you have a place to belong to. Allows more freedom to work, choose leaders, and better yourself and your family." During the follow-up interview I reviewed this comment with Yer and then asked if he would feel a greater sense of membership in American society when he became a citizen. He responded:

Yer: That's the feeling. Now it's just immigrant, aliens from another country who don't belong yet. You have to strive more to belong to this country. But getting citizenship, then you have some sense of belonging. It's different from my parents [who say], "Even though you are here you have to be careful." They feel that way, that they have to be wary of people because they were mistreated.

Author: What type of mistreatment?

Yer: For older Hmong either mistreatment here or there. But with us [younger Hmong], it's just here, it doesn't carry over from Thailand. They have that in them already. That's where it starts from, the Vietnam War. I read some horrible things that the Vietnamese soldiers did [to the Hmong in Laos]. [Yer pauses and looks somber.] The generation in that Vietnam War is the generation that raises us now.

Yer's insights on his parents' generation indicate how older Hmong have difficulty obtaining a "sense of belonging" from citizenship due to their ethnic origins. Harsh experiences in Southeast Asia predispose them to emphasize the durability of ethnic boundaries, something that naturalization is powerless to change. Nonetheless, Yer feels that younger Hmong like him are not as constrained in their social identities as the older generation. He associates citizenship with increased social integration ("you have some sense of belonging") primarily because it replaces stigmatized identities like "alien."

Ka, Sopot, and Yer unambiguously state that their parents' ethnicity shapes their own responses to naturalization. For these young adults, emphasizing a new social identity would create a familial conflict, since their parents are very traditional and have not acculturated as much as they have. Citizenship, therefore, is only one part of a much more complex process in which younger Cambodians and Hmong evaluate their own ethnic identity by taking into account the ethnic identity of significant others, such as peers and parents.

Similarly, older Cambodians and Hmong can be influenced by a spouse's decision to naturalize as well as consideration of how citizenship will affect their children's social identity. In Milwaukee, Kelly explained, "My husband was becoming a citizen so I went with him." Her family had an even greater influence on her attitudes toward citizenship than this statement suggests because she then added:

I want to teach my children to have a voice like American people, to vote. If they don't agree with Congress, the Senate, they can vote like white people. I teach my children that we are in this country, if there is ever a war we will help. If I learn more professional words, then I can help American people. "You are Hmong American, children, that's why Daddy and I became an American citizen." That's what I tell them. If I don't teach them that they still think Hmong, think they don't have rights. I teach them step by step. They have the right to vote, to help this country even though we can't change our hair or eyes to a white person.

Kelly's remarkable statement illustrates how significant others (as well as race) lead to an instrumental conception of citizenship. Given this context, her response to my question "Did citizenship make you feel more American, like calling yourself Hmong American?" was predictable: "I never thought that," she said.

Even less immediate kin than members of the nuclear family influence the meaning of citizenship for Cambodians and the Hmong. In Rochester, Phen's lengthy response to my questions on citizenship reveals how interaction within the Cambodian community shapes views of U.S. citizenship. When I asked him whether becoming an American citizen would make him feel more American he responded:

> It won't change things one bit. There is no advantage or disadvantage, only for traveling outside the country. That's what I'm told by other Cambodians. They told me other countries are more liable if you are a citizen, that it's easier to travel. I guess I agree with that. You see the reason is, in Rochester, a lot of [Cambodian] people become citizens because many Cambodian men and women go to Cambodia to find a spouse and then sponsor them to the United States. But for me, I don't need to be an American citizen [because I'm already married], maybe just to make it easier to fill out a form at work. I'll always be Cambodian. But as I grow older I believe in politics more, to help the United States choose who is running the country. Being able to vote may get me going. And the [application] fee keeps going up every year. So there's no reason to wait any longer. Most of my family on my wife's side, they are citizens already. It's not that they intimidate me, they just mention it, so it's "Okay, I'll do it if you are." But becoming American? No.

Phen unambiguously explains how kin and members of the ethnic community define the meaning of U.S. citizenship for individual refugees. His description makes it is easier to appreciate the significance of the brief remarks made by several survey respondents. One Cambodian woman in Chicago answered the survey question on the meaning of becoming a citizen by using a Khmer idiom which the Cambodian interviewer translated as "Go with the flow: other people do it so I might as well." Asked why he had become a citizen, a Hmong man in Milwaukee simply stated: "Because everyone else did it." When citizenship results from social conformity it is much more likely to produce an instrumental view of national identity than a profound feeling of membership in American society.

Some Cambodians and Hmong, particularly those who live in small cities, do associate U.S. citizenship with greater integration into American society. Yet even these informants still overwhelmingly prioritize the legal dimension of citizenship and explain that becoming a U.S. citizen cannot make them American.

Local Citizenship

Chong is midway through the naturalization process. He has passed the Bureau of Citizenship and Immigration Services (BCIS) interview but has not yet attended the swearing-in ceremony. During the follow-up interview in Eau Claire he told me, "Being an American citizen means I belong to this country." This expression of social integration is common among refugees in small midwestern cities, where local race and ethnic relations make them feel like foreigners. In such environments, citizenship offers a way to gain a status enjoyed by the larger white community. Yet in response to my question—"Will becoming a citizen make you feel more American, like calling yourself Hmong American?"— Chong also conveys the limits of U.S. citizenship. He said: "My feelings will not change, not be any different. Hmong American, we sometimes call Hmong American too because there are Hmong from Canada, Australia. Sometimes we call Hmong American, but not if you are not a citizen yet. Otherwise it's just Hmong."

Chong has just revealed something fascinating about how Southeast Asian refugees use the word American: not only does he show the influence of the Hmong diaspora, but he explains that "American" is a residential designation rather than an indication of social membership. To natives it may seem obvious that the refugees now have a home in the United States. But these international migrants have moved so often in the recent past that obtaining a sense of place does not come easily. Their uprooting began with war-induced migration within their homeland, then flight to a refugee camp in Thailand, then being shipped to a transit camp in Indonesia or the Philippines for Americanization courses, and finally arrival in the United States. These experiences explain why Chong uses "American" to mean literally residence in the United States, not membership in a new people and culture.

Elizabeth, a Cambodian resident of Rochester, also uses U.S. citizenship to express putting down roots and ending her refugee saga. On the survey she stated that becoming a citizen "makes me feel part of America," referring to a place (the United States of America) rather than the American people. I asked her if she felt more American after becoming a citizen several years ago:

> Elizabeth: Actually, way back then, the most important reason was to sponsor my husband's sister. Second, travel and job privileges, the right to a better deal. I feel I have more rights, feel part of America.
>
> Author: What was it that made you feel that way?

Elizabeth: I just don't have to carry the green [permanent resident] card. That A [alien] number, now they don't have to ask for it. "That A number, do you have that number?" [spoken in an intimidating bureaucratic voice]. All those questions. So now they don't ask those questions. I just check "citizen."

Elizabeth obviously felt out of place in a small midwestern city such as Rochester. As a result, shedding the permanent resident card that identified her as an "alien" became a significant rite of passage in her life course. Yet the "better deal" she referred to was not a new ethnicity, such as being American. Instead, her feeling of greater membership in American society stemmed from reducing the number of occasions when she is labeled foreign-born.

In Eau Claire, You provides an even more emphatic description of how refugees in small towns use citizenship to decrease their marginality. On the survey she cited "to feel part of the community" as one reason for wanting to become a citizen. By the time of the follow-up interview she and her husband had completed the citizenship application form but had not yet had their submission confirmed by the BCIS. Like Elizabeth, You feels that the act of checking "permanent resident" instead of "citizen" on a document significantly affects her sense of membership: "On applications, whatever, it asks that. I don't feel good to say no. I would feel better being a citizen so I can do anything, be part of the family here." You's use of the family metaphor is one of the strongest suggestions by any informant that naturalization can augment feelings of affinity with natives. Yet in response to a follow-up question You clearly stated that although naturalization would convey the same rights as natives, it would not affect her perceptions of ethnic identity: "It won't change how I feel. I am Hmong and I can't change to American. I can just do more things like Americans can. It won't change my views from Hmong to American. I don't feel I am like them."

For informants like Chong, Elizabeth, and You, naturalization is more than a change in their legal status and yet falls short of conferring a sense of national identity, as many policy makers hope for. In Eau Claire, Robert's perceptions of U.S. citizenship help explain this gap. On the survey he stated that he had become a citizen to "get more respect from the majority people," the quintessential expression of what membership means when refugees experience hospitality and hate in a white community. In the follow-up interview I therefore expected Robert to state that he began feeling like an American when he became a citizen. Instead, he confirmed feeling politically equal to Americans, but avoided identifying himself as an American: "I felt more confidence. I felt more comfortable being with groups of whites, like I am the same, almost the same as them, vote, do anything. You feel you have more power than a regular refugee."

Robert's wonderfully alliterative phrase "regular refugee" conveys the sense of marginality that Southeast Asians experience in places like Eau Claire and Rochester. He expresses a far greater sense of membership in American society through the idiom of citizenship than do informants who live in the urban pecking order. I learned the reason when I asked him why he uses an American first name, which he adopted when he became a citizen:

> Honestly, I don't know if using Robert makes a difference for American people. But if an American citizen uses the name Robert it would be . . . American people might feel I'm Americanized, acculturated, assimilated. Then I would feel more accepted by the majority people. People would like me more, I would feel more comfortable. I don't know how they feel, it may make some difference. But I kept my last name for my identity. I don't want to be Robert Smith [he laughs]. I'm still Hmong, one-half Hmong. Even if I changed my last name I'm not American. I took the name Robert to be more accepted.

Cambodian refugees in Chicago's Uptown and Hmong refugees on Milwaukee's Near North Side are much less likely to reach the conclusion that Robert did in Eau Claire: taking an American name upon naturalizing promotes social integration into the local community. In small cities refugees like Robert observe that race and ethnic relations center on the issue of foreigners creating diversity rather than merely being the latest representatives of diversity in the process of urban ethnic succession. Some therefore think of citizenship as a way to diminish what makes them different.

Carl, a Cambodian resident of Rochester, provides a final insight into how refugees in small cities use the idiom of citizenship to diminish the stigma of being outsiders. Since he arrived in the United States at the age of seven, and was now twenty-four years old, I expected a positive answer to my question "Did becoming a citizen make you feel more American?" Yet Carl halfheartedly answered: "You get a little sense of more belonging." Surprised by his response, I probed to determine the reason by asking whether he called himself Cambodian American. He replied, "Actually I wouldn't. I would say I'm originally from Cambodia. Because when I first came here I heard a few racist remarks, yelling, 'Go back.' . . . So that's part of why I wanted to become an American citizen, so I could think I was part of something."

Carl clearly reveals how U.S. citizenship can counteract small-town nativism by erasing one big difference between the refugees and whites in the community. Nonetheless, he disavows the name "Cambodian

American," despite acknowledging that wanting to be "part of something" had motivated him to become a citizen. Even in small cities where naturalization becomes a local rite of passage, Cambodian and Hmong refugees do not think they become Americans when they become U.S. citizens.

Conclusion

Cambodian and Hmong refugees are surprisingly similar in their views of U.S. citizenship—an aspect of their adaptation that does not support the ethnic-origins hypothesis. Members of both groups tend to have an instrumental attitude, in which they value naturalization for its legal advantages rather than as the source of a new social identity. Not one of the twenty-eight individuals I interviewed answered yes to the question "Would [or Did] becoming an American citizen make you feel more American?" Instead, Cambodians and the Hmong are more likely to view citizenship as similar to passing a driving test to get a license, a pattern consistent with the postnational perspective on citizenship.

This instrumental attitude to citizenship is not a recent development, as is suggested by the postnational perspective. A comparison of immigrants in the first and last thirty years of the twentieth century reveals the "continuing pragmatic view of cost and benefits of naturalization, rather than an awakening of patriotism" (Schneider 2001, 76). Cambodian and Hmong refugees do not point to globalization to explain why they rarely associate gaining U.S. citizenship with acquiring an American identity. Instead they observe that racial divisions in American society erase commonalities based only on a piece of paper. They also note that peers, kin, and other members of the ethnic community influence both their decision to naturalize and the degree to which this potential sign of Americanization could cause familial and communal conflict. Thus, the racial hierarchy in the United States and the importance of social networks for all immigrants largely negate variation in ethnic origins when it comes down to having an affinity for U.S. citizenship.

Despite the ways race and social conformity circumscribe citizenship, Cambodians and the Hmong are not emotionally neutral toward it. Most consider becoming a U.S. citizen a significant stage in their racial and ethnic adaptation. Some even feel a new sense of membership in American society because citizenship confers legal equality with natives. A few even call themselves Cambodian American or Hmong American as a result, although they use "American" as a territorial designation rather than an ethnic identity. Even if U.S. citizenship does not have the social and cultural significance for Cambodians and the Hmong that some policy makers hope for, many of the refugees consider it valuable. They disagree with social scientists who claim that U.S. citizenship confers "few privileges beyond those already granted to permanent residents" (Joppke 1999, 632) and that "the marginal benefits to most aliens of moving from legal resident status to full membership are slight" (Schuck 1999, 169).

Although the refugees generally have an instrumental view of citizenship, there are some specific differences between Cambodians and the Hmong that support the ethnic-origins hypothesis. The Hmong are much more likely than Cambodians to consider naturalization a necessity due to their exile from Laos rather than a choice about identities. They often cite their historic lack of a nation-state of their own when discussing reasons for becoming U.S. citizens. Hmong respondents who explain that they want to become a citizen "because I have no country, I have to live here" are not just describing current political conditions but are invoking a worldview shaped by their diaspora from China. Ethnic origins clearly influence some of the meanings Cambodians and the Hmong attach to U.S. citizenship, a pattern that the postnational perspective on the nation-state does not wholly account for.

Where refugees resettle in the United States also influences this dimension of their racial and ethnic adaptation, a point missed by the transnational perspective when it overemphasizes the ability of people to transcend geography. Those in small cities are more likely than those in big cities to think of naturalization as a transformative experience leading to a new sense of membership. Even as transnational trends erode the significance of naturalization, in places like Eau Claire and Rochester refugees consider citizenship a milepost in their acculturation because it reduces feeling foreign. Marginality is not a problem for the refugees in Chicago and Milwaukee, owing to the extensive racial and ethnic diversity of these environments. Nevertheless, in the urban pecking order U.S. citizenship has only a limited capacity to promote social integration.

Social identities based on pan-ethnicity and nationality are only one aspect of immigrants' racial and ethnic adaptation. In addition to identities, diversity in our society regrettably means social inequality. Charles Tilly (1998, 25, emphasis in original) defines social inequality as:

the uneven distribution of costs and benefits—that is *goods* broadly defined. Relevant goods include not only wealth and income but also such various benefits and costs as control of land, exposure to illness, respect from other people, liability to military service, risk of homicide, possession of tools, and availability of sexual partners.

Among the disparate items on this list readers will surely pause to ponder the significance of "respect from other people" in the case of immigrants. To understand what happens when some groups receive more or less social respect requires shifting analysis from the boundaries between Asian and white, foreigner and citizen, to the effects of these differences. Tilly (1998, 84) eloquently summarizes this linkage as "categorical pairs and the mechanisms of inequality." The next four chapters examine Cambodians' and the Hmong's perceptions of and reactions to various mechanisms of racial and ethnic inequality in American society.

= Part V =

Inequalities

═ Chapter 9 ═

Societal Racism

"The American dilemma" is one of the most enduring phrases to emerge from twentieth-century social-science research. Gunnar Myrdal (1944/1962) coined this term in his landmark study of African Americans' inequality in the United States. His book quickly became "an epoch-making work [that] brought to broad public notice for the first time the fact that . . . Jim Crow segregation was unjustified and indeed un-American" (Fredrickson 2002, 167). A Swedish economist with an outsider's perspective of American race relations, Myrdal was struck by a contradiction in the United States (McKee 1993), which he dubbed "the American dilemma": American democracy values freedom, justice, and equal opportunity, but white racism ranks whites above other groups.

Becoming aware of the American dilemma is among the most fundamental challenges that immigrants face during their racial and ethnic adaptation. Yet social scientists vehemently disagree over whether Myrdal's insight about white racism and black inequality can be generalized to mean that all nonwhites in the United States—including recent immigrants from Asia—face the same kind of hardships as African Americans. The sociologist Joe Feagin, a president of the American Sociological Association, has spent decades analyzing American race relations. He concludes (Feagin 2000, 204) that systemic racism against blacks "has been extended and tailored for each new non-European group brought into the sphere of white domination." Ronald Takaki (1979, 1989, 1993), a historian and one of the most respected authorities on the Asian American experience, agrees that white racism victimizes Asian Americans just as it does African Americans. As evidence of a shared pattern of inequality he cites events such as the U.S. government's denial of citizenship to Asians in the 1920s and the internment of Japanese Americans in the 1940s. After reviewing the history of race relations since World War Two, the sociologist Howard Winant (2000, 309) reached the same verdict: "By and large the descendants of slaves, indigenous and occupied peoples, refugees, and migrants continue to be subjugated to the descendants of landholders and slavemasters, occupiers and European settlers."

Other social scientists see greater complexity in the experiences of nonwhites in the United States. The sociologist Robert Blauner's (1969, 1972) early distinction between colonized and immigrant minorities is the basis for several arguments that the American dilemma affects blacks in a unique way. The anthropologist John Ogbu (1978, 1991b), a leading authority on school culture, argues that African Americans respond to inequality by collectively resisting repression and seeking to change mainstream institutions. Asian Americans, by contrast, attempt to overcome adversity by assimilating into the institutions controlled by whites.

The political scientist Andrew Hacker (1992, 9–10) goes even further in this line of reasoning, stating that Asian Americans do not experience the inequality at the heart of the American dilemma: "Most Asian immigrants arrive in this country ready to compete for middle-class careers. . . . [So even] if Asians are not literally 'white,' they have the technical and organizational skills expected by any 'Western' or European-based culture." A similar theory is advanced to explain why immigrants from Taiwan and the Philippines obtain better jobs through their social networks in the United States than do immigrants from China. It results from "the tendency of both Taiwanese and Filipinos to arrive relatively well versed in Western culture and social practices" (Sanders, Nee, and Sernau 2002, 299).

The political scientist Lawrence Fuchs (1990), who has extensive policy experience at the national level, presents the strongest argument that the American dilemma is not the rule for all nonwhites, but is an exceptional problem that affected only African Americans. He believes that the civil rights era of the 1960s fundamentally reformed the American civic culture: the legal framework and political consensus protecting civil rights and ethnic diversity in the United States (Almond and Verba 1965). According to Fuchs, this period of social change largely resolved the American dilemma just prior to the new immigration that began in the 1970s. Thus Fuchs concludes that contemporary Asian Americans— nearly 70 percent of whom are immigrants—skipped the publicly sanctioned racism that so scarred African Americans. The sociologists Richard Alba and Victor Nee agree (2003, 58) with this view, noting that in contrast to African Americans, today's immigrants are "much less burdened by the legacies of the historic norms and etiquette governing race relations. The examples of the Asian American groups offer the most compelling testimony."

Despite these positive assessments, the U.S. Commission on Civil Rights reported in 1992 (190): "Contrary to the popular perception that Asian Americans have overcome discriminatory barriers, Asian Americans still face wide-spread prejudice, discrimination, and denials of equal opportunity." We can turn to Cambodian and Hmong refugees for help in evaluating these competing claims about immigrants' experiences of the American dilemma. They arrive in this country with an idealized notion of American society's political freedoms and economic riches, but then they experience racial and ethnic inequality in both big and small cities.

The Best and Worst Things About the United States

When contrasting life in their homeland with life in the United States, Cambodian and Hmong survey respondents emphasize what is better about their new home far more than what is worse (see table 9.1). They prize the intangible components of the American civic culture—democratic freedom and public education—above the material advantages of the American way of life, such as living standards and food supply. The low ranking of economic opportunity among the best things about the United States is partly explained by the political causes of the refugees' migration from Southeast Asia, which made Cambodians and the Hmong more likely to value American civil liberties. In addition, Cambodians and the Hmong are among the lowest income groups in the United States (Southeast Asian Resource Action Center 2004). In my sample, 46 percent of respondents earn or receive in public assistance less than $10,000 a year. Only 2 percent earn more than $40,000. These refugees are far removed from the affluence of American society and are thus much less likely to perceive economic opportunity.

Table 9.1   Responses to the Statement, "Describe Some of the Best and Worst Things About Life in the United States Compared to Life in Cambodia/Laos" (Percentages, Multiple Responses Accepted)[a]

Best		Worst	
Education	68	Assimilation	30
Freedom	56	Racism	29
Standard of living	44	Crime	23
Physical safety	29	Gangs	21
Health care	29	Economic hardships	19
Food supply	27	Family conflict	16
Economic opportunity	23	Weather	6
New culture	9	Other	19
Other	17		

Source: Author's compilation.
Note: N = 178
[a]Responses were assigned to one or more categories based on content analysis.

Given Cambodians' and the Hmong's low socioeconomic status it is understandable that much of the social-science literature on contemporary immigrants examines their occupational attainment and earnings. Yet economic pressures such as low pay and too many bills are cited by a comparatively small proportion of survey respondents. As with their perceptions of the positive features of the United States, cultural and social issues, not material conditions, lead the list of negatives.

The refugees' primary worry about living in the United States is the struggle to assimilate a new culture, particularly learning English. Familial conflict is a specific form of cultural adjustment cited by about one in six respondents. Parents are particularly concerned that their children have too much freedom in the United States, which weakens their authority. Co-ethnic and inter-ethnic gangs are a specific form of crime cited by about one-fifth of respondents. Some respondents describe the gang problem in conjunction with family problems, such as the inability of parents to use corporal punishment to deter their children from illegal activity lest they be accused of child abuse.

Natives' negative reactions to diversity are also prominent among those things that Cambodians and the Hmong dislike about the United States. Twenty-four respondents specifically listed the terms "prejudice," "discrimination," or "racism" when asked to describe some of the worst things about American society. Others gave examples of prejudicial attitudes or discriminatory actions, or described their minority status, such as "a feeling of being unwanted in the white community." Thus, more than one-quarter of the refugees spontaneously articulated the American dilemma by qualifying their positive perceptions of the United States with the observation that racial and ethnic inequality is a problem.

Places and Problems

What the refugees dislike about the United States is very much dependent on where they live (see table 9.2). In Chicago and Milwaukee their biggest problems stem from the urban pecking order, but in small cities their concerns involve race and ethnicity. More than one-third of Cambodians in Rochester and Hmong in Eau Claire describe assimilation as a problem; only about one-fifth of refugees in big cities report this problem ($p < .05$). Many are perturbed by their linguistic handicap, such as an elderly Hmong man in Eau Claire who poignantly states: "I am frustrated because I don't speak English and have no job. You have a mouth but you can't talk." Conversely, refugees in big cities are much less likely to be troubled by limited English proficiency because they create their own enclaves and live among other immigrants.

Table 9.2   Top Two Worst Aspects of Life in the United States Compared to Life in Homeland, by Ethnicity and City (Percentages, Multiple Responses Accepted)

Hmong				Cambodians			
Milwaukee		Eau Claire		Chicago		Rochester	
Crime	26	Racism	55	Crime	55	Assimilation	39
Economic hardship	26	Assimilation	36	Gangs	47	Racism	20[a]

Source: Author's compilation.
Note: N = 48 in Eau Claire, 49 in Rochester, 31 in Milwaukee, and 50 in Chicago.
[a]Twenty percent of Cambodians in Rochester also listed family conflict among the worst aspects of life in the United States.

Prejudice and discrimination are also more serious problems for the refugees when they live in small cities rather than in big ones (the interaction of ethnicity and urban context is fully examined in chapters 10 and 11). Whereas the Hmong in Eau Claire rank racism as their biggest concern about living in the United States, those in Milwaukee list it third, tied with assimilation and family problems. Cambodians in Rochester named racism as their second biggest problem, while it is ranked fourth among Cambodians in Chicago.

Philomena Essed (1990, 257) first used the name "everyday racism" to describe "the situations, attitudes and customs that produce racial inequality in daily life." Subsequent analysis by Feagin (1991) and others (Byng 1998; Essed 1991; Feagin and Sikes 1994) revealed several types of face-to-face discrimination against African Americans, the most common of which are avoidance, rejection, and verbal harassment. Cambodians in Rochester and the Hmong in Eau Claire experience all of these problems.

Avoidance is an action to increase physical distance or limit social interaction. It is a particular problem for young black males, who are often stereotyped as violent criminals, but it is also experienced by a wide range of Hmong and Cambodians in small cities. For example, a Cambodian woman in Rochester reported an incident that occurred when she was forty-eight years old: "One time I was walking along the sidewalk as exercise. An American man walking toward me got away from the sidewalk and his face seemed not to like me or say hi to me. I felt so sad about it and then I thought to myself it's because I am a refugee and came from a different country."

A more aggressive form of avoidance experienced by refugees in small cities is the look of contempt termed the "hate stare"—also well known to African Americans. Complete strangers at times engage in this

behavior by making hostile facial expressions that convey their unwill-
ingness to engage in social interaction. Neighbors, however, are a more
common source for this type of avoidance. In Eau Claire many Hmong
report that their white neighbors refuse to associate with them and withhold the usual exchange of pleasantries. The following excerpt, from a
father of five children, is representative: "Our neighbor seems to hate us
very much. She has never said hi or smiled to us. She said that we should
not park our car on her spot on the street even though it belongs to the
public. She seems to hate our black hair people a lot." Avoidance involving neighbors is particularly painful for Hmong and Cambodians. It
tends to occur over a long period of time, cannot be ignored because of
physical proximity, and affects their children.

Rejection is poor, disrespectful, or otherwise unequal service in public accommodations such as stores. The incidents that make Hmong and
Cambodians in small cities feel like undesirable customers closely match
those of African Americans. Sometimes the staff in a store reject customers in subtle ways. In Eau Claire, a Hmong man in his thirties
described a diurnal pattern of rejection:

> In a superstore, gas station, sometimes they are surprised at me, a totally
> different race, especially at night. Like when I punch gas [use a self-serve
> gas pump and then go inside to pay]. They don't say anything, it's just my
> feeling. They suspect you might do something bad. They don't say that,
> it's just in my mind. They're afraid, suspect a bad person. During the day
> it should be fine.

Rejection in public accommodations can also be much more direct. A
Hmong man in Eau Claire, who had recently graduated from the local
university, spontaneously used the word "reject" to describe his worst
discriminatory experience in the United States. Although it occurred nine
years prior to the date of the interview this young man vividly recalled
it because it initiated him into the reality of racism in the United States:

> The worst thing that ever happened to me was rejecting me at a sporting
> goods store in 1988. It happened when I was in high school. Americans,
> Caucasians hated me for who I am. I was in a small store. The owner never
> took his eyes off me. I can still picture that now. It made me so nervous I
> was scared to touch anything. I realized that in a small town, they are not
> familiar with other cultures, they are still afraid. That incident showed me
> that discrimination exists even though I had Caucasian friends and would
> hang with them.

The hostile nonverbal communication described by this Hmong man
in Eau Claire is only one variant of rejection in public accommodations.
Another form is for staff to withhold the usual courtesies that they

would normally extend to customers, such as asking, "Are you finding everything you need?" Being followed by store staff is the most egregious form of rejection, according to Hmong and Cambodians. A Cambodian woman in Rochester reported an event that occurred when she was twenty-seven years old: "One time back in 1994 I was really badly mistreated in the Wal-Mart store. When I just walked into the store they sent a security guard to follow me all the time because I have different color skin and hair from them."

Verbal harassment is the use of speech to demean and stigmatize a member of a racial or ethnic minority. It often involves highly offensive epithets that denote inferiority. In small cities anonymous strangers sometimes verbally harass Cambodians and Hmong in public places. A young Hmong woman in Eau Claire described an event she experienced as a teenager: "No one in my family knew how to drive, so we had to walk to the grocery store. When Americans drove past they would blow their horn at us and stick their head out the window and yell very bad words at us. They would say bad things like, 'Go back to your country, your dark skin doesn't belong here!' "

Although any public place can become the site of verbal harassment, it appears from the reports of the Hmong and Cambodians that students in public schools are frequently the targets of offensive name-calling. For example, a Cambodian woman initially resettled in San Antonio with her parents. Then the family moved to Dallas and finally to Rochester. Upon arriving in Rochester at the age of ten she made a terrible discovery in a city that four years later would be named by *Money* magazine as the best American city to live in:

> When I moved to Rochester in 1989 my family's [migration] problems were over but there was another problem that I was going to go through. The problem was that I saw prejudice here in Rochester that I didn't know of. When I went to school a couple of Americans would tell me to go back to my own country, that I don't belong here. They would call me all kinds of names. A couple of my neighbors were like that too. That made me angry and sad. They made me feel like I didn't belong here. I just wanted to move back to Texas.

A Hmong woman in Eau Claire provides a remarkably similar account of verbal harassment. Now in her twenties, she reported an experience that occurred when she was a teenager: "When I went to middle school and high school, many American students bothered me and called me bad names. Sometimes I was angry and had some tears. Sometimes they spat on me and my Hmong friends. We were afraid. We did not do anything because we were afraid of them. It seemed like they didn't really like us at all."

The Hmong's and Cambodians' experiences of avoidance, rejection, and verbal harassment are identical to the ostracism documented among African Americans (Byng 1998; Essed 1990, 1991; Feagin 1991; Feagin and Sikes 1994). Yet their accounts of face-to-face discrimination in public also reveal an additional dimension of micro-level inequality not reported in this literature: nativism, which ranks the native-born above the foreign-born by portraying immigrants as aliens whose birth in another society prevents them from being legitimate members of American society (Higham 1974). The irrationality of racism means that even a native-born minority such as African Americans can be subjected to the nativist taunt "Go back to Africa." But the Hmong in Eau Claire and the Cambodians in Rochester are even more vulnerable to nativism because they think of themselves as refugees who were invited to resettle in someone else's country.

"Go Back to Your Country"

The refugees' reports of verbal harassment in small midwestern cities unambiguously reveal that in addition to being targeted because they are not white they are also harassed because they are foreign-born. In Rochester, a forty-six-year-old Cambodian man's description of verbal harassment in 1990 actually contains the definition of nativism: "One day when I went to the grocery store a few American boys came up to me and said: 'Hey you! Go back to your country. This is our land. You don't belong here.' I felt so bad and mad but I tried to be patient by walking away from them."

Some cases of verbal harassment combine both racism and nativism. In Eau Claire a Hmong man now in his twenties described an event in school that occurred when he was sixteen years old. It clearly illustrates the intersection of racism and nativism: "Someone called me gook and told me to go back to my country. That was back in 1989. I ended up in a violent fight with that person." Verbal harassment invoking racial epithets and nativism is also described by a Hmong woman in Eau Claire when asked about her worst experience of discrimination: "It happened during my junior year in high school. I was shopping with my cousins. Some junior high girls followed us into the mall and continued to harass us by calling us names: 'Chinese, slanted eyes, go back to your country.' It made me feel bad."

As these quotations indicate, Hmong and Cambodians are vulnerable to verbal harassment because of both their physical appearance and natives' assumption, correct or incorrect, that they are foreign-born. Many instances of verbal harassment express only nativism, however. Numerous respondents in small cities confirmed that verbal harassment against Hmong and Cambodians is often intended to stigmatize their being foreign. Telephone harassment almost always has a nativist dimension and is reported only by the Hmong in Eau Claire and Cambodians in Rochester. Apparently, the ethnic diversity in Milwaukee and Chicago thwarts would-be harassers since there are so many foreign-sounding names. But in small cities non-European surnames stand out in the phone book, with unfortunate consequences. In Eau Claire a Hmong man in his thirties described a particularly devious anonymous phone call that was exclusively nativist rather than racist:

> Someone called me on the phone and pretended to ask questions like a survey. He said my cousin did not speak English so he wanted to talk to me about the survey. But after a while he said mean things to me. First he asked, "Do you eat rice?" I said, "Yes." Then he said if I wanted to eat rice I should go back to my country because there is only enough rice here for Americans. I was very angry but tried to be calm.

The limited number of Hmong surnames in the Eau Claire phone book makes the refugees easy targets for verbal harassment by telephone (there are only eighteen clan names in the total Hmong population). But Cambodians in Rochester also report this experience even though they have a much greater diversity of surnames. A Cambodian woman in her forties described the following incident as her worst experience of discrimination:

> One time in 1987 one American man called me and asked me, "How are you? How many children do you have? How old are you? Do you want me to buy underwear for you? Can you go out to a bar and dance with me?" At that time I felt very angry because my daughter was listening on another phone and interpreting for me because I only understood a little English. But she understood and wanted me to put down the phone.

This instance of telephone harassment reveals a variant of nativism that targets Asian women, not men: stereotypes about their sexuality. As the previous quotation suggests, some native men think that Asian women's birth in an "exotic" country trains them to be sexually submissive. This stigma connecting nativism and sexism is conveyed in a young Cambodian woman's account of a particularly bad day in Rochester in 1995:

> When I went out with my friends a bunch of white guys came up to us and started calling us gook and other names. Later on that day when I was walking to get something to eat with my friends a different group of guys came by in a car and asked us if we wanted to go into a hotel with them. We all just ignored them and kept on walking. Then they called us hookers and

said that in my country we give up to men so easily and why can't we do it to them now. I got so mad that I walked home crying. They made me feel like I was so easy to them.

Another uniquely nativist dimension of verbal harassment of Southeast Asians in small cities is the invention of new derogatory terms to stigmatize the fact that they are foreign-born. In addition to the widely known racial epithets "gook" and "chink," Cambodians in Rochester report being taunted with the label "boat people," a term coined by the media in 1979 to describe the flight of Vietnamese refugees across the South China Sea. Now the term has turned up in Rochester, where some whites use "boat people" to stigmatize Cambodians—of course, it is a complete misnomer, since Cambodians crossed into Thailand by land, not sea. A Cambodian man reported what happened to him in 1984, just a few years after the mass arrival of Vietnamese refugees in the United States during 1980 to 1981:

One time in middle school two or three American students said some words to me, calling me names. "Go back to your country, boat people." One guy spit saliva. All these things made me so upset and angry. I shook both my hands and wanted to fight back but at that time I was very new to living in United States and my English wasn't enough to explain to the teachers that something had happened.

Apparently, the phrase "boat people" became an enduring stigma for Cambodians in Rochester. Cambodians reported hearing it in verbal harassment during the late 1980s and into the 1990s. A Cambodian woman described the derogatory use of this phrase in an incident of verbal harassment that occurred in 1995:

One American boy in my school said, "You go back to your country" and he called me "boat people." It made me very angry and then I went to the principal and told him what he said and the principal solved this problem. But I still felt so sad when I came back home. I told my parents and they said, "It's because we came to their country, that's why they look down on us." I tried to control myself and calm down but I still hated that guy.

What is significant about these cases of nativist verbal harassment of the Hmong and Cambodians is that their aggressors seek to shame them through their status as refugees by asserting that they are trespassers on someone else's land, not by making negative references to their bodies. Small cities generate this form of inequality much more than do big cities, where anonymity and diversity limit claims to space.

Country of Origin Social Structure and American Opportunity

Conditions in the refugees' homelands strongly influence what they like most about American society (see table 9.3). Although both Cambodians and the Hmong value the American civic culture, the distinct social structures of Cambodia and Laos determine what they most appreciate, and why.

The Hmong in both Milwaukee and Eau Claire think that the best feature of the United States is access to public education, particularly for children but also for college and university students. Although many Cambodians praise the educational opportunities in the United States (54 percent) they do so at a level significantly below that of the Hmong— 86 percent (p < .001).

Cambodians in both Chicago and Rochester think that democratic freedoms are the best aspect of the United States—77 percent of Cambodians list freedom as a positive attribute of American society, versus only 29 percent of the Hmong, a very significant difference (p < .001). Finally, almost twice as many Hmong (59 percent) as Cambodians (31 percent) think the material standard of living (such as plumbing) is one of the best things about the United States. I used follow-up interviews to determine how homeland conditions shape the refugees' perceptions of the American civic culture and also to directly ask informants about the seriousness of racism.

"In Cambodia If a Party Has the Army They Win"

Cambodians' faith in the U.S. system of government stems from a history of negative experiences with their homeland government. They lived under an authoritarian government from 1970 to 1975 (the Lon Nol

Table 9.3 Top Two Best Aspects of Life in the United States Compared to Life in Homeland, by Ethnicity and City (Percentages, Multiple Responses Accepted)

Hmong				Cambodians			
Milwaukee		Eau Claire		Chicago		Rochester	
Education	81	Education	89	Freedom	69	Freedom	86
Standard of living	59	Standard of living	60	Education	45	Education	63

Source: Author's compilation.
Note: N = 48 in Eau Claire, 49 in Rochester, 31 in Milwaukee, and 50 in Chicago.

regime, installed by a U.S.-backed coup) and then the totalitarian genocide of the Khmer Rouge from 1975 to 1978 (Becker 1986). The Vietnamese invasion in December 1978 removed the Khmer Rouge but then established another authoritarian regime under Hun Sen, the leader of the Cambodian People's Party. A quasi-democratic form of government returned to Cambodia in 1993, under the auspices of an election supervised by the United Nations. But Hun Sen refused to relinquish his grip on power and initiated a coup in 1997. Some Cambodians now feel they are living under a dictatorship and cite flagrant human rights violations as examples.[1]

Suom, a Cambodian living in Chicago, explains how past and present political conditions in Cambodia shape his views of the American dilemma. On the survey he listed "freedoms" and "good government system" among four positive features of the United States. His three entries under negative features were prejudice, discrimination, and racism. During the follow-up interview I reminded him of his responses to the survey question and asked how both could be true. Suom replied:

> I don't understand the system completely, but there are two or three parties in the United States. The majority picks and what they pick is good. That is what they call democracy. In Cambodia it's not like that. If a party has the army they win. Even if people all over vote for another party, they lose. Since I was born [in 1945] the majority has never won. The army always wins. The people with arms, soldiers, they win.

Suom's description of authoritarian regimes in Cambodia makes it easy for us to understand why he greatly values the democracy he has found in the United States. In turn, this appreciation for American political institutions shaped his views of racism in American society. When I asked him whether racism is strong enough to take away the freedoms of some people in the United States, he immediately responded, "Racism is still in America from a long time ago and it is still here now. The system of government makes laws to cover it up so we don't see it, so it's not free to discriminate, not free to be racist. The laws protect against racism but don't cure it. They just don't let it grow."

Buon, another Chicago resident, provides an even clearer statement of Cambodians' perception that the U.S. government guarantees civil liberties for everyone. In responding to the survey question on the best and worst things about the United States, she listed terms that directly name the American dilemma. Her short list of best things included "opportunity to go to school" and "able to apply for loans" while her equally brief negative list included "discrimination." I asked Buon how both of these traits could exist simultaneously. She laughed as I used my hands to show two sides of a scale tipping up and down in a futile attempt to balance dissimilar objects and then said:

> Buon: Discrimination, I meant the way people look at me, common peo-
> ple. The government has to be fair because it's the law. People around me,
> the way they look and treat me, it's as if I don't have any education, can't
> speak English.

> Author: Can you give me an example of that?

> Buon: Sometimes when I'm in line they ask [serve] the American behind
> me before they ask me. They ask the American first, not the one who's first
> on line.

For Buon the American dilemma is a disjuncture rather than a contradiction. She expects fair treatment from the government and in areas
of life governed by laws. Yet routine personal interactions in public are
regulated by what sociologists term folkways or unwritten norms of
conduct. Here Buon fears she will be judged by her appearance and folkways will be broken, such as "first come, first served." Thus, both Suom
and Buon describe the rule of law in general to explain why racism is
kept at bay in American society.

Two Cambodians in Rochester specifically cite affirmative action
when I asked about their views of equality versus racism in the United
States. Phen works in a hospital and is impressed by its employment
policies, stating: "I believe strongly that Cambodians, whites, blacks
have the same opportunity. It depends on the individual's personality."
Rebecca shares Phen's impression that there is a system in place to
reduce racism's impact. On the survey she listed "more opportunity to
survive and educate myself" as the best qualities of the United States,
but did not list any form of racism among the worst qualities. I asked
Rebecca, "Do you think that people who aren't white have less opportunity?" She answered, "In Rochester most people try to be more fair to
minorities, people of color. They create a lot of programs to help, to
make some opportunity with schools, grants. The Mayo Clinic creates
that with equal opportunity."

Like other Cambodians, Rebecca believes that policy triumphs over
prejudice and cites affirmative action as an example. Sokorn, a blue-
collar worker in Chicago, is also impressed by workplace regulations,
such as workers' compensation. He stated on the survey, "I like the U.S.
laws," as well as "We can have what we want as long as we work for it."
He did not list any form of racism among the negative aspects of life in
the United States. In the follow-up interview Sokorn explained how his

perception of American law shapes his response to the American dilemma:

> When I came here I felt close to the U.S. rules. Rules about the government. If I lose my job I will get unemployment money. Rules that if bad people steal the police will take care of them. If you own a store you pay taxes to the government to support the rules [his wife runs a video-rental business].

> Author: But some people say the good things in the U.S. are easier to get if you are white. If you are black or Asian then you have a harder time getting these good things.

> Sokorn: Sometimes the laws don't protect. But if you get a [legal] job, the type of job where you pay taxes, then the laws protect you. If you work for cash and don't pay taxes then you don't get protection. If you pay taxes then you get the benefits, like money if you are laid off and retirement when you are old.

Phen, Rebecca, and Sokorn clearly believe that democracy, civil rights, and the rule of law create far more opportunities than are lost to racism. They focus on government protection to resolve the American dilemma, whereas the Hmong tend to focus on education as the reason why racism is not an insurmountable problem for them.

"In Laos Only Rich People Could Go to School"

The isolation of the Hmong in the highlands of Laos meant that they had a degree of political autonomy at the local level. Government for the Hmong in Laos rarely amounted to more than a village chief or clan leader who handled disputes among villagers numbering only about two hundred (although military decisions became increasingly centralized following U.S. intervention). Resettlement in the United States thus requires the Hmong to adjust to an extraordinarily intrusive state that regulates many aspects of everyday life.

A number of Hmong survey respondents feel that government regulations are one of the worst things about life in the United States. Some cite the fiscal power of government. One Hmong woman in Milwaukee states, "You are not always free for everything. You always pay taxes each year for the things you own." Others cite the legal power of government to intervene in family life. A Hmong man in Milwaukee states that one of the worst things about the United States is that there are "so many laws protecting children. So much freedom for children. Children have no respect for parents. Parents cannot discipline children." A Hmong man in Eau Claire provides an eloquent summary of Sucheng

Chan's classic 1994 book, *Hmong Means Free:* "In Laos some of the best things are that we live in harmony in the mountains. We were under no control or under any law. We can hunt as many animals as we want. We never have any bills. We never experience crime, violence, and gangs. We work hard physically but we don't have emotional and psychological problems."

As these quotations suggest, many Hmong believe that their village democracy in Laos provided greater independence than does the centralized democratic state in the United States. As a result, the Hmong are less likely than Cambodians to perceive freedom as one of the best things about American society. What does impress them much more than Cambodians are the educational opportunities in the United States, particularly for children but also for young adults.

The Hmong in Laos did not have a written form of their language until the 1950s and usually they lacked access to schools. According to Yang Dao (Yang 1975/1993, 83), "Traditional Hmong society is marked by the notable absence of any formal educational system, which explains its very low level of education. The illiteracy rate is, even today [1969 to 1970], estimated at more than 99 percent in certain mountain regions of Laos." By 1960 there were only one hundred village schools in areas where the Hmong lived. In Cambodia, however, by the 1950s the country had a public educational system comprising almost 1,500 schools attended by more than 300,000 students (Steinberg 1959). Most male youths gained additional literacy through temporary sojourns in Buddhist temples. As a result, about 60 percent of the Cambodian population attained at least basic literacy. These vast differences in educational opportunities in Laos and Cambodia explain why the 2000 U.S. census found that 45 percent of the Hmong over the age of twenty-five had no formal schooling compared to only 26 percent among Cambodians (Southeast Asian Resource Action Center 2004).

The views of Kelly, a Milwaukee resident, illustrate how homeland conditions influence Hmong perceptions of the American dilemma. On the survey she listed "education" and "equal opportunities" as the best features of this country but did not list any form of racism among the worst. Before broaching the issue of racism, I decided I should learn more about her list of positive attributes:

Author: What did you mean by equal opportunity as one of the best things in the United States, as compared to Laos?

Kelly: There is equal opportunity here. There are schools out there. There is no limitation to certain people only. That's a big opportunity. In Laos only rich people could go to school. The poor could not afford it. Here the government has grants. Everyone has the opportunity to pursue an education.

Author: Do you think there is more opportunity for whites?

Kelly: I went to school, the opportunity is there. I don't feel whites have more opportunity than others. If parents make more money then their children have to pay more tuition. If parents don't make so much then the children can get grants. I don't feel whites get more grants. I personally know some of their parents. They are doctors, professors. They have to pay.

Kelly resolves the American dilemma by citing her own educational achievement (a B.A. degree) and government policy to promote equal access to higher education. Sy, another Milwaukee resident, is also extremely impressed with the educational opportunities available to the Hmong. He stated on the survey that "the best thing about life in the United States was when I went to receive my B.A. in school." When I asked him whether prejudice and discrimination diminished opportunities for the Hmong, he answered:

For education, that barrier, I don't see much [prejudice and discrimination]. That depends on individual talent. But in Laos education was very limited. You had to have a good relationship with the clan leader to get a job. In Laos you didn't have to have an education to own a farm. You already had the freedom to own a farm, you didn't need an education to do that. Everyone has freedom there to do what they want. It's similar to this country. But in this country more depends on education. We do have freedom within this country, but freedom is based on your education, based on your behavior and if you follow the rules. Actually, my children say, "This is freedom country." I say, "It's not freedom." If there is a red light you have to stop for that light. But in Laos we have no red lights. This country has freedom but only if you follow the rules. If you talk about freedom, there's not as much as in Laos. If there really was [complete] freedom then you wouldn't have red lights.

Sy's extraordinary insights into the American dilemma emphasize the values of individualism and meritocracy that are prized by the American civic culture. Ironically, like other Hmong, he also perceives the plethora of government rules (traffic lights in his analogy) as reducing freedom. Individualism is most actualized, according to Sy, through the greater educational opportunities in the United States compared to those in Laos. In fact, he thinks the Hmong benefit when they selectively assimilate the value of individualism since he perceives opportunity in Laos as largely determined by the powerful group norms of Hmong clans. But in the United States clans have far less power to distribute resources, although the Hmong still value clans as a form of kinship.

Younger Hmong are also enthusiastic about the educational opportunities offered by American society. Yer, a college student in Milwaukee, focuses on the different generations of Hmong in the United States to explain how education creates opportunities that largely negate the effect of racism. Among the best features of life in the United States he cites "more opportunities to better one's self and one's family." He did not list any form of racism among the worst features. When I ask him if prejudice and discrimination limited opportunities for the Hmong he responds:

> With the older generation that's a problem. Cultural differences, language barrier. They have a different view. With us it's not so much a problem. Just work at it. Other than biases against us it's not much of a problem.
>
> Author: The biases don't limit opportunity?
>
> Yer: Maybe hinder, but if you work hard that won't come into play. It's the older generation that doesn't have as much opportunity.
>
> Author: So the biases aren't strong enough to limit opportunity for younger Hmong?
>
> Yer: If you really want to better yourself that's more a motivation to strive. That's my motivation to better myself, my family, and my culture.

Yer clearly values the educational component of the American civic culture and believes that schools, particularly colleges and universities, present opportunities to youths regardless of race. His optimistic view of the achievements of younger Hmong, and Kelly's and Sy's favorable views of American schools, explain why the Hmong believe education resolves the American dilemma between opportunity and racism.

Conclusion

The ethnic-origins hypothesis does not accurately predict perceptions of societal racism among Cambodians and the Hmong. Both groups tend to emphasize the positive aspects of the American civic culture far more than social problems, and their concerns about racism are primarily the result of urban locale, and not their ethnicity. The Cambodians in Rochester and the Hmong in Eau Claire report all of the varieties of face-to-face discrimination by whites that have been documented for contemporary African Americans. In some respects the refugees' exposure to small-town hate is even more dire than the experiences of blacks in large cities. Cambodians and the Hmong are targets for antipathy not only because of their race but also because they are comparatively recent arrivals who attract nativist impulses. The prevalence of "everyday racism" in small cities with no prior experience of daily contact between minority and dominant groups suggests that the American dilemma will always exist at the micro-level.

A very different conclusion is warranted when considering what the refugees think about the American civic culture at the macro-level. Despite experiencing racism, Cambodians and the Hmong still prize political freedom and public education and believe that these institutions facilitate their incorporation into American society. In fact, they appreciate these aspects of the civic culture above material conditions such as higher living standards and even physical safety from political violence. Public policy and popular culture often portray economic opportunity as the feature of the United States most valued by immigrants, but this is one of the most infrequently cited items among those things that Cambodians and the Hmong consider the best. Instead, they are most impressed by the rule of law and the possibility of self-improvement through an accessible educational system.

Thus, at the macro-level, the refugees endorse the American civic culture rather than perceiving an American dilemma like that confronting African Americans. Their views will apparently surprise some policy makers. Among its many recommendations, the U.S. Commission on Immigration Reform (1997, vi) issued a "call for the Americanization of new immigrants, that is, the cultivation of a shared commitment to the American values of liberty, democracy and equal opportunity." Similarly, the chief of the U.S. Office of Citizenship believes that "our nation must ensure that immigrants understand and identify with the constitutional principles that define the term 'American'" (Aguilar 2004, 2). Cambodians and the Hmong do not require this sort of indoctrination; they already endorse these ideals because they intuitively recognize that American society has many positive attributes absent from their homelands.

Yet the refugees' appraisal of the American civic culture is not monolithic. Consistent with the transnational perspective, homeland experiences shape what Cambodians and the Hmong like most about the United States. Because the educational system in Laos was so rudimentary, the Hmong focus on American schools to explain how they will overcome racism. For Cambodians, government protection of political freedom is the way racism is held at bay, a legacy of their experiences with dictatorship and human rights abuses under authoritarian and totalitarian governments. Conversely, some Hmong feel that they have less freedom in the United States than they had in their semi-autonomous villages in the highlands of Laos, where government traditionally meant a single chief.

These differences between how Cambodians and the Hmong evaluate American society result from their homelands' social structures, and thus do not support the ethnic-origins hypothesis: education in Laos and government in Cambodia are institutions rather than ethnic boundaries and identities. Nevertheless, variation between what Cambodians and the Hmong like most about the United States compared to their homeland supports the underlying premise of the ethnic-origins hypothesis derived from the transnational perspective: homeland experiences shape how international migrants adapt to new identities and inequalities in the host society.

= Chapter 10 =

Group Stereotypes

In everyday life, inequality often manifests itself as prejudice, a pre-judging of individuals on the basis of their group membership. Stereotyping is one of the central mechanisms in prejudice (Fiske 1998). People with prejudices have preexisting negative beliefs about particular groups, and they apply these stereotypical generalizations to individuals whom they identify as members of these groups. Coming to terms with group stereotypes is thus an inevitable part of immigrants' racial and ethnic adaptation.

Walter Lippmann (1922/1965) provided one of the first widely accepted definitions of stereotypes, and he emphasized that they are irrational. Lippmann contrasted their origins in our imagination with their reduction via factual learning: "We are told about the world before we see it. We imagine most things before we experience them. And those preconceptions, unless education has made us acutely aware, govern deeply the whole process of perception" (59). Stereotypes can be completely false depictions of groups but they can also be inaccurate exaggerations based on a few real, but rare, events. Social scientists have concluded that prejudiced people ignore evidence refuting stereotypes in order to preserve rigid generalizations about the social world (Allport 1958).

Stereotypes, although false or inaccurate, remain a powerful component of social inequality because people use them to rank one group above another, usually to justify existing inequalities (Bobo and Massagli 2001). For example, whites in Los Angeles have group-specific stereotypes about blacks ("prefer to live off welfare"), Latinos ("speak English poorly") and Asians ("tend to discriminate against others") rather than broad stereotypes about all nonwhites (Bobo and Johnson 2000). The same group-specific stereotypes are prevalent in different regions of the United States, leading Lawrence Bobo and Michael Massagli (2001, 132) to caution "against a view of stereotypes as highly localized and context-specific."

Research on racial and ethnic stereotypes usually seeks to explain why some people endorse them (Bobo and Massagli 2001; Fiske 1998). Much less is known about how the targets of stereotypes react to them. For second-generation Asian Americans, anti-Asian stereotypes lead to feelings of vulnerability and displays of hyper-Americanism in order to disassociate themselves from recent immigrants whose "foreignness" is often the raw material for these stereotypes (Kibria 2002; Tuan 1998). For those recent immigrants from Asia, learning about the existence of anti-Asian stereotypes is part of their racial and ethnic adaptation. Most Cambodians and Hmong in the Midwest know that some Americans think they eat dogs, lack a work ethic, and don't belong here because they are foreign-born. Two videographers, Kati Johnston and Taggart Siegel, in their extraordinary film *Blue Collar and Buddha* (1987), captured on film groups of whites in Rockford, Illinois, expressing these views. Surprisingly, the refugees exhibit a wide range of emotional reactions to these blatantly offensive stereotypes. Some feel angry while others do not. Their different ethnic origins, and to a lessor degree the different places where they live, explain this variation.

Responses to Stereotypes

Cambodian and Hmong survey respondents rated their reactions to three stereotypes: "An American who thinks Cambodians/the Hmong eat dogs"; "An American who thinks Cambodians/the Hmong don't want to work"; and "An American who thinks Cambodians/the Hmong should go back to Cambodia/Laos." On a scale of 0 (not bothered) to 10 (extremely angry), all the numbers were chosen—and 10 percent of respondents picked all 10s. Twenty-two percent, however, selected a score of 0 for at least one of the three stereotypes. The refugees' perceptions of anti-Asian stereotypes are clearly very nuanced and also vary by ethnicity and place of settlement in the United States (see table 10.1).

Table 10.1   Sensitivity to Anti-Asian Stereotypes, by Ethnicity and City, on a Scale of 0 (Not Bothered) to 10 (Extremely Angry)

	Hmong		Cambodians	
	Eau Claire	Milwaukee	Rochester	Chicago
"Eat dogs"	6.5[a]	6.0	6.1	4.7
"Should go back"	7.0	7.8[a]	7.1[a]	5.6
"Don't want to work"	8.9[a,b]	8.5[a,b]	7.0	6.3
Mean score*	22.4[a]	22.3[a]	20.2[a]	16.6

Source: Author's compilation.
Note: N = 48 in Eau Claire, 49 in Rochester, 32 in Milwaukee, and 50 in Chicago.
*Scores range from 0 to 30 representing the sum of responses to all three stereotypes.
[a]Significantly higher than Cambodians in Chicago (p < .05 or less).
[b]Significantly higher than Cambodians in Rochester (p < .01).

When the scores for all three stereotypes are combined, the Hmong in Milwaukee have a significantly stronger reaction than do Cambodians in Chicago (p < .001). Similarly, Cambodians in Rochester have a stronger reaction than their compatriots in Chicago (p < .05). Thus, the refugees' sensitivity to anti-Asian stereotypes appears to be correlated with both their ethnicity and where they live.

Sociologists will generally not accept a correlation between two variables, such as ethnicity or city size and sensitivity to stereotypes, without first checking for the effect of other variables. For example, perhaps this correlation could really be the result of the fact that the Hmong in my sample have more years of U.S. education than Cambodians or of Cambodians in Rochester reporting greater proficiency in English than those in Chicago (see appendix A). If these differences strongly influence respondents' attitudes then sociologists would call the initial relationship between ethnicity, city size, and sensitivity to stereotypes a misleading or spurious correlation.

Many sociologists use a statistical technique called multiple-regression analysis to resolve such questions. This technique can determine whether it is still reasonable to conclude that two variables are correlated with each other after having taken into account or controlled for the influence of other variables. What variables should be controlled for in analyzing the relationship between ethnicity, city, and sensitivity to anti-Asian stereotypes? Sociologists know that being male or female is one of the most significant determinants of a person's social experiences and thus must be controlled for. Other variables are suggested by theories about immigrants' racial and ethnic adaptation.

According to ethnic-competition theory, immigrants with higher socioeconomic status compete most directly with natives and thus should be more sensitive to stereotypes. Years of U.S. education is a good measure of socioeconomic status. It also takes into account length of U.S. residence (refugees can't have many years of U.S. education if they have just arrived) and age (younger refugees have more U.S. education than their seniors). Years of U.S. education is also strongly correlated with higher incomes among the refugees (r = .32; p < .001). Thus Hmong and Cambodians with many years of U.S. education are exactly the type of immigrants that ethnic competition theory predicts will know the most about American society and will interact and compete the most with natives. They are younger, have lived in the country for a considerable period of time, have learned about the United States in schools, and have higher incomes.

Assimilation theory offers a different explanation for how immigrants adapt to American race and ethnic relations. According to this perspective, immigrants who are socially and culturally integrated into a host society should be less sensitive to stereotypes because they feel accepted. Having become a U.S. citizen (rather than remaining a permanent resident) and identifying as a Christian (rather than with a homeland religion) are good indicators of the refugees' assimilation.

Even when controlling for variables suggested by ethnic competition and assimilation theory, a multiple-regression analysis confirms the important ethnic and urban differences in the refugees' reactions to stereotypes (see table 10.2). Living in a big city reduces anger at anti-Asian stereotypes, whereas living in a small city increases their offensiveness. But the most powerful variable explaining why some respondents are less upset by stereotypes and others are very upset is being Cambodian or Hmong. Another interesting finding is that refugees who have become U.S. citizens are more offended by the prejudice shown by natives than those who have not, the opposite of the pattern predicted by assimilation theory.

An even more precise way of statistically verifying the relationships among variables is to check for interaction effects, which means combining two related independent variables into one. Since the Hmong in both big and small cities have views of stereotypes much like those of Cambodians in a small city, it is logical to disaggregate Cambodians in a big city into a single variable. Thus, the variable "big city × Cambodian" compares the Cambodians in Chicago with all others (see table 10.3).

This analysis confirms that Cambodians in Chicago are much less angry about anti-Asian stereotypes even when taking into account other factors such as years of U.S. education and having become a U.S. citizen.

Table 10.2   Standardized OLS Coefficients for Regression of Stereotype-Sensitivity Score on Ethnicity, City, and Other Variables

	Model 1	Model 2	Model 3	Model 4
Years of U.S. education	.12			.05
Christian		.02		−.08
U.S. citizen		.16*		.17*
Female				.12
Big city			−.16*	−.13
Cambodian				−.23**
R^2	.01	.03	.02	.12**

Source: Author's compilation.
Note: N = 179
* $p < .05$; ** $p < .01$

Table 10.3   Standardized OLS Coefficients for Regression of Stereotype-Sensitivity Score on Interaction of City and Ethnicity

	Model 1	Model 2
Years of U.S. education		.07
Christian		−.10
U.S. citizen		.14
Female		.11
Big city × Cambodian	−.28*	−.27*
R²	.08*	.11*

Source: Author's compilation.
Note: N = 179
* p < .001

Ironically, a separate analysis reveals that those Cambodians who identify themselves as Christian have almost identical responses to stereotypes as those who identify as Buddhist, a testament to the enduring influence of Buddhism in Cambodians' ethnic origins even after conversion. Whatever new religious name Cambodians give themselves, their ethnic origins continue to minimize angry responses to stereotypes, particularly when they live in a diverse urban pecking order.

Multiple-regression analysis is a sophisticated statistical technique that can tell us with a high degree of confidence that Cambodians living in a big city are much less upset by anti-Asian stereotypes than are the Hmong in both big and small cities and Cambodians in small cities. But the technique cannot explain why the Hmong have very similar views of prejudice regardless of where they live whereas Cambodians vary when they live in a big or small city. Qualitative data are needed to answer that question. When I conducted follow-up interviews I asked informants to explain why they picked particular numbers to represent their reactions to stereotypes about their food, work ethic, and nativity.

"All the Hmong Suffer"

In Milwaukee, Sy explained how he carefully evaluated different forms of native prejudice rather than just dismissing them all. Asked what he thought about while picking numbers on the 0-to-10 scale, Sy answered:

> I do have a friend who said, "Hmong people eat dogs." I responded, "Not me! Some people may say yes. What others say I don't know." So when I picked that it was not for the Hmong as a group, it was for myself. So I have not eaten dogs. But when I picked a few of the other numbers like

[for the question on] "the Hmong don't want to work" . . . I don't believe that. Most Hmong do want to work. They don't want to stay on welfare. But because the Hmong are still in a low or poverty level we do need welfare assistance from the state and federal level.

In this statement Sy reveals how different anti-Asian stereotypes trigger different emotional responses. He uses the personal pronoun "me" as the basis for his response to the dog eating stereotype but uses the collective pronoun "we" to talk about the work stereotype. Sy is less angered by the dog-eating stereotype because he has a more personal response ("Not me!"). He even explains that this reaction "was not for the Hmong as a group, it was for myself." He then shifts to a collective perspective to explain why he is much more offended by the work stereotype and states, "Most Hmong do want to work."

This distinction between individualized and collective perceptions of prejudice explains why the Hmong in both big and small cities have very similar emotional reactions to anti-Asian stereotypes. The Hmong tend to interpret experiences with inequality through the lens of their ethnic group rather than thinking of such incidents as isolated, personal tragedies. Teng, in Eau Claire, illustrates the profoundly collective view that the Hmong have of stereotypes. Like Sy he was deeply offended by the work stereotype, which he ranked a 9 on the scale. When I asked Teng why that stereotype angered him the most his answer took the form of a macro-level economic analysis of Hmong adaptation patterns:

About that one on work, mostly they [Americans] don't know my culture, parents. I think their parents, grandparents are similar. They used to be like us [immigrants]. We have a lot of kids because we are a different culture. We came to the United States but still use our own culture. Not so much the young, the young are changing. But people who came older than twenty or thirty years old, they don't have a good education, can't write and read, so they are not working. They think that the amount of money they would make from working and from the government helping their family is similar. They think if they work they will have to ask their brother to take care of their kids. They are not lazy. In my culture, in Laos, everyone worked, there was no welfare. Twenty-, fifteen-, ten-year-old kids worked. When that family comes to the United States, the middle-aged and older people, they cannot change. They still are like farmers, like the culture in Laos.

The remarkable feature of Teng's statement is its total focus on the Hmong as an ethnic group and the complete absence of any expression of his own feelings or experiences. Chou, another Eau Claire resident, provides a similar example of the way Hmong informants refer to their ethnic group to explain their reactions to stereotypes. She ranked her response to all three stereotypes as 10s, one of only seventeen survey respondents to do so. In the follow-up interview Chou asked her eighteen-year-old daughter to interpret for her, even though Chou is proficient in English, because she finds making even minor grammatical mistakes embarrassing. When I asked Chou why she picked 10s for all three stereo-types the following exchange occurred:

> Mother [as interpreted by daughter]: I'm very angry if they say that.
>
> Daughter [interjecting her own response]: Those are narrow-minded people. It bothers me, they don't know but they choose to say like that. They don't want to change. They're ignorant and don't want to change, be more open.
>
> Author: None bother you more than the others?
>
> Mother [as interpreted by daughter]: The ones that really bother me the most are go back and don't want to work. They don't appreciate why we came here, all the hardships in living. We should be able to live without that harassment. The great majority of Hmong work but they don't see that, all they think about are the ones on welfare. But we pay taxes just like white people but they refuse to see that.

Chou's use of the pronouns "we" and "they" seven times in her last statement indicates that she is drawing upon a polarized conception of groups when reacting to stereotypes.

Another way Hmong informants in both big and small cities express a collective interpretation of prejudice is by citing the experiences of Hmong people they know. Even when Cambodian informants refer to their ethnic group to explain their reactions to stereotypes they rarely discuss specific individuals other than themselves. Hmong informants, however, are much more likely to do that, particularly using close kin as examples to refute a stereotype. In Milwaukee, Ka is deeply offended by the work stereotype and explains her feelings by discussing the situations of other Hmong:

> Well for the Hmong it's not like they don't want to work, but old people got involved in the war, the Vietnam War. It affected them. Some [natives] say, "They only want food stamps." But my mom was old when she got here so it doesn't mean they don't want to work, they just can't. But when they do work they work the best to try to make Americans happy. They don't feel lazy.

Close kin are also the focus of You's explanation for why she is angered by the "don't want to work" stereotype. A resident of Eau Claire, she commented during the follow-up interview: "We want to work, like my parents, grandfather, grandmother. They don't speak English or drive a car so it's hard for them to work." I then asked her why the other two stereotypes (which she ranked an 8 and a 10) seemed to bother her about as much. You immediately answered:

They bother me because we don't want other people to think we are lazy. If a friend says that to you, you will think that even though you don't know me. You will take his word and think [she is] lazy even though you don't know me. You just heard that from him. So it goes around. Lazy. Don't want to work. They don't know so they think we are lazy. But most Hmong work and go to school.

You's strong kinship ties amplify the offensive content of the work stereotype since she interprets it not just in relation to herself but for significant others in her social network. She also invokes the Hmong as an ethnic group and is concerned about the stereotype's impact on her community ("We don't want other people to think we are lazy"). Indeed, You has such a collective perspective of these stereotypes that she also examines them from the point of view of the out-group. She addresses me directly and takes my point of view as a native-born European American in order to show how friendship networks can transmit stereotypes ("So it goes around").

In Milwaukee, Kelly provides a final and even more compelling illustration of how the Hmong respond to stereotypes by weaving together their personal feelings, the relevance of the stereotype for close kin, and its impact on the Hmong community as a whole. She is equally offended by all three stereotypes (she ranked all three as 10s), and her explanation for these reactions focuses on other Hmong. I began by asking about her reactions to "an American who thinks the Hmong don't want to work":

Kelly: Don't want to work?! Before I worked with a Hmong lady who had five or six children. People our age do not have that problem. But those Hmong ladies and men who are older, they have that problem. I took one to social services and they said that to my face.

Author: Who said that?

Kelly: An African American and a white receptionist. I translated that. It was very negative. They [older Hmong] want to work but they don't have a driver's license, they have young children. How can they work with no license, no baby-sitter? If the government wants them to work it should provide a baby-sitter. I'm very bothered by that. Many Hmong families cry. I feel bad whenever that happens.

Author [pointing to questionnaire]: Do you feel the same way about the statement "The Hmong should go back to Laos"?

Kelly: It bothers me. Hmong people were not willing to come to this country, they came by force, not the opportunity for school. Now there is no public assistance [due to recent changes in eligibility standards], so all the Hmong suffer. I feel so bad.

Kelly's poignant statement "All the Hmong suffer. I feel so bad" clearly expresses how Hmong informants link their own feelings about a stereotype to its effects for other Hmong. Cambodian informants, however, tend to have more individualistic interpretations and thus their social environment has a bigger influence on their emotional responses to anti-Asian stereotypes than the Hmong.

"People Like That, They Look Down on Me"

In Chicago, Sokorn illustrates the personal response to stereotypes typical of Cambodians. He ranked from 5 to 10 the items describing Americans who believe negative things about Cambodians. I asked Sokorn what he was thinking about when he chose these numbers:

Sokorn: I don't want to talk to people like that. If I do I will just get into a fight. People who talk like that think crazy.

Author: So what was the reason you put down a ten for one of these but a five for this other one?

Sokorn: Because I'm angry. People like that, they look down on me. They think I came here to take their job. But the government brought me here because of the war. I came with a passport, I got here by the rule.

Sokorn's remarks focus exclusively on his emotional response to prejudiced natives and he frequently uses the pronouns "I" and "me." In sharp contrast to Hmong informants, Sokorn makes no reference to members of his ethnic group to explain his feelings about anti-Asian stereotypes.

The difference between the collective-oriented views of the Hmong and the individual-oriented views of Cambodians is one of degree rather than opposites. Some Cambodian informants do express their reactions to stereotypes in ways that are indistinguishable from those of the Hmong. In Chicago, Buon was extremely angered by all three stereotypes, which she ranked 9 and 10. During the follow-up interview I asked why, and she exploded, emotionally and verbally: "They should not say those words! It offends us. Not all eat dog. Not all are lazy. I work hard. They look down on us. Is it just Cambodians who are like that? There are a lot of bad Americans, too, who don't work."

The collective sentiments in Buon's remarks are obvious. They reveal that the responses of Cambodians and the Hmong to native prejudice do overlap a continuum from collective- to individual-orientations. Nonetheless, it is Cambodians who overwhelmingly occupy the individual end. Heng, another Chicago resident, is a good example of Cambodians' highly personalized reactions to anti-Asian stereotypes, particularly when they live in a big city. He ranked the examples of negative stereotypes with two 0s and a 5. I asked Heng why he chose these numbers:

Heng: If you judge me, why should I jump back, fight back? Why should I judge others? Why should I care about other people? It just stresses out yourself. If you say Cambodians eat dogs, that's okay. It's not true. If you say Cambodians don't want to work, maybe, maybe not. There are different types of people in the world. In the refugee camp I knew one guy. All he did was drink [alcohol]. There are rich people and poor people. There are a lot of types of people.

Author: Is "angry" the right word to describe your feelings about negative things some Americans think?

Heng: You should not get angry. Think good things even if they hate you. Think why they do that.

Among the many fascinating features of Heng's comments is the total absence of any reference to his ethnic group. Instead he focuses exclusively on his own emotions and state of mind. Although Heng is an extreme example of how Buddhist values create a personalized response to suffering, the views of other Cambodian informants are much closer to his than to Buon's.

In Rochester, Carl's explanation for why he is deeply offended by the work stereotype (which he ranked 10) reveals what can happen when Cambodians live in a small city. When I asked him why that stereotype angered him, he stated, "That's preposterous. It just gets you upset. It's not true." In responding to a follow-up question, however, Carl discloses an additional basis for his attitude:

Author: Okay, but there could be many reasons why it makes you angry.

Carl: It just identifies you. It comes back to race, puts you in that category. "Cambodians don't want to work." Maybe that's true for some, but everybody wants to better themselves and get educated. So if they know you are Cambodian then people will identify you with comments they are making. I mean, just that comment, it's just a stereotype and people who hear comments like this from the media assume you are like that too.

Carl is clearly concerned with the lack of factual accuracy of the "lazy" stereotype, wavering between rejecting it entirely for that reason ("It's not true") and admitting that it may be "true for some." But in response to my follow-up question Carl reveals a second approach to evaluating the offensiveness of a stereotype: its consequences. He emphasizes that the work stereotype has the potential to cause him harm ("People . . . assume you are like that"). In fact, Carl goes so far as to state that it "puts you in that category," a way of indicating how in small cities ethnic boundaries can become more polarized for Cambodians. But like Cambodians in Chicago, Carl uses the personal pronoun "you" rather than "we."

Contrast Carl's views with that of Nao, a Hmong resident of Eau Claire with whom he shares many social characteristics. Both are single males in their early twenties who arrived in the United States less than ten years old and are now college graduates. On the survey Nao ranked the dog stereotype with a 0 but picked 10 to indicate his intense anger at the doesn't-work stereotype. In the follow-up interview I asked him why he had such different reactions:

That one about dogs, that's not much offensive, a little bit negative. We are human beings and eat normal food. It bothers me but it's [speech] like freedom of the press. These two questions [work and go back], they're different, they bother me [he says "bother" slowly to accentuate the negativity]. It's a first impression. It's just like Caucasians, they just picture us one way and it affects the whole community. That bothers me big time. They're uneducated. They don't put it on the table and see if it's true. Maybe some of us are creative, maybe they could learn from our community.

Nao's explanation for his strong reactions to the work and nativist stereotypes is completely different from Carl's. Nao states that stereotypes "affect the Hmong community." His use of the collective pronoun "us" and reference to "our community" clearly differs from the more individualistic perception of Carl and other Cambodians.

Conclusion

Ethnic origins strongly influence perceptions of anti-Asian stereotypes among Southeast Asian refugees in the Midwest. In both Eau Claire and Milwaukee the Hmong refer to their community to contextualize the meaning of native prejudice. They often use the pronoun "we" when discussing why a stereotype is offensive and describe how other Hmong are affected by it. Linking personal experiences with the fate of the ethnic group as whole amplifies angry reactions to stereotypes. This collective perspective stems from the Hmong's hermetic ethnic boundary and their polarized conception of group identities. In both Rochester and Chicago, however, Cambodians' ethnic origins foster an individualistic perception of American prejudices. Their reactions are more personal and psychological and rarely include a consideration of how the stereotype affects other Cambodians. All immigrants experience a process of resocialization as they confront inequalities in the United States, but historical, political, and cultural experiences in their homelands shape how they adapt to social problems such as stereotypes.

In addition, Cambodians' perceptions of prejudice are also shaped by where they live—in a big urban center with a pecking order or in a provincial city where they experience small-town hate. Those who reside in a small city feel greater anger than those residing in a big city. This finding is an important reminder that ethnic origins do not predetermine immigrants' racial and ethnic adaptation but form the basis from which they interact with their new social environment. Cambodians arrive in this country already thinking of group boundaries as porous and group identities as liminal; the diversity in Chicago confirms this worldview. Although some African Americans and Hispanic Americans do express prejudice toward Cambodians in Chicago, a diverse social environment provides a buffer for the refugees.

The same prejudices are deemed more offensive when expressed by whites in small cities, where the refugees perennially feel like foreigners. Although the content of group-specific stereotypes reflects national history and macro-level hierarchies (Bobo and Massagli 2001), local context can influence emotional responses by members of target groups to being stigmatized. And localized stereotypes do exist. Whites generally do not think Asians as a whole prefer welfare to being self-supporting (Bobo and Massagli 2001), but in the Midwest this is a common belief about Southeast Asian refugees.

The variation between Cambodians' and the Hmong's perceptions of anti-Asian stereotypes supports the ethnic-origins hypothesis, but in one respect the two groups are similar. Since the 1920s social scientists have considered stereotypes to be an expression of irrational thinking. But Cambodians and the Hmong do not react irrationally; instead they respond to anti-Asian stereotypes in a highly logical and reasoned manner. Most of them carefully evaluate the implications of each stereotype on the basis of their personal experiences and often that of other members of their ethnic group. Very few Cambodians and Hmong have identical reactions to stereotypes about their food, work ethic, and right to reside in the United States. Two percent of my sample of 179 respondents report that they are completely unperturbed by the stereotypes; 10 percent state that all three stereotypes make them feel extremely angry; and the remaining 88 percent of respondents have more complex responses and usually consider the stereotype that they prefer public assistance to work more offensive than the stereotype that they eat dogs. For most Cambodians and Hmong, racial and ethnic adaptation involves a thoughtful assessment of natives' prejudices toward immigrants rather than a simple rejection of them.

= Chapter 11 =

Institutional Discrimination

Racial and ethnic stereotypes are among the vilest manifestations of social inequality, but the actual deprivation of rights results from discrimination, which means unequal treatment. Discrimination often involves the abuse of power by individuals whose positions in institutions enable them to make decisions that harm other people (Jones 1997). One of the most central aspects of immigrants' racial and ethnic adaptation to American society is recognizing the existence of such institutional discrimination in the United States.

Immigrants' perceptions of discrimination in a host society are usually explained by examining events that occur after their arrival. Ethnic-competition theory posits that awareness of inequality increases among immigrants as they adapt to a new society and have more contact and rivalry with a dominant group. There is substantial empirical support for this theory. With some exceptions (Aguirre, Saenz, and Hwang 1989; Hwang and Murdock 1991; Stepick et al. 2001), research on immigrants' perceptions of discrimination demonstrates that those with higher socio-economic status report the most discrimination (Floyd and Gramman 1995; Itzigsohn, Giorguli, and Vazquez 2005; Kasinitz, Battle, and Miyares 2001; Kuo 1995; Portes 1984; Portes and Bach 1985; Portes and McLeod 1996; Roberts 1988). Rather than feeling more accepted because of their educational and occupational achievements in the United States, these immigrants face more rejection as they start to compete directly with natives.

In ethnic-competition theory, however, ethnicity is seen largely as an outcome of material conditions in the host society. Using theories of intergroup behavior, psychologists have shown that individuals who strongly identify with a racial or ethnic minority group perceive more discrimination than those with weaker identification (Operario and Fiske 2001; Sellers and Shelton 2003). The ethnic-origins hypothesis, therefore, predicts that immigrant groups that develop a hermetic ethnic boundary and polarized identity in their homeland will perceive more institutional discrimination in a host society than will groups that arrive with a porous ethnic boundary and a liminal identity. Among

Cambodians and the Hmong in the Midwest there are numerous discriminatory experiences to examine in order to evaluate this claim.

Generalizations About Institutional Discrimination

Cambodians and the Hmong have very precise assessments of how much institutional discrimination their ethnic groups are likely to encounter. They reported their perceptions of institutional discrimination by ranking, on a scale of 0 to 10, the frequency of discrimination against Cambodians or the Hmong in vignettes involving an American employer, landlord, and police officer (among the refugees the name American means natives of the United States). The question on employment in the survey read: "If a Cambodian/Hmong person applied for ten jobs at ten different businesses run by Americans, and he or she was qualified to do the jobs, about how many times out of ten would the Hmong person not be hired because the Americans think the Hmong are not good workers?" The question on housing read: "If a Cambodian/ Hmong family called to rent an apartment from ten different American landlords, about how many times out of ten would the landlords say the apartment is not vacant because they do not want to rent to a Cambodian/ Hmong family?" The question on law enforcement read: "If ten different Cambodian/Hmong drivers got into a small car accident with American drivers, about how many times out of ten would the American police officer believe what the American driver said and not the Cambodian/ Hmong driver?" Respondents picked every number on the scale of 0 (never) to 10 (always) for all three items (although five individuals did not answer one or two questions).

What can account for respondents' perceptions that institutional discrimination is rare or common for their ethnic group? Ethnic origins and urban locale are two important explanations (see table 11.1). Regardless of where they live, the Hmong perceive more discrimination on the part of employers, landlords, and the police than do Cambodians (Sizemore and Milner [2004] also found ethnic variation in perceptions of discrimination among Hispanics). In addition, the Hmong who experience small-town hate conclude that institutional discrimination occurs more frequently than do their compatriots who live in a large city. This difference is not apparent for Cambodians: those in Chicago and Rochester have very similar views concerning how often members of their ethnic group are treated unfairly by authorities with decision-making power.

It is important to examine other variables before concluding that ethnic origins and type of urban locale shape immigrants' generalizations about the probability of institutional discrimination. What else could

Table 11.1   Perceived Prevalence of Institutional Discrimination, by
Ethnicity and City, on a Scale of 0 (Never) to 10 (Always)

	Hmong		Cambodians	
	Eau Claire	Milwaukee	Rochester	Chicago
By employers	7.2[a]	4.8	4.0	4.0
By landlords	7.0[a]	4.4	4.0	2.8
By police	6.5[b]	6.5[b]	4.3	3.9
Mean score*	20.7[a]	15.7[b]	12.3	10.7

Source: Author's compilation.
Note: N = 48 in Eau Claire, 48 in Rochester, 29 in Milwaukee, and 49 in Chicago
*Scores range from 0 to 30 representing the sum of responses to all three types of institutional discrimination.
[a]Significantly higher than Hmong in Milwaukee and Cambodians in Rochester and Chicago (p < .001).
[b]Significantly higher than Cambodians in Rochester and Chicago (p < .01 or less).

differentiate the respondents who, for example, think that employers would never or almost never mistreat members of their ethnic group from those who think that discrimination would always or almost always occur? An obvious explanation is having personally experienced some form of institutional discrimination and survey respondents were asked whether this had ever happened to them. In addition, ethnic-competition theory predicts that discrimination-prevalence scores will be higher among refugees with higher socioeconomic status. Years of U.S. education is a good measure of the refugees' socioeconomic status, since it is strongly correlated with their income ($r = .32$, $p < .001$) and especially employment in laborer, production, service, technical service, or professional jobs ($r = .63$, $p < .001$). Assimilation theory predicts that scores will be lower among refugees who have become U.S. citizens (rather than remain permanent residents) and have converted to Christianity (rather than retain their traditional religion). Multiple-regression analysis can determine the influence of each of these variables when holding constant the others (see table 11.2).

Consistent with other research on perceived group discrimination (Kleugel and Bobo 2001; Sizemore and Milner 2004), the Cambodians and the Hmong who report having experienced some type of institutional discrimination are much more likely to conclude that their ethnic group faces a high level of unfair treatment. Similarly, the more years of U.S. education the refugees have achieved the greater the prevalence of institutional discrimination they believe occurs (Kleugel and Bobo [2001] found the same pattern among Asians in Los Angeles). When other

Table 11.2   Standardized OLS Coefficients for Regression of Institutional-Discrimination Score on Ethnicity, City, and Other Variables

	Model 1	Model 2	Model 3	Model 4
Discriminated against	.32*			.17*
Years of U.S. education		.20*		.08
Christian			.11	−.07
U.S. citizen			.05	.05
Female				.07
Big city				−.27**
Cambodian				−.45**
R^2	.11**	.04*	.02	.40**

Source: Author's compilation.
Note: N = 174
* $p < .01$; ** $p < .001$

variables are controlled, there is no longer a statistically meaningful correlation between years of U.S. education and perceptions of discrimination because, consistent with ethnic-competition theory, more educated respondents are more likely to report having been discriminated against. In addition, ethnicity and city size strongly influence how the refugees think about unfair treatment even when they have or have not been personally discriminated against by an employer, landlord, or police officer. Cambodians tend to perceive less discrimination than the Hmong, as do refugees living in big cities.

The importance of both ethnicity and city size for the refugees' perceptions of unfair treatment suggests that the effects of homeland history, politics, and culture depend on the social structure in which they now live. An interaction variable is an ideal measure of this possibility, since it combines two related independent variables into one. Cambodians and the Hmong perceive the most discrimination when they live in small cities. The Hmong gave higher estimates than Cambodians for the frequency of institutional discrimination. Therefore, it is reasonable to use the variable "small city × Hmong" to contrast the views of Hmong refugees in Eau Claire with all the other respondents.

Multiple-regression analysis confirms the explanatory power of the interaction variable (see table 11.3). The marginality created by small-town hate greatly increases feelings of being a target for the Hmong because their ethnic origins already conceptualize boundaries as hermetic and identities as polarized. Thus, immigrants' ethnic origins interact with their new social environments during their racial and ethnic

Table 11.3   Standardized OLS Coefficients for Regression of Institutional-Discrimination Score on Interaction of City and Ethnicity

	Model 1	Model 2
Discriminated against		.19*
Years of U.S. education		.11
Christian		.01
U.S. citizen		.10
Female		.10
Small city × Hmong	.58**	.54**
R^2	.33**	.41**

Source: Author's compilation.
Note: N = 174
* p < .01; ** p < .001

adaptation. Being Cambodian or Hmong, and living with small-town hate or within the urban pecking order, shapes how these newcomers generalize about the likelihood of experiencing discrimination by employers, landlords, and the police.

Ethnic Origins Filter Institutional Discrimination

During follow-up interviews I asked informants why they chose particular numbers when answering the survey questions and discovered how ethnic origins filter perceptions of institutional discrimination. In fact, before I even began the follow-up interviews I noticed a surprising pattern in how survey respondents answered the question "Have you ever been treated unfairly by an American landlord, employer, or police officer?" Seven Hmong respondents (but no Cambodian respondents) answered no, but then described what they had heard from other members of their ethnic group. Some commented specifically on the experiences of their kin. In Eau Claire a Hmong man stated, "I haven't had any problems yet, but my relatives had an accident. When the police came they only listened to the white person because they can speak and make up a story." Similarly, in Milwaukee a Hmong woman reported that she had never been discriminated against but then added, "My sister had an accident. It was not her fault but the officer gave her a ticket. It happened in Stevens Point [Wisconsin]."

These statements indicate that some Hmong consider the discriminatory experiences of others relevant to a question about their own experiences. Additional evidence of this collective perception comes from Hmong respondents who report on a much wider ethnic social network. A Hmong man in Milwaukee stated, "I have never experienced this personally but I have heard a lot from other people." A Hmong man in Eau Claire said, "I have never had any problem. But I heard a lot from Hmong people about police treating them unfairly and some landlords getting mad at some Hmong people." The follow-up interviews provide even stronger evidence that the Hmong have a more collective view of discrimination than do Cambodians.

In Chicago, Sokorn typifies the individualistic perception of discrimination among Cambodians. I reviewed with him his responses to the survey questions on the likelihood of discrimination—from 0 to 5—and then asked him to explain his choices. Sokorn responded:

> Landlords know about you before they rent to you. They call where you lived before. Some of them think Cambodians are not clean because of one family. They say all Cambodians are like that but that's not fair. I keep my apartment clean. So if they call to find out about me, they say this guy good, clean. Then they will rent to me. It's the same at work. When I was laid off I looked for another job. They [a prospective employer] called my old company. They asked, "Is Mr. Keo a hard worker?" And they said "He's a hard worker." So they hired me right away.

Sokorn believes that there is prejudice against Cambodians. Yet his response emphasizes his own merit as a tenant and worker to explain why he would not suffer discrimination. Sokorn thus distances himself from other Cambodians rather than emphasizing what they have in common or that their experiences could be relevant to him.

In Rochester, Elizabeth also illustrates Cambodians' penchant for personalizing discrimination rather than connecting their experiences to those of other members of the ethnic group. On the survey she reported having been discriminated against when seeking to purchase a trailer home. During the follow-up interview I asked her to elaborate on this incident and she discussed it at length:

> Elizabeth: My husband and I went to deposit two hundred dollars for a trailer. That way we would have one week to decide if we wanted to buy it. So the same day I went back to pick up the receipt because I had left the receipt at the table. Well, [she mimics the actions of the salesman]: "I don't know where the receipt is. If you want the trailer get it. If not you don't get your money back. If you want it back see my lawyer." I was so frustrated, confused. My trust to people here. . . . I was born really trusting. In our culture we never use receipts, just trust, and I carry that over with me. And that's how I learned not to trust. Doctors. Rich people. I don't care. Get a signature, a written piece of paper.

Author: Would you call what happened racism?

Elizabeth: I'm not sure racism. It's more. . . . Maybe he thought I was stupid, that I can't fight back because I didn't have the receipt.

Although the encounter does have a degree of ambiguity, in the context of what social scientists know about race and economic exploitation it would be entirely reasonable for Elizabeth to attribute the unfair treatment she experienced to racial antipathy. But she did not do so. Curious to discover why she instead personalized the problem, I asked Elizabeth to elaborate on what she meant by the statement "I was born really trusting," and she answered:

In our country it's the way we are raised. We never need a receipt, just trust. I'm sure some people do cheat but most of them don't. In Buddhism, something that does not belong to you, it's stealing, it's a sin to take it. When you rip off somebody else. . . . We believe in reincarnation, so in the next life we will owe that other person. We believe that what goes around comes around back to you.

Elizabeth explicitly cites Buddhist values to explain why collective terms such as "racism," "white," and "Asian" do not help her interpret an incident that some would assume to be a blatant example of racial discrimination. Instead, Elizabeth focuses on the individual qualities of her antagonist, such as his greed, and not his race.

Despite Cambodians' tendency to minimize the importance of group differences, small-town hate can lead some Cambodians to recognize the salience of ethnic boundaries. On the survey, Sopot mentioned experiencing unfair treatment and even commented, "If I become an American citizen I know that the Americans will always keep me as an immigrant and treat me the same as they always will." During the follow-up interview I asked her how serious discrimination was in Rochester. She answered, "It depends where you go to school or work. It depends on the crowd of people you are with, who you work with. Some people around here are racist. Some teachers are racist. They won't give you a good grade just because of the fact it's you. Someone might tell the manager on you to get you fired." This injustice had happened to her:

Once, awhile ago, I tried to get some jobs. Because I'm Cambodian, from another culture, I didn't get hired. They said the job was already taken. The next day I went there and saw them giving an interview. I asked [the person giving interviews] why I couldn't get the job. He looked at me strange and walked away.

Sopot's statement is surprisingly strong, given Cambodians' proclivity to disregard group differences. She clearly emphasizes the strength of ethnic boundaries in her remark "I'm Cambodian, from another culture." Thus experiencing small-town hate can change the individualistic worldview that Cambodians arrive with. Yet Sopot still remains reluctant to generalize about groups since she qualifies her assessment of inequality with the phrases "it depends" and "some people."

Unlike Cambodians, the Hmong tend to emphasize group differences as they adapt to racial and ethnic inequality, particularly when they live in a small city. Contrast Sopot's description of her experiences in Rochester with that of Robert's for Eau Claire. Asked whether he thought discrimination would prevent the Hmong from moving ahead he responded:

> For a company that knows the Hmong, Hmong workers, they keep hiring them. They like Hmong people and they have a good relationship. But a company that never hires them has a feeling Hmong people are bad, lazy. They don't like you, hate you, don't want contact. Those companies will discriminate. Prejudice will prevent the Hmong from succeeding [in those companies]. There is prejudice and discrimination but I don't know how much. If you don't know someone you may have a strange feeling. People who don't know you have a stereotype and discriminate. There's discrimination out there but you have to work to make communication. If you break through it goes around like a circle. Hmong people work hard at Hutchinson [Technology] and the boss, supervisor, manager, they will have no prejudice. It will travel to the whole Eau Claire community and companies will like the Hmong to work anywhere.

Robert's views of Asians' employment opportunities in a small city are quite different from Sopot's. He quickly affirms the importance of group differences by acknowledging the prevalence of stereotypes against the Hmong as well as discrimination in the hiring process. Indeed, Robert feels that it is nearly inevitable that people from different racial and ethnic groups would initially look at each other as "strange." His solution to this problem is not only improved communication, which is an individualistic approach. According to Robert, the Hmong need to prove themselves as a group to the "Eau Claire community."

You, another Eau Claire resident, also reveals how the marginalization experienced by the Hmong in a small city exacerbates their feeling that groups are inevitably differentiated by strong ethnic boundaries. When I asked You why she picked particular numbers when answering the survey questions about discrimination she answered:

> I heard a lot from my cousins. They say when they called to rent an apartment they are told it's rented even though it's in the paper. They call again but they are still told it's rented. Maybe they [landlords] say it's rented

because they think, "It's just the Hmong, we don't do that." The Hmong have the feeling that Americans don't want to rent to them. So it hasn't happened to me, just other Hmong. But it would make me feel bad if they would not rent it to me and gave it to other people. My cousins feel bad, it makes them feel bad. They make a joke, "If we ever have apartments to rent and Americans call, we will say 'Already rented.' " They joke like that.

You's discussion of inequality in Eau Claire includes numerous references to groups, such as "my cousins," "the Hmong" and "Americans." Small-town hate accentuates the Hmong's sense of being distinct from other groups and thus intensifies their perceptions of discrimination. Yet even when the Hmong live in a big city, they still have a collective view of inequality. Kelly, a Milwaukee resident, used the phrase "our people" when asked to explain her responses to the survey questions. She began by describing an incident that had happened to another woman:

> One time I invited an officer to speak to the group [a Hmong self-help association]. A lady said [to him], "I had an accident and the police said I'm at fault. But I don't speak English. The officer didn't give the other person a ticket even though he crossed the stop sign." This bothers me. It shouldn't happen to our people. Why didn't that officer call for a translator? Even though you don't speak English you should not be treated unequally.

Kelly then linked this woman's mistreatment with an incident she had experienced. She described what happened once while driving her son to a doctor's appointment:

> I did not watch a sign and went straight when it said turn only. I tried to explain to the police officer but he ignored me and said, "Just because you're in trouble you try to say all those things." I'm telling him the thing I did, not making the thing up to get away. I felt so mad. I wanted to go to court but it was sixty-seven dollars and I thought "That will not make us poor forever." Something like this happens to other Hmong people. I wish I could help so they don't have that problem. Why do they have to suffer?

The strong sense of in-group solidarity so evident in Kelly's statement is largely absent from the remarks of Cambodian informants. Even Cambodians who have personally experienced discrimination rarely connect the incident to the experiences of other members of their ethnic group. Samnang, a Chicago resident, is one of the exceptions. A college senior majoring in business administration, she has already encountered the glass ceiling, the barriers that prevent women and other minorities from receiving promotions in the workplace. Samnang reported:

> I applied for an assistant-manager position where I work. It was narrowed down to ten people. I was interviewed three times but they picked another

candidate. He is white. I asked why and they said they had a strong feeling he would accomplish things quicker, had better communication. How do they know that? They didn't say the real reason because of the laws. They just said he had more variety of experiences. They think I am a minority. The same thing happened to a Cambodian friend. He is a supervisor. They promoted a white guy over him who had only been there a couple of months. Now he is over him. My friend had been there over ten years and moved up only little by little. But this white guy was picked.

Samnang's reference to the discrimination against a compatriot is unusual among Cambodians, who tend to personalize social inequality. Even so, her statement "I am a minority" is revealing since she could have said "Cambodians are a minority." Where the Hmong think of discrimination in its social context, Cambodians minimize the relevance of group differences even when directly confronted by unequal treatment.

Conclusion

Ethnic origins profoundly influence how Cambodians and the Hmong interpret discrimination by employers, landlords, and police officers. Of course, those who have experienced discrimination perceive a significantly higher level of discrimination against their ethnic group than those who have not. Yet even when taking past discrimination into account, ethnic origins continue to shape this dimension of the refugees' racial and ethnic adaptation. The Hmong perceive a significantly greater likelihood of unfair treatment than do Cambodians and experiencing small-town hate compounds the Hmong's feelings of unequal treatment even more.

How do ethnic origins affect perceptions of unfair treatment in work, housing, and the criminal justice system? They influence the way individuals make inferences about the macro-level inequality faced by their respective groups. The porous ethnic boundary among Cambodians leads to a more individualistic perception of discrimination that focuses on their interaction with the perpetrator. As a result, they typically think of discriminatory incidents as isolated rather than connected by the common ethnicity of the victims. Cambodians therefore tend to perceive less discrimination than the Hmong.

Hmong ethnic origins have the opposite influence. The hermetic ethnic boundary of the Hmong creates a collective worldview. When Hmong individuals think about discrimination, they tend to recall not only their own experiences but also those of other members of their ethnic group. From this perspective the victim of discrimination is the group as a whole, even though the incident happens to an individual. Since the Hmong associate one incident with others because of the victims' ethnicity they perceive unfair treatment to be more prevalent than do Cambodians.

This finding, and those in chapter 10, have important implications for ethnic-competition theory. One aspect of social inequality fits the theory's predictions, but a second aspect does not. Among both Cambodian and Hmong refugees, those who have the greatest contact and rivalry with Americans because of higher levels of U.S. education think that institutional discrimination occurs more often than those with less U.S. education. Refugees with more years of U.S. education are also much more likely to report being the victims of institutional discrimination. As demonstrated in chapter 10, however, level of U.S. education is not associated with the refugees' sensitivity to anti-Asian stereotypes. This pattern suggests that ethnic-competition theory works well as an explanation for material conflicts that arise during immigrants' racial and ethnic adaptation but not for conflicts involving symbols and interpersonal communication.

Although Cambodians' and the Hmong's perceptions of institutional discrimination vary with their ethnic origins and urban locale, the larger process of racial and ethnic adaptation is quite similar. Members of both groups have very specific beliefs about the extent to which natives abuse the power conferred on them by institutions. The refugees carefully evaluate their own experiences of discrimination and those of other people in their social networks. Even if they have never personally experienced unfair treatment, both Cambodians and the Hmong nonetheless develop generalizations about how often it happens to their ethnic group. Such perceptions are noteworthy because before their arrival in the United States the refugees knew little or nothing about the occurrence of institutional discrimination in American society. After arrival each one eventually develops an explicit cognition of the probability that people like them will encounter unfair treatment by employers, landlords, and police officers.

═ Chapter 12 ═

Political Mobilization

Severe prejudice and discrimination against a people transform them into a minority group because they are more likely than other people in the society to repeatedly experience social inequality. In the first social science definition of the concept minority, the sociologist Louis Wirth (1945, 34) noted that "the existence of a minority group implies the existence of a dominant group enjoying higher social status and greater privileges."

American history demonstrates that minority groups sometimes fight back, and immigrants' political reactions to inequality are an important component of their racial and ethnic adaptation. Members of a disadvantaged community often discuss the inequalities they experience. Many agree that something needs to be done. Some formulate plans for social change. Sociologists who study social movements call these activities "mobilization." Once mobilized, a community can collectively challenge the practices of a dominant group that perpetuate inequality. In the literature on social movements this behavior is known as "collective action."

Law and public policy often dramatize the inequality experienced by a minority group and the need for social change. Such was the case in 1996, when the U.S. Congress overhauled the provision of public assistance to the poor by passing the Personal Responsibility and Work Opportunity Reconciliation Act (PRWORA). This legislation developed during a period of heightened nativist sentiment in the United States. In 1993, 64 percent of the American public believed that immigrants "mostly hurt the economy by driving wages down for many Americans," and in 1994, 57 percent agreed that "immigrants cost the taxpayers too much by using government services" (Jones 2000, 66). Immigrants inevitably became ensnared in the politics of welfare reform.

Among its many provisions, the PRWORA made non–U.S. citizens ineligible for some federal social welfare programs during their first five years in the United States and permanently excluded them from others (see Fix and Passel 2002 and Singer 2004 for a detailed analysis of the PRWORA's impact on immigrants). Previously, these programs had been open to all legal residents of the United States even if they had not yet naturalized. Since passage of the PRWORA, many immigrants who arrive legally, work, and pay federal income taxes cannot receive federal aid should they lose a job through layoffs or disability. Depending on the program, immigrants remain ineligible until they become a U.S. citizen, a multi-year process fraught with delay due to bureaucratic indifference and incompetence at the U.S. Bureau of Citizenship and Immigration Services.

After reviewing the PRWORA's impact, the President's Advisory Commission on Asian Americans and Pacific Islanders (2001, 67) concluded that the restriction of aid to U.S. citizens only was "harsh and unfair to many legal-immigrant families and had nothing to do with the goal of welfare reform, which was to move people from welfare to work." The law did not apply to refugees during their first five to seven years in the United States. Most Hmong and Cambodians, however, had arrived during the 1980s and did not benefit from this provision. They tended to have higher rates of illness, disability, and poverty than natives and other immigrants, so many refugee families received aid from one or more federal social-welfare programs (Cho and Hummer 2001; Hao and Kawano 2001; Jensen 1988).

Passage of the PRWORA in 1996 caused intense apprehension among Cambodians and the Hmong. Subsequent legislation amended the PRWORA and exempted all immigrants who arrived prior to enactment. Despite this modification, the law remains a reminder of the refugees' minority status because those who arrived after 1996 are subject to its provisions. Responding to the assertion that immigrants take advantage of the social welfare system, the Hmong community leader Lee Pao Xiong stated at a public forum in St. Paul, "My aging father cannot work. I pay taxes, and I expect that he will get assistance. If you deny him assistance, because he is an immigrant, then I want my taxes back, so I can help him."[1]

In previous chapters I used survey and personal-interview data to analyze the refugees as individuals. In this chapter I examine them as members of communities. I present data obtained from a variant of the focus-group methodology, called a peer-group conversation, in which a small number of people who have similar life experiences carry on an unstructured discussion about a controversial political issue (Gamson 1994).

The PRWORA is an obvious choice of topic for Cambodian and Hmong peer-group conversations. I analyzed the resulting transcripts to determine to what degree participants constructed and used three "collective-action frames" to evaluate the impact of the PRWORA on them and their communities (see Gamson 1994, 6–8, for definitions and discussion of collective-action frames). The first possible frame is an injustice frame. In the case of the PRWORA, a peer group that creates an injustice frame interprets the policy as unfair because it is harmful. An identity frame then concretizes the harm by specifying an adversary responsible for it, thus mobilizing individuals in a we-they conflict. Finally, an agency frame empowers individuals to feel that they can make a difference and endorses collective action to confront the adversary. A peer group's level of political activism can be gauged by the intensity of its feeling of injustice, we-they conflict, and agency. For Cambodians and the Hmong, peer-group discussions about the PRWORA revealed that the groups' respective ethnic origins shaped their mobilization and collective action. I present the results from four groups. Cambodian and Hmong men in big cities and Cambodian and Hmong women in small cities (see appendix A).

Cambodian Men in Chicago: "The Government Will Not Let Us Die"

The Cambodian men in Chicago exhibited the weakest political mobilization of the four groups. They did not reach a consensus that the PRWORA is unjust. Nor did they view the U.S. government as an adversary whose actions are causing harm to their ethnic group. And they certainly did not evidence a sense of empowerment to engage in collective action and confront their adversary.

At the start of the peer-group conversation two men explained why the new law would not adversely affect Cambodians. Savuth observed that the law treats refugees better than immigrants and that the Cambodian Association of Illinois would help those in need. Khuon believed that the PRWORA was in fact necessary, since "if the government keeps giving assistance to the immigrants then people outside of the United States would see this as an opportunity and they would flood into the United States." None of the other three men in the group disagreed with this statement. The co-ethnic facilitator then probed the reasons for this complacency. To prompt some discussion and find out why the group appeared reluctant to invoke an injustice frame he noted, "There is a great number of people who want to protest and demand justice so that these new laws can be changed." In response Sarom and Khoun argued that some Cambodians were abusing the social-welfare system:

> Sarom: Most people, including me when I just came to the United States, are supported by the government and most of the time they have a lot of free time. These people don't want to go to school even though the school is so close to their home. Not just the elderly people, young people don't even want to go to school either. They believe that they still get benefits even though they don't go to school. So I think these people are not con-

tributing to the society. They just want to depend on government assistance. So if the government speaks directly to them they would think the government is too harsh on them. The government has many techniques. So it created the law that requires people to become citizens before they can be eligible for assistance. That means the government wants people to make some effort to help themselves.

Khuon: Now Congress is making the laws tougher by requiring people to become citizens.

Sarom: Yes, becoming citizens enables people to learn and to speak English.

Khuon: If they learn they will pass the test and be able to become citizens.

Sarom: I am not blaming the elders, but I am blaming the young people because young people have the ability to learn.

Khuon: Yes, young people have the ability to learn, but some of them are just lazy.

The Cambodian men formed a consensus that the law was not unjust because it was intended to address a real social problem. At only one point later in their discussion did a participant raise concerns about the law:

Darith: This government action has some negative effect on many people because there are a lot of families who have children and the head of these families have no education or skills. For example, Mr. Prak's family. He has many children and he does not have any skill. If the government cuts their assistance they will have a lot of difficulties. It would be too hard for them to survive in America. Mr. Yimsut's family has the same problem.

Khuon: That's because they did not prepare from the beginning. Now it's almost too late. If they had started [looking for work] from the beginning it would not be too difficult to adjust to changes.

Darith: But in the beginning it was too easy for them.

Khuon and Sarom [simultaneously]: Yes, it was too easy.

The reactions of other participants to Darith's injustice frame is revealing. Once again the group did not view the PRWORA as unfair. While Khuon and Sarom seemed to concur that the two families cited by Darith may be hurt by the law, they assigned responsibility for this problem to the families. Even though Darith agreed that the PRWORA may cause hardships for Cambodians ("This government action has some negative affect"), he still viewed the law as a rational response to welfare dependency ("in the beginning it was too easy" for refugees to get public assistance).

Not only did these Cambodian men rarely invoke an injustice frame but they also did not evince an identity frame. Rather than viewing the U.S. government as an adversary that had inflicted harm on their ethnic group, they clearly accepted the legitimacy of its action. This positive view of the state emerged most strongly after one participant mentioned that Congress passed the PRWORA to reduce the deficit, which a second participant stated was a serious problem. Savuth then commented on the new law and initiated the following discussion:

> Savuth: When the top government tries to reduce [the national] debt it affects the poor people, like refugees. So from now on we must try harder to be independent because the welfare laws are getting tougher every day. We must keep reminding our people about these new laws. But for refugees like us, the government will not let us suffer financially. It will not let us die because refugees were brought here by the government. After five years, if their benefits are cut, there would be some other program to assist the poor people. They should find out about that at agencies like the Cambodian Association of Illinois, get more information about the programs.
>
> Facilitator: Sarom, do you agree with that too?
>
> Sarom: I have no objection to it. But I would like to say this. People who are not citizens will be affected by the new laws. But they should not be worried too much about it because the government will not let us die. Life is precious. For example, when a person dies the government still wants to find out the cause of death [by conducting an autopsy]. So the government thinks that life is precious. In this case it wants to make laws tougher, but it will find different ways to help people. It will not close its eyes to let people die.
>
> Khuon: I heard on the radio that each state has a surplus of federal grants for public assistance. Each state still has a lot of funds to support the programs. So America is not a poor country. Now America has reached a golden age, just like the era of the Khmer Empire [circa A.D. 800 to 1431].

This portion of the discussion reveals a complex set of reasons why this male Cambodian peer group did not create an identity frame through which to view the U.S. government as an adversary. First, a reoccurring theme is that "the government will not let us die." In contrast to these men's experiences during the horrific Khmer Rouge revolution and even the authoritarian regimes before it, the U.S. government, they say, unambiguously evinces a concern for the welfare of its citizens. To them a change in a social welfare policy is a minor inconvenience. What is significant is the very existence of social-welfare programs, which are absent in Cambodia. Other reasons for viewing the U.S. government as legitimate include a faith that a paternalistic government will look after the refugees it admitted and the reasonableness of asking individuals to sacrifice for the national good (for example, to reduce the deficit). Finally, the men appreciate living in a powerful country that they see as comparable to Cambodia's renowned civilization, which built the famed temples of Angkor Wat.

Lacking both injustice and identity frames, the Cambodian men did not develop an agency frame. Early in the discussion, Sarom stated, "We don't want these changes, but Congress would probably not listen to us if we want to protest." Khuon then tamely replied, "They probably want to hear our reactions, though," and the subject of the conversation then changed to the actual provisions of the law. When the facilitator directly asked a question to gauge the group's level of agency—should Cambodians "keep quiet or should they fight?"—the men's responses clearly indicate little interest in collective action:

> Khuon: In my opinion there should be a work program that pays working people. I want to see a program that can help people get started before cutting off their benefits. If their benefits are cut without providing any work program, people would face problems. Government work programs can benefit a lot of unskilled workers.

> Darith: Whatever the jobs may be.

No other participants suggested proposals for modifying the PRWORA, and only Darith voices support for Khuon's idea. Rather than a sense of empowerment, the Cambodian men conveyed a sense of acceptance and even apathy.

Hmong Men in Milwaukee: "We Have the Right to Fight for Change"

In contrast to the Cambodian men in Chicago, the Hmong men in Milwaukee displayed extensive mobilization in their peer-group conversation about the PRWORA. They immediately reached a consensus that the law was harmful, thus establishing an injustice frame. They then created an identity frame by agreeing that the law adversely affects the Hmong more than other groups. Finally, they endorsed specific actions to confront the government and change the law, a clear indication of an agency frame.

After the facilitator read a description of the PRWORA to the four participants, the first topic they discussed was the difficulty that older Hmong had in passing the citizenship test in order to qualify for aid. They briefly shared examples of this problem and then invoked an injustice frame to articulate why the law was harmful. According to Song, "If the law is implemented, it will affect all our parents. It will only affect some [other] people but it will affect all the Hmong people." Chai agreed that "this is a hard time not only for us [in Milwaukee] but for others [Hmong in the United States] as well." The other men concurred and the facilitator then probed to determine the basis for this consensus, asking, "So if you were going to write a letter to the government, what would you say to them?" Chai responded that he would remind members of Congress that some refugees brought less human capital with them than others:

> When they design this law it supposedly will not affect the Hmong, but ironically it turns out that it affects the Hmong. Other groups such as Vietnamese and Laotians, it won't affect them as much as the Hmong because they are more educated and literate than us before they came to this country. The majority of them have an educated background so the law won't affect them as much. But the Hmong, it will not only affect one person but everyone, from a blue-collar worker to a white-collar worker, and from our clan leaders to our Hmong leaders [in formal organizations]. This is the big concern for us.

There was an obvious consensus among these men that the law was unjust because it limited much-needed social-welfare assistance. They also exemplified an identity frame by concluding that the law was particularly harmful to the Hmong. The strongest evidence of this we-they or adversarial perspective occurred when the group turned to the topic of why the Hmong migrated to the United States in the first place and discussed the U.S. government's military mobilization of the Hmong during the Vietnam War. Vue was the first participant to establish an identity frame in this way:

> When you think about it the truth is that it [the PRWORA] affects us Hmong the most. The fact is that it affects our parents the most. I see that it affects them the most because in the past when they lived in their country, they didn't have much education. When they were at the age of eleven or twelve and knew how to hold a gun, General Vang Pao and his crew came and made soldiers out of them. They didn't get to go to school. That is why our parents are uneducated. It's not just that they don't know how to read and write in English, they also don't know how to read and write Hmong and Lao. They only know to speak Hmong and sometimes Lao. And now when they have this law it affects many of them. I heard that many of our parents committed suicide when this law was passed.

Shortly after Vue made these comments the facilitator asked the group, "What should we tell the lawmakers about our concerns?" In response Song again raised the topic of the U.S. government's obligations to the Hmong because of the so-called Secret War in Laos:

> The reason the Hmong are here is because our people were devastated in our country. The Americans and their CIA got the Hmong involved in the war in Southeast Asia, that's why the Hmong are here. So when a problem like this one happens the Hmong have to cooperate and go talk to the government and fight for it because it will be more beneficial if a group fights rather than each individual. I see that whatever we do in this country, Americans will always have a law that will affect us, but we also have the right to fight for change if we are willing to fight for it. We lived in our own country. Why you bother me? This is my point. Why you come to bother me? You guys bother to get involved with us so now you guys should solve the problem for us [of laws that disproportionately hurt us].

The strong sense of injustice and solidarity that these Hmong men communicated allowed them easily to formulate an agency frame. They agreed that the Hmong should take collective action to change a public policy that adversely affects their group. When the facilitator asked, "Is there a possible way that the Hmong can fight back?" the response was unanimously affirmative:

> Chai: Yes, there will be a way. If the Hmong don't like it, Hmong will be able to fight for their rights.

> Vue: I think our Hmong people are getting to use the Constitution. If we are unhappy about anything we are no longer complaining alone at home. We go as a group to protest so the government can see why we are unhappy. If each individual complains alone the government won't pay any attention to us. But if we do it in a group then the government will check out to see why we are not happy with the law.

> Dee: Cooperate.

> Vue: Like last time, the letters we wrote to the White House [when the PRWORA was first passed in 1996]. There's almost two hundred thousand Hmong [in the United States], right?

> Dee: Two hundred and fifty thousand.

> Vue: Two hundred and fifty thousand Hmong population lives in this country. I think at least about twenty to thirty thousand Hmong wrote to the White House. Someone asked me how many letters the Hmong wrote to the White House. I told them that a house won't be able to hold them all!

Dee: You know, that many letters is just enough to make them hear what our problem is.

The feeling of empowerment so evident among these Hmong men in Milwaukee contrasts sharply with the absence of any sense of group efficacy among the Cambodian men in Chicago. In addition to their strong injustice and identity frames, the Hmong men evince a strong agency frame and thus great potential to participate in a social movement.

Cambodian and Hmong Women in Small Cities

Cambodian and Hmong men in big cities had nearly opposite reactions to a public policy that disenfranchised most members of their respective ethnic groups. The discussion of the PRWORA by Cambodian women in Rochester and Hmong women in Eau Claire revealed less pronounced differences in their views. Both female groups created injustice, identity, and agency frames. Although the two groups were similar in many respects, the Hmong women displayed greater mobilization than the Cambodian women because they had a more expansive injustice frame, a more specific identity frame, and a more activist agency frame.

Narrow Versus Expansive Injustice Frames

The Cambodian men in Chicago rarely invoked an injustice frame when discussing the PRWORA, but the Cambodian women in Rochester felt that the law seriously harmed some of their close relatives. Several women reported moving stories of hardship, starting with Kristi, who noted that the older Cambodians who receive public assistance have no job skills and little English proficiency yet are expected to "fill out tons and tons of paper[work] and sometimes they can't read it." Sothy concurred and cited her mother as an example: "If she had a choice of working, she'd rather work than just stay home and get all these forms and fill it out and give it back every month and sometimes they have people follow her just to make sure she's sick [disabled] and staying at home." Sothy also commented that the four hundred dollars a month her mother received was often inadequate to meet her needs. Lakhena then chimed in:

> Well my mom's the same thing. She'd rather work than get a monthly check because like she [Sothy] said, it's not enough. And like every month they send these papers to fill out and you have to meet with them and the whole thing. And I think, too, some of the questions they ask on the form are very demeaning. And it sometimes puts you down, you know, it's like looking down on those people that are getting public assistance. And I

know the people that are getting it, they said they'd rather be spending money off their sweat and work for it than getting these checks that make them look really bad or really guilty.

These quotations vividly convey the Cambodian women's outrage toward the PRWORA. The group clearly built an injustice frame to analyze its unfairness and that of the American social-welfare system in general. The main feature of this injustice frame is the stigma attached to recipients of aid. Other features include the bureaucratic procedures for receiving aid, the small amount of financial assistance, and negative treatment by case workers. Although all of these harms predate the PRWORA, the women use them to build a consensus that the new law is unjust because it exacerbates existing problems.

The Hmong women in Eau Claire created an even stronger injustice frame than the Cambodian women of Rochester. Their discussion of the PRWORA began similarly, by portraying the law as unfair because it harms their relatives. When asked by the facilitator, "Has this law affected you, your family, relatives, or friends?" the Hmong women unanimously agreed that it had. But unlike the Cambodian women, the Hmong women launched into a much broader critique of the federal government. Mayseng led off, stating:

I know they change that law a little, too, but it affects everybody. Even everybody here. We have some family members who are on some kind of assistance, some kind of help, and we are very angry about it. And now there is the law of deportation for people that are not citizens and the government is sending those people back into a country that they fled from, from persecution. And it's not right.

Kaolee: For people that are elderly, they can't read and write and they can't just become a citizen.

Julie: And they make their citizenship process such a hard and expensive process.

Mayseng: It's so long. Three years for me [after sending the application].

Kaolee: It took me three years, too. But see, if they want everybody to become a citizen don't charge them a lot of money. I mean where . . . Some of them are on public assistance.

Mayseng: They can't afford it.

Kaolee: They can't afford it. That money is enough for their family for the whole month. They have to get two hundred dollars to get their U.S. citizen application, all the pictures and fingerprints, and it's driving all the way out there [to Milwaukee].

These Hmong women presented a much more extensive list of injustices whereas the Cambodian women had a narrower and highly individualistic view of the PRWORA's harmful effects. As a result, the Cambodian women restricted their critique to personal harms, such as the stigma of receiving aid and the lack of compassion among the congressional supporters of the PRWORA. The Hmong women developed a more expansive injustice frame by critiquing multiple aspects of the U.S. state. Where the Cambodian women focused exclusively on the unfairness of the social-welfare system, the Hmong women incorporated a larger range of problems within their frame, including naturalization procedures and the policy of deporting permanent residents convicted of a felony in the United States even though some of these refugees arrived as young children and have no memory of their native country. This variation in the strength of injustice frames can actually be observed in how the Cambodian and Hmong women communicated with each other. Where a Cambodian woman stated, "I don't like their law," a Hmong woman stated, "We are very angry about it."

General Versus Specific Identity Frames

Not only did the Hmong women create a stronger injustice frame than the Cambodian women, but their identity frame also was far more specific about the we-they conflict responsible for this injustice. The Hmong women first identified this conflict when discussing why Congress passed the PRWORA. They concluded that the U.S. state is controlled by powerful groups pursuing their own interests at the expense of others. This surprisingly radical identity frame is best conveyed by a long quotation from the peer group transcript:

> Julie: What U.S. history has taught us is that whenever the United States is in a prosperous position they tend to go down on minorities because the economy is prosperous. And then when everyone is poor, we're in a recession or something, everybody is trying to help the poor and everything. And it doesn't seem fair that when we are in a good economy and everybody is getting jobs or stuff we turn our backs on those people that need us the most. And it's just not good. The welfare, AFDC, Food Stamps came out of the Great Depression and now we are in a prosperous position to help those people and yet the government is punishing them for being poor, for being unable to read and write and . . . It's just not right.

> Mayseng: I feel like the government does things according to the rich people ordering them to do.

> Julie: Yes, yes!

Mayseng: They always . . . Like, they are not straightforward. They are not doing what their heart tells them to do. They are doing it because other people are sponsoring them. If you do this, you vote for his tax, vote for that, you gonna be reelected for senator or whatever position in Washington, D.C. And a lot of people are doing that and they don't know or don't understand that it's affecting so many people's lives. You know?

Kaolee: See, the people that are poor, they can't really have a voice. And the people who have a voice are the middle class, upper-middle class, and the very rich people. Those are the people that have voices. And if they would let the poor people have their voice, that would be different.

Julie: See, but the more rich they are the richer they want to be. You know they didn't want their taxes to be taken away. So of course, I'm rich, I have the power, you know?

Mayseng: And one thing the government thinks is that we will give all this tax-break money to the rich people so they can provide jobs for the poor people.

Julie: But that's not true.

Mayseng: I know and they think that it works that way but—

Julie: Because when you do that, well, those rich people hire the rich people or the middle-class people to work and the poor don't get jobs.

These women obviously had a very specific identity frame based on class that enables them to concretize the injustices they experience by naming an adversary. In fact, a sociologist would call it a neo-Marxist critique of the U.S. state and the power elite.

The strength of the Hmong women's identity frame was further evidenced by their ability to switch from one group identity to another as a basis for analyzing social inequality. At one point in their discussion the women shifted their identity frame from class to race and ethnicity. Julie noted that the congressional supporters of the PRWORA probably pictured the Hmong as "people sitting at home with kids and on welfare." Bao, who had been silent for much of the conversation, then commented, "From what I heard, they said our Hmong people are lazy and just stay home, make many babies, and depend on their money. We Hmong people don't want to stay on welfare, like so many American people do."

By citing stereotypes the women showed a concern with the stigmatizing affects of the U.S. social-welfare system quite similar to the injustice frame used by the Cambodian women. But the Cambodian women only saw the stigma as affecting their relatives. The Hmong women, however, extended the stigma to stereotypes about their ethnic group ("they said our Hmong people are lazy") and thus constructed a far stronger and more specific identity frame. In fact, no portion of the Cambodian women's peer-group conversation revealed a we-they opposition based on class, race, and ethnicity. The closest the Cambodian group came to a specific rather than general identity frame was when participants responded to the facilitator's question "What other group of people do you think this law affected?" Several Cambodian women immediately gave an answer:

Lakhena: Any group that's not citizens, like minorities.

Sothy: Like people from Southeast Asian countries. Vietnamese and Hmong and Laotians.

Lakhena: Immigrants.

Sothy: Like right now, we have a lot of Bosnians and Somalians that are here and they don't speak much English. How are you gonna get started without any money in a new country? The only way that they do it is to get some public assistance to help them start out.

Sambo: My manager was saying, like, imagine her going to Cambodia at her age and trying to go to school and learn. And if we do the same thing to them, she said she would not pass the test and she would not, you know, she would just starve. You know she can't go through what we go through and she can't imagine that. It's really hard.

These statements do indicate an identity frame since the women name particular ethnic groups as disproportionately impacted by the new law. Yet the very inclusion of so many diverse groups undermined their ability to frame the issue as a we-they conflict. What groups like Cambodians, Somalis, and Bosnians have in common, according to the Cambodian women, is a temporary disadvantage due to being newcomers rather than an enduring inequality due to a racial and ethnic hierarchy. Their identity frame was so general that participants could even incorporate within it the hypothetical experience of an American immigrating to Cambodia. In short, the "we" and "they" expressed by the Cambodian women was far less specific than the class, racial, and ethnic identities expressed by the Hmong women.

Reform Versus Activist Agency Frames

The moderate we-they opposition in the Cambodian women's identity frame was matched by moderate plans for collective action when they discussed how to respond to the PRWORA. Unlike the Cambodian men, who seemed resigned to the law or actually felt it was legitimate, the Cambodian women quickly created an agency frame by reaching a consensus that it is appropriate to voice their concerns. In fact, they raised the topic of changing the law prior to the facilitator's question specifically designed to assess the group's level of agency ("What to do about it?"). When the facilitator asked, "What would you tell the people who passed this law?" Sambo answered:

> I think people who want to do something about this law should get ahold of their representatives and congressmen, legislative, and let them know that people, not just Cambodians but any minorities who are disabled, should get disability [aid] no matter if they're a citizen or not. Because if they don't know how to speak, read, or write English they have no income, no supporting anyhow. How can they live?

> Sothy: That's right. I agree.

> Kristi: I think, my opinion is that Cambodian people, not only Cambodian people but minorities, should get together in a group and think about, you know, writing letters to a congressman to consider about the law that people who are not American citizens cannot get assistance or SSI [Supplemental Security Income]. I think that's what the people, Cambodian or minorities, should do. That's what I think.

> Facilitator: So they need to get together and do something about it?

> Kristi: As a group, yes. Write a letter to a congressman and say that they should reconsider the new law because it affected a lot of people. Especially old people, mental people, or deaf people.

> Sambo: The younger generation needs to speak for the older generation that cannot speak English. So we need to do something about it in order for it to get changed.

> Kristi: Yeah, the more people we can gather the more it makes a difference, you know? Keep writing letters to congressmen.

These women clearly wanted change, and phrases like "minority" and "as a group" appeared for the first time, an indication of a strengthening identity frame. Yet even at their peak level of mobilization the women suggested only the most moderate forms of collective action, such as writing elected officials.

The reformist quality of Cambodian women's agency frame became even more apparent after Sothy suggested that Cambodians in each state pick a highly educated representative from the community who could write a petition, get signatures from other Cambodians, and then send it to the president of the United States. Several women simultaneously interrupted her with expressions of incredulity, with one saying "How do we get to the president?" Sothy then defensively responded: "You can write to the president. He can do something because, you know, the people who pass the law, they would probably listen to the president more than us. They are like, we are a bunch of nobodies. Who cares?"

The group's exchange over Sothy's suggestion reveals the limitations of the Cambodian women's agency frame. Several of them deemed too radical the idea of actually writing to the president. All that their agency frame invokes is the proper working of a representative democracy in which those given power by the people take the time to become acquainted with their constituents' needs. Even Sothy, the most militant of the group, hoped that writing letters would get members of Congress to "visit the state and look at these people that are on public assistance and visit a home. They aren't going to understand otherwise." Here she appeals to the empathy of the powerful, rather than emphasizing the power of her ethnic group to initiate social change through collective action.

The reformist agency frame among the Cambodian women is in marked contrast to the strong activism among the Hmong women. The Hmong group initially constructed their agency frame just as the Cambodian group did, by advocating writing letters to and meeting with members of the city council, state assembly, and the U.S. Congress. Paly then changed the rhetoric of the discussion by stating, "Have them contact the Hmong association and educate the Hmong people. If a struggle happens, where do we have to go to? Do we have to go as the first step to the city manager and then the council and go up a higher step?"

Paly's brief remark is noteworthy for its mention of a community organization and shows that the Hmong women want to use their clout to put pressure on those in power. Immediately following Paly's suggestion to organize through the Hmong Mutual Assistance Association (HMAA), Mayseng raised the topic of voting: "I know that many of us are U.S. citizens. We can vote. The people in the government need to come to the HMAA so we can see who they are so we can vote for them." A short digression followed on the difficulty of knowing which candidates to vote for. Then the women directly described the process of ethnic mobilization:

Bao: If you go vote you need to see the real candidate there and ask them straight in person so you can find out what exactly they have done and are going to do. If you just talk to those people that work for them, he or she is not going to help or do anything different.

Mayseng: They don't even come to Eau Claire. They go to a big city like Madison, Milwaukee. . . .

Bao: That candidate that people will vote for, he has to come right away so people can say what they don't like, so he understands what they don't like. That way he can try to change himself.

Kaolee: And so he knows that I have a lot of support. These people are the one's who vote for me. I need to work for them.

Mayseng: I think that will come when more Hmong people become U.S. citizens.

Julie: More working in [government] offices, departments, and voting.

Mayseng: Yes, because Wisconsin has the third highest Hmong population and the government should listen to us.

The activist agency frame among the Hmong women is evidenced by their strong feeling of political efficacy, since they insisted on grilling a candidate for office in person. Similarly, forming a Hmong voting block is a far higher level of ethnic mobilization than that proposed by the Cambodian women, who wanted a single representative from their ethnic group to deliver a petition. These different agency frames are most evident in how the two groups of women articulated their sense of empowerment. Where the Cambodian women tended to feel "we are a bunch of nobodies," the Hmong women believed "the government should listen to us."

Conclusion

Intra-ethnic communication about inequality is an essential aspect of immigrants' racial and ethnic adaptation. It reveals what immigrants consider an injustice, whether they attribute injustice to a dominant group, and their willingness to confront an adversary. These reactions to minority-group status indicate immigrants' capacity for participation in a social movement. The ethnic-origins hypothesis predicts that homeland ethnic boundaries and identities can augment or diminish immigrants' political mobilization and collective action in a host society.

This prediction proves accurate in the case of the PRWORA: Hmong and Cambodian peer groups have substantially different reactions to it. On all three ways of framing a political issue the Hmong groups display more mobilization than the Cambodian groups. First, the Hmong groups tend to perceive the PRWORA as more unjust and causing more serious social inequality. Where Cambodian men focus on the hardships of a few families, the Hmong men critique the entire social-welfare system. Where Cambodian women focus on the stigma attached to recipients of public aid, Hmong women see the injustices of the social-welfare system as part of a larger pattern of state-sanctioned inequality.

Second, the Hmong groups are more likely than the Cambodian groups to view the PRWORA as a we-they conflict. Both Hmong men and women see the law as specifically harming their ethnic group. Cambodian men give no indication of having this view and Cambodian women tend to see the law as harming all immigrants equally. Where the Hmong use ethnicity, race, and class to describe an adversarial relationship with the PRWORA's supporters, Cambodians rarely view the anti-immigrant provision of the law as part of an unequal relationship between a minority and a dominant group.

Finally, the Hmong groups articulate a much stronger challenge to the legitimacy of the political process that produced the PRWORA than the Cambodian groups. The Hmong not only have a greater consensus than Cambodians that the PRWORA is wrong but also propose more militant collective action for getting the U.S. Congress to change the law. Cambodian men suggest a federal employment program to assist people whose public aid is cut; Hmong men advocate mass letter writing by the Hmong to amend the law itself. Cambodian women want an ethnic representative to bring a petition to government officials; Hmong women endorse forming a Hmong voting block to put pressure on politicians.

These patterns provide strong evidence that ethnic origins influence not only individuals' perceptions of prejudice and discrimination but also the ways minority groups mobilize as communities to challenge social inequality. Immigrants, such as the Khmer, who arrive with a porous ethnic boundary and a liminal ethnic identity may recognize social inequality and mobilize against it. But they will be hindered by their individualistic view of racial and ethnic adaptation. Immigrants, such as the Hmong, who arrive with a hermetic boundary and polarized identity can more easily discern how social inequality affects them. They can then draw upon preexisting in-group solidarity to initiate collective action.

Given these differences in ethnic origins, one can better appreciate what happened when House Speaker Newt Gingrich attended a Republican Party fund-raiser in Minneapolis in February 1996. Gingrich was the architect of the *Contract with America,* which first proposed the policies that became the PRWORA: "to further reduce welfare spending, welfare assistance (AFDC, SSI, food stamps, housing, and a host of other public assistance) is denied to noncitizens" (Republican National Committee 1994, 73). Outside the fund-raiser venue, about 175 Hmong protesters rallied against the PRWORA and scuffled with security staff in an attempt to disrupt Gingrich's speech.[2] One police officer discharged pepper spray, causing nine protesters to be briefly hospitalized.

= Part VI =

Implications

Chapter 13

Conclusion

Policy makers, journalists, and social scientists often attribute the new challenges of diversity in the United States to the fact that blacks, Hispanics, and Asians are becoming a larger proportion of the population in major cities, populous states, and American society as a whole. Many note that this change is occurring at a time of heightened scarcity and competition brought on by the globalization of the post-industrial economy. These are the headlines that attract the most attention, but demography and economics alone cannot explain why American society confronts additional racial and ethnic dilemmas before it has resolved older ones.

The Hmong and Cambodians in big and small midwestern cities help us understand the symbolic dimension of the new American dilemmas. They reveal that each group of immigrants arrives with distinctive ethnic origins that shape their responses to new identities and inequalities. Ethnic origins comprise homeland histories, politics, and cultures and define for immigrants what it means to be a member of society. Cambodians come from a hybrid nation-state, whereas the Hmong were an isolated, highland minority that arrived in Laos through a diaspora. Cambodian kinship norms and religious values tilt toward individualism and discretionary social networks; those of the Hmong emphasize groups and obligation. Finally, Cambodians killed each other following a civil war in which the U.S. military remained largely in Air Force planes. In Laos, in contrast, the U.S. military organized a Hmong army to fight Lao and Vietnamese forces, who then persecuted the Hmong after the war. As a result of this variation in ethnic origins, Cambodian and Hmong refugees arrive in the United States with very different ways of thinking about ethnic boundaries and identities.

The Hmong and Cambodians also show us what happens when immigrants from different ethnic groups settle in the same urban environments. In larger cities such as Chicago and Milwaukee, American society takes the form of an urban pecking order among different ethnic and racial groups. Here, Cambodians and the Hmong are the most recent arrivals in a chain of ethnic successions and become vulnerable to established minority groups stressed by social inequality. Although often victimized, in big cities both groups of refugees are able to create robust enclaves that contribute to urban renewal. In small, racially homogeneous towns such as Eau Claire and Rochester, American society manifests as small-town hospitality and hate. Here Cambodians and the Hmong encounter extraordinary generosity from some whites motivated by Christian faith and civic pride, but they also experience virtually every form of white racism known to contemporary African Americans.

Given the enormous differences between the urban pecking order and small-town hospitality and hate one would expect that urban locale largely determines Cambodians' and the Hmong's responses to identities such as Asian American and inequalities such as discrimination. In some respects this assumption turns out to be correct, but the refugees' racial and ethnic adaptation is also heavily shaped by their ethnic origins. Cambodians residing in Rochester have views of American society much like those of Cambodians in Chicago and often quite different from those of the Hmong in Eau Claire. The same pattern exists for the Hmong: they have similar responses to American society regardless of where they live, and often differ substantially from Cambodians even when residing in the same type of social environment.

The ethnic-origins hypothesis helps make sense of this pattern, in which there is more variation by ethnicity than by urban locale. International migrants arrive in a host society with preexisting conceptions of diversity and adversity derived from the histories, politics, and cultures of their homelands. These worldviews shape immigrants' resocialization during the process of racial and ethnic adaptation and explain why the United States has more racial and ethnic dilemmas than it did in the past. This development is not the result of immigrants having increased the total "minority population," but because immigrants are redefining identities such as "Asian" and "American citizen" and reinterpreting features of inequality such as racism, stereotypes, and discrimination. What it means to be a member of a minority group in American society is changing as the histories, politics, and cultures of people around the world come to the United States.

Caveats on Cases

Several reasonable objections can be raised about the generalizability of my findings on Cambodians and the Hmong in the Midwest to other immigrants in the United States. One concerns the fact that Cambodians and the Hmong are refugees. On a migration continuum ranging from permanent exile to circular migration, both groups are closest to "permanent exile." The political violence that marked their departure created a deep rupture with their homelands, and neither Cambodians nor the Hmong can easily return for a visit. War and political conflict were the main deterrents in the 1980s and early 1990s. The remaining barriers are the vast geographic distance separating the United States from Southeast Asia and the high cost of air travel for these low-income groups. Many other ethnic groups in the United States—such as Mexicans in the U.S. Southwest, Dominicans in New York City, and Cubans in South Florida—are closer to the "circular migration" end of the continuum, exhibiting much more transnationalism. Yet if ethnic origins matter for groups like Cambodians and the Hmong who have limited contact with their homeland, they may be even more important for groups with sustained contact. Since these refugees were forced to make a very sharp break with their country of origin, they provide an extremely conservative test of the effects of homeland history, politics, and culture for immigrants' adaptation in the United States.

We might also ask ourselves whether the Cambodians or the Hmong or both are so unique that we can learn little from them about immigrants in general. The Hmong are certainly a distinctive group. In Laos they were a highland minority that practiced animism and organized kinship through clans. Rather than eliminate the Hmong from immigration research on the basis of specific anthropological criteria, we should ask whether there are other immigrant groups who arrive with similar ethnic origins: a hermetic ethnic boundary and a polarized ethnic identity. I think there are. Likely candidates would be immigrants who were a minority in their homeland, because of an earlier diaspora, religion, or both. Examples of such "pre-minorities" include ethnic Chinese from Southeast Asia (Hein 1988) and Muslims from India (Kurien 2001). Immigrants from groups that have struggled for greater regional autonomy or a nation-state of their own are also likely to share some of the Hmong's views of boundaries and identities, such as the Maya (Fink 2003) and Palestinians (Aoudé 2001). There are obviously other immigrants like the Hmong who left precarious positions in their homeland.

Similarly, before concluding that Cambodians are fairly typical of immigrants in the United States it would be worth systematically determining which other newcomers arrive thinking of ethnic boundaries as porous and ethnic identities as liminal. Some obviously do. The Burmese, Thai, and Lao share significant traits with the Khmer (Theravada Buddhism and bilateral kinship). Filipinos also share some characteristics with the Khmer, principally loose kinship norms and a hybrid culture incorporating elements from Spain, Islam, the United States, and other traditions. Immigrants from East Asia, on the other hand, such as Koreans, Japanese, Taiwanese, and the Han of China, have very different kinship patterns and nation-state histories than immigrants from Southeast Asia. The Khmer are not representative of all Asians, so they certainly do not typify all immigrants who arrive in the United States. One aspect of Cambodian history that sets them apart is the atrocities they experienced during the Khmer Rouge revolution.

Both Cambodians and the Hmong, however, are distinctive because they are perfect examples of their respective ethnic origins: one group having a porous ethnic boundary and a liminal ethnic identity, the other characterized by a hermetic ethnic boundary and a polarized ethnic identity. To invoke Max Weber's famous concept of an ideal type, both groups represent nearly experimentally perfect examples of different sociological cases because their histories, politics, and cultures are aligned in opposite directions. Hmong ethnic origins consist of a diaspora, lack of a nation-state, prior minority status, inter-ethnic violence, a form of ancestor worship, and patrilineal clan kinship. Khmer ethnic origins consist of a hybrid nation-state, status as a culturally dominant group, intra-ethnic violence, notions of merit making and individual karma, and bilateral kinship with limited emphasis on ancestry and lineage. Most other ethnic groups show more polyvalent forms of ethnic origins. For example, Tibetan refugees in the United States share some Buddhist values with the Khmer but share the struggle for highland autonomy with the Hmong. Analysis of ethnic groups that do not represent ideal types will require more sophisticated comparative methodologies and a more elaborate conceptualization of ethnic boundaries than I have used in this book.

A more practical caveat than the anthropological uniqueness of the Khmer or Hmong concerns the locations in which I studied these refugees. It might be argued that these cities are not sufficiently distant to fully test the affect of urban setting on immigrants' racial and ethnic adaptation. There is some merit to this argument. The Hmong in Eau Claire are about two hundred forty miles from those in Milwaukee, and about three hundred fifty miles separate the Cambodians in Rochester from those in Chicago. Only ninety miles separate the Hmong in Eau Claire from those in St. Paul, who constitute the largest Hmong community in the United States. Social networks, ethnic nonprofit organizations, ethnic media, and the Internet connect the Hmong living in different parts of the United States, as well as Cambodians, and a few hundred miles is not much of a barrier.

While conceding the point that ethnic communities are less isolated than maps may make them appear, Rochester is not Chicago and Eau Claire is not Milwaukee. Urban locale does shape Cambodians' and the Hmong's racial and ethnic adaptation in some important respects. Residing in a small city makes the refugees more likely to think that becoming a U.S. citizen promotes their social integration, whereas a purely instrumental view of naturalization is more common among the refugees in metropolitan areas.

Living in a big or small city has an even greater impact on Cambodians' and the Hmong's perceptions of inequalities than it does on their social identities. Place of residence greatly influences what they consider to be the worst attributes of this country compared to their homeland. In large cities the refugees cite crime. Those in small cities state that assimilation problems and racism are their biggest problems in the United States. In fact, small- or large-city residence is a better predictor of emotional responses to anti-Asian stereotypes and perceptions of institutional discrimination than is sex, citizenship, years of U.S. education, and being Christian rather than Buddhist or animist. Living in a small city even increases the refugees' estimates of how often employment, housing, and police discrimination occur more than does actually having experienced such discrimination! Controlling for how many large cities the refugees have lived in prior to moving to Eau Claire or Rochester (since some initially resettled elsewhere) does not diminish the impact of currently residing in a small city. Some of the data presented in this book therefore indicate that immigrants' racial and ethnic adaptation is profoundly shaped by living in an urban pecking order or with small-town hospitality and hate. Nonetheless, ethnic origins have a distinctive influence on the refugees' responses to American diversity and adversity. This finding has several implications for theories that seek to explain adaptation among immigrants.

Ethnic Origins and Theories of Immigrant Adaptation

Both the quantitative and qualitative data presented in this book establish that Cambodian and Hmong refugees' racial and ethnic adaptation is primarily shaped by their ethnic origins, to some degree by their urban locale and also by the interaction of past and place. These findings suggest the need to extend assimilation, modes of incorporation, and ethnic-competition theories to include homeland history, politics, and culture.

The theory of segmented assimilation (Portes and Zhou 1993) is the most important innovation in research on immigrants since Milton Gordon's *Assimilation in American Life* (1964), which first suggested the possibility of multiple adaptation outcomes. Its principal contribution is explaining how immigrants' human capital and place of settlement in the United States affect their children's acculturation and thus educational attainment. Yet in the original presentation of the theory,

Alejandro Portes and Min Zhou (1993) curiously avoid using the concept culture to analyze patterns of acculturation among immigrants and the second generation. Instead, they focus on the strengths and weaknesses of ethnic communities as measured by economic and demographic resources.

A broadly accurate typology of ethnic communities can be derived from variables measuring human and social capital. In its most recent formulation (Portes and Rumbaut 2001), segmented assimilation theory characterizes both Cambodian and Hmong communities as "concentrated" and "poor" compared to the Filipino community (50–51) but also "more solidary" than the Mexican community (110). Analyzing the ethnic origins of Cambodians and the Hmong, however, reveals significant differences between them. Chapters 3 and 4 indicate that religiosity, political activism, kinship ties, and the formation of self-help associations lead Hmong communities to have a denser and more cohesive social organization compared with Cambodian communities. Similarly, chapter 7 demonstrates that the Hmong evince a higher level of ethnic solidarity in the United States than do Cambodians. Finally, chapters 10 and 11 reveal that when the refugees describe their reactions to stereotypes and institutional discrimination, the Hmong are more likely than Cambodians to use the pronoun "we" and refer to the experiences of co-ethnics. Culture, as well as history and politics in the homeland, shape social ties in immigrant communities, but the effects of immigrants' cultures are not addressed by segmented assimilation theory.

Ironically, Portes and Zhou (1993) do apply the concept culture to native-born members of American society. They warn that the "second generation [is] at risk of bypassing white or even native black middle-class models to assimilate into the culture of the underclass" (92). In a subsequent elaboration of segmented assimilation theory Portes and Rubén Rumbaut (2001, 59–60) even describe a "counterculture" in American inner cities: "Proliferation of female teenage pregnancy, high involvement of youngsters in crime, and the disappearance of work habits and discipline are common traits in these areas." Regardless of whether one agrees or disagrees with this cultural perspective of poverty, we can insist on logical consistency. If the behavior of the ghetto poor is explained by values and norms concerning family, deviance, and work, then surely the cultural variation among Asian, Latin American, and Caribbean immigrants needs to be theorized as well.

Instead, segmented assimilation theory (Portes and Rumbaut 2001) emphasizes the universal and positive traits among immigrants, such as "original immigrant ambition" (282) and "an immigrant achievement drive" (281). This approach creates two theoretical problems. First, it implies that only denizens of the "ghetto" have "norms of behavior inimical to upward mobility" (61) and that there are none among immigrants until they experience "downward assimilation" (59). Yet as shown in chapter 5, the extremely patriarchal gender roles in traditional Hmong culture can be devastating for Hmong girls and women in the United States, particularly for their chances of completing high school and attending college. Second, we do not need the concept culture to predict which groups will be winners and losers in the post-industrial economy. Race, human capital, and state policy—concepts central to segmented assimilation theory—have sufficient explanatory power to achieve that theoretical objective. We need the concept culture to explain variation in social meaning, such as immigrants' feelings about their homelands, ethnicity, and membership in American society.

In this respect the data supporting the ethnic-origins hypothesis corroborate a premise underlying the "new assimilation theory" as set forth in *Remaking the American Mainstream: Assimilation and Contemporary Immigration*, by Richard Alba and Victor Nee (2003). They note that "immigrants and their descendants act in accordance with mental models shaped by cultural beliefs that mold perceptions of self-interest. They follow rule-of-thumb heuristics in solving problems" (39). Although culture makes almost no other analytical appearance in the remainder of the book, its mere mention is a promising development for theories of immigrant adaptation.

The ethnic-origins hypothesis delineates some of the historical, political, kinship, and religious factors that shape immigrants' assimilation into American society. For example, intermarriage is common among the Khmer in the United States (Chan 2004; Ong 2003) but rarer for the Hmong, in part because the tradition of arranged marriage has declined much more for the Khmer (Smith-Hefner 1999) than for the Hmong (Donnelly 1994). In addition, bilateral Khmer kinship norms mean that a multiracial child will be perceived as Khmer, whereas the patrilineal kinship norms of the Hmong create barriers to recognizing Hmong ancestry and clan affiliation when a Hmong woman marries a man from another ethnic group. The Khmer's history of cultural amalgamation compared to the Hmong's history of cultural preservation may also explain this variation in rates of exogamy.

Some aspects of the new assimilation theory, however, need revision in light of the empirical support for the ethnic origins hypothesis. The theory's emphasis on "self-interest" tilts it in an overly rational direction. Alba and Nee (2003, 43) define norms as "the problem-solving activity of individuals striving to improve their chances for success through cooperation." This conceptualization of norms distorts the meaning of religion and kinship for immigrants in two ways. First, religion primarily shapes immigrants' cultural identity (Zhou, Bankston, and Kim 2002), while kinship primarily shapes socio-emotional interaction between parents and children (Bacon 1996) and husbands and wives (Hondagneu-Sotelo 1994). Second, both religion and kinship are often sources of conflict among immigrants (see chapter 6 on the schisms in Cambodian Buddhist temples and chapter 4 on clan rivalry within Hmong communities). Norms cannot be equated with social utilitarianism.

Another needed modification of new assimilation theory concerns the distinction between "individual" and "primary-group" mechanisms of assimilation (Alba and Nee 2003, 38). Among immigrants, the concepts "individual" and "group" are variables rather than constants. Owing to variation in their ethnic origins, immigrants such as Cambodians and Hmong differ tremendously in how they conceptualize the relationship between the individual and groups such as family and community. Cambodians balance personal choice and collective commitments in a way that privileges the individual over the group, whereas the reverse is true for the Hmong, as seen in their allegiance to their clan. A telling example of this pattern is the refugees' different approaches to Christianity. Cambodians tend to become Christian as individuals and consider conversion a path to assimilation (Smith-Hefner 1994) and thus "a rite of passage to self-reinvention" (Ong 2003, 217). The Hmong tend toward collective conversion via kin groups and then create Hmong-language congregations that promote the retention of Hmong ethnicity by emphasizing Christian symbols of mutual aid, family, and patriarchy (Duchon 1997; Tapp 1989b; Winland 1992). As a result, conversion is more common for the Hmong than Cambodians (Chan 2004). The study of ethnic origins can greatly advance understanding of the cultural dimension of immigrants' assimilation.

The data supporting the ethnic origins hypothesis also validate the central insight of the modes of incorporation theory: historic group position in a nation-state is a better predictor of perceptions of racial and ethnic inequality than are individual-level characteristics (Bobo and Hutchings 1996). The question remains: Which nation-state? According to Lawrence Bobo and Vincent Hutchings (1996, 957), "The longer the history of relations between dominant and subordinate group members, the more fully crystallized is the sense of group position; the shorter the history of group contact and interaction, the less well crystallized the sense of group position is likely to be." But group position is not defined only by events in the host nation-state. Immigrants arrive with fully crystallized conceptions of inequality that are based on the history and politics of their homeland. Khmer and Hmong refugees often have profoundly different assessments of their relationship with the dominant group in the United States. It is important to analyze not only whether a group became part of American society through coercion or immigration to achieve a better life, but also the cultural variation among "voluntarily incorporated subordinate groups" (956).

Recognizing ethnic variability among immigrants is particularly pertinent to ethnic-competition theory (Nagel and Olzak 1982; Olzak 1992) and the reactive-ethnicity hypothesis derived from it (Portes 1984; Portes and Rumbaut 2001). Following Nathan Glazer and Daniel Moynihan (1963), this theory posits that American society transforms immigrants into ethnic groups through economic and political conflict. Of course, immigrants have experienced such conflict in their homelands, and it is one of the main components of their ethnic origins—perhaps the very reason for their emigration. Cambodians and the Hmong have different assessments of the probability of mistreatment by employers, landlords, and police officers, even when self-reported experiences of institutional discrimination are controlled for. Discriminatory incidents dissipate in Cambodians' more personalized worldview and looser social networks; the same events are amplified by the collective worldview and dense social networks of the Hmong. Thus, immigrants' ethnic origins shape their approaches to racial and ethnic conflict well before they begin competing with natives.

Ethnic origins also influence immigrants' behavior during political struggles over material resources, such as the 1996 restriction of federal social welfare programs to U.S. citizens only. As described in chapter 12, Hmong peer groups discussing this law display a much higher level of mobilization and more aggressive plans for collective action than do Cambodian peer groups. Ethnic origins even influence actual community organizing and political involvement among Cambodians and the Hmong. During the early years of the migration the Hmong established many more nonprofit organizations (one per 478 Hmong) than did Cambodians (one per 1,024 Cambodians), indicating a far more collective approach to the adaptation process (Khoa and Bui 1985). Similarly, the Hmong in the United States have displayed far greater electoral participation (Yang 2003) than Cambodians (Chan 2003, 2004). For example, since 1996 three Hmong men in Eau Claire have been elected to at-large seats on the city council. Three others have run for the local school board. In 2004 a Hmong man narrowly lost a bid for election to the state assembly from a predominantly white district. Conversely, Cambodians have been conspicuously absent from local politics in Chicago and Rochester. One told me, "I hate political meetings because they remind me of those nights when the Khmer Rouge would lecture us about being good workers and then torture and kill people to prove their point."

The corporate quality of Hmong ethnicity gained public attention in November 2004, after Chai Vang admitted shooting eight white hunters in northern Wisconsin while hunting for deer himself. Vang lived in

St. Paul and news of the shooting immediately triggered a response from the Hmong community in the city well before the national media amplified the story. A spokesman for General Vang Pao, who was residing in the St. Paul area at the time, denounced Chai Vang at a news conference and the influential 18-Council, an organization of representatives from Hmong clans, established a fund for the victims' families.[1] These reactions were intended to placate the white community but upset some members of the Hmong community, particularly since Chai Vang reported that the white hunters yelled racial epithets at him and then fired the first shot.[2] Yet the traditional leaders were simply expressing the Hmong worldview developed in Laos: ethnic boundaries need to be vigilantly protected when threatened even if that means sacrificing an individual for the greater good of the community.

Not only do ethnic origins influence the communal resources and individual attitudes that immigrants bring to ethnic competition, but there is mounting evidence that ethnic origins also define competition outcomes such as socioeconomic status. As Julie Canniff (2001) persuasively demonstrates, even though Cambodians in the United States value common American measures of success, such as self-reliance and a high income, these goals are circumscribed by Buddhist values and kinship norms. Cambodians see children's commitment to education as a way of showing respect for parents. Education means not just scholastic achievement but also learning ethical conduct. Such findings do not support a cultural explanation for socioeconomic progress or lack thereof, but they do suggest that immigrants evaluate their material conditions in the United States within the context of their ethnic origins.

These revisions to theories of immigrant adaptation based on assimilation, ethnic competition, and modes of incorporation are all consistent with the transnational perspective. Scholars who intensively study immigrants' homelands will not be surprised that places like Eau Claire and Rochester are less important than ethnic origins in shaping racial and ethnic adaptation. The ethnic-origins hypothesis therefore is among the emerging family of explanations within the transnational perspective. This perspective provides a corrective for policy makers, journalists, and social scientists who still think about immigrants (those who arrive) more often than emigrants (those who leave) and thus conceptualize newcomers only on the basis of their destination, rather than their place of departure as well.

Even so, the ethnic-origins hypothesis is not entirely at home within the transnational perspective. Many proponents of this perspective are content to use broad terms such as "the less-developed world," "periphery in the world system," and "postcolonial countries," even though their analytical power is quite limited. For example, all of these characterizations apply to both Cambodia and Laos, and yet the Khmer and the Hmong often have very different patterns of racial and ethnic adaptation in the United States.

The ethnic-origins hypothesis is even less compatible with a variant of the transnational perspective that argues against using the nation-state as a unit of analysis (Wimmer and Glick Schiller 2003) and for replacing the concept of social identity with that of "social fields" (Levitt and Glick Schiller 2004). Thus, some advocates of the transnational perspective may consider the concept of ethnic origins to be anachronistic, since it is explicitly based on distinctions between types of homeland nation-states and the forms of ethnic identity that arise from them. In the final analysis, transnationalism's essential insight is to study "there" and not just "here" as well as the links between the two. The strength of these links does not erase the importance of place.

Ethnic Origins and Metatheoretical Issues

The concept of ethnic origins suggests resolutions for a range of meta-theoretical problems in the fields of immigration, race, and ethnicity and ways of improving public policy in these areas. Four of the most prominent challenges concern aggregate names, balancing analysis of race with ethnicity, primordial versus constructionist conceptions of ethnicity, and a materialist bias in research on immigrants.

The Aggregation Fallacy

Despite the undisputed increase in American diversity many policy makers, journalists, and social scientists only analyze racial and ethnic groups as aggregates. According to the President's Advisory Commission on Asian Americans and Pacific Islanders (2001, 34):

> The vast majority of data collection and analysis efforts that consider Asian Americans and Pacific Islanders still employ a single categorical designation for the entire population. Such aggregation fails to recognize the diversity that characterizes the Asian and Pacific Islander communities, and leads to improper generalizations and inaccurate evaluations.

The tendency to fit immigrants into categories such as black, white, Hispanic, or Asian ignores important ethnic differences among specific groups. For example, the authors of an article in Social Forces, a top-tier sociology journal, found no differences among minority groups' access to supervisory jobs but conceded, "One explanation for this nonfinding is that our broad racial and ethnic categories failed to capture the 'true' effects of ethnic concentration—results would have been different if we had examined, say, Chinese as opposed to Asians, Mexicans as opposed to Hispanics, and so forth" (Smith and Elliott 2002, 272).

Generic terms like Asian and Hispanic are unavoidable to some extent and are even necessary for some purposes, such as describing macro-level patterns in the demographic transformation of the American population. Aggregates become problematic when they are default terms that shape our perception of diversity. Using the names Asian and Hispanic is convenient for policy makers, journalists, and social scientists since they reduce complexity. But a tidy image of diversity is a disservice at a historical moment when the meanings of diversity are changing. One need not agree with Roger Waldinger and Jennifer Lee (2001, 69) that "Asian is a cover-all category of limited sociological meaning" to nonetheless conclude that the social sciences have reached the point where aggregate names obscure more than they reveal.

Another pernicious consequence of aggregates is the misleading assumption that immigrants become minorities simply because they can be given a name that distinguishes them from whites of European ancestry. Minority status results from inequality, not simply being different from European Americans. Members of a minority group are more likely to encounter stigma and stereotypes about prominent features of their culture and body. They also face an increased chance of discriminatory treatment in everyday public encounters and by people who work for powerful institutions. Assigning immigrants minority status through a tally sheet of aggregate names conceals the real inequalities they experience.

Using names like black, Asian, and Hispanic also implies that the minority experience has a single meaning for all the groups subsumed within an aggregate. A good example disproving this fallacy is Cambodian and Hmong refugees' reactions to the Personal Responsibility and Work Opportunity Reconciliation Act of 1996 (PRWORA). It created a nativist hierarchy in the social-welfare system by denying benefits to noncitizens even if they were legal immigrants who worked and paid taxes. The law also had racial overtones, since European Americans in the U.S. Congress used their power to deprive many Asian and Hispanic Americans of access to public programs funded in part through their taxes. Yet the Cambodians and the Hmong evaluate the PRWORA in different ways because of their ethnic origins. When the Hmong discuss the PRWORA and what to do about it they exhibit a much higher level of mobilization and collective action than do Cambodians. Immigrants can be demographically aggregated upon arrival—and thus instantly labeled a minority—but their subjective understanding of minority status is something learned gradually and heavily influenced by their ethnic origins. The most serious problem with aggregate names, however, is that they prioritize race over ethnicity.

Race . . . and Ethnicity

There is an obvious pattern in the aggregate names white, black, Asian, and Native American. They are racial classifications. Hispanic, of course, is an ethnicity referring to ancestry in Latin America. But policy makers and social scientists usually use it as a de facto racial name by contrasting Hispanics with blacks and whites and merely appending a footnote indicating that "Hispanics may be of any race." This practice encourages the public to think of Hispanics as a race, as do forms requesting demographic information that list Hispanic alongside the categories black, white, and Asian. Thus aggregate names cause many people in American society to implicitly define diversity as racial differences and minimize or even ignore ethnic differences.

A glaring instance of this problem is the very name for President Clinton's Advisory Board on Race, which obviously does not include the concept ethnicity. More than an issue of semantics, the Board's exclusive focus on race became one of its most severe shortcomings. For example, it asserts: "Skin color more than culture or language influences the way immigrants and their offspring become incorporated into our society" (President's Advisory Board on Race 1998, 90). Sociologists know that race is one of the most important determinants of socio-economic status in the United States. But the Board's overemphasis on immigrants' race prioritizes an obsession in American society and ignores immigrants' conceptions of ethnicity derived from experiences in their homelands.

The concept ethnic origins resolves this problem by analyzing how immigrants use their homeland history, politics, and culture to understand their experiences in American society. In doing so it points to one of the most important ways in which contemporary immigrants are changing the meaning of diversity in the United States. Similarities and differences based on religion, language, food, and other aspects of ethnicity are now just as central as race in shaping how natives interact with immigrants and how immigrants interact with each other. The social sciences, however, still tend to prioritize race over ethnicity, often for purely methodological convenience in statistical analysis since "race" is easy to categorize with a few labels while ethnicity is not so easily measured. Yet the public is already quite sophisticated in its ability to distinguish cultural variation among immigrants. To take just one example, guidebooks for Chicago (Fodor's Travel Publications 1995; Passport Books 1993) encourage tourists to visit Korean, Indian, and Vietnamese neighborhoods and describe each cuisine in great detail. Few indeed are the denizens of American cities who need a guidebook to recognize the cultural differences among immigrants from Asia and other parts of the world.

Douglas Massey (1995) is among the first sociologists to question the conventional wisdom that race is more important than ethnicity. He observes that ethnic identity is gaining a new durability because "immigration has become a permanent structural feature of the post-industrial society of the United States" (643). This seemingly irreversible trend means that "the character of ethnicity will be determined relatively more by immigrants and relatively less by later generations, shifting the balance of ethnic identity toward the language, culture, and ways of life of the sending society" (645). Other sociologists point to urban concentration, transnational ties, and the multicultural trend in public policy and popular culture to explain why they think immigrants are more likely now than in the past to transmit their culture to subsequent generations born in the United States (Min 2002).

Policy makers, journalists, and social scientists have been slow to recognize this trend. Many still prioritize receiving society conceptions of race over sending society notions of ethnicity, thus seriously distorting our image of contemporary American diversity. In its final report the President's Advisory Board on Race stated that "racial differences and discrimination obstruct our ability to move beyond race and color to recognize our common values and goals" (President's Advisory Board on Race 1998, 2). This point is valid for physical appearance but not for other forms of diversity. Substituting the phrase "culture and ethnicity" for the phrase "race and color" in the statement results in an absurdity: "to move beyond culture and ethnicity to recognize our common values and goals." Obviously, culture and ethnicity are sources of values and goals, some shared and others distinctive. They cannot be dismissed as myths or social constructions to be overcome—as race can—in order to achieve greater national unity. Unfortunately, giving ethnicity the same prominence as race in our thinking about American diversity runs counter to some assumptions in the social sciences.

One of the most unquestioned assumptions is the taboo against cultural explanations of immigrant adaptation. It is indeed peculiar that social science theories about immigrants abandoned the concept culture just as the American population started becoming more ethnically diverse in the 1970s. Adding to the irony of culture's demise in the fields of immigration, race, and ethnicity is the fact that at several points during the twentieth century progressives and the Left needed the concept culture. Sociologist Robert Park developed the assimilation model in the early 1900s to argue that immigrants stigmatized as culturally inferior at the time (southern and eastern Europeans) would in fact become culturally indistinguishable from those very natives who prided themselves on ancestry from northern and western Europe. In the 1970s, historian Herbert Gutman turned to culture to refute the myth of rapid

Americanization among nineteenth-century immigrants and to demonstrate the vibrancy of anticapitalist immigrant subcultures. These examples should encourage social scientists to bring culture back in to theories about immigrant adaptation despite its current misuse by neoconservatives. Without culture we cannot adequately conceptualize ethnicity, and without ethnicity we are left with racial aggregates. Better to start the difficult work of unpacking the black box of ethnicity than to continue relying on racial names while railing at the myth of race.

The Black Box of Ethnicity

Jhumpa Lahiri is a Pulitzer Prize–winning author of fiction about immigrants from India. Although she has lived almost all of her life in the United States, Lahiri has publicly stated that she finds it difficult to think of herself as an American. When a reporter asked her why, she explained, "Mainly because my parents didn't think of themselves as American. You inherit that idea of where you're from" (Glassie 2003, 19). Lahiri's comment exemplifies what sociologists mean when they refer to ethnicity as a "black box," something that has recognizable external features but whose internal workings remain mysterious. We can understand what "inherit" means for biology, but what does it mean in the case of an ethnic identity?

To "unpack" the black box of ethnicity, sociologists must explain how this complex phenomenon works, and not just show that it works. As an example of the latter tendency, the variable nationality rather than ethnicity is commonly used in statistical analyses of immigrants. This substitution conveniently sidesteps the issue of culture, values, and norms. Often the analysis finds significant differences among nationality groups even when other variables are controlled for. To explain this variation, researchers end up speculating about the influence of some complex of unspecified factors associated with national origin, thus leaving ethnicity "packed."

The sociologist Charles Tilly has suggested one ingenious way of unpacking the black box of ethnicity. Since the mid-1980s, social scientists have recognized that immigrants adapt not only as individuals but also as members of households, families, communities, and other types of social networks. Tilly (1990, 84) encapsulates this consensus in one of his trademark gnomic aphorisms: "Networks migrate; categories stay put; and networks create new categories." It is now conventional wisdom that whereas social ties are "portable," since immigrants maintain membership in networks even when they move, social identities such as ethnicity quickly gain new meaning in a new context. Obviously, being Khmer or Hmong in the United States is not the same as being Khmer in Cambodia or Hmong in Laos.

Yet Tilly's statement on the relationship between social networks and ethnic identity is a guide, not a formula. The experiences of Cambodians and the Hmong in midwestern cities indicate that categories don't always "stay put." For example, the Hmong were an ethnic minority in China and carried this experience to Laos, where it was reinforced, and then to the United States. It certainly seems that some elements of this diasporic worldview have moved with them. Similarly, religion is a highly portable category, since it can take the form of a text, food taboos, and other deeply embedded values and norms that immigrants carry with them. Among Cambodian refugees, early childhood socialization in Cambodia can sustain elements of a Buddhist worldview in the United States, even when they lose touch with monks and temples. Finally, a kinship system, such as a Hmong clan, embodies a worldview about membership in the in-group and out-groups. The clan is the quintessential social network. Yet it would be misleading to depict the importance of clan membership for the Hmong in the United States as solely the creation of a social network, since it is also a cultural norm brought from their homeland.

Among social scientists, reification means incorrectly attributing the power to act or influence to something that is really just a concept or abstraction. In arguing for the durability of homeland social categories I acknowledge the risk of reifying norms and values such as "Xiong clan" and "Buddhist." Social networks may be the ideal mechanism by which to explain how interaction among people produces social categories. Yet the motivation for this interaction in the first place often comes back to preexisting norms and values.

Emphasizing durability too much, however, risks a deterministic argument that presents ethnicity as primordial. Also undesirable is an extreme version of the social constructionist perspective, in which ethnicity has no inherent substance and is merely a context-dependent choice or option. The ethnic-origins hypothesis illustrates how to balance constructionist and primordial perspectives. Rather than having to choose one view or the other, I have made that theoretical decision for each element of Khmer and Hmong ethnic origins instead of for ethnicity in general.

Of the factors I have used to explain variation in the ethnic origins of Cambodians and the Hmong, kinship norms undoubtedly are the closest to being primordial. Practices like patrilineal clans or bilateral kin ancestry are not options, and they change slowly. Indeed, immigrants commonly feel constrained by the durability of kinship norms. Hmong youths in the United States face considerably more parental involvement in their selection of a spouse than do Cambodian youths.

Much less primordial but still not primarily constructionist is the influence of Theravada Buddhism for Cambodians and the diaspora from China for the Hmong. Both of these components of ethnic origins have been in place for hundreds of years. Nonetheless, they can be used to construct new identities. For Cambodians, the multifaceted qualities of Buddhism facilitate their ability to make their beliefs compatible with other worldviews. Similarly, there is variation among the Hmong in the ties they feel to the Hmong population in China. In both cases individuals do have considerable discretion in how they use these group characteristics to fashion a personal sense of ethnicity.

Politics is the most malleable component of ethnic origins. For Cambodians, it involves their experiences and memories of intra-ethnic killing fields; for the Hmong, it concerns being abandoned by their U.S. allies. The meanings of these past events are largely determined by a polyphonic discourse in the present. Yet they ought not to be thought of as optional identities since they will remain potent symbols for future generations of Cambodians and the Hmong in the United States. Immigrants sometimes wish that homeland experiences would "stay put" and not follow them. But historical trauma, the German novelist W. G. Sebald (2001, 258) eloquently reminds us, has a peculiar durability: "We also have appointments to keep in the past, in what has gone before and is for the most part extinguished, and must go there in search of places and people who have some connection with us on the far side of time."

The Materialist Bias

The greatest potential of the ethnic-origins hypothesis is shifting the focus of research on immigrant adaptation from materialist to symbolic outcomes. Most of the social-science literature on immigrants seeks to explain attributes of class such as educational achievement, employment, and income. This goal is epitomized in the title of Stanley Lieberson's (1981) classic work about social mobility among blacks and European immigrants, *A Piece of the Pie: Blacks and White Immigrants Since 1880*.

Twenty years later, Roger Waldinger (2001a, 4) speaks for many social scientists and policy makers when he explains that the subject of his book *Strangers at the Gates* "is the issue at the heart of the contemporary immigration debate: can today's newcomers make it?" The meaning of "making it," however, is open to several interpretations. For Waldinger and others it is unambiguous: "Sociologists now agree that economic progress is the linchpin of assimilation, driving all other shifts in the social structure of ethnicity" (Waldinger 2001a, 15). Similarly, Portes and Rumbaut's (2001, 282–83) analysis of immigrant youths focuses on "paths of mobility across generations" to explain why "some groups manage to make it into the middle classes." Although Alba and Nee (2003, 41) are critical of Portes and Rumbaut's conclusions, their new assimilation theory actually rests on the same assumption, that success means "pursuit of familiar goals—a good education, a good job, a nice place to live." Despite the enormous contributions to the immigration literature that all five sociologists have made, David Hernández and Evelyn Glenn (2003) argue persuasively that studies of individual mobility among immigrants reinforce the conventional status-attainment model in this field and implicitly exclude other paradigms for analyzing social inequality, such as group advancement through social movements.

Political mobilization and collective action is a reasonable alternative conceptualization of what "making it" means in the United States, but I suggest a third possibility: successful communication about racial and ethnic differences in an increasingly pluralistic society. In fact, the need "for a new language of diversity" was one of the main obstacles confronted by the President's Advisory Board on Race (1998, 56). Finding a new language of diversity has been an elusive goal for many reasons. One reason is the materialist bias in social-science research on immigrants and the assumption that symbolic outcomes such as ethnic identity and perceptions of inequality lack policy relevance. When social scientists think of public policy they usually define it narrowly as the goals of federal departments and agencies. Given the importance of federal funding for social-science research, it is not surprising that policy relevance is typically equated with labor, housing, public assistance, health, crime, and education.

At the local level, however, race and ethnic relations are common public policy concerns. A survey of municipal elected officials found that 24 percent often or very often were involved in public discussions about race, ethnicity, and racism; another 40 percent reported occasional involvement (National League of Cities 1996). A similar survey in 2005 (Brennan, Wheel, and Hoene 2005) revealed that 47 percent of these officials considered population changes and migration a moderate or major problem in their cities, a level of concern above that for violent crime (44 percent) and only slightly below the quality of education (50 percent). To address racial and ethnic issues, mayors, city councils, and other municipal officials invite residents to serve on commissions and task forces to promote dialogue among diverse groups (National League of Cities 1999). This interactionist goal reached the federal level in 1997, when President Clinton formed the President's Advisory Board on Race (1998). The Board encouraged hundreds of community leaders to support its "One America Conversations" series, which resulted in about 1,400 meetings involving more than 18,000 participants in 113 cities. From these gatherings the board concluded that "the shifting characteristics of racial and ethnic groups and their deeper meanings make it hard to have a concrete conversation about what race means to any one group" (56). Understanding immigrants' ethnic origins is thus vital to decoding the new language of American diversity.

Despite the challenges faced by President Clinton's national initiative, local initiatives to promote better race and ethnic relations remain common. For example, in January 2005, the State Council on Asian-Pacific Minnesotans sponsored a day-long meeting entitled "Asian Pacific American Dialogue on Race and Reconciliation." According to the organizers, the event was designed "to help community members to share their own experiences of racism with others; talk about the effect racism has had on them; take ownership of their stories and experiences; and be healed and empowered to take action to make a difference."[3] Social scientists could not ask for a more concise statement of how research on the symbolic dimension of race, ethnicity, and immigration addresses the aspirations of some segments of the American public.

Beyond the First Generation

The empirical support for the ethnic-origins hypothesis suggests a number of ways of improving theory and policy about immigrants' racial and ethnic adaptation. But it is also important to mention the theory's greatest limitation: the ethnic-origins hypothesis is most applicable to first-generation immigrants. Theories based on assimilation, segmented assimilation, modes of incorporation, and ethnic competition are well positioned to examine developments among the second generation—the immigrants' native-born children.

Despite this caveat, ethnic origins may be relevant beyond the first generation. Sociologists commonly call immigrants who arrive in the United States at the age of twelve years or younger the 1.5 generation because they fall in the middle, being born abroad but experiencing most or all of their formative socialization here. Of the 179 survey respondents analyzed in this book, 40 belong to the 1.5 generation. Only one of them, however, stated that she was unable to answer the question "Describe some of the best and worst things about life in the United States compared to life in Cambodia/Laos." Immigrants who arrive as young children retain strong impressions of their homeland, owing to early childhood experiences there; familial, peer, and communal socialization in the United States; and sometimes return visits to their country of origin. I therefore give the last word on ethnic origins to a particularly eloquent member of the 1.5 generation:

I think the most important thing is not discrimination and other races but who you are. It's more important to understand who you are so then people know you. If I have kids I wouldn't have to teach them about discrimination. They will experience it no matter what I say so it's better to know who you are, where I'm from, what language I speak, my culture. Our culture has been drowned in the United States, it cannot compare. American culture is so much more aggressive. Because of freedom, Americans say whatever they believe. They rebel against their own parents a lot here. But for us it's very crucial to respect parents. Culture, religion, all that comes down from parents to us. For us to break against parents is like breaking our culture.

= Appendix A =
Overview of Methodologies

Archival Sources

I examined articles about the Hmong, Cambodians, and other Southeast Asian refugees in the *Eau Claire Leader-Telegram, Rochester Post-Bulletin, Milwaukee Journal Sentinel*, and several citywide and neighborhood newspapers in Chicago. I have not provided page numbers for quotations from these newspaper articles for two reasons. First, I obtained many of the newspaper articles from on-line databases rather than the original newspaper. There is often no way to determine page numbers from the electronic version of an article. Second, articles from clipping files at a library or the office of the newspaper itself often do not contain page numbers. It would have been inconsistent to cite page numbers for quotations from some newspaper articles but not others. I do, of course, cite page numbers for all quotations from books, journals, and magazines.

Standardized Survey

Between 1996 and 1999, five co-ethnic interviewers administered the survey questionnaire following the principle of dimensional sampling (Arnold 1970). They took between six and twelve months to complete this activity in each city, starting with Eau Claire and ending with Milwaukee. The interviewers used a community profile checklist I created to select respondents based on sex, age, marital status, years of U.S. residence, and employment. Once the quota for a category had been filled, such as twenty-five males, the remaining respondents had to be from the other category. Although not a random sample, this dimensional sampling produced an extremely diverse quota sample (see tables A.1, A.2, and A.3).

Semistructured Personal Interviews

I conducted semistructured face-to-face interviews in English with 28 of the 179 survey respondents (whom I call informants when they spoke to

Table A.1   Social and Demographic Characteristics of Survey Sample,
1996 to 1999

Variable	Hmong			Cambodians		
		Mini-mum	Maxi-mum		Mini-mum	Maxi-mum
Percentage foreign-born	100	—	—	100	—	—
Percentage living in small city	60	—	—	50	—	—
Percentage male	49	—	—	46	—	—
Percentage never married	18	—	—	26	—	—
Mean current age	36	18	76	39	18	70
Mean age at arrival	23	1	65	26	2	53
Mean years of U.S. residence	13	2	23	13	4	21
Percentage U.S. citizens	44	—	—	41	—	—
Percentage Christian	34	—	—	17	—	—
Mean level of English[a]	2.0	0	3	1.9	0	3
Percentage speaking no English	8	—	—	2	—	—
Percentage speaking English very well	41	—	—	24	—	—
Mean years of U.S. education[b]	5.6	0	20	3.6	0	16
Percentage with no U.S. education	42	—	—	51	—	—
Percentage with B.A. or M.A. Degree	24	—	—	6	—	—
Mean occupational level[c]	2.3	0	5	1.7	0	5
Percentage laborers	14	—	—	18	—	—
Percentage professionals	26	—	—	8	—	—

Source: Author's compilation.
Note: N = 80 Hmong, 99 Cambodians.
[a]Respondents' self-designated level of proficiency: none (0), only a little, difficulty speaking and make many mistakes (1), enough to make myself understood but still make mistakes (2), speak very well, can almost always say what I mean (3).
[b]Education in primary, middle, and high school in U.S., as well as two- and four-year colleges, and graduate school. Excludes English as a Second Language classes.
[c]Type of current job or last job if currently unemployed: never employed (0), laborer (1), production (2), service (3), technical service (4), professional (5).

Table A.2   Distribution by Neighborhood of Survey Sample in Chicago and Milwaukee (as Percentage of Sample)

Neighborhood	Cambodians	Hmong
Chicago		
Uptown	56	—
Albany Park	42	—
Other	2	—
Milwaukee[a]		
Near North Side	—	63
Near South Side	—	22
Other	—	13

Source: Author's compilation.
Note: N = 32 Hmong, 50 Cambodians
[a]Data are missing for one respondent.

me in person). Extending a technique used by Mary Waters (1990) to understand how European Americans answer the U.S. census question on ancestry, I used several of my survey questions as the outline for the interviews. I asked each informant about her or his answers to some of the closed-ended and open-ended survey questions and, if necessary, I probed to determine what specific experiences were the basis for her or his assessment of American race and ethnic relations. I intentionally chose informants from both sexes, a range of age groups, and different

Table A.3   Distribution of Clans in Hmong Survey Sample (as Number of Respondents)

Hmong Clans[a]	Hmong
Xiong	20
Vang	16
Yang	14
Lee or Ly	9
Lor	6
Her	4
Moua	4
Thao	3
Vue	3
Cha	1

Source: Author's compilation.
Note: N = 80
[a]The Xiong, Vang, and Yang clans are the three largest clans, in that order, in both Eau Claire and Milwaukee (*Hmong American Residence and Business Directory* 1999).

Table A.4   List of Informants Interviewed, 1997 to 1999

Name	Sex	Ethnicity	City	Age	Occupation
Buon	F	Khmer	Chicago	40	Public school teacher
Carl	M	Khmer	Rochester	24	Health program student
Cher	F	Hmong	Milwaukee	37	Public school teacher
Chong	M	Hmong	Eau Claire	37	Social-service worker
Chou	F	Hmong	Eau Claire	35	Teacher's aide
Elizabeth	F	Khmer	Rochester	30	Health-care worker
Heng	M	Khmer	Chicago	24	Fast-food worker
Kantal	M	Khmer	Chicago	52	Social-service worker
Ka	F	Hmong	Milwaukee	18	College student
Kelly	F	Hmong	Milwaukee	31	Public school teacher
Kouy	F	Khmer	Rochester	19	Unemployed
Margaret	F	Khmer	Chicago	46	Public school teacher
Mee	F	Hmong	Eau Claire	22	College student
Nao	M	Hmong	Eau Claire	21	Sales representative
Phen	M	Khmer	Rochester	29	Health-care worker
Rebecca	F	Khmer	Rochester	30	Health-care worker
Robert	M	Hmong	Eau Claire	31	Retail-store manager
Roun	F	Khmer	Chicago	29	At-home mother of two
Samnang	F	Khmer	Chicago	28	College student
Sokorn	M	Khmer	Chicago	46	Factory worker
Sombat	M	Khmer	Chicago	24	College student
Suom	M	Khmer	Chicago	51	Factory worker
Sopot	F	Khmer	Rochester	18	Factory worker
Sy	M	Hmong	Milwaukee	34	Church pastor
Teng	M	Hmong	Eau Claire	36	Factory worker
Yer	M	Hmong	Milwaukee	19	College student
Ying	M	Hmong	Milwaukee	34	Grocery-store owner
You	F	Hmong	Eau Claire	20	Teacher's aide

Source: Author's compilation.

classes and have given each one a Khmer, Hmong, or American pseudonym depending on the real name they gave to the co-ethnic interviewer at the time of the survey (see table A.4).

Peer-Group Conversations

Seven co-ethnic facilitators organized and moderated peer-group conversations for Cambodians in Rochester and Chicago, and for the Hmong in Eau Claire and Milwaukee (see Gamson 1994 for an overview of the peer-group methodology). Each facilitator recruited a minimum of four and a maximum of five individuals, none of whom had taken part in the survey nor the semistructured interviews. I stipulated that participants not include close relatives or leaders of ethnic self-help associations, and that separate peer groups be held for men and women. But I did not use a quota system to determine whom they recruited as participants since, as Gamson argues, selecting friends or acquaintances from similar backgrounds promotes conversation. I did provide the facilitators with topics and questions to initiate the discussion, which they tape-recorded. Tables A.5, A.6, A.7, and A.8 provide background information on each of the four peer-group conversations analyzed in this book. I have given all participants a Khmer, Hmong, or American pseudonym depending on the name they gave to their co-ethnic facilitator.

Table A.5   Participant Characteristics of Cambodian Men's Peer Group, Chicago, 1997

Name	Age	Years in United States	U.S. Education	Current Occupation
Sarom	55	15	Associate's Degree	Retired
Khuon	55	15	In College	College student
Chath	23	13	In College	Computer consultant
Darith	41	11	ESL classes	Real estate agent
Savuth	55	16	Associate's Degree	Retired

Source: Author's compilation.
Notes: Facilitator: Self-employed male interpreter and translator, with B.A. degree
Location: Cambodian Association of Illinois
Language used by participants: Khmer

Table A.6   Participant Characteristics of Hmong Men's Peer Group, Milwaukee, 1999

Name	Age	Years in United States	U.S. Education	Current Occupation
Song	32	19	M.A. degree	Social worker
Chai	36	19	M.A. degree	Social worker
Dee	30	18	M.A. degree	Accountant
Vue	42	16	—[a]	Small-business owner

Notes: Facilitator: Male case worker at an ethnic nonprofit association, with M.A. degree
Location: Facilitator's home
Language used by participants: Hmong
[a]Information not provided by participant.

Table A.7   Participant Characteristics of Cambodian Women's Peer Group, Rochester, Minnesota, 1999

Name	Age	Years in United States	U.S. Education	Current Occupation
Lakhena	26	16	Some college	School counselor
Kristi	21	17	High school	Food service
Sothy	20	16	Some college	Salesperson
Sambo	29	18	Associate's degree	Medical technician
Sinath	25	—[a]	Associate's degree	Data entry

Source: Author's compilation.
Notes: Facilitator: Female health-care worker, with associate's degree
    Location: Facilitator's home
    Language used by participants: English
[a]Information not provided by participant.

Table A.8   Participant Characteristics of Hmong Women's Peer Group, Eau Claire, Wisconsin, 1999

Name	Age	Years in United States	U.S. Education	Current Occupation
Julie	39	19	B.A. degree	Patient services
Mayseng	30	21	B.A. degree	Teacher's aide
Paly	25	19	B.A. degree	Social worker
Kaolee	26	13	B.A. degree	Small-business owner
Bao	24	5	None	None

Source: Author's compilation.
Notes: Facilitator: Female membership-services director at an American nonprofit
    association, with B.A. degree
    Location: Hmong Mutual Assistance Association
    Language used by participants: English and Hmong

Appendix B

Details of Methodologies

omparing two ethnic groups in the four cities quickly convinced me of the need to use more than one methodology. Ever since the formation of quantitative and qualitative camps in the 1950s, some social scientists have advocated using multiple methods to achieve "mutual validation" (Vidich and Shapiro 1955, 30) through "a triangulation of measurement processes" (Webb et al. 1966/1981, 35). Advantages of this approach include maximizing the efficiency of each method (Zelditch 1962), compensating for the limitations inherent in any single method (Campbell and Fiske 1959; Denzin 1970), and actually integrating diverse methods to produce a new methodology (Sieber 1973). Several different models exist for combining quantitative and qualitative methods (Axinn, Fricke, and Thornton 1991; Louis 1982; Pearce 2002). I follow the multimethod, multisite research model called an ethnosurvey (Massey 1987; Massey and Zenteno 2000).

My ethnosurvey of Cambodians in Chicago and Rochester, Minnesota, and the Hmong in Milwaukee and Eau Claire, Wisconsin, began in 1996 and ended in 1999. I first examined archival sources to determine how Cambodian and Hmong refugees arrived in each research site and the patterns of race and ethnic relations that unfolded with their settlement. I then used a standardized survey to obtain identical statistics on the refugees in each place. After the survey I conducted semistructured follow-up interviews with survey respondents to obtain qualitative data. Finally, I organized peer-group conversations in each city with new participants in order to have multilevel qualitative data. The resulting database provides the in-depth historical information necessary to understand the social structure of particular places. It also provides the quantitative data necessary to statistically test whether ethnicity, urban locale, and other factors are significantly correlated with a range of immigrant adaptation outcomes. Finally, the database contains the qualitative data necessary to explain these correlations and to allow Cambodian and Hmong refugees to use their own words to express their experiences with American diversity.

Archival Sources

An ethnosurvey typically employs ethnography and fieldwork to document the social structure of each research site (Massey 1987). Given the historical dimension of Cambodian and Hmong refugees' resettlement in the upper Midwest from the mid-1970s to the early 1990s, I turned to contemporaneous newspaper articles for information about the four cities.

At the time of my research, the on-line database of the *Eau Claire Leader-Telegram* included articles dating back to 1991; the *Rochester Post-Bulletin* database contained articles dating back to 1990. The on-line database for the *Milwaukee Journal Sentinel* only went back to 1999.[1] I pursued several strategies for procuring earlier newspaper coverage of Cambodians and the Hmong in these three cities.

In Eau Claire and Rochester I went to the office of the local newspaper to read relevant clipping files from the 1970s and 1980s. At the *Eau Claire Leader-Telegram* this was a single file named "Hmong." At the *Rochester Post-Bulletin* I read a series of files labeled "Refugees—Asia," "Refugees—Southeast Asia," and so on for "Cambodia," "Hmong," "Laos," and "Vietnam."

The *Milwaukee Journal Sentinel*'s clipping files are not open to the public, but with the help of a reporter I obtained copies of the articles indexed under the heading Hmong; most of them were published during the mid-1980s through the early 1990s. I also located a subject index for the *Milwaukee Journal* for the years 1976 (produced by the Bell & Howell Company Indexing Center) and for 1979 to 1980 (produced by the Indexing Software Group) in the Special Collections Department of the library at the University of Wisconsin–Eau Claire. At the main branch of the Milwaukee Public Library I found other newspaper articles in the clipping file "Hmong in Wisconsin" and "Vietnamese in Wisconsin." Various neighborhood-history files at the library contained additional newspaper articles, as well as some very valuable secondary sources. Perhaps my most important archival discovery was at the reference section of the library at the University of Wisconsin–Whitewater, where I located a CD-ROM of indexed *Milwaukee Journal Sentinel* articles from 1990 to 1998.

A search of the *Chicago Tribune* and *Chicago Sun-Times* websites produced very few articles on Cambodians in the city, which is not surprising, given that they number only 5,000 out of a total population of 2 million. Fortunately, I had done fieldwork and participant observation in the Cambodian community in Uptown for a previous study (Hein 1995), and also located an excellent secondary source on the topic (Hansen and Hong 1991). In addition, I read the materials, mostly newspaper articles, in the relevant files at the Sulzer Regional Chicago Public

Library, the Chicago Historical Society, and the municipal reference section of the Chicago Public Library's Harold Washington Center. At each archive I examined the files "Ethnic Groups—Asian," "Ethnic Groups—Cambodian," "Ethnic Groups—Vietnamese," "Communities—Uptown," and "Communities—Albany Park."

Standardized Survey

Generally, an ethnosurvey obtains quantitative data from an event-history questionnaire administered by means of a survey (Massey 1987). Collecting life histories is important for documenting longitudinal decision making related to marriage, work, and migration. Since the process of immigrants' incorporation into a host society's race and ethnic relations does not follow a discrete sequence, I used the traditional cross-sectional approach to collecting quantitative data. I planned to survey a total of two hundred Cambodians and Hmong, fifty in each of the four research sites. I hired one or two bilingual co-ethnic interviewers in each city to conduct in-person interviews with other Cambodians and Hmong, using a questionnaire containing sixty-eight closed-ended and seven open-ended questions.

With subsamples of this size I deemed it unrealistic to attempt a random sample. For example, even if picked randomly, 50 Hmong could not "represent" the 15,000 Hmong in Milwaukee. I therefore allowed the co-ethnic interviewers to select the respondents for the sample on the basis of their contacts in the ethnic community.

Given the statistical techniques I planned to apply to the quantitative data, I considered it unacceptable to have a snow-ball sample. Instead I created a quota sample by following the principle of dimensional sampling (Arnold 1970). I gave the co-ethnic interviewers five stipulations to ensure that the respondents they picked produced a varied and balanced sample.

First, respondents had to be foreign-born; age eighteen or over; could not come from the same household; and could not be current employees of an ethnic association. I intended this last stipulation to exclude ethnic leaders who might report attitudes that they wished outsiders to have of their community rather than their personal views.

Second, I used data from the 1990 U.S. census, the most current one at the time, to create a profile of the Cambodian and Hmong population in each research site. I then created a community profile checklist for the co-ethnic interviewers to use in selecting respondents. The checklist itemized sex, age, marital status, years of U.S. residence, and employment. For example, the checklist contained places to mark off twenty-five men and twenty-five women. Once the quota of twenty-five males had been recruited, all of the remaining respondents had to be female. A similar procedure was used for the remaining four respondent characteristics: age group; year of arrival; marital status; and work status (or receiving public assistance). It became more difficult for the co-ethnic interviewers to complete the quotas as the number of survey respondents increased (for example, finding a married, working woman who arrived in the United States prior to 1980). Once the survey was completed, deviation from the quotas proved to be minor, with the required number of respondents off by no more than five for any category and typically only two or three.

Third, for the surveys in Chicago and Milwaukee I asked the co-ethnic interviewers to seek respondents from the different neighborhoods where the refugees live. The community profile checklist for these sites therefore included Uptown and Albany Park for Chicago and the Near North Side and Near South Side for Milwaukee. I did not seek neighborhood variation in the samples from Eau Claire and Rochester.

Fourth, Hmong communities are segmented by kinship groups. I therefore asked the co-ethnic interviewers to select Hmong respondents in Eau Claire and Milwaukee from as many different clans as possible. I did not, however, list specific clans on the community profile checklist.

Fifth, I stipulated that Cambodian respondents could not be members of minority groups from Cambodia, such as Cham (Muslims), Chinese, or Vietnamese (though people of mixed ancestry were included). I made this stipulation because I wanted to compare refugees who were from a minority group in their homeland (the Hmong in Laos) to those from a dominant cultural group in their respective homeland (the Khmer in Cambodia).

After extending the survey completion deadline several times, the sample finally totaled 179 individuals. I will call these people respondents because they completed a questionnaire. This group comprised 50 Cambodians in Chicago; 49 Cambodians in Rochester, Minnesota; 32 Hmong in Milwaukee; and 48 Hmong in Eau Claire, Wisconsin.

The five co-ethnic interviewers who administered the survey questionnaire all had extensive knowledge of and contacts in their ethnic communities. Three of them worked for a Cambodian or Hmong mutual assistance association, and two others were active community members who frequently organized self-help and cultural events. I met with each one in person to review the questionnaire, coach them on interviewing techniques (particularly for the open-ended survey questions), and explain how they should administer the human subjects' research consent form. I paid the co-ethnic interviewers twenty dollars for each completed interview. As explained in appendix A, I allowed the co-ethnic interviewers to pick respondents to fill quotas on the basis of sex, age, length of U.S. residence, marital status, and source of income. While not a random sample, this dimensional sampling produced an extremely diverse sample in terms of demographic and socioeconomic characteristics (see tables A.1, A.2, and A.3).

A potential for bias in the sample was the possibility of co-ethnic interviewers' picking respondents from their own kin and friendship networks. If the co-ethnic interviewers had just chosen their friends and family members, they would have been able to quickly recruit respondents and rapidly complete the survey. I do not think this problem occurred. In fact, it took the interviewers from six months to a year to complete the interviews in each locale. One interviewer, in Milwaukee, was unable to complete the project, largely owing to the demands of his full-time job at an ethnic self-help association. When one year had elapsed and he had only interviewed thirty-two individuals, I terminated the effort to recruit more Hmong respondents in Milwaukee; for this reason the number of completed questionnaires at this site is substantially lower than those in Chicago (fifty), Rochester (forty-nine), and Eau Claire (forty-eight). A payment of thirty dollars to each respondent was a final factor that helped diversify the sample. The payment reduced sampling bias by providing a financial incentive for participation rather than relying on respondents' ties to the co-ethnic interviewers.

Semistructured Personal Interviews

Qualitative data can be obtained at any stage of an ethnosurvey, since its primary purpose is to increase the external validity of the research by adding "historical depth, richness of context, and the intuitive appeal of real life" (Massey 1987, 1504). To maximize this outcome, I chronologically linked the multisite survey with multisite follow-up interviews. After the co-ethnic interviewers completed the survey I conducted semistructured face-to-face interviews with 28 of the 179 respondents (whom I call informants when describing what they said to me in person).

I also thematically linked the survey with the follow-up interviews. Surveys are often supplemented with qualitative methods to investigate anomalies in the survey data (Pearce 2002). To increase the internal validity of the survey data I extended a technique used by Mary Waters (1990). When she interviewed European Americans she asked how they would have answered the U.S. census question on ancestry (in 1980 only 5 percent of the population was asked this question). Waters then used probing questions to determine why respondents picked specific ancestry names, such as Irish or German, and what those names meant to them.

Like Waters, I used survey questions as the outline for my semistructured interviews. Unlike her, I actually knew my informants' answers to these questions prior to the interview. I asked each informant to explain why she or he had given particular answers to some of the closed-ended and open-ended survey questions. When necessary I probed to determine what specific experiences were the basis for an informant's assessment of American race and ethnic relations. My informants' responses provide a wealth of quotations that immeasurably enrich the statistical findings from the survey.

I planned to conduct follow-up interviews with 40 of the 179 survey respondents (10 from each city). The final survey question asked whether respondents would be willing to be contacted again, and 22 percent said no, thus reducing the number of potential informants to 140. Due to my lack of foreign language skills, I could only interview respondents who were somewhat or very proficient in English. This limitation excluded 30 percent of the remaining survey respondents, leaving only 98 individuals as potential informants. Some of these had moved and could not be contacted. A few others whom I contacted declined to be interviewed again or canceled the interview at the last moment for personal reasons. I also needed to conduct interviews in four different cities, which further reduced the pool to about 25 potential informants at each site. Finally, I sought to interview equal numbers of men and women from different class backgrounds and at different points in the life cycle. Within this pool of potential informants I prioritized those who had given lengthy and detailed responses to the open-ended questions on the survey.

The twenty-eight informants who provided follow-up interviews are evenly divided by sex and include unmarried young adults, parents who have young children, and parents with adult children (see table A.4). The informants vary considerably by occupation. Most are factory workers, health-care providers, college students, and public school teachers. Informants also include an unemployed woman, an at-home mother of two young children, a fast-food worker, two social service providers, a chain-store manager, a minister, and a self-employed owner of an ethnic grocery store. The interviews lasted one to three hours, largely determined by the amount of time informants could spare from their busy lives. Interviews usually took place in respondents' homes or in the offices of Cambodian or Hmong nonprofit associations. Two were held in a nearly empty university cafeteria and one took place in the informant's workplace. I paid each follow-up interviewee twenty dollars.

Transcription Philosophy for Semistructured Interviews

In order to have a transcript of each of the twenty-eight semistructured interviews I took detailed notes during the interview but did not tape-record them. I began learning the art of the personal interview in 1983 from Howard S. Becker during my first year of graduate study in the Department of Sociology at Northwestern University. Unless the goal is conversational analysis, Becker advised students not to use a tape recorder. He felt that a tape recorder inhibits informants from expressing their true feelings and is surprisingly prone to technical problems despite its apparent simplicity. Becker believed that with practice an interviewer could take written notes in sufficient detail during the interview to be able to type up a nearly verbatim transcript after the interview. He stipulated, however, that the typed transcript must be completed as soon as possible after completing the interview. For Becker this meant no longer than a few hours. He emphasized that, whenever possible, the interviewer must type the transcript before sleeping, which he felt impaired memory of the interview. I followed Becker's advice when I conducted and transcribed the interviews for this book.

The most difficult issue I faced concerned the best way to produce transcripts of interviews with people who speak English as a second language. Some scholars follow a transcription philosophy that seeks to portray informants' speech the way they would speak if they had perfect command of their second language. This edited-language approach to interview transcription has several advantages. It provides clear and unambiguous prose for readers. It may be consistent with an informant's desire to be presented as a highly articulate speaker of English. Finally, the edited-language approach avoids inadvertently invoking stereotypes, such as the prejudicial portrayal of Asian Americans as speakers of "broken English." Sucheng Chan (1994; 2003, xxiv), an advocate of the edited-language approach, argues that "Purists who transcribe every hem and haw, every nonstandard usage, are not ensuring authenticity but are, rather, fetishizing 'exotic' speech. I find such a stance paternalistic and condescending."

Despite these valid considerations, I follow Amy Tan's (1995) natural-language approach to linguistic diversity. She emphasizes the need to retain the different voices expressed by various forms of "Englishes." I thus transcribed the personal interviews to reflect as closely as possible my informants' actual spoken English. I have, however, made minor grammatical corrections to facilitate communication with readers, such as the use of articles, verb tense, and plural or singular nouns. I found several other reasons to make minor editorial changes. I have deleted a few sentences from the quotations presented in this book to maintain an informant's anonymity or when the informant briefly went off on a tangent and then resumed the thread of the conversation. I have also made a few changes in sentence sequence that violate the actual chronology of the interview but clarify incidents and experiences when the informant refers to previously mentioned statements. Aside from these few technical alterations I kept editorial alterations to a bare minimum in order to retain what Joyce Carol Oates (1999, 13) has called "the immediate, impressionistic fluidity of speech."

The primary advantage of this approach is that it conveys the feeling of what it is like to have a conversation with an informant during a personal interview. For example, I use ellipses within quotations from the follow-up interviews to indicate when an informant stopped speaking in midsentence; the ellipses do not indicate the omission of a word or phrase from the quotation. To further give readers the sense that they are present with an informant I often include my questions to informants. In addition, I provide brief parenthetical comments where appropriate to indicate the tone in which an informant made a statement (such as irony or anger).

There are additional reasons for following the natural-language approach. Oddly enough, I found the most persuasive rationale for presenting unpolished quotations in Todd Gitlin and Nanci Hollander's classic book on urban Appalachians. As the authors of *Uptown: Poor Whites in Chicago* explain (1970, xxvi–xxvii):

> We have maintained enough dialect to ensure that you do not forget these are foreigners who are speaking to you, and who would speak to your face as foreigners if they had the chance: foreigners in many senses, at least in that they have codes and meanings and experience, condensed into language, which are not yours. . . . [Remember that] transcriptions of our own speech would betray more slurring and uneven contraction than writers and others of the literate class like to take credit for.

Charles Tilly, who surely ranks as one of the most eloquent sociologists of the late twentieth and early twenty-first centuries, is one member of the literati who has owned up to Gitlin and Hollander's assessment of our speech. He makes a revealing admission about speech in an essay on the error-correction process in social institutions (Tilly 1996). Early in his teaching career Tilly provided tapes and transcripts of his classroom lectures to his students, hoping to reduce their note taking and increase their attention in class. He quickly abandoned this experiment (594):

> Tapes and transcripts reveal something I should have known, but had never quite recognized: lecturing from notes, however orderly, I hardly ever uttered a complete sentence. Even intact sentences often mixed metaphors or switched grammatical direction. I interrupted myself, introduced new points that suddenly came to mind, modified or even contradicted arguments incessantly. . . . I had discovered the difference between

writing and conversation. I could not bear to distribute accurate transcripts, and found myself staying up very late, like Louis XIV, to rewrite the record of what happened in my domain. I never taped another course.

A final reason I chose gritty over polished transcripts is that, unlike a classroom lecture, an interview is a special type of conversation. When conversations are about complex subjects like experiencing discrimination they contain a tangled mixture of the abstract and the concrete, statements of general beliefs and anecdotal descriptions of past events. The social-science interview creates even greater experimentation in expressing meaning. An informant may not have previously articulated an opinion about one or more of the issues raised by the interviewer. The nuances of speech are multiplied even further when the informant is using English as her or his second language. One need not move to full conversational analysis, where every pause and "uh" is preserved in the written record, to appreciate the spontaneity of speech in face-to-face settings. To convey this unrehearsed quality of a conversation I refrained as much as possible from making editorial changes to the transcripts.

Peer-Group Conversations

An ethnosurvey obtains multilevel data by gathering information on both individuals and households (Massey 1987). I took the ethnosurvey one step further toward the goal of compiling multilevel data. After reviewing the data from the survey and semistructured interviews, I concluded that they only tapped the individual rather than collective dimensions of race and ethnic relations. As Rick Fantasia (2002, 123) notes: "When people are entirely represented in interviews, the only social relationships that we observe are those that can be constituted in, and by their words, but practices speak louder than words, or differently than words, or they may play a role in influencing what words are chosen or permitted." I share Fantasia's concerns and therefore used a variant of the focus group that William Gamson (1994) calls a peer-group conversation to provide a more interactionist account of racial and ethnic adaptation among Cambodians and the Hmong. According to Gamson (17), "The greatest advantage [of the peer-group conversation] is that it allows us to observe the process of people constructing and negotiating shared meaning using their natural vocabulary."

To implement Gamson's (1994) methodology I recruited seven coethnic facilitators to organize and moderate peer-group conversations for Cambodians in Rochester and Chicago and for the Hmong in Eau Claire and Milwaukee. Some of the facilitators were staff members at local ethnic nonprofit associations and some were individuals who were well known in the ethnic community because of their volunteer work during social and cultural events. Only one facilitator had been involved in the survey phase of the project. I met in person with each facilitator and explained how she or he should select participants, administer the human-subjects research consent form, distribute a one-page demographic questionnaire to each participant, and promote discussion in the group (which I would not be attending).

Each facilitator recruited a minimum of four and a maximum of five individuals. The co-ethnic facilitators then organized and moderated the peer-group conversations. The topic of the conversation was a contro-versial political issue affecting immigrants. The resulting transcripts yielded exceptionally rich collective discourses on race and ethnic rela-tions in the United States.

A peer-group conversation works best when it involves "familiar acquaintances rather than strangers" and is "held on participants' own turf rather than in a bureaucratic setting" (Gamson 1994, 193). I there-fore allowed the facilitators to select the location for the group. Similarly, I did not closely regulate how the facilitators recruited participants (as I did for survey respondents), since selecting friends or acquaintances from similar backgrounds would actually promote conversation. I stip-ulated only that none of the participants could be survey respondents nor follow-up interview informants. In addition, none of the partici-pants could be facilitators' close relatives, or be currently employed by an ethnic self-help association, in order to avoid conflicts of interest among participants (see tables A.5, A.6, A.7, and A.8).

I also stipulated that separate peer-group conversations be held for men and women. Since men's and women's communication styles vary, mixing men and women could have created unnecessary dissonance among participants. The patriarchal gender roles among Cambodians and the Hmong might have dissuaded some women from speaking freely in front of men. With one exception I used male facilitators for the male groups and female facilitators for the female groups. In Chicago I chose a self-effacing young man as the facilitator for the women's group. He had an excellent reputation in the Cambodian community, and his prior work as a co-ethnic interviewer for the survey demonstrated a nonsexist communication style.

When the peer groups met, the co-ethnic facilitators first determined whether participants wished to communicate in their native language, English, or both. They then moderated the approximately one-and-a-half-hour conversation using questions I provided to stimulate discussion. The facilitators made two tape recordings for each peer-group conversation and then sent them to me for transcription and, if necessary, translation. The facilitators paid each participant fifty dollars and I paid each facilitator seventy-five dollars. Ultimately I obtained tape recordings of a male and a female group of Hmong in Eau Claire; a male and a female group of Hmong in Milwaukee; a male and a female group of Cambodians in Chicago; and a female group of Cambodians in Rochester.

I terminated the effort to hold a male peer-group conversation for Cambodians in Rochester after two attempts did not yield the minimum of four participants. On both occasions only two or three men out of the five who had agreed to participate actually showed up at the facilitator's home. They were thanked and paid twenty-five dollars and told the group could not be held for lack of numbers.

The tapes from the female Hmong group in Milwaukee unfortunately proved unusable. One of the two tape recorders failed to produce a recording and the second tape had such poor sound quality that it could not be translated.

The Cambodian women in Rochester conversed exclusively in English. An American university student produced a verbatim transcription of this tape. The Hmong women's group in Eau Claire also spoke in English, except for one participant who spoke in Hmong and some short responses by other participants in Hmong. The Hmong university student who transcribed this tape therefore had little translation work. When it was necessary he followed the natural-language approach, to be consistent with the verbatim transcription of the English speech on the tape. The Cambodian translator for the Chicago men's and women's peer-group conversations followed the edited-language approach advocated by Chan (1994). Thus, his transcripts present a more formal and refined pattern of communication. The Hmong translator of the Milwaukee men's peer group used a natural-language approach and produced a transcript that is closer to ordinary speech.

I made only minor editorial revisions to the transcripts of the peer-group conversations. Most of these revisions involved punctuation, particularly adding commas to clarify pauses between phrases. I also removed pauses and utterances such as "uh" when the transcribers used these excessively. Concerning vocabulary, I changed a small number of words in the transcript of the Cambodian men and women in Chicago, where I felt the translator had relied excessively on a Cambodian-English dictionary to render speech into text. The translation of the conversation among the Hmong men in Milwaukee required even fewer word changes, but in several places I made minor changes to maintain consistency in a participant's manner of speech.

═══ Notes ═══

Preface

1. Available at: www.cnn.com/ALLPOLITICS/1998/06/09/poll (accessed November 3, 2005).

2. Naming ethnic groups is a complex task because each choice represents a different perspective. Laotian refers to citizens of Laos, but the Lao are a distinct ethnic group, as are the Hmong. Similarly, Cambodian technically refers to citizens of Cambodia, while the Khmer are the majority ethnic group that speaks the Khmer language, in contrast to Vietnamese and Chinese-speaking minority groups. Among the Khmer in the United States, however, the name Khmer is used only when actually speaking in Khmer, and the name Cambodian is used when speaking in English. I therefore use the name Cambodian most often in this book but in places prefer the more anthropologically accurate name Khmer. There are also grammatical issues involved in naming ethnic groups. Hmong is both a collective noun, similar to the Irish, and an adjective, such as Hmong music. The plural is the Hmong, not the Hmongs, but the possessive case requires an apostrophe "s" for clarity, such as the Hmong's role in the Vietnam War, although this use of an "s" is awkward to our ear. For these reasons, I often use the phrase "Cambodians and the Hmong" even though it is a nonparallel construction.

Chapter 1

1. A literal rendition of this Buddhist aphorism is "Lose, go to 'preah.' Win, go to 'meah.' " "Preah" is an informal Khmer word for the Buddha ("preah putth"). "Meah" is an idiom for "mie" (evil doers). It also refers to Mara, the evil deity who attempted to spoil the Buddha's enlightenment by provoking him into aggression. By not retaliating against provocation, the Buddha attained enlightenment, although his passivity made it appear as if he was losing a fight.

2. Hmong clans are kinship groups based on surnames. There are eighteen Hmong clans. A clan recognizes descent from an original ancestor (for example, the first Vang) and practices exogamy (a Vang may not marry a Vang).

3. Some sociologists object to the phrase "race and ethnic relations" because it seems to imply harmony. Yet as Georg Simmel (1908/1955) observed, conflict

265

is one type of relationship. I therefore use the phrase "American race and ethnic relations" or the shorthand "American diversity" to mean contested identities and inequalities based on perceived physical and cultural differences in the United States.

4. Ellen Hume, "Indochinese Refugees Adapt Quickly in U.S.," *Wall Street Journal,* March 21, 1985.

5. Lizette Alvarez, "Census Director Marvels at the New Portrait of America," *New York Times,* January 1, 2001.

Chapter 3

1. [n.a.], "Old U.S. Bomb Kills Children," *Asian American Press,* September 12, 2003.

Chapter 4

1. Amy Doeun, "Roma Delegation Visits Hmong Community," *Hmong Times,* April 16, 2005.

2. Tou Vang, "Will the Kurds Be Our Next Forsaken Allies?" *Asian American Press,* January 10, 2003.

3. [n.a.], "Salute to the Hmong Veterans," *Hmong Tribune,* May–June 2000, 1.

4. [n.a.], "Proving Genocide," *Asian American Press,* August 9, 2002.

5. [n.a.], "Laos Rebels Starving, Says Freed Reporter," *Asian American Press,* July 18, 2003.

Chapter 5

1. Aleta Freimark, "Rochester 4-H Club 'Adopts' Chinese Cambodian Family," *Rochester Post-Bulletin,* September 18, 1982.

2. Jodi Schneider, "Hmong Preserve Culture with Celebration of New Year," *Eau Claire Leader-Telegram,* November 10, 1980.

3. [n.a.], "Refugee Aid Group Nominated for Presidential Volunteer Award," *Eau Claire Leader-Telegram,* March 8, 1983.

4. Mary Vitacenda, "Refugee Finds Rewarding Career," *Rochester Post-Bulletin,* March 8, 1976.

5. Arnie Hoffman, "Altoona Family 'Shares' with Orphans," *Eau Claire Leader-Telegram,* April 19, 1975.

6. Susan Halena, "City's Cambodian Refugees Finding Help in Adjusting," *Rochester Post-Bulletin,* October 13, 1981.

7. Pauline Walle, "Lobbyist for Refugees Makes Plea," *Rochester Post-Bulletin,* March 18, 1985.

8. George W. Cornell, "Refugees' Trials Recall Migrant Bethlehem Birth," *Rochester Post-Bulletin*, December 22, 1986.

9. Barbara Ketcham, "Woman Enjoys Reaching Out to Help Others," *Eau Claire Leader-Telegram*, January 21, 1984.

10. Doug Mell, "Second Laotian Refugee Family Arrives in Menomonie," *Eau Claire Leader-Telegram*, February 4, 1979.

11. Arnie Hoffman, "Family Hosts Refugees to Pay Back Blessings," *Eau Claire Leader-Telegram*, February 25, 1980.

12. Mike Klein, "City Expects 67 Hmong," *Eau Claire Leader-Telegram*, August 9, 1986.

13. Aleta Freimark, "Resettling Joint Effort Works Well," *Rochester Post-Bulletin*, September 13, 1982.

14. Martha Helgerson, "Outreach Program Helps Bring School to Refugees," *Rochester Post-Bulletin*, February 25, 1983.

15. Steve Andrist and Ron Drevlow, "Sponsors Keep Busy Planning for Families," *Rochester Post-Bulletin*, November 12, 1985.

16. [n.a.], "Event Honors Those Who Helped," *Rochester Post-Bulletin*, December 29, 1995.

17. Karen Harder, "Maureen Homstad Mother to Hmong in Their New Home," *Eau Claire Leader-Telegram*, November 16, 1987.

18. Dennis R. Getto, "All-American Wausau Is a Red-White-and-Blue City," *Milwaukee Journal*, July 1, 1984.

19. Susan M. Halena, "City's Cambodian Refugees Finding Help In Adjusting," *Rochester Post-Bulletin*, October 13, 1981.

20. Tom Weber, "Prejudice, Language Hamper Refugees' Struggle," *Rochester Post-Bulletin*, June 1, 1985.

21. Steve Andrist, "Refugees Encounter Some Bias," *Rochester Post-Bulletin*, November 14, 1983.

22. Aleta Capelle, "Survey Shows Racial Bias in Olmsted," *Rochester Post-Bulletin*, September 7, 1990.

23. [n.a.], "Durenberger: Refugees a Hardship," *Rochester Post-Bulletin*, April 24, 1986.

24. [n.a.], "Man's Attitude Reflects Strong Racial Bias Against Refugees," *Wausau Daily Herald*, October 28, 1997.

25. Christopher Terry, "Anonymous Postcard Sent City Official," *Eau Claire Leader-Telegram*, November 10, 1993.

26. Bill Gharrity, "Harassment of Hmong Stirs Concern Among Police," *Eau Claire Leader-Telegram*, June 15, 1982.

27. Bill Gharrity, "Hmong Eagerly Learn English," *Eau Claire Leader-Telegram*, June 8, 1982.

28. Bill Gharrity, "Hmong Often Treated Badly in New Home," *Eau Claire Leader-Telegram*, June 7, 1982.

29. Steve Andrist and Ron Drevlow, "Many Southeast Asians Find Refuge in Rochester," *Rochester Post-Bulletin*, November 12, 1983.

30. Steve Andrist, "Refugees Encounter Some Bias," *Rochester Post-Bulletin*, November 14, 1983.

31. Tom Weber, "Prejudice, Language, Hamper Refugees' Struggle," *Rochester Post-Bulletin*, June 1, 1985.

32. [n.a.], "Showdown at Zumbro Ridge," *Rochester Post-Bulletin*, July 22, 1998.

33. [n.a.], "Mobile Home Residents Say Managers Are Unfair," *Rochester Post-Bulletin*, July 23, 1998.

34. Mike Klein, "Refugees Find Hunt for Home Difficult," *Eau Claire Leader-Telegram*, September 25, 1989.

35. Eric Lindquist, "Test Shows Blatant Rental Discrimination," *Eau Claire Leader-Telegram*, March 21, 1993.

36. Jack Norman, "Rental Firm to Pay Record Settlement in Bias Case." *Milwaukee Journal*, November 30, 1994.

37. James Walsh, "Housing Discrimination Does Exist in Rochester," *Rochester Post-Bulletin*, March 3, 1989.

38. James Walsh, "Car Driven by Southeast Asian Forced Off the Road, Six Arrested," *Rochester Post-Bulletin*, April 3, 1989.

39. [n.a.], "Man: Attack Racially Motivated," *Rochester Post-Bulletin*, May 15, 1989.

40. [n.a.], "Hmong Women Report Being Harassed in Park," *Eau Claire Leader-Telegram*, May 31, 1990.

41. Lynne Miller, "Cross Burned in Minority Area," *Eau Claire Leader-Telegram*, May 6, 1996.

42. Tom Weber, "Refugees' Plight Poses Challenges for Sponsors," *Rochester Post-Bulletin*, June 3, 1985.

43. Janice Gregerson, "Asian Gangs Using Strong-Arm Tactics May Be in Rochester," *Rochester Post-Bulletin*, February 3, 1989.

44. Janice Gregerson, "6 Vietnamese Said Threat to Asian Community," *Rochester Post-Bulletin*, March 4, 1989.

45. [n.a.], "Rochester Citizens Confront Gang Problem," *Rochester Post-Bulletin*, August 11, 1992.

46. [n.a.], "Juveniles Robbed of Gold Chains," *Rochester Post-Bulletin*, May 8, 1990.

47. [n.a.], "Fear Leads Some to Gang Involvement," *Rochester Post-Bulletin*, October 26, 1993.

48. [n.a.], "Gangs a Part of Everyday Life in Junior High School," *Rochester Post-Bulletin*, November 16, 1993.

49. [n.a.], "Fear Leads Some to Gang Involvement," *Rochester Post-Bulletin*, October 26, 1993.

50. Tom Weber, "Survey Shows 57% of Asian Students Suffer Harassment," *Rochester Post-Bulletin*, December 10, 1984.

51. Tom Weber, "Teacher Group Urges Effort to Fight Prejudice Against Refugee Students," *Rochester Post-Bulletin*, June 5, 1985.

52. James Walsh, "Police Break Up Fight Among 100 Youths at Barclay Square," *Rochester Post-Bulletin*, April 1, 1989.

53. [n.a.], "Student Charged in Assault at School," *Rochester Post-Bulletin*, July 2, 1991.

54. Julie Speltz, "Fear, Anger Show Up in Race Survey," *Rochester Post-Bulletin*, July 11, 1991.

55. [n.a.], "Culture Clash: Students Speak Out," *Rochester Post-Bulletin*, July 11, 1991.

56. Elizabeth Hoff and Mary Vitacenda, "Refugees, Teachers Overcome Challenges to Learn Together," *Rochester Post-Bulletin*, March 9, 1976.

57. Lynne Miller, "Ganging Up," *Eau Claire Leader-Telegram*, September 19, 1993.

58. Julian Emerson, "Gang Activities Spark Concern," *Eau Claire Leader-Telegram*, March 9, 2002.

59. [n.a.], "Police Seek Man After Abduction," *Eau Claire Leader-Telegram*, January 8, 1987.

60. Joe Knight, "Hmong Custom Misunderstood," *Eau Claire Leader-Telegram*, February 3, 1987.

61. Joe Knight, "Hmong, Officials Discuss Conflicting Customs, Laws," *Eau Claire Leader-Telegram*, February 17, 1987.

62. Joe Knight, "Hmong, Officials Discuss Conflicting Customs, Laws," *Eau Claire Leader-Telegram*, February 17, 1987.

63. Joe Knight, "Hmong, Officials Discuss Conflicting Customs, Laws," *Eau Claire Leader-Telegram*, February 17, 1987.

64. [n.a.], "Hmong Try to Keep Customs," *Eau Claire Leader-Telegram*, May 3, 1987.

65. Mike Klein, "Girl Kidnapped for Marriage: Sources Say 'Bride Capture' a Tradition in Hmong Culture," *Eau Claire Leader-Telegram*, October 11, 1989.

66. Mike Klein, "Hmong Custom of Marrying Young Hinders Girls," *Eau Claire Leader-Telegram*, May 6, 1990.

67. [n.a.], "Girl Says Asian Ritual Forced Marriage," *Milwaukee Journal Sentinel*, October 12, 1989.

68. Bob Brown, "Judge Hopefuls Say They'd Be Sensitive," *Eau Claire Leader-Telegram*, January 28, 1994.

69. Thomas Pfankuch, "Cultures Define Crime, Attitude Toward Officers," *Eau Claire Leader-Telegram*, January 10, 1993.

70. Richard Meryhew and Mary Lynn Smith, "Tragedy Leaves Eau Claire Grasping for Explanations," *Minneapolis Star Tribune*, June 14, 1998.

71. [n.a.], "Man Arrested after Kidnapping Claim," *Eau Claire Leader-Telegram*, October 31, 2005.

72. Thomas Pfankuch, "Cultures Define Crime, Attitude Toward Officers," *Eau Claire Leader-Telegram*, January 10, 1993.

73. Mike Klein, "Attorney: Hmong More Aware of Rights," *Eau Claire Leader-Telegram*, May 16, 1990.

74. Thomas Pfankuch, "Cultures Define Crime, Attitude Toward Officers," *Eau Claire Leader-Telegram*, January 10, 1993.

75. Stephen Kinzer, "Motive in Hunting Deaths Is a Riddle," *New York Times*, November 23, 2004; Stephen Kinzer, "Hunter Tells Police He Was Threatened," *New York Times*, November 24, 2004; Stephen Kinzer and Monica Davey, "A Hunt Turns Tragic, and Two Cultures Collide," *New York Times*, November 28, 2004.

76. Julian Emerson, "Hunter to Hmong: Stay Away," *Eau Claire Leader-Telegram*, December 17, 2004.

77. Stephen Kinzer and Monica Davey, "A Hunt Turns Tragic, and Two Cultures Collide," *New York Times*, November 28, 2004.

78. Tom La Venture, "Chai Vang Guilty on Nine Counts," *Asian American Press*, September 23, 2005.

79. Christina T. O'Brien, "Adding Fresh Voices," *Eau Claire Leader-Telegram*, March 5, 2002.

80. Julian Emerson, "Hmong Told Federal Welfare Cutbacks Will Mean Changes," *Milwaukee Journal Sentinel*, April 12, 1997.

81. [n.a.], "Eau Claire Loses 13 Year Old Hmong Radio Program," *Hmong Times*, July 16, 2002.

82. Mike Klein, "Hmong Protest in Support of Rebels," *Eau Claire Leader-Telegram*, February 2, 1990.

83. Joe Knight, "Gunderson Hears Hmong Concerns," *Eau Claire Leader-Telegram*, November 14, 1993.

84. Jodi Schneider, "Hmong Preserve Culture with Celebration of New Year," *Eau Claire Leader-Telegram*, November 10, 1980.

85. Jodi Schneider, "Hmong People Try to Topple Cultural Barriers," *Eau Claire Leader-Telegram*, December 22, 1980.

86. [n.a.], "Hmong Church Raising Funds to Purchase Van," *Eau Claire Leader-Telegram*, October 3, 1986.

87. Blythe Wachter, "Rough Times Tested Faith of Hmong Pastor." *Eau Claire Leader-Telegram,* September 15, 1990.

88. Blythe Wachter, "Faith in a New Religion," *Eau Claire Leader-Telegram,* March 9, 2002.

89. Eric Lindquist, "Master Mediators," *Eau Claire Leader-Telegram,* March 8, 2002.

90. [n.a.], "Cambodians Here Dance into New Year," *Rochester Post-Bulletin,* April 19, 1982.

91. Dawn Schuett, "New Year's Fete Includes Visitors from Cambodia," *Rochester Post-Bulletin,* April 16, 1999.

92. Julie Speltz, "Band Finds Cultural Music, Dance Ease Homesickness," *Rochester Post-Bulletin,* August 5, 1988.

93. [n.a.], "Cambodian Artists to Perform Friday," *Rochester Post-Bulletin,* August 15, 1996; Dawn Schuett, "Popular Cambodian Singers to Perform in Rochester," *Rochester Post-Bulletin,* December 17, 1999.

94. [n.a.], "Cambodians," *Rochester Post-Bulletin,* October 23, 1995.

95. [n.a.], "Cambodia on the Air," *Rochester Post-Bulletin,* March 25, 1996.

96. [n.a.], "A Weekend for Picnics," *Rochester Post-Bulletin,* 1985 [n.d.].

97. [n.a.], "Cambodians Take Time to Celebrate," *Rochester Post-Bulletin,* August 24, 1987.

98. [n.a.], "Rochester's Cambodians Find a Place to Worship," *Rochester Post-Bulletin,* March 7, 1992.

99. [n.a.], "Refugees Raise Funds to Build Schools in Cambodia," *Rochester Post-Bulletin,* February 13, 1996.

100. Aamer Madhani and Pauline Walle, "A Most Challenging Ministry," *Rochester Post-Bulletin,* July 25, 1997.

101. [n.a.], "Faith Profile: Rochester First Church of the Nazarene," *Rochester Post-Bulletin,* July 19, 1997.

102. [n.a.], "Keeping the Faith," *Rochester Post-Bulletin,* October 26, 1993.

103. Tom Weber, "Area Buddhists Greet Leader," *Rochester Post-Bulletin,* January 12, 1987.

Chapter 6

1. Lesley Sussman, "Agencies Admit Refugees Housed in Slum Buildings," *North Town News,* December 23, 1981.

2. Jerry De Meth, "Things Getting Better in Uptown," *Chicago Sun-Times,* December 5, 1976; Dorothy Stark, "Residents Want Their Pride Back," *Today,* April 2, 1972.

3. Michael Miner and Sam Washington, "The Promise of Progress," *Sun Times*, March 25, 1971.

4. Lester Jacobson, "Uptown's Future Is Bright, Residents Say," *Uptown News*, April 22, 1975.

5. Leonard Aronson, "Uptown Doesn't Fit Plan," *Today*, January 24, 1973; Jerry De Meth, "Things Getting Better in Uptown," *Sun Times*, December 5, 1976; Gary Washburn, "Uptown Seen as Possible Extension of Newtown," *Chicago Tribune*, June 17, 1973.

6. Jess Carlos, "Argyle Strip Sees New Life," *Sunday Star*, January 29, 1984.

7. [n.a.], "Vietnamese Reviving a Chicago Slum," *New York Times*, January 2, 1985.

8. [n.a.], "Vietnamese Reviving a Chicago Slum," *New York Times*, January 2, 1985.

9. Barry Pearce, "Argyle Sets New Pattern," *Apartments and Homes*, October 15, 1993.

10. Robert Kurson, "Feisty New Enclave Is a Bazaar of Bargains," *Chicago Sun-Times*, February 16, 1996.

11. [n.a.], "Cambodians Worry Community Will Be Split by Apartment Complex," *Chicago Tribune*, February 28, 1992.

12. Brian Edwards, "Albany Park Offers Diversity, Housing Bargains," *Chicago Tribune*, March 15, 1991.

13. [n.a.], "Refugees Get Reorientation," *Milwaukee Journal*, April 27, 1980.

14. Marilynn Marchione, "Major Employers Have Not Hired Hmongs [*sic*], Leader Charges," *Milwaukee Journal*, April 24, 1992.

15. Steve Hannah, "US Culture Alien to Laotian Tribe," *Milwaukee Journal*, July 22, 1980.

16. Steve Schultze, "The Most Crime," *Milwaukee Journal Sentinel*, March 11, 1996.

17. Steve Schultze, "The Most Crime," *Milwaukee Journal Sentinel*, March 11, 1996.

18. [n.a.], *Milwaukee Journal*, "Agenda," March 26, 1992.

19. Whitney Gould, "The Rezzas," *Milwaukee Journal Sentinel*, October 20, 1996.

20. Lesley Sussman, "Agencies Admit Refugees Housed in Slum Buildings," *North Town News*, December 23, 1981.

21. Ken Wysocky, "Meeting Set to Defuse Hmong, Hispanic Tension," *Milwaukee Sentinel*, July 16, 1986.

22. Melita Garza, "Hmong Tension Is Disputed," *Milwaukee Journal*, July 31, 1986.

23. Ken Wysocky, "Hmong Must Combat Harassment While Adjusting to an Alien Culture," *Milwaukee Sentinel*, July 14, 1986.

24. Michele Derus, "A New Start in an Old Neighborhood," *Milwaukee Journal Sentinel*, July 7, 1996.

25. William Janz, "Nun Shares Dreams, Nightmares of Asian Refugees," *Milwaukee Sentinel,* October 14, 1992.

26. Jessica McBride, "Culture Clash, Harassment Blamed for Gunshots," *Milwaukee Journal Sentinel,* July 8, 1996.

27. Michele Derus, "A New Start in an Old Neighborhood," *Milwaukee Journal Sentinel,* July 7, 1996.

28. Kevin Harrington, "Fatal Shooting Shatters Laotian Couple's Search for Peace," *Milwaukee Journal,* June 16, 1991.

29. [n.a.], "Firing of Officers Hailed by Some as Restoring Police Accountability," *Milwaukee Journal,* September 7, 1991.

30. [n.a.], "Police Report," *Milwaukee Journal Sentinel,* September 19, 1996.

31. Julian Emerson, "Gang Activities Spark Concern," *Eau Claire Leader-Telegram,* March 9, 2002; Mary Beth Murphy, "City's Asian Families Eye New Enemy," *Milwaukee Sentinel,* September 2, 1993.

32. Tom Held, "Mourning Parents Feel Helpless," *Milwaukee Sentinel,* May 17, 1993.

33. Fran Bauer, "Activists Go Their Own Ways in Purging Areas of Drugs," *Milwaukee Journal,* June 18, 1991.

34. Colleen Krantz, "Forum Focuses on Asian Children," *Milwaukee Journal Sentinel,* March 29, 1998.

35. Mary Beth Murphy, "City's Asian Families Eye New Enemy," *Milwaukee Sentinel,* September 2, 1993.

36. Fran Bauer, "A Place They Can Call Home," *Milwaukee Journal,* March 21, 1990; Gary Rummler, "Old Ways Tested in a New Land," *Milwaukee Journal,* October 15, 1992.

37. Fran Bauer, "Elderly Sellers, Low-Income Buyers Get Help," *Milwaukee Journal,* October 28, 1992.

38. Michele Derus, "A New Start in an Old Neighborhood," *Milwaukee Journal Sentinel,* July 7, 1996.

39. Wendy S. Tai, "Hmong Families Torn by Collision of Old and New," *Minneapolis Star Tribune,* February 8, 1993.

40. Marie Rohde, "Church on Mission to Lift Community," *Milwaukee Journal,* October 31, 1994.

41. Michele Derus, "A New Start in an Old Neighborhood," *Milwaukee Journal Sentinel,* July 7, 1996.

42. Michele Wucker, "Family Angry After Hearing Tapes," *Milwaukee Sentinel,* August 2, 1991.

43. Steven Walters and Jesse Garza, "Panel Approves English," *Milwaukee Journal Sentinel,* February 21, 1996.

44. Fran Bauer, "Busloads Take Their Concerns to Lawmakers in Madison," *Milwaukee Journal Sentinel,* January 5, 1996.

45. Dennis R. Getto, "Hmong Emigrants Hear War's Echoes," *Milwaukee Journal,* September 30, 1990; "No Price Is too High for Hmong Fighters," *Milwaukee Journal,* October 1, 1990.

46. Michael S. Bayer, "Hmong Ring In the New Year," *Milwaukee Sentinel,* November 29, 1991.

47. Gary Rummler, "Old Ways Tested in a New Land," *Milwaukee Journal,* October 15, 1992.

Chapter 8

1. [n.a.], "Lao Government Under Fire," *Milwaukee Journal Sentinel,* December 27, 1999.

Chapter 9

1. [n.a.], "King Tells Cambodians Not to Fear Vote Violence," Reuters, January 17, 2002; [n.a.], "Opposition Angered by Election Results," *Chicago Tribune,* September 2, 1998. Available on the website of the Cambodian Funcinpec party, www.funcinpec.org.

Chapter 12

1. Andreas Jurewitsch, "Panel Discusses Findings of Mondale Study on Community and Immigration," *Hmong Times,* January 1, 2005.

2. Thomas Morley, "Hmong Protesters Disrupt Newt Gingrich Appearance," *Asian American Press,* February 16, 1996.

Chapter 13

1. Wameng Moua, "Hunting Tragedy Puts Focus on Hmong Community," *Hmong Today,* November 18, 2004.

2. Wameng Moua, "Hunting Tragedy Puts Focus on Hmong Community," *Hmong Today,* November 18, 2004; Va-Megn Thoj, "Stereotypes Feed Bigotry in Small Midwestern Towns," *Pioneer Press,* December 29, 2004; Gaoib Xiong, "Hunting Tragedy Opens Up Questions of Race, Class, Sanity, Competence, and Tradition," *Hmong Times,* December 1, 2004.

3. [n.a.], "APA Dialogue on Race and Reconciliation," *Asian American Press,* January 14, 2005.

Appendix B

1. www.leadertelegram.com; www.postbulletin.com/archive; www.jsonline.com.

═ References ═

Adams, James P., and William W. Dressler. 1988. "Perceptions of Injustice in a Black Community: Dimensions and Variation." *Human Relations* 41(10): 753–67.

Aguilar, Alfonso. 2004. "Welcoming New Americans: Challenges and Opportunities for the U.S. Office of Citizenship." *Refugee Reports* 25(7): 1–2.

Aguirre, Adalberto, and Jonathan H. Turner. 1998. *American Ethnicity: The Dynamics and Consequences of Discrimination.* Boston: McGraw-Hill.

Aguirre, B. E., Rogelio Saenz, and Sean-Shong Hwang. 1989. "Discrimination and the Assimilation and Ethnic Competition Perspectives." *Social Science Quarterly* 70(3): 594–606.

Ainsworth-Darnell, James W., and Douglas B. Downey. 1998. "Assessing the Oppositional Culture Explanation for Racial/Ethnic Differences in School Performance." *American Sociological Review* 63(4): 536–53.

Alba, Richard. 1990. *Ethnic Identity: The Transformation of White America.* New Haven: Yale University Press.

Alba, Richard, and Victor Nee. 2003. *Remaking the American Mainstream: Assimilation and Contemporary Immigration.* Cambridge, Mass.: Harvard University Press.

Alexander, June G. 1988. Review of *For Bread with Butter: Life-Worlds of East Central Europeans in Johnstown, Pennsylvania, 1890–1940,* by Ewa Morawska. *International Migration Review* 22(3): 143–44.

Allen, Irving L. 1993. *The Language of Ethnic Conflict: Social Organization and Lexical Culture.* New York: Columbia University Press.

Allport, Gordon. 1958. *The Nature of Prejudice.* Garden City, N.Y.: Doubleday/ Anchor Books.

Almond, Gabriel A., and Sidney Verba. 1965. *The Civic Culture: Political Attitudes and Democracy in Five Nations.* Boston: Little, Brown.

Aoudé, Ibrahim G. 2001. "Maintaining Culture, Reclaiming Identity: Palestinian Lives in the Diaspora." *Asian Studies Review* 25(2): 153–67.

Arnold, David O. 1970. "Dimensional Sampling: An Approach for Studying a Small Number of Cases." *The American Sociologist* 5(2): 147–50.

Asian American Services of Chicago. 1986. *Asian American Demographics: Chicago Metro, Estimated 1986 Population.* Chicago: Asian American Services of Chicago.

Axinn, William, Thomas E. Fricke, and Arland Thornton. 1991. "The Micro-demographic Community-Study Approach: Improving Survey Data by Integrating the Ethnographic Method." *Sociological Methods and Research* 20(2): 187–217.

Bacon, Jean. 1996. *Life Lines: Community, Family, and Assimilation Among Asian Indian Immigrants.* Chicago: University of Chicago Press.

Bailey, Thomas, and Roger Waldinger. 1991. "Primary, Secondary, and Enclave Labor Markets: A Training Systems Approach." *American Sociological Review* 56(4): 432–45.

Barkan, Elliott R. 1995. "Race, Religion, and Nationality in American Society: A Model of Ethnicity—From Contact to Assimilation." *Journal of American Ethnic History* 14(2): 38–75.

Barney, G. Linwood. 1957. "The Meo: An Incipient Church." *Practical Anthropology* 4: 31–50.

Barrera, Mario. 1979. *Race and Class in the Southwest: A Theory of Racial Inequality.* Notre Dame, Ind.: University of Notre Dame Press.

Barth, Fredrik. 1969a. "Introduction." In *Ethnic Groups and Boundaries: The Social Organization of Culture Difference,* edited by Fredrik Barth. Boston: Little, Brown.

———. 1969b. "Pathan Identity and Its Maintenance." In *Ethnic Groups and Boundaries: The Social Organization of Culture Difference,* edited by Fredrik Barth. Boston: Little, Brown.

Basch, Linda, Nina Glick Schiller, and Cristina Szanton Blanc. 1994. *Nations Unbound: Transnational Projects, Post-Colonial Predicaments, and Deterritorialized Nation-States.* Amsterdam: Gordon & Breach Science Publishers.

Bauböck, Rainer. 1994. *Transnational Citizenship: Membership and Rights in International Migration.* Aldershot, U.K.: Edward Elgar.

Beck, David R. 1996. "Native Americans." In *The Ethnic Handbook: A Guide to the Cultures and Traditions of Chicago's Diverse Communities,* edited by Cynthia Linton. Chicago: Illinois Ethnic Coalition.

Becker, Elizabeth. 1986. *When the War Was Over: Cambodia's Revolution and the Voices of Its People.* New York: Touchstone Books.

Becker, Howard S. 1992. "Cases, Causes, Conjunctures, Stories, and Imagery." In *What Is a Case? Exploring the Foundations of Social Inquiry,* edited by Charles C. Ragin and Howard S. Becker. New York: Cambridge University Press.

———. 1998. *Tricks of the Trade: How to Think About Your Research While You're Doing It.* Chicago: University of Chicago Press.

Bell, Myrtle P., David A. Harrison, and Mary E. McLaughlin. 1997. "Asian American Attitudes Toward Affirmative Action in Employment: Implications for the Model Minority Myth." *Journal of Applied Behavioral Science* 33(3): 356–77.

Bensman, David. 1988. Review of *For Bread with Butter: Life-Worlds of East Central Europeans in Johnstown, Pennsylvania, 1890–1940,* by Ewa Morawska. *Contemporary Sociology* 17(2): 173–74.

Beverstock, Frances, and Robert P. Stuckert, eds. 1972. *Metropolitan Milwaukee Community Fact Book: 1970,* Milwaukee: Milwaukee Urban Observatory.

Blauner, Robert. 1969. "Internal Colonialism and Ghetto Revolt." *Social Problems* 16(4): 392–408.

———. 1972. *Racial Oppression in America.* New York: Harper & Row.

Bloemraad, Irene. 2004. "Who Claims Dual Citizenship? The Limits of Postnationalism, the Possibilities of Transnationalism, and the Persistence of Traditional Citizenship." *International Migration Review* 38(2): 389–426.

Bobo, Lawrence D., and Vincent L. Hutchings. 1996. "Perceptions of Racial Group Competition: Extending Blumer's Theory of Group Position to a Multiracial Social Context." *American Sociological Review* 61(6): 951–72.

Bobo, Lawrence D., and Devon Johnson. 2000. "Racial Attitudes in a Prismatic Metropolis: Mapping Identities, Stereotypes, Competition, and Views on Affirmative Action." In *Prismatic Metropolis: Inequalities in Los Angeles*, edited by Lawrence D. Bobo, Melvin L. Oliver, James H. Johnson, and Abel Valenzuela. New York: Russell Sage Foundation.

Bobo, Lawrence D., and Michael P. Massagli. 2001. "Stereotyping and Urban Inequality." In *Urban Inequality: Evidence from Four Cities*, edited by Alice O'Connor, Chris Tilly, and Lawrence D. Bobo. New York: Russell Sage Foundation.

Bodnar, John. 1985. *The Transplanted: A History of Immigration in Urban America*. Bloomington: Indiana University Press.

Bonnell, Victoria E., and Lynn Hunt. 1999. "Introduction." In *Beyond the Cultural Turn: New Directions in the Study of Society and Culture*, edited by Victoria E. Bonnell and Lynn Hunt. Berkeley: University of California Press.

Bozorgmehr, Mehdi. 1997. "Internal Ethnicity: Iranians in Los Angeles." *Sociological Perspectives* 40(3): 387–408.

Brennan, Christiana, Elizabeth Wheel, and Christopher Hoene. 2005. *The State of America's Cities 2005: The Annual Opinion Survey of Municipal Elected Officials*. Washington, D.C.: National League of Cities.

Brewer, Marilynn B., and Rupert J. Brown. 1998. "Intergroup Relations." In *The Handbook of Social Psychology*, edited by Daniel T. Gilbert, Susan T. Fiske, and Gardner Lindzey. Boston: McGraw-Hill.

Brubaker, Rogers. 2005. "The 'Diaspora' Diaspora." *Ethnic and Racial Studies* 28(1): 1–19.

Brune, Tom, and Eduardo Comacho. 1983. *Race and Poverty in Chicago*. Chicago: Community Renewal Society.

Bueker, Catherine S. 2005. "Political Incorporation Among Immigrants from Ten Areas of Origin: The Persistence of Source Country Effects." *International Migration Review* 39(1): 103–40.

Burstein, Daniel. 1983. "Caught in the Crossfire: The Ordeal of the Hmong Tribe." *Boston Globe New England Magazine*, December 4, 1.

Burton, Eve. 1983. "Khmer Refugees in Western Massachusetts: Their Impact on Local Communities." *Migration Today* 11(2–3): 29–34.

Byng, Michelle D. 1998. "Mediating Discrimination: Resisting Oppression Among African-American Muslim Women." *Social Problems* 45(4): 473–87.

Cambodian Association of Illinois. 2000. *Campaign for Hope and Renewal*. Chicago: Cambodian Association of Illinois.

Campbell, Donald T., and Donald Fiske. 1959. "Convergent and Discriminant Validation by the Multitrait-Multimethod Matrix." *Psychological Bulletin* 56(2): 81–105.

Canniff, Julie G. 2001. *Cambodian Refugees' Pathways to Success: Developing a Bi-Cultural Identity*. New York: LFB Scholarly Publishing.

Caplan, Nathan, John K. Whitmore, and Marcella H. Choy. 1989. *The Boat People and Achievement in America: A Study of Family Life, Hard Work, and Cultural Values*. Ann Arbor: University of Michigan Press.

Chan, Sucheng. 1994. *Hmong Means Free: Life in Laos and America*. Philadelphia: Temple University Press.

————. 2003. *Not Just Victims: Conversations with Cambodian Community Leaders in the United States*. Urbana: University of Illinois Press.

————. 2004. *Survivors: Cambodian Refugees in the United States*. Urbana: University of Illinois Press.

Chandler, David. 1996. *A History of Cambodia*. Boulder: Westview Press.

Chindarsi, Nusit. 1976. *The Religion of the Hmong Njua*. Bangkok: Siam Society.

Cho, Youngtae, and Robert A. Hummer. 2001. "Disability Status Differentials Across Fifteen Asian and Pacific Islander Groups and the Effect of Nativity and Duration of Residence in the U.S." *Social Biology* 48(3–4): 171–95.

Chouléan, Ang. 1988. "The Place of Animism Within Popular Buddhism in Cambodia: The Example of the Monastery." *Asian Folklore Studies* 47: 35–41.

Clifford, James. 1994. "Diasporas." *Cultural Anthropology* 9(3): 302–38.

Clinton, Bill. 1997. Partial Transcript of the President's Speech on Race. Commencement address, University of California–San Diego, June 16. Transcript. *NewsHour with Jim Lehrer*. Available at: www.pbs.org/newshour/bb/race_relations/jan-june97/race_6-16a.html (accessed December 9, 2005).

Coe, Michael D. 2003. *Angkor and the Khmer Civilization*. New York: Thames & Hudson.

Coedès, George. 1968. *The Indianized States of Southeast Asia*. Honolulu: University of Hawaii Press.

Coffey, Zimmerman, and Associates. 1985. *An Evaluation of the Highland Lao Initiative*. Washington: U.S. Office of Refugee Resettlement.

Cohen, Robin. 1997. *Global Diasporas: An Introduction*. Seattle: University of Washington Press.

Conquergood, Dwight. 1992. "Life in Big Red: Struggles and Accommodations in a Chicago Polyethnic Tenement." In *Structuring Diversity: Ethnographic Perspectives on the New Immigration*, edited by Louise Lamphere. Chicago: University of Chicago Press.

Cornell, Stephen. 1996. "The Variable Ties that Bind: Content and Circumstances in Ethnic Processes." *Ethnic and Racial Studies* 19(2): 265–89.

Culas, Christian. 2004. "Innovation and Tradition in Rituals and Cosmology: Hmong Messianism and Shamanism in Southeast Asia." In *Hmong/Miao in Asia*, edited by Nicholas Tapp, Jean Michaud, Christian Culas, and Gary Y. Lee. Chaing Mai, Thailand: Silkworm Books.

Culas, Christian, and Jean Michaud. 2004. "A Contribution to the Study of Hmong (Miao) Migrations and History." In *Hmong/Miao in Asia*, edited by Nicholas Tapp, Jean Michaud, Christian Culas, and Gary Y. Lee. Chaing Mai, Thailand: Silkworm Books.

Cutler, Irving. 1982. *Chicago: City at Mid-Continent*. Dubuque, Iowa: Kendall-Hunt.

D.C. Everest Area Schools. 2000. *Hmong Oral Histories from the Hmong of Central Wisconsin*. Wausau, Wis.: D.C. Everest Area Schools.

Dang, Nghiem Van. 1993. "The Flood Myth and the Origin of Ethnic Groups in Southeast Asia." *Journal of American Folklore* 106(421): 304–37.

Dawley, Alan. 1976. *Class and Community: The Industrial Revolution in Lynn*. Cambridge, Mass.: Harvard University Press.

del Pinal, Jorge, and Audrey Singer. 1997. *Generations of Diversity: Latinos in the United States.* Washington, D.C.: Population Reference Bureau.

Demo, David H., and Michael Hughes. 1990. "Socialization and Racial Identity Among Black Americans." *Social Psychology Quarterly* 53(4): 364–74.

Denton, Nancy A., and Douglas S. Massey. 1989. "Racial Identity Among Caribbean Hispanics: The Effect of Double Minority Status on Residential Segregation." *American Sociological Review* 54(5): 790–808.

Denzin, Norman K. 1970. *The Research Act: A Theoretical Introduction to Sociological Methods.* Chicago: Aldine.

Dommen, Arthur J. 2001. *The Indochinese Experience of the French and the Americans: Nationalism and Communism in Cambodia, Laos, and Vietnam.* Bloomington: Indiana University Press.

Donnelly, Nancy D. 1994. *Changing Lives of Refugee Hmong Women.* Seattle: University of Washington Press.

Duchon, D. A. 1997. "Home Is Where You Make It: Hmong Refugees in Georgia." *Urban Anthropology* 26(1): 71–79.

Dunnigan, Timothy. 1986. "Processes of Identity Maintenance in Hmong Society." In *Hmong in Transition,* edited by Glenn L. Hendricks, Bruce T. Downing, and Amos S. Deinard. New York: Center for Migration Studies.

Dunnigan, Timothy, Douglas P. Olney, Miles A. McNall, and Marline Spring. 1997. "Hmong." In *Case Studies in Diversity: Refugees in America in the 1990s,* edited by David W. Haines. Westport, Conn.: Praeger.

Ebaugh, Helen R., and Janet S. Chafetz. 2000. *Religion and the New Immigrants: Continuities and Adaptations in Immigrant Congregations.* Walnut Creek, Calif.: AltaMira Press.

Ebihara, May M. 1968. *Svay: A Khmer Village in Cambodia.* Ph.D. diss., Columbia University. Ann Arbor, Mich.: University Microfilms.

Espiritu, Yen L. 1992. *Asian American Panethnicity: Bridging Institutions and Identities.* Philadelphia: Temple University Press.

————. 2003. *Home Bound: Filipino American Lives Across Cultures, Communities, and Countries.* Berkeley: University of California Press.

————. 2004. "Asian American Panethnicity: Contemporary National and Transnational Possibilities." In *Not Just Black and White: Historical and Contemporary Perspectives on Immigration, Race, and Ethnicity in the United States,* edited by Nancy Foner and George M. Fredrickson. New York: Russell Sage Foundation.

Essed, Philomena. 1990. *Everyday Racism: Reports from Women of Two Cultures.* Alameda, Calif.: Hunter House.

————. 1991. *Understanding Everyday Racism: An Interdisciplinary Theory.* Newbury Park, Calif.: Sage.

Everingham, John. 1980. "One Family's Odyssey to America." *National Geographic,* May, 643–61.

Fantasia, Rick. 2002. Review of *The Dignity of Working Men: Morality and the Boundaries of Race, Class, and Immigration,* by Michèlle Lamont. *Contemporary Sociology* 31(2): 122–25.

Faruque, Cathleen Jo. 2002. *Migration of Hmong to the Midwestern United States.* Lanham, Md.: University Press of America.

Feagin, Joe R. 1991. "The Continuing Significance of Race: Antiblack Discrimination in Public Places." *American Sociological Review* 56(1): 101–16.

———. 2000. *Racist America: Roots, Current Realities, and Future Reparations.* New York: Routledge.

Feagin, Joe R., and Melvin P. Sikes. 1994. *Living with Racism: The Black Middle-Class Experience.* Boston: Beacon Press.

Fein, Helen. 1987. *Congregational Sponsors of Indochinese Refugees in the United States, 1979–1981: Helping Beyond Borders.* Cranbury, N.J.: Associated University Presses.

Fine, Gary A. 1993. "The Sad Demise, Mysterious Disappearance, and Glorious Triumph of Symbolic Interactionism." *Annual Review of Sociology* 19: 61–87.

Fink, Leon. 2003. *The Maya of Morganton: Work and Community in the Nuevo New South.* Chapel Hill: University of North Carolina Press.

Fiske, Susan T. 1998. "Stereotyping, Prejudice, and Discrimination." In *The Handbook of Social Psychology,* edited by Daniel T. Gilbert, Susan T. Fiske, and Gardner Lindzey. Boston: McGraw-Hill.

Fix, Michael, and Jeffrey Passel. 2002. *The Scope and Impact of Welfare Reform's Immigrant Provisions.* Washington, D.C.: Urban Institute.

Floyd, Myron F., and James H. Gramman. 1995. "Perceptions of Discrimination in a Recreational Context." *Journal of Leisure Research* 27(2): 192–99.

Fodor's Travel Publications. 1995. *Fodor's 95 Chicago.* New York: Fodor's Travel Publications.

Foner, Nancy. 2000. *From Ellis Island to JFK: New York's Two Great Waves of Immigration.* New Haven and New York: Yale University Press and Russell Sage Foundation.

Fordam, Signithia, and John U. Ogbu. 1986. "Black Students' School Success: Coping with the Burden of 'Acting White.' " *The Urban Review* 18(3): 176–206.

Fredrickson, George M. 2002. *Racism: A Short History.* Princeton: Princeton University Press.

Fu, Charlene L. 1986. "Anti-Asian Violence in Uptown." Unpublished research paper, Medill School of Journalism. Evanston, Ill.: Northwestern University.

Fuchs, Lawrence H. 1990. *The American Kaleidoscope: Race, Ethnicity, and the Civic Culture.* Hanover, N.H.: University Press of New England.

Gamson, William A. 1994. *Talking Politics.* New York: Cambridge University Press.

Gans, Herbert. 1979. "Symbolic Ethnicity: The Future of Ethnic Groups and Cultures in America." *Ethnic and Racial Studies* 2(1): 1–20.

Geertz, Clifford. 1963. "The Integrative Revolution: Primordial Sentiments and Civil Politics in the New States." In *Old Societies and New States,* edited by Clifford Geertz. Glencoe, Ill.: Free Press.

Georges, Eugenia. 1990. *The Making of Transnational Community: Migration, Development, and Cultural Change in the Dominican Republic.* New York: Columbia University Press.

Geron, Kim, Enrique de la Cruz, Leland T. Saito, and Jaideep Singh. 2001. "Asian Pacific Americans' Social Movements and Interest Groups." *Political Science and Politics* 34(3): 619–24.

Gitlin, Todd, and Nanci Hollander. 1970. *Uptown: Poor Whites in Chicago.* New York: Harper & Row.

Glassie, John. 2003. "Crossing Over." *The New York Times Magazine,* September 7: 19.

Glazer, Nathan. 1971. "Blacks and Ethnic Groups: The Difference, and the Political Difference It Makes." *Social Problems* 18(4): 444–61.

Glazer, Nathan, and Daniel P. Moynihan. 1963. *Beyond the Melting Pot: The Negroes, Puerto Ricans, Jews, Italians, and Irish of New York City.* Cambridge, Mass.: MIT Press.

Glick Schiller, Nina, Linda Basch, and Cristina Blanc–Szanton. 1992. "Transnationalism: A New Analytic Framework of Understanding Migration." In *Towards a Transnational Perspective on Migration: Race, Class, Ethnicity, and Nationalism,* edited by Nina Glick Schiller, Linda Basch, and Cristina Blanc-Szanton. New York: New York Academy of Sciences.

Glick Schiller, Nina, Linda Basch, and Cristina Szanton–Blanc. 1995. "From Immigrant to Transmigrant: Theorizing Transnational Migration." *Anthropological Quarterly* 68(1): 48–63.

Gonlag, Ruth. 1985. "Protectiveness Modified in a Shared-Life Relationship: Sponsoring Hmong Families in Eau Claire, Wisconsin." *Wisconsin Sociologist* 22(4): 124–28.

Gordon, Milton. 1964. *Assimilation in American Life: The Role of Race, Religion, and National Origins.* New York: Oxford University Press.

Grasmuck, Sherri, and Patricia R. Pessar. 1991. *Between Two Islands: Dominican International Migration.* Berkeley: University of California Press.

Griswold, Wendy. 2004. *Cultures and Societies in a Changing World.* Thousand Oaks, Calif.: Pine Forge Press.

Gurda, John. 1976. *The Latin Community on Milwaukee's Near South Side.* Milwaukee: University of Wisconsin–Milwaukee, Milwaukee Urban Observatory.

———. 1999. *The Making of Milwaukee.* Milwaukee: Milwaukee County Historical Society.

Gutman, Herbert. 1973. "Work, Culture, and Society in Industrializing America, 1815–1919." *American Historical Review* 78(June): 531–88.

———. 1976. *The Black Family in Slavery and Freedom, 1750–1925.* New York: Vintage Press.

Hacker, Andrew. 1992. *Two Nations: Black and White, Separate, Hostile, Unequal.* New York: Ballantine Books.

Hamilton-Merritt, Jane. 1993. *Tragic Mountains: The Hmong, the Americans, and the Secret Wars for Laos, 1942–1992.* Bloomington: Indiana University Press.

Handlin, Oscar. 1951/1973. *The Uprooted: The Epic Story of the Great Migrations That Made the American People.* Boston: Little, Brown.

———. 1962. *The Newcomers: Negroes and Puerto Ricans in a Changing Metropolis.* Garden City, N.Y.: Anchor Press.

Hannan, Michael T. 1979. "The Dynamics of Ethnic Boundaries in Modern States." In *National Development and the World System,* edited by John W. Meyer and Michael T. Hannan. Chicago: University of Chicago Press.

Hansen, Marcus Lee. 1940/1964. *The Immigrant in American History.* New York: Harper & Row.

Hao, Lingxin, and Yukio Kawano. 2001. "Immigrants' Welfare Use and Opportunity for Contact with Co-Ethnics." *Demography* 38(3): 375–89.

Harrington, Michael. 1962/1986. *The Other America: Poverty in the United States.* New York: Penguin Books.

Hassoun, Jean-Pierre. 1997. *Hmong du Laos en France: Changement social, initiative et adaptations.* Paris: Presses Universitaires de France.

Headley, Robert K. 1990. "The Society and Its Environment." In *Cambodia: A Country Study,* edited by Russell R. Ross. Washington: Library of Congress, Federal Research Division.

Healy, Joseph F. 1997. *Race, Ethnicity, and Gender in the United States.* Thousand Oaks, Calif.: Pine Forge Press.

Hein, Jeremy. 1988. "State Incorporation of Migrants and the Reproduction of a Middleman Minority Among Indochinese Refugees." *The Sociological Quarterly* 29(3): 463–78.

———. 1993. *States and International Migrants: The Incorporation of Indochinese Refugees in the United States and France.* Boulder: Westview Press.

———. 1994. "From Migrant to Minority: Hmong Refugees and the Social Construction of Identity in the United States." *Sociological Inquiry* 64(3): 281–306.

———. 1995. *From Vietnam, Laos, and Cambodia: A Refugee Experience in the United States.* New York: Twayne Publishers.

Hein, Jeremy, and Randall R. Beger. 2001. "Legal Adaptation Among Vietnamese Refugees in the United States: How International Migrants Litigate Civil Grievances During the Resettlement Process." *International Migration Review* 35(2): 420–48.

Hernández, David M., and Evelyn N. Glenn. 2003. "Ethnic Prophecies: A Review Essay." *Contemporary Sociology* 32(4): 418–26.

Hickey, Gerald C. 1964. *Village in Vietnam.* New Haven: Yale University Press.

Higham, Charles. 2001. *The Civilization of Angkor.* Berkeley: University of California Press.

Higham, John. 1974. *Strangers in the Land: Patterns of American Nativism, 1860–1925.* New Brunswick, N.J.: Rutgers University Press.

———. 1982. "Review of *Ethnic America: A History,* by Thomas Sowell." *American Historical Review* 87(5): 1452.

Hinton, Alexander L. 2005. *Why Did They Kill: Cambodia in the Shadow of Genocide.* Berkeley: University of California Press.

Hmong American Residence and Business Directory. 1999. St. Paul: L&W Communications.

Hoang, Mai. 1992. "Asian American Republicans in Houston." *Asian Business and Community News* 10(8): 17.

Hochschild, Jennifer L. 1995. *Facing Up to the American Dream: Race, Class, and the Soul of the Nation.* Princeton: Princeton University Press.

Hondagneu-Sotelo, Pierrette. 1994. *Gendered Transitions: Mexican Experiences of Immigration.* Berkeley: University of California Press.

Hopkins, MaryCarol. 1996. *Braving a New World: Cambodian (Khmer) Refugees in an American City.* Westport, Conn.: Bergin & Garvey.

Hout, Michael, and Joshua R. Goldstein. 1994. "How 4.5 Million Irish Immigrants Became 40 Million Irish Americans: Demographic and Subjective Aspects of the Ethnic Composition of White Americans." *American Sociological Review* 59(1): 64–82.

Houtart, François. 1977. "Theravada Buddhism and Political Power: Construction and Destruction of Its Ideological Function." *Social Compass* 24(2–3): 207–46.

Howard, Judith A. 2000. "Social Psychology of Identity." *Annual Review of Sociology* 26: 367–93.

Hurtado, Aida, Patricia Gurin, and Timothy Peng. 1994. "Social Identities—A Framework for Studying the Adaptations of Immigrants and Ethnics." *Social Problems* 41(1): 129–51.

Hwang, Sean-Shong, and Steve H. Murdock. 1991. "Ethnic Enclosure or Ethnic Competition: Ethnic Identification Among Hispanics in Texas." *The Sociological Quarterly* 32(3): 469–76.

Immigration and Refugee Services of America. 1986a. "Refugees Help Rebuild Chicago Neighborhood." *Refugee Reports* 7(5): 8–10.

———. 1986b. "Refugees Learn to Flex Political Muscle." *Refugee Reports* 7(11): 1–7.

———. 2003. "U.S. State Department Holds Public Meeting on Refugee Resettlement." *Refugee Reports* 24(5): 1–8.

Isaacs, Harold R. 1975. *Idols of the Tribe: Group Identity and Political Change.* New York: Harper & Row.

Itzigsohn, José, Silvia Giorguli, and Obed Vazquez. 2005. "Immigrant Incorporation and Racial Identity: Racial Self-Identification Among Dominican Immigrants." *Ethnic and Racial Studies* 28(1): 50–78.

Izikowitz, Karl G. 1969. "Neighbors in Laos." In *Ethnic Groups and Boundaries: The Social Organization of Culture Difference,* edited by Fredrik Barth. Boston: Little, Brown.

Jackson, James S., Wayne R. McCullough, Gerald Gurin, and Clifford L. Broman. 1991. "Racial Identity." In *Life in Black America,* edited by James S. Jackson. Newbury Park, Calif.: Sage.

Jackson, Karl D. 1989. "The Ideology of Total Revolution." In *Cambodia, 1975–1978: Rendezvous with Death,* edited by Karl D. Jackson. Princeton: Princeton University Press.

Jaret, Charles. 1979. "Recent Patterns of Chicago Jewish Residential Mobility." *Ethnicity* 6(3): 235–48.

Jasso, Guillermina, and Mark R. Rosenzweig. 1990. *The New Chosen People: Immigrants in the United States.* New York: Russell Sage Foundation.

Jensen, Leif I. 1988. "Patterns of Immigration and Public Assistance Utilization, 1970–1980." *International Migration Review* 23(1): 51–83.

Jones, James M. 1997. *Prejudice and Racism.* New York: McGraw- Hill.

Jones, Jeffrey M. 2000. "Americans Remain Split on Immigration, but Significantly More Positive Than in Mid-1990s." *The Gallup Poll Monthly,* September: 64–66.

Jones-Correa, Michael, and David L. Leal. 1996. "Becoming 'Hispanic': Secondary Panethnic Identification Among Latin American–Origin Populations in the United States." *Hispanic Journal of Behavioral Sciences* 18(2): 214–54.

Johnston, Kati, and Taggart Siegel. 1987. *Blue Collar and Buddha.* Video. Evanston, Ill.: Siegel Productions.

Joppke, Christian. 1998. "Immigration Challenges the Nation-State." In *Challenge to the Nation-State: Immigration in Western Europe and the United States*, edited by Christian Joppke. New York: Oxford University Press.

———. 1999. "How Immigration Is Changing Citizenship: A Comparative View." *Ethnic and Racial Studies* 22(4): 629–52.

Kandel, William, and Douglas S. Massey. 2003. "The Culture of Migration: A Theoretical and Empirical Analysis." *Social Forces* 80(3): 981–1004.

Karnow, Stanley. 1983. *Vietnam: A History*. New York: Penguin Books.

Kasinitz, Philip, Juan Battle, and Inés Miyares. 2001. "Fade to Black? The Children of West Indian Immigrants in Southern Florida." In *Ethnicities: Children of Immigrants in America*, edited by Rubén G. Rumbaut and Alejandro Portes. Berkeley: University of California Press.

Kazal, Russell A. 1995. "Revisiting Assimilation: The Rise, Fall, and Reappraisal of a Concept in American Ethnic History." *American Historical Review* 100(2): 437–71.

Kent, Mary M., Kelvin M. Pollard, John Haaga, and Mark Mather. 2001. *First Glimpse from the 2000 U.S. Census*. Washington, D.C.: Population Reference Bureau.

Khoa, Le Xuan, and Diana D. Bui. 1985. "Southeast Asian Mutual Assistance Associations: An Approach for Community Development." In *Southeast Asian Mental Health: Treatment, Prevention, Services, Training, and Research*, edited by T. C. Owan. Washington, D.C.: National Institute of Mental Health.

Kibria, Nazli. 1993. *Family Tightropes: The Changing Lives of Vietnamese Americans*. Princeton: Princeton University Press.

———. 1997. "The Construction of 'Asian American': Reflections on Intermarriage and Ethnic Identity among Second-Generation Chinese and Korean Americans." *Ethnic and Racial Studies* 20(3): 523–44.

———. 1998. "The Contested Meaning of 'Asian American': Racial Dilemmas in the Contemporary United States." *Ethnic and Racial Studies* 21(5): 939–58.

———. 1999. "College and Notions of 'Asian American': Second-Generation Chinese and Korean Americans Negotiate Race and Identity." *Amerasia Journal* 25(1): 29–51.

———. 2000. "Race, Ethnic Options, and Ethnic Binds: Identity Negotiations of Second-Generation Chinese and Korean Americans." *Sociological Perspectives* 43(1): 77–95.

———. 2002. *Becoming Asian American: Second-Generation Chinese and Korean American Identities*. Baltimore: Johns Hopkins University Press.

Kiernan, Ben. 1996. *The Pol Pot Regime: Race, Power, and Genocide in Cambodia Under the Khmer Rouge, 1975–97*. New Haven: Yale University Press.

———. 2004. *How Pol Pot Came to Power: Colonialism, Nationalism, and Communism in Cambodia, 1930–1975*. New Haven, Conn.: Yale University Press.

Kleugel, James R., and Lawrence D. Bobo. 2001. "Perceived Group Discrimination and Policy Attitudes: The Sources and Consequences of the Race and Gender Gaps." In *Urban Inequality: Evidence from Four Cities*, edited by Alice O'Connor, Chris Tilly, and Lawrence D. Bobo. New York: Russell Sage Foundation.

Koltyk, Jo Ann. 1998. *New Pioneers in the Heartland: Hmong Life in Wisconsin.* Boston: Allyn & Bacon.

Kraybill, Donald B., and Carl F. Bowman. 2001. *On the Backroad to Heaven: Old Order Hutterites, Mennonites, Amish, and Brethren.* Baltimore: Johns Hopkins University Press.

Kristol, Irving. 1966. "The Negro Today Is Like the Immigrant Yesterday." *The New York Times Magazine,* September 11: 50.

Kulke, Hermann. 1984. "Max Weber's Contribution to the Study of 'Hinduization' of India and 'Indianization' of Southeast Asia." In *Recent Research on Max Weber's Studies of Hinduism,* edited by Detlef Kantowsky. Munich: Weltforum Verlag.

Kuo, Wen H. 1995. "Coping with Racial Discrimination: The Case of Asian Americans." *Ethnic and Racial Studies* 18(1): 109–27.

Kurien, Prema. 2001. "Religion, Ethnicity, and Politics: Hindu and Muslim Indian Immigrants in the United States." *Ethnic and Racial Studies* 24(2): 263–93.

Kyle, David. 2000. *Transnational Peasants: Migrations, Networks, and Ethnicity in Andean Ecuador.* Baltimore: Johns Hopkins University Press.

Lamont, Michèle. 2000. *The Dignity of Working Men: Morality and the Boundaries of Race, Class and Immigration.* New York: Russell Sage Foundation.

Landale, Nancy S., and R. S. Oropesa. 2002. "White, Black, or Puerto Rican? Racial Self-Identification among Mainland and Island Puerto Ricans." *Social Forces* 81(1): 231–54.

Lay, Sody. 2004. "Lost in the Fray: Cambodian American Youth in Providence, Rhode Island." In *Asian American Youth: Culture, Identity, and Ethnicity,* edited by Jennifer Lee and Min Zhou. New York: Routledge.

Lee, Gary. 1994–95. "The Religious Presentation of Social Relationships: Hmong World View and Social Structure." *Lao Study Review* 2. Available at: www.global.lao.net/laostudy/hmrelate.htm (accessed December 12, 2005).

———. 2004. "Transnational Adaptation: An Overview of the Hmong in Laos." In *Hmong/Miao in Asia,* edited by Nicholas Tapp, Jean Michaud, Christian Culas, and Gary Y. Lee. Chaing Mai, Thailand: Silkworm Books.

Lee, Sharon M. 1998. *Asian Americans: Diverse and Growing.* Washington, D.C.: Population Reference Bureau.

Lee, Stacey J. 1996. "Perceptions of Panethnicity Among Asian American High School Students." *Amerasia Journal* 22(2): 109–25.

———. 2001. "More than 'Model Minorities' or 'Delinquents': A Look at Hmong American High School Students." *Harvard Educational Review* 71(3): 505–28.

Lemoine, Jacques. 1972. *Un village Hmong vert du haut Laos.* Paris: Editions du Centre National de la Recherche Scientifique.

Levine, Lawrence W. 1977. *Black Culture and Black Consciousness: Afro-American Folk Thought from Slavery to Freedom.* New York: Oxford University Press.

Levitt, Peggy. 2001. *The Transnational Villagers.* Berkeley: University of California Press.

Levitt, Peggy, Josh DeWind, and Steven Vertovec. 2003. "International Perspectives on Transnational Migration: An Introduction." *International Migration Review* 37(3): 565–75.

Levitt, Peggy, and Nina Glick Schiller. 2004. "Conceptualizing Simultaneity: A Transnational Social Field Perspective on Society." *International Migration Review* 38(3): 1002–39.

Lewis, Oscar. 1959. *Five Families: Mexican Case Studies in the Culture of Poverty.* New York: Basic Books.

———. 1965. *La Vida: A Puerto Rican Family in the Culture of Poverty—San Juan and New York.* New York: Random House.

Lie, John. 1995. "From International Migration to Transnational Diaspora." *Contemporary Sociology* 24(4): 303–6.

Lieberson, Stanley. 1980. *A Piece of the Pie: Blacks and White Immigrants Since 1880.* Berkeley: University of California Press.

Lien, Pei-te, M. Margaret Conway, and Janelle Wong. 2003. "The Contours and Sources of Ethnic Identity Choices Among Asian Americans." *Social Science Quarterly* 84(2): 461–81.

Light, Ivan. 1988. Review of *For Bread with Butter: Life-Worlds of East Central Europeans in Johnstown, Pennsylvania, 1890–1940,* by Ewa Morawska. *American Journal of Sociology* 94: 453–55.

Lippmann, Walter. 1922/1965. *Public Opinion.* New York: Free Press.

Livo, Norma J., and Dia Cha. 1991. *Folk Stories of the Hmong: Peoples of Laos, Thailand, and Vietnam.* Englewood, Colo.: Libraries Unlimited.

Lo, Fungchatou T. 2001. *The Promised Land: Socioeconomic Reality of the Hmong People in Urban America (1976–2000).* Lima, Ohio: Wyndham Hall Press.

Loewen, James W. 1971/1988. *The Mississippi Chinese: Between Black and White.* Prospect Heights, Ill.: Waveland Press.

Lopez, David, and Yen Espiritu. 1990. "Panethnicity in the United States: A Theoretical Framework." *Ethnic and Racial Studies* 13(2): 198–224.

Louis, Karen S. 1982. "Multisite/Multimethod Studies: An Introduction." *American Behavioral Scientist* 26(1): 6–22.

Lucke, Joyce J. 1995. "We All Agree: A Study of Cultural Consensus in a Hmong Community." Ph.D. diss., University of Wisconsin–Milwaukee.

Ly, Choua. 2001. "The Conflict Between Law and Culture: The Case of the Hmong in America." *Wisconsin Law Review* 2: 471–99.

Lyden, Jacki, and Chet Jakus. 1980. *Landmarks and Legends of Uptown.* Chicago: Jacki Lyden and Chet Jakus.

Lyman, Thomas A. 1990. "Proverbs and Parables in Mong Njua (Green Miao)." *Zeitschrift der Deutschen Morgenländischen Gesellschaft* 140(2): 326–42.

———. 2004. "A Note on the Ethno-Semantics of Proverb Usage in Mong Njua (Green Hmong)." In *Hmong/Miao in Asia,* edited by Nicholas Tapp, Jean Michaud, Christian Culas, and Gary Y. Lee. Chaing Mai, Thailand: Silkworm Books.

Marger, Martin N. 1997. *Race and Ethnic Relations: American and Global Perspectives.* Belmont, Calif.: Wadsworth.

Martin, Philip, and Elizabeth Midgley. 2003. *Immigration: Shaping and Reshaping America.* Washington, D.C.: Population Reference Bureau.

Massey, Douglas S. 1981. "Dimensions of the New Immigration to the United States and the Prospects for Assimilation." *Annual Review of Sociology* 7: 57–85.

————. 1987. "The Ethnosuvey in Theory and Practice." *International Migration Review* 21(4): 1498–1522.

————. 1995. "The New Immigration and Ethnicity in the United States." *Population and Development Review* 21(3): 631–52.

Massey, Douglas, Rafael Alarcón, Jorge Durand, and Humberto González. 1987. *Return to Aztlan: The Social Process of International Migration from Western Mexico.* Berkeley: University of California Press.

Massey, Douglas S., Joaquín Arango, Graeme Hugo, Ali Kouacouci, Adela Pellegrino, and J. Edward Taylor. 1998. *Worlds in Motion: Understanding International Migration at the End of the Millennium.* Oxford: Clarendon Press.

Massey, Douglas S., and Nancy J. Denton. 1993. *American Apartheid: Segregation and the Making of the Underclass.* Cambridge, Mass.: Harvard University Press.

Massey, Douglas S., and Rene Zenteno. 2000. "A Validation of the Ethnosurvey: The Case of Mexico–U.S. Migration." *International Migration Review* 34(3): 766–93.

Mattison, Wendy, Laotou Lo, and Thomas Scarseth. 1994. *Hmong Lives: From Laos to La Crosse.* La Crosse, Wis.: Pump House.

McBee, Susanna. 1984. "Asian Americans, Are They Making the Grade?" *U.S. News and World Report,* April 2: 41–47.

McKee, James B. 1993. *Sociology and the Race Problem: The Failure of a Perspective.* Urbana: University of Illinois Press.

McLemore, Romo. 1998. *Racial and Ethnic Relations in America.* Boston: Allyn & Bacon.

McNall, Miles, Timothy Dunnigan, and Jeylan T. Mortimer. 1994. "The Educational Achievement of the St. Paul Hmong." *Anthropology and Education Quarterly* 25(1): 44–65.

Men, Chean R. 2002. "The Changing Religious Beliefs and Ritual Practices Among Cambodians in the Diaspora." *Journal of Refugee Studies* 15(2): 222–33.

Menjívar, Cecilia. 2000. *Fragmented Ties: Salvadoran Immigrant Networks in America.* Berkeley: University of California Press.

————. 2002. "The Ties That Heal: Guatemalan Immigrant Women's Networks and Medical Treatment." *International Migration Review* 36(2): 437–66.

Milwaukee Department of City Development. 1984a. "Midtown." Poster.

————. 1984b. "Walker's Point." Poster.

Min, Pyong Gap. 2002. "Contemporary Immigrants' Advantages for Intergenerational Cultural Transmission." In *Mass Migration to the United States: Classical and Contemporary Periods,* edited by Pyong Gap Min. Walnut Creek, Calif.: Altamira Press.

Mitchell, Roger. 1987. "The Will to Believe and Anti-Refugee Rumors." *Midwestern Folklore* 13(1): 5–15.

Miyares, Ines M. 1998. *The Hmong Refugee Experience in the United States: Crossing the River.* New York: Garland.

Moghaddam, Fathali M., Donald M. Taylor, Wallace E. Lambert, and Amy E. Schmidt. 1995. "Attributions and Discrimination: A Study of the Attributions to the Self, the Group, and External Factors Among Whites, Blacks, and Cubans in Miami." *Journal of Cross-Cultural Psychology* 26(2): 209–20.

Montgomery, David. 1979. *Control in America: Studies in the History of Work, Technology, and Labor Struggles.* Cambridge: Cambridge University Press.

Morawska, Ewa. 1985. *For Bread with Butter: Life-Worlds of East Central Europeans in Johnstown, Pennsylvania, 1890–1940.* Cambridge: Cambridge University Press.

Mortland, Carol. 1996. "Khmer." In *Case Studies in Diversity: Refugees in America in the 1990s,* edited by David W. Haines. Westport, Conn.: Praeger.

Moynihan, Daniel P. 1967. "The Negro Family: The Case for National Action." In *The Moynihan Report and the Politics of Controversy,* edited by William L. Rainwater. Cambridge, Mass.: MIT Press.

Murray, Charles. 1984. *Losing Ground: American Social Policy, 1950–1980.* New York: Basic Books.

Mustaphi, Rita. 2005. "Katha Dance Theatre Presents the Ramayana Project: A Pan-Asian Collaboration." Press release. Available at: http://www.kathadance.org/Press_Release_Ramayana.doc.

Myrdal, Gunnar. 1944/1962. *An American Dilemma.* New York: McGraw-Hill.

Nagel, Joane. 1994. "Constructing Ethnicity: Creating and Recreating Ethnic Identity and Culture." *Social Problems* 41(1): 152–76.

Nagel, Joane, and Susan Olzak. 1982. "Ethnic Mobilization in New and Old States: An Extension of the Competition Model." *Social Problems* 30(2): 127–43.

National League of Cities. 1996. *The State of America's Cities: The Thirteenth Annual Opinion Survey of Municipal Elected Officials.* Washington, D.C.: National League of Cities.

———. 1999. *Undoing Racism: Fairness and Justice in America's Cities and Towns.* Washington, D.C.: National League of Cities.

Ngor, Haing. 1987. *Haing Ngor: A Cambodian Odyssey.* New York: Warner Books.

Nhat Hang, Thich. 1998. *The Heart of the Buddha's Teaching: Transforming Suffering into Peace, Joy, and Liberation.* New York: Broadway Books.

North, David, and Nim Sok. 1989. *Profiles of Some Good Places for Cambodians to Live in the United States.* Washington, D.C.: U.S. Office of Refugee Resettlement.

Oates, Joyce Carol. 1999. "Crime and Punishment." *The New York Times Book Review,* September 19: 13.

Ogbu, John U. 1978. *Minority Education and Caste: The American System in Cross-Cultural Perspective.* New York: Academic Press.

———. 1991a. "Minority Coping Responses and School Experience." *Journal of Psychohistory* 18(4): 433–56.

———. 1991b. "Immigrant and Involuntary Minorities in Comparative Perspective." In *Minority Status and Schooling: A Comparative Study of Immigrant and Involuntary Minorities,* edited by Margaret A. Gibson and John U. Ogbu. New York: Garland.

Okamoto, Dina G. 2003. "Towards a Theory of Panethnicity: Explaining Asian American Collective Action." *American Sociological Review* 68(6): 811–42.

Olzak, Susan. 1992. *The Dynamics of Ethnic Competition and Conflict.* Palo Alto, Calif.: Stanford University Press.

Omi, Michael, and Howard Winant. 1994. *Racial Formation in the United States: From the 1960s to the 1990s.* New York: Routledge.

Ong, Aiwha. 2003. *Buddha Is Hiding: Refugees, Citizenship, the New America.* Berkeley: University of California Press.

Ono, Hiromi. 2002. "Assimilation, Ethnic Competition, and Ethnic Identities of U.S.-Born Persons of Mexican Origin." *International Migration Review* 36(3): 726–45.

Operario, Don, and Susan T. Fiske. 2001. "Ethnic Identity Moderates Perceptions of Prejudice: Judgments of Personal Versus Group Discrimination and Subtle Versus Blatant Bias." *Personality and Social Psychology Bulletin* 27(5): 550–61.

Osborne, Milton. 1988. *Southeast Asia: An Illustrated Introductory History.* Sydney, Australia: Allen & Unwin.

———. 2000. *The Mekong: Turbulent Past, Uncertain Future.* New York: Atlantic Monthly Press.

Oxnam, Robert B. 1986. "Why Asians Succeed Here." *The New York Times Magazine,* November 30: 72.

Paige, Jeffrey. 1975. *Agrarian Revolution: Social Movements and Export Agriculture in the Underdeveloped World.* New York: Free Press.

Park, Robert E. 1914/1967. "Racial Assimilation in Secondary Groups." In *Robert E. Park on Social Control and Collective Behavior,* edited by Ralph H. Turner. Chicago: University of Chicago Press.

———. 1950. *Race and Culture.* Glencoe, Ill.: Free Press.

Passport Books. 1993. *Guide to Ethnic Chicago.* Chicago: Passport Books.

Peang-Meth, Abdulgaffar. 1991. "Understanding the Khmer: Sociological-Cultural Observations." *Asian Survey* 31(5): 442–55.

Pearce, Lisa D. 2002. "Integrating Survey and Ethnographic Methods for Systematic Anomalous Case Analysis." *Sociological Methodology* 32(1): 103–32.

Pedraza, Sylvia. 1994. "Introduction from the Special Issue Editor: The Sociology of Immigration, Race, and Ethnicity in America." *Social Problems* 41(1): 1–8.

Perlmann, Joel. 1988. *Ethnic Differences: Schooling and Social Structure among the Irish, Italians, Jews, and Blacks in an American City, 1880–1935.* New York: Cambridge University Press.

Pfaff, Tim. 1995. *Hmong in America: Journey from a Secret War.* Eau Claire, Wis.: Chippewa Valley Museum Press.

Pokorny, Gary. 1991. "Ministry to Hispanics in the Archdiocese of Milwaukee." In *Milwaukee Catholicism: Essays on Church and Community,* edited by Steven M. Avella. Milwaukee: Knights of Columbus.

Ponchaud, François. 1989. "Social Change in the Vortex of Revolution." In *Cambodia, 1975–1978: Rendezvous with Death,* edited by Karl D. Jackson. Princeton: Princeton University Press.

Portes, Alejandro. 1984. "The Rise of Ethnicity: Determinants of Ethnic Perceptions Among Cuban Exiles in Miami." *American Sociological Review* 49(3): 383–97.

———. 2003. "Conclusion: Theoretical Convergences and Empirical Evidence in the Study of Immigrant Transnationalism." *International Migration Review* 37(3): 874–92.

Portes, Alejandro, and Robert L. Bach. 1985. *Latin Journey: Cuban and Mexican Immigrants in the United States.* Berkeley: University of California Press.

Portes, Alejandro, and Dag MacLeod. 1996. "What Shall I Call Myself? Hispanic Identity Formation in the Second Generation." *Ethnic and Racial Studies* 19(3): 523–47.

Portes, Alejandro, and Rubén G. Rumbaut. 1990. *Immigrant America: A Portrait.* Berkeley: University of California Press.

———. 2001. *Legacies: The Story of the Immigrant Second Generation.* Berkeley: University of California Press.

Portes, Alejandro, and Min Zhou. 1993. "The New Second Generation: Segmented Assimilation and Its Variants." *Annals of the American Academy of Political and Social* Science 530(November): 74–96.

Pou, Saveros. 1992. "Indigenization of the Ramayana in Cambodia." *Asian Folklore Studies* 51: 89–102.

President's Advisory Board on Race. 1998. *One America in the 21st Century, Forging a New Future: The Advisory Board's Report to the President.* Washington: U.S. Government Printing Office.

President's Advisory Commission on Asian Americans and Pacific Islanders. 2001. *Asian Americans and Pacific Islanders: A People Looking Forward.* Rockville, Md.: Office of the White House Initiative.

Prpic, George J. 1987. Review of *For Bread with Butter: Life-Worlds of East Central Europeans in Johnstown, Pennsylvania, 1890–1940,* by Ewa Morawska. *American Historical Review* 92(3): 760–61.

Quincy, Keith. 1988. *Hmong: History of a People.* Cheney: Eastern Washington University Press.

———. 2000. *Harvesting Pa Chay's Wheat: The Hmong and America's Secret War in Laos.* Spokane: Eastern Washington University Press.

Ragin, Charles C. 1987. *The Comparative Method: Moving Beyond Qualitative and Quantitative Strategies.* Berkeley: University of California Press.

———. 1992. " 'Casing' and the Process of Social Inquiry." In *What Is a Case? Exploring the Foundations of Social Inquiry,* edited by Charles C. Ragin and Howard S. Becker. New York: Cambridge University Press.

Rainwater, William L. 1967. *The Moynihan Report and the Politics of Controversy.* Cambridge, Mass.: MIT Press.

Ramirez, Anthony. 1986. "America's Super Minority." *Fortune,* November 24, 148–58.

Reeves, Terrance J., and Claudette E. Bennett. 2004. *We the People: Asians in the United States.* Washington: U.S. Department of Commerce.

Reimers, David M. 2005. *Other Immigrants: The Global Origins of the American People.* New York: New York University Press.

Republican National Committee. 1994. *Contract with America: The Bold Plan by Rep. Newt Gingrich, Rep. Dick Armey, and the House Republicans to Change the Nation.* New York: Random House.

Richie, Martha F. 2000. *America's Diversity and Growth: Signposts for the 21st Century.* Washington, D.C.: Population Reference Bureau.

Ritchie, Laura. 2005. "Miss Hmong Wisconsin." *Future Hmong,* January: 10–11.

Roberts, Alden E. 1988. "Racism Sent and Received: Americans and Vietnamese View One Another." *Research in Race and Ethnic Relations* 5: 75–97.

Robinson, W. Courtland. 1998. *Terms of Refuge: The Indochinese Exodus and the International Response.* London: Zed Books.

Rockler, Naomi R. 2003. "Entertainment, the Personal, and the Political: Therapeutic Rhetoric and Popular Culture Controversies." *The Communication Review* 6(2): 97–115.

Rolland, Barbara, and Houa Vue Moua. 1994. *Trail Through the Mists.* Eau Claire, Wis.: Eagles Printing.

Rose, Peter I. 1983. *Working with Refugees.* New York: Center for Migration Studies.

Ruefle, William, William H. Ross, and Diane Mandell. 1992. "Attitudes Towards Southeast Asian Immigrants in a Wisconsin Community." *International Migration Review* 26(3): 877–98.

Rumbaut, Rubén. 1997. "Paradoxes (and Orthodoxies) of Assimilation." *Sociological Perspectives* 40(3): 481–511.

Rutledge, Paul. 1986. "Southeast Asian Religions: A Perspective on Historical Buddhism with the Developing States of Southeast Asia." *East Asian Journal of Theology* 4(2): 138–56.

Safran, William. 1991. "Diasporas in Modern Societies: Myths of Homeland and Return." *Diaspora* 1(1): 83–99.

Said, Edward W. 1978. *Orientalism.* New York: Pantheon Books.

Sánchez, George J. 1997. "Face the Nation: Race, Immigration, and the Rise of Nativism in Late Twentieth Century America." *International Migration Review* 31(4): 1009–1030.

Sanders, Jimy M. 2002. "Ethnic Boundaries and Identity in Plural Societies." *Annual Review of Sociology* 28: 327–57.

Sanders, Jimy M., Victor Nee, and Scott Sernau. 2002. "Asian Immigrants' Reliance on Social Ties in a Multiethnic Labor Market." *Social Forces* 81(1): 281–314.

Santoli, Al. 1988a. *New Americans: An Oral History; Immigrants and Refugees in the United States Today.* New York: Viking.

———. 1988b. "How They Saved a Neighborhood." *Chicago Tribune (Parade) Magazine,* August 14.

Sassen, Saskia. 1991. *The Global City.* Princeton: Princeton University Press.

Schein, Louisa. 1998. "Forged Transnationality and Oppositional Cosmo-politanism." In *Transnationalism from Below,* edited by Michael P. Smith and Luis E. Guarnizo. New Brunswick, N.J.: Transaction Publishers.

———. 2004. "Hmong/Miao Transnationality: Identity Beyond Culture." In *Hmong/Miao in Asia,* edited by Nicholas Tapp, Jean Michaud, Christian Culas, and Gary Y. Lee. Chaing Mai, Thailand: Silkworm Books.

Schneider, Dorothee. 2001. "Naturalization and United States Citizenship in Two Periods of Mass Migration: 1890–1930, 1965–2000." *Journal of American Ethnic History* 21(1): 50–82.

Schuck, Peter. 1999. *Citizens, Strangers, and In-Betweeners: Essays on Immigration and Citizenship.* Boulder: Westview Press.

Scott, George M. 1986. "Migrants Without Mountains: The Politics of Socio-cultural Adjustment Among the Lao Hmong Refugees in San Diego." Ph.D. diss., University of California–San Diego.

———. 1987. "The Lao Hmong Refugees in San Diego: Their Religious Transformation and Its Implications for Geertz's Thesis." *Ethnic Studies Report* 5(2): 32–46.

———. 1988. "To Catch or Not to Catch a Thief: A Case of Bride Theft Among the Lao Hmong Refugees in Southern California." *Ethnic Groups* 7(2): 137–51.

———. 1990. "Hmong Aspirations for a Separate State in Laos: The Effects of the Indo-China War." In *Secessionist Movements in Comparative Perspective,* edited by Ralph R. Premdas, S. W. R. de A. Samarasinghe, and Alan B. Anderson. New York: St. Martin's Press.

Sebald, W. G. 1998. *The Rings of Saturn.* New York: New Directions Books.

———. 2001. *Austerlitz.* New York: Random House.

Sellers, Robert M., and J. Nicole Shelton. 2003. "The Role of Racial Identity in Perceived Racial Discrimination." *Journal of Personality and Social Psychology* 84(5): 1079–92.

Sewell, William H. 1999a. "Geertz, Cultural Systems, and History: From Synchrony to Transformation." In *The Fate of Culture: Geertz and Beyond,* edited by Sherry B. Ortner. Berkeley: University of California Press.

———. 1999b. "The Concept(s) of Culture." In *Beyond the Cultural Turn: New Directions in the Study of Society and Culture,* edited by Victoria E. Bonnell and Lynn Hunt. Berkeley: University of California Press.

Shawcross, William. 1977. *Side-Show: Nixon, Kissinger, and the Destruction of Cambodia.* New York: Pocket Books.

Shigagawa, Larry H., and Gin Y. Pang. 1996. "Asian American Panethnicity and Intermarriage." *Amerasia Journal* 22(2): 127–52.

Sieber, Sam D. 1973. "The Integration of Fieldwork and Survey Methods." *American Journal of Sociology* 78(6): 1335–59.

Sigelman, Lee, and Susan Welch. 1992. *Black Americans' Views of Racial Inequality: The Dream Deferred.* New York: Cambridge University Press.

Simmel, Georg. 1908/1955. *Conflict and the Web of Group Affiliations.* Translated by Kurt H. Wolff and Reinhard Bendix. New York: Free Press.

Singer, Audrey. 1999. "U.S. Citizenship Applications at All-Time High." *Population Today* 27(October): 4–5.

———. 2004. "Welfare Reform and Immigrants: A Policy Review." In *Immigrants, Welfare Reform, and the Poverty of Policy,* edited by Philip Kretsedemas and Ana Aparicio. Westport, Conn.: Praeger.

Sizemore, David S., and Wesley T. Milner. 2004. "Hispanic Media Use and Perceptions of Discrimination: Reconsidering Ethnicity, Politics, and Socioeconomics." *The Sociological Quarterly* 45(4): 765–84.

Smelser, Neil J., William J. Wilson, and Faith Mitchell, eds. 2001. *America Becoming: Racial Trends and Their Consequences.* Washington, D.C.: National Academy Press.

Smith, Anthony D. 1986. *The Ethnic Origins of Nations.* New York: Basil Blackwell.

Smith, Ryan A., and James R. Elliott. 2002. "Does Ethnic Concentration Influence Employees' Access to Authority? An Examination of Contemporary Urban Labor Markets." *Social Forces* 81(1): 255–79.

Smith-Hefner, Nancy J. 1994. "Ethnicity and the Force of Faith: Christian Conversion Among Khmer Refugees." *Anthropological Quarterly* 67(1): 24–37.
———. 1999. *Khmer American: Identity and Moral Education in a Diasporic Community.* Berkeley: University of California Press.
Southeast Asian Resource Action Center. 2004. *Southeast Asian American Statistical Profile.* Washington, D.C.: Southeast Asian Resource Action Center.
Sowell, Thomas. 1981. *Ethnic America: A History.* New York: Basic Books.
———. 1996. *Migrations and Culture: A World View.* New York: Basic Books.
Soysal, Yasemin. 1994. *Limits of Citizenship: Migrants and Postnational Membership in Europe.* Chicago: University of Chicago Press.
State Council on Asian-Pacific Minnesotans. 2004. *Clarity of Purpose: A Strategic Plan for the Council on Asian-Pacific Minnesotans.* St. Paul: Council on Asian-Pacific Minnesotans.
Steinberg, David J. 1959. *Cambodia: Its People, Its Society, Its Culture.* New Haven: HRAF Press.
Steinberg, Stephen. 1981/1989. *The Ethnic Myth: Race, Ethnicity, and Class in America.* Boston: Beacon Press.
———. 2000. "The Cultural Fallacy in Studies of Racial and Ethnic Mobility." In *Immigrants, Schooling and Social Mobility: Does Culture Make a Difference?*, edited by Hans Vermeulen and Joel Perlmann. New York: St. Martin's Press.
Stepick, Alex, Carol Dutton Stepick, Emmanuel Eugene, Deborah Teed, and Yves Labissier. 2001. "Shifting Identities and Intergenerational Conflict: Growing Up Haitian in Miami." In *Ethnicities: Children of Immigrants in America*, edited by Rubén G. Rumbaut and Alejandro Portes. Berkeley: University of California Press.
Sutton, Constance R. 1987. "The Caribbeanization of New York City and the Emergence of a Transnational Sociocultural System." In *Caribbean Life in New York City: Sociocultural Dimensions*, edited by Constance R. Sutton and E. Chaney. New York: Center for Migration Studies.
Sutton, Constance R., and Susan R. Makiesky. 1975. "Migration and West Indians' Racial and Ethnic Consciousness." In *Migration and Development: Implications for Ethnic Identity and Political Conflict*, edited by Helen I. Safa and Brian M. du Toit. The Hague: Mouton Publishers.
Swidler, Ann. 1986. "Culture in Action: Symbols and Strategies." *American Sociological Review* 51(2): 273–86.
Takaki, Ronald. 1979. *Iron Cages: Race and Culture in Nineteenth Century America.* New York: Alfred A. Knopf.
———. 1989. *Strangers from a Different Shore: A History of Asian Americans.* Boston: Little, Brown.
———. 1993. *A Different Mirror: A History of Multicultural America.* Boston: Little, Brown.
———. 1994. *From Different Shores: Perspectives on Race and Ethnicity in America.* New York: Oxford University Press.
Tan, Amy. 1995. "Mother Tongue." In *Under Western Eyes: Personal Essays from Asian America*, edited by Garrett Hongo. New York: Anchor Books.

Tapp, Nicholas. 1986a. "Geomancy as an Aspect of Upland-Lowland Relationships." In *Hmong in Transition*, edited by Glenn L. Hendricks, Bruce T. Downing, and Amos S. Deinard. New York: Center for Migration Studies.

———. 1986b. "Buddhism and the Hmong: A Case Study in Social Adjustment." *Journal of Developing Societies* 2(1): 68–88.

———. 1989a. "Hmong Religion." *Asian Folklore Studies* 48(1): 59–94.

———. 1989b. "The Impact of Missionary Christianity Upon Marginalized Ethnic Groups: The Case of the Hmong." *Journal of Southeast Asian Studies* 20(1): 70–95.

———. 1989c. *Sovereignty and Rebellion: The White Hmong of Northern Thailand.* New York: Oxford University Press.

Tenhula, John. 1991. *Voices from Southeast Asia: The Refugee Experience in the United States.* New York: Holmes & Meier.

Terkel, Studs. 1967. *Division Street: America.* New York: Pantheon.

Thernstrom, Stephan. 1964/1975. *Poverty and Progress: Social Mobility in a Nineteenth Century City.* New York: Atheneum.

Tillema, Richard G. 1981. "Starting Over in a New Land: Resettling a Refugee Family." *Public Welfare* 39(1): 35–41.

Tilly, Charles. 1990. "Transplanted Networks." In *Immigration Reconsidered: History, Sociology, and Politics*, edited by Virginia Yans-McLaughlin. New York: Oxford University Press.

———. 1996. "Invisible Elbows." *Sociological Forum* 11(4): 589–601.

———. 1998. *Durable Inequality.* Berkeley: University of California Press.

Tuan, Mia. 1998. *Forever Foreigners or Honorary Whites? The Asian Ethnic Experience Today.* New Brunswick, N.J.: Rutgers University Press.

U.S. Commission on Civil Rights. 1992. *Civil Rights Issues Facing Asian Americans in the 1990s.* Washington: U.S. Commission on Civil Rights.

U.S. Commission on Immigration Reform. 1997. *Becoming an American: Immigration and Immigrant Policy.* Washington: U.S. Commission on Immigration Reform.

U.S. Department of the Army. 1970. *Minority Groups in Thailand.* Washington: U.S. Department of the Army.

U.S. Department of Commerce. 1993. *1990 Census of Population: Asians and Pacific Islanders in the United States.* Washington: U.S. Department of Commerce.

U.S. House of Representatives. 2000. "Hmong Veterans Naturalization Act." *Congressional Record*, Tuesday, May 2, 2000, 106th Congress, 2nd session, vol. 146, no. 52.

———. 2001. "Expressing the Sense of Congress that the President Should Issue a Proclamation Recognizing a National Lao-Hmong Recognition Day." March 27, 2001. 107th Congress, 1st session, H. Con. Res. 88. Available at: www.frwebgate.access.gpo.gov.

van den Berghe, Pierre L. 1981. *The Ethnic Phenomenon.* New York: Praeger.

van Niekerk, Miles. 2004. "Afro-Caribbeans and Indo-Caribbeans in the Netherlands: Premigration Legacies and Social Mobility." *International Migration Review* 38(1): 158–83.

VanGeest, Jonathan, and Ariela Royer. 1995. "Albany Park." In *Chicago Local Community Fact Book.* Chicago: Academy of Chicago Publishers.

Vecoli, Rudolph J. 1964. "*Contadini* in Chicago: A Critique of *The Uprooted.*" *Journal of American History* 51(December): 404–17.

Vermeulen, Hans, and Joel Perlmann, eds. 2000. *Immigrants, Schooling and Social Mobility: Does Culture Make a Difference?* New York: St. Martin's Press.

Vertovec, Steven. 2004. "Migrant Transnationalism and Modes of Transformation." *International Migration Review* 38(3): 970–1001

Vidich, Arthur J., and Gilbert Shapiro. 1955. "A Comparison of Participant Observation and Survey Data." *American Sociological Review* 20(1): 28–33.

Waldinger, Roger. 2001a. "Strangers at the Gates" In *Strangers at the Gates: New Immigrants in Urban America,* edited by Roger Waldinger. Berkeley: University of California Press.

———. 2001b. "Conclusion: Immigration and the Remaking of Urban America." In *Strangers at the Gates: New Immigrants in Urban America,* edited by Roger Waldinger. Berkeley: University of California Press.

Waldinger, Roger, and Jennifer Lee. 2001. "New Immigrants in Urban America." In *Strangers at the Gates: New Immigrants in Urban America,* edited by Roger Waldinger. Berkeley: University of California Press.

Warner, R. Stephen. 1998. "Immigration and Religious Communities in the United States." In *Gatherings in Diaspora: Religious Communities and the New Immigration,* edited by R. Stephen Warner and Judith G. Wittner. Philadelphia: Temple University Press.

Warner, Roger. 1996. *Shooting at the Moon: The Story of America's Clandestine War in Laos.* South Royalton, Vt.: Steerforth Press.

Warner, W. Lloyd, and Leo Srole. 1945. *The Social Systems of American Ethnic Groups.* New Haven, Conn.: Yale University Press.

Waters, Mary C. 1990. *Ethnic Options: Choosing Identities in America.* Berkeley: University of California Press.

———. 1999. *Black Identities: West Indian Immigrant Dreams and American Realities.* Cambridge, Mass.: Harvard University Press.

Webb, Eugene T., Donald T. Campbell, Richard Schwartz, Lee Sechrest, and Janet B. Grove. 1966/1981. *Nonreactive Measures in the Social Sciences.* Boston: Houghton Mifflin.

Welaratna, Usha. 1993. *Beyond the Killing Fields: Voices of Nine Cambodian Survivors in America.* Palo Alto, Calif.: Stanford University Press.

Whitaker, Donald P. 1979. *Laos: A Country Study.* Washington: U.S. Government Printing Office.

Wilson, William J. 1987. *The Truly Disadvantaged: The Inner City, the Underclass, and Public Policy.* Chicago: University of Chicago Press.

Wimmer, Andreas, and Nina Glick Schiller. 2003. "Methodological Nationalism, the Social Sciences, and the Study of Migration: An Essay in Historical Epistemology." *International Migration Review* 37(3): 576–610.

Winant, Howard. 2001. *The World Is a Ghetto: Race and Democracy Since World War II.* New York: Basic Books.

Winland, Daphne N. 1992. "The Role of Religious Affiliation in Refugee Resettlement: The Case of the Hmong." *Canadian Ethnic Studies* 24(1): 96–119.

Wirth, Louis. 1945. "The Problem of Minority Groups." In *The Science of Man in the World Crisis,* edited by Ralph Linton. New York: Columbia University Press.

Yancey, William, Eugene Erickson, and Richard Juliani. 1976. "Emergent Ethnicity: A Review and Reformulation." *American Sociological Review* 41(3): 391–403.

Yang, Dao. 1975/1993. *Hmong at the Turning Point.* Minneapolis: WorldBridge Associates.

Yang, Doua, and David North. 1988. *Profiles of the Highland Lao Communities in the United States.* Washington: U.S. Office of Refugee Resettlement.

Yang, Kao-Ly. 2004. "Problems in the Interpretation of Hmong Clan Surnames." In *Hmong/Miao in Asia,* edited by Nicholas Tapp, Jean Michaud, Christian Culas, and Gary Y. Lee. Chaing Mai, Thailand: Silkworm Books.

Yang, Kou. 2003. "Hmong Diaspora of the Post-War Period." *Asian Pacific Migration Journal* 12(3): 271–300.

Yang, Philip Q. 1994. "Explaining Immigrant Naturalization." *International Migration Review* 28(3): 449–77.

Yoshino, William. 1996. "Japanese Americans." In *The Ethnic Handbook: A Guide to the Cultures and Traditions of Chicago's Diverse Communities,* edited by Cynthia Linton. Chicago: Illinois Ethnic Coalition.

Young, Crawford. 1976. *The Politics of Cultural Pluralism.* Madison: University of Wisconsin Press.

Zarestsky, Eli, ed. 1976. *The Polish Peasant in Europe and America: A Classic Work in Immigration History.* Urbana: University of Illinois Press.

Zeidler, Frank P. 1991. "Catholicism and Political Life in Milwaukee." In *Milwaukee Catholicism: Essays on Church and Community,* edited by Steven M. Avella. Milwaukee: Knights of Columbus.

Zelditch, Morris. 1962. "Some Methodological Problems of Field Studies." *American Journal of Sociology* 67(5): 566–76.

Zhou, Min. 1997. "Segmented Assimilation: Issues, Controversies, and Recent Research on the New Second Generation." *International Migration Review* 31(4): 975–1008.

———. 2001. "Straddling Different Worlds: The Acculturation of Vietnamese Refugee Children." In *Ethnicities: Children of Immigrants in America,* edited by Rubén G. Rumbaut and Alejandro Portes. Berkeley: University of California Press.

Zhou, Min, and Carl L. Bankston. 1998. *Growing Up American: How Vietnamese Children Adapt to Life in the United States.* New York: Russell Sage Foundation.

Zhou, Min, Carl L. Bankston, and Rebecca Y. Kim. 2002. "Rebuilding Spiritual Lives in the New Land: Religious Practices Among Southeast Asian Refugees in the United States." In *Religions in Asian America: Building Faith Communities,* edited by Pyong G. Min and Jung H. Kim. Walnut Creek, Calif.: Altamira Press.

Zunz, Oliver. 1982. *The Changing Face of Inequality: Urbanization, Industrial Development, and Immigrants in Detroit, 1880–1920.* Chicago: University of Chicago Press.

$=$ Index $=$